Praise for Tracey Marino and Vance Marino

Tracey and Vance have written the most informative book about media music that I've ever read. This is a supportive, fun, and positive guide through what can be a brutal industry. The book is a sync world epic—kind of like Homer's *Odyssey*, except I can actually understand and learn from every page.

—**John Houlihan**, Music Supervisor

Songwriters and composers who want to have their music synchronized need information that can be difficult to find. This book is a complete guide for those who want to write successfully for production music libraries.

—**Adam Taylor**, President of APM Music, Chairman of the PMA

Kudos to Tracey and Vance Marino for leveraging their industry experience to compile such a comprehensive and valuable resource for composers! This book contains a veritable wealth of information and tips on everything from licensing and publishing to composing and recording, plus networking, contracts, metadata, and more. A must-read for any aspiring media composer!

—**Ron Mendelsohn**, President and CEO of Megatrax

As a veteran in this business who has built and sold many production music libraries, I have seen this couple/team make it their business to meet everyone and glean wisdom from many. This is a definite go-to for those who need clarity on how to make a living in the film and TV business.

—**Cassie Lord**, SyncStories, PMA Board Member

Not gonna lie! I *need* this book! I've been a successful songwriter for over thirty years, and there is so much I still don't understand—but could learn—from reading it! I will definitely be buying a copy!

—**Allan Rich**, award-winning Hit Songwriter

In their book *Hey! That's My Song!* Tracey and Vance have written a classic reference book for all things dealing with music for sync. The Marinos have put a positive spin on their years of trials and tribulations in a concise and comprehensive book that is a pleasure to read—and will be enjoyed by both beginners and pros alike.

—**Brian Thomas Curtin**, Composer and Songwriter, Eaglestone Music

Sync placements continue to be a reliable source of income for songwriters and music rights owners. However, securing a coveted placement requires navigating a minefield of eclectic music business professionals, confusing terminology, and extremely tight deadlines. In *Hey! That's My Song!* Tracey and Vance provide a road map on how to be successful by providing relevant examples through their years of experience filled with hits and misses. This is a must-read for songwriters, composers, or anyone else interested in making money in sync placements.

—**David Quan**, Vice President, Business Affairs, Angry Mob Music,
Past President of the California Copyright Conference

Hey! That's My Song! is a complete instruction manual on the inner workings of writing appropriate and highly placeable music for production music libraries. The book is informally written, very easy to read, and jam-packed with essential information. Tracey and Vance have covered every related topic. This book is truly *a must-read* for anyone considering involvement with production music libraries.

—**Tom Villano**, Emmy®-winning Music Editor and Music Supervisor, Instructor, Musicians Institute

Tracey and Vance prove how combining good music and grace, along with effective networking, leads to the best results!

—**Juan Carlos Quintero**, Composer and Producer, Moondo Music LLC

It's always a pleasure to receive music from Tracey and Vance because I know it will be master quality, well-written and performed, and easy to clear. For a catalog owner, knowing that the submission will be professional, as well as good, is simply a blessing.

—**Beth Wernick**, Imaginary Friends Music Partners

Tracey and Vance are true professionals with vast knowledge about the music industry. They are master networkers with an innate ability to make everyone around them feel valued. They genuinely care about people and want to help everyone succeed, so it is no surprise that they wrote this book to guide others on the journey. They generously share their expertise with readers, collating and condensing information that they spent years acquiring, into the pages of this book. I will definitely recommend this to the artists I work with and the songwriting community!

—**Nitanee Paris**, Award-Winning Songwriter, and Partner and Director of A&R, ArtistMax

Sync world veterans Tracey and Vance Marino are breaking it down for you in *Hey! That's My Song!* Everything you need to know to be successful in the sync world is here: creative, marketing, and business. They put their twenty-plus years of experience in a no-nonsense, easy-to-digest guide.

—**Suzan Koç**, Publisher and Songwriting Mentor

In *Hey! That's My Song!* as one can tell from the slightly irreverent title, Tracey and Vance will entertain, as well as educate, all who avail themselves of this wonderful new resource. A great primer in this very competitive music space, Tracey and Vance are generous in offering up lessons they have learned and relevant information they have garnered over the years in their professional experience. *Hey! That's My Song!* is most definitely a book for my industry library and an easy recommendation.

—**Garrett M. Johnson**, Esq., Past President of the California Copyright Conference

You are so lucky to have two wonderful people in Tracey and Vance to guide you on the journey into the world of music for sync.

—**Richard Harris**, Artist, Songwriter, and Producer

Tracey and Vance walk the walk! Not only do they fight for fair pay for songwriters and composers through their amazing work with creators' rights organizations, like NSAI and SONA, but they are incredibly generous with their knowledge of how the music industry works, particularly on how creators can make money through sync. We writers are so lucky to have them as advocates and as educators.

—**Michelle Lewis**, Singer-Songwriter and Composer, Creators' Rights Advocate,
Executive Director of Songwriters of North America (SONA), ASCAP Board Member,
and Recording Academy L.A. Chapter Board Member

Hey! That's My Song!

A Guide to Getting Music Placements in Film, TV, and Media

TRACEY MARINO AND VANCE MARINO

Edited by Ronny S. Schiff

To access the online media visit:
www.halleonard.com/mylibrary

Enter code: 4703-8562-0804-3959

Essex, Connecticut

An imprint of Globe Pequot, the trade division of The Rowman & Littlefield Publishing Group, Inc.
4501 Forbes Blvd., Ste. 200
Lanham, MD 20706
www.rowman.com

Distributed by NATIONAL BOOK NETWORK

Copyright © 2022 by Tracey J. Marino and Vance K. Marino
All audio composed by Tracey and Vance Marino, Copyright © 2021 by SongMaker Productions

All rights reserved. No part of this book may be reproduced in any form or by any electronic or mechanical means, including information storage and retrieval systems, without written permission from the publisher, except by a reviewer who may quote passages in a review.

Edited by Ronny S. Schiff

Additional Credits:
Alexis Tia Diller: "About the Authors" photography
T. Bannister and M. Weddleton: Badges photography
Chris Armes/Green Ribcage Graphics: Cartoon icons and chart diagrams
Charylu Roberts/O.Ruby Productions: Keyboard diagrams

The information, forms, and contracts provided in this book (the "Information") are intended for informational and educational purposes only and should not be used without the advice from a qualified attorney. Any use of the of the Information is at the sole risk of the reader, and the reader hereby freely assumes the risk of using the Information and any damages or loss that may occur as a result thereof. The authors and publisher and their respective heirs, assigns, employees, officers, and representatives shall not be held responsible for any loss or damages that may occur as a result of the use of the Information herein.

British Library Cataloguing in Publication Information available

Library of Congress Cataloging-in-Publication Data

Names: Marino, Tracey, author. | Marino, Vance, author. | Schiff, Ronny S. editor.
Title: Hey! that's my song! : a guide to getting music placements in film, TV, and media / Tracey and Vance Marino ; edited by Ronny S. Schiff.
Description: Lanham : Backbeat Books, 2022. | Includes index.
Identifiers: LCCN 2021021620 (print) | LCCN 2021021621 (ebook) | ISBN 9781493061112 (paperback) | ISBN 9781493061129 (epub)
Subjects: LCSH: Music trade. | Musicians' contracts. | Licensing agreements. | Music—Marketing. | Music—Production and direction. | Sound recordings—Production and direction. | Music trade—Vocational guidance.
Classification: LCC ML3790 .M3502 2022 (print) | LCC ML3790 (ebook) | DDC 781.5/4—dc23
LC record available at https://lccn.loc.gov/2021021620
LC ebook record available at https://lccn.loc.gov/2021021621

∞™ The paper used in this publication meets the minimum requirements of American National Standard for Information Sciences—Permanence of Paper for Printed Library Materials, ANSI/NISO Z39.48-1992.

This book is dedicated to our moms, dads, families, and friends who encourage us to dream and create.

Contents

FOREWORD

Hey! This Is the Foreword!

Dan Kimpel

It would be highly unlikely to be an active member of the composing and songwriting communities in Hollywood and not have met Tracey and Vance Marino. From industry conferences to confabs, screenings to socials, and panels to parties, they are present at absolutely everything.

As the author of books on music industry networking, I will testify that they are experts at working the room. But there is substance to their style. They radiate with positive energy that is consistently authentic, welcoming, and gravitational. By presenting opportunities and supporting advocacy for their colleagues, the Marinos *play* it forward with love.

While I admire their interpersonal skills and ambassadorial stewardship, I also have some questions. With all of their social and nonprofit commitments, when do they have time to write and record over three thousand titles as noted in their repertoire, with over a thousand-plus placements? On how many occasions has the duo traveled from their home base near San Diego to Los Angeles? What is their secret to staying awake on these trance-inducing drives on the 405 freeway? And, lastly, how can there be enough hours remaining in their days to write this book?

Let me spare you the hackneyed Thomas Edison–attributed trope about perspiration and inspiration. It is no secret that music endeavors come without guarantees. This industry is not for the faint of heart. Commitment and resilience are necessary attributes.

The authors endured years of rebuffs as they developed thick skins. They revised, analyzed, and sought advice from sage mentors. Irrepressibly upbeat and deeply committed, they persisted. Correspondingly, every day, somewhere in this world, their music plays on television, in films, in commercials, and on other media. Their determination paid off for them, and the invaluable knowledge they share in these pages will pay off for you too, if you are willing to put in the work.

The music-for-sync industry is immense. The cast includes composers, songwriters, musicians, music editors, publishers, music supervisors, and a lengthy list of decision-makers. While a livelihood in this lucrative enterprise requires an aptitude for composing and recording music, there is an equivalent knowledge base. Successful creators are businesspeople, responsible for marketing themselves, and navigating intricate income streams. Modern music makers need both a connection to the muse and a command of the metadata.

Tracey and Vance Marino are authorities who navigate this complex ecosystem. They now graciously offer you their knowledge, to inspire, educate, and awaken you with a hefty wallop of reality.

May your music become ever more syncable. May your optimism and ambition be equally unsinkable.

Dan Kimpel is author of *Networking Strategies for the New Music Business, It All Begins with the Music: Developing Artists and Careers for the New Music Business* (with Don Grierson), *Electrify My Soul: Songwriters and the Spiritual Source, How They Made It: True Stories of How Music's Biggest Stars Went from Start to Stardom!*, and *Networking in the Music Business.*

Introduction

WHO NEEDS THIS BOOK?

This guide is for *music creators*—songwriters, composers, musicians, singers, and anyone else whose dream it is to make money with their music and hear it playing in film, TV, and other media.

WHY DID WE WRITE THIS BOOK?

We wrote this book for *you*. Why? Because we've been there. We know what it's like to work so hard on a song, only to be told by a publisher, "I'm just not feeling it" or "It's great, but I don't know what to do with it."

Another reason for writing this book is so you may avoid some of the mistakes we made at the start of our sync music careers. This is the book we wish we'd had back then. It is our goal to provide you with helpful information that we have gathered from multiple sources into one convenient place. In doing so, we hope music creators will make better-informed decisions, which will benefit them as well as the sync music business as a whole.

Our backgrounds include being music teachers, so we get a thrill passing along information and seeing the light bulb go off in a student's head. We're proud of the person who takes our advice and becomes successful.

The clearest way we have found to communicate musical ideas is to play the Audio Examples that demonstrate these concepts. Throughout this book, the "Hey! Listen to This!" sidebars are included to clarify the points being discussed in the text. One of the most important aspects of writing for sync is being able to dissect and extract crucial elements and hear how they work together synergistically.

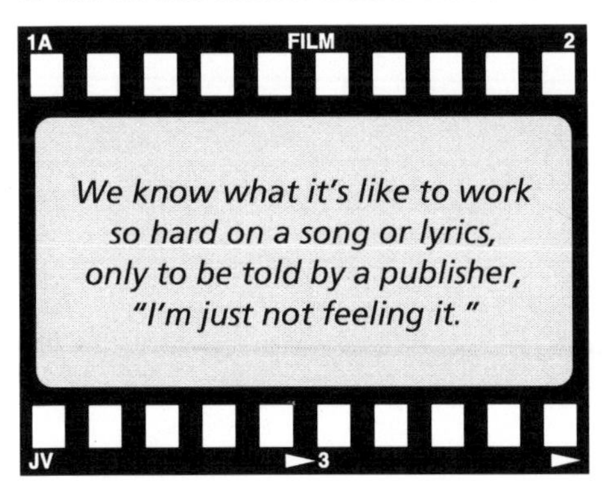

So, why listen to us? We were struggling, full-time musicians who'd played extra gigs and finally scraped up enough money to go to a music convention known as the TAXI Road Rally. We had no idea what to expect. Shyly, we sat in the ballroom listening to various speakers, afraid to talk with anyone, but we enjoyed the experience.

However, one panel, titled "TAXI Success Stories," was so life-changing, it put our music career on a completely different course.

We listened to a musical montage by Matt Hirt, who was, and arguably still is, one of TAXI's most successful members. We'd seen the ads in music magazines featuring Matt and watched his videos, but we still had our doubts. We listened intently to Matt's Latin music, an Asian cue, and his happy, inspirational track. We were moved by his high-intensity, heart-pounding chase music.

Matt wrote in many different genres, and it was all great. As his music reel ended, we looked at each other in amazement, because, at that exact moment, we both knew: This was what we'd always wanted to do. We hadn't even known this was a possible career path. This was our destiny! This will be easy! We'll be rich!

THE LONG AND WINDING ROAD: THIS JOURNEY MAY TAKE MANY YEARS

It took more than seven years before we'd even make a dollar—and two more years before we got our first BMI royalty statement, which was a total of $200 between the two of us! During those first nine years, we spent thousands of dollars on studio equipment and software, going to music conventions, buying dozens of how-to-write-songs books (and the life-saving book *Producing in the Home Studio with Pro Tools*; thank you, David Franz), taking recording classes, treating music industry people to coffee or lunch, and networking. Our families thought we had gone off the deep end and needed some serious intervention.

However, this was, and still is, a journey. And we've learned a lot on this journey, good and not so good, from every music industry person we've met—so much, in fact, that we wanted to share our story and knowledge with you so you can perhaps avoid some of the pitfalls that held us back for many years. You're welcome.

I CAN'T WAIT: PATIENCE AND MORE PATIENCE

Looking back, we wouldn't change anything, even though we had a mountain of rejections and frustrations in those early years (and still get them from time to time). The trade-off was, we met some incredibly helpful people who have become our trusted sources and confidants. Matt Hirt ended up becoming a dear friend. With Matt, in 2011, we started a monthly "L.A. Hang Group," a think tank/support group of like-minded composers and songwriters from around the world that still exists today. Matt would offer encouragement with a phrase we still use: "You need to have superhuman patience." He was right. Many times, when we were on the brink of giving up, we'd recite Matt's words of wisdom; we'd hang in there; and, to our amazement, something wonderful would happen. Then there was that magical day when we both exclaimed, "Hey! That's our song, and it's in a feature film!" We want *you* to be able to say, "Hey! That's my song!" as well. It's an incredible feeling. It is our sincere hope that you read this book knowing that if we can be successful at licensing our music, you can, too.

AUTHORS' NOTE REGARDING THE HEADINGS

Several of the headings throughout this book are twists on lyrics, titles of songs and TV shows, and movie quotes that have impacted us in some meaningful way. Most of the songs have been covered by artists and became popular again, or they have been getting placements in various projects for decades. It's likely these songs will continue to be synced for years to come.

A good song is a good song.

PART 1: CREATIVE

Hey! How Do I Write Music for Sync?

Steps to Writing and Recording Highly Placeable Songs and Instrumentals

CHAPTER 1

Understanding the World of Sync

WHAT IS THE "SYNC WORLD"?

If you do an Internet search for "sync," you'll find many definitions and spellings. However, *sync* is simply the term short for *synchronization*. This means "matching the music to the picture," which in this case would be a scene from a film, TV show, commercial, video game, podcast, or other media. *Media* is defined as "the means by which something is communicated."

The sync world consists of three entities:

1. *Music creators.* Songwriters, lyricists, topliners, composers, musicians, singers, artists, bands, music producers, mixers, and recording and mastering engineers.
2. *The companies that place music.* Production music libraries, sync agencies, and music publishing companies.
3. *Music users.* Music supervisors, music editors, video editors, filmmakers, TV directors, content producers, video game development companies, ad agencies, and showrunners.

They all work together to place music in projects, and, in order to be successful, there are standards and expectations within all of these groups (see the glossary for definitions). There are several different terms for "music placement," the most common being: "music licensing" and "getting sync."

Music for media is different than music made for radio and streaming, which is referred to as "listening music." This is when the listener is listening to music for enjoyment, and often with no video accompaniment, unless there's a music video. If there is a music video, the music (such as a hit pop song) is created first, and then the video is created around the music. Therefore, this is not the same as sync music, where the video (the picture) is created first, and then the music is added.

WHAT A FEELING: THE PURPOSE OF SYNCED MUSIC

Synced music has to create a feeling or emotion for the viewer, and it needs to do this quickly. Synced music should enhance and elevate the scene (the picture).

How do you write music that's easily placed or synced? The best advice is to watch, listen, pay attention, and really analyze the shows that use the type of music you would like to write. It's easier to (1) watch a show first to understand the story being told and then (2) watch it again to focus on how the music was used (while not being distracted by the story).

Many reality TV shows don't have a single person who writes all of the music. The music is provided by a production music library or a sync agency. (More about these in part 2.) Because of the number of opportunities in this area, we watch a lot of reality shows, listen to the types of cues that are playing, and go from there.

If you like writing *trailer music*, watch and study trailer music. There is a formula and style you need to know to be successful.

If you want to write music for video games, then play video games. The music is used differently.

If you are a movie fan and would like to hear your song played during the end credits of a major feature film, then you'll need to study how songs are used in this way.

BOTH SIDES NOW: TWO COPYRIGHTS—COMPOSITION AND RECORDING

There are two sides (known as "halves" in the music supervisor's jargon) to a recorded song's copyrights: the composition and the recording. Technically, a sync license allows a visual media producer to use (1) a *composition* (the written song or instrumental—meaning the lyrics, chords, and melody) and (2) a *recording* of the composition (also known as the *master recording*) in their project. It's important to be clear about the terms of licensing and ownership of these two copyrights in your transactions. Most of the time, this license is for a specific use of your music in a specific project, for a specific amount of time, in a specific territory.

A sync license is somewhat like borrowing a library book: the music user will be borrowing or using your music, but you still own your music, just like the library still owns the book. The term *sync* is used, in general, to refer to both of these types of licenses. Read your contracts carefully, and, if you have co-writers, make sure you have a signed *songwriter split sheet*, also known as a *writers' split agreement* or *writer splits*. (See appendix B.)

It's important to be absolutely sure that *you* are the owner of, and can control, your music composition and your master recording. If you had a couple of co-writers help you write the song, then they may own part of the song's *composition* copyright. If you had someone else record your song, then that person may actually be the owner or co-owner of the *master recording*, unless you have proof otherwise. Most, if not all, reputable music publishing companies will ask for signed agreements from everyone involved with the music before signing it themselves. The company needs to know everyone is in agreement about what's being done with the music. This is because the publisher needs to assure the music supervisor or music editor that the musical composition *and* the recording of the music can be cleared for use.

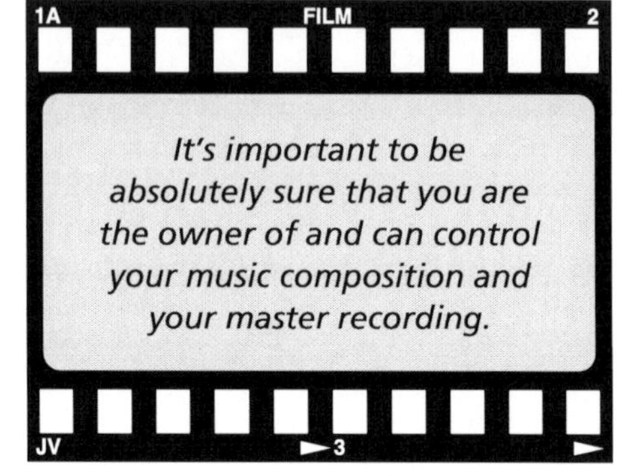

THE ROLES SYNC MUSIC PLAYS

It's important to know the different roles sync music plays and the ones for which you'd like to write. A common mistake is to watch a crime drama on network TV and then write similar music to submit to the show's music supervisor. The problem is that the show already has a score composer, who will likely write the score for upcoming episodes, so the production company doesn't need instrumentals that sound like the score. However, crime dramas do need additional music, such as source music. Here are the different types of syncable music:

- *Score* is the instrumental music you hear throughout most films or TV shows. It is written by a score composer who receives a video of the show and writes customized music. Generally, the score composer must answer to a director *and* the producers. Many times, the score composer is not at liberty to write whatever they feel or desire, but instead has a temp score, specs, or direct input from the director and music editor. A score composer must meet certain expectations and can have very demanding deadlines. One music industry professional said on a panel that a well-known composer "missed a major deadline on a feature film and never worked in Hollywood again." Harsh, but it's the reality of score composing.
- *Source* is music that can be heard by the characters in a show as well as the audience. It comes from a "source"—visible or implied, like a jukebox, a piano player, a band on stage, or a group of musicians or singers. Typically it is used to set the scene and put the viewer in the room with the characters. Many production music libraries started as a result of a show needing source music (more about production music libraries later).

- *Scource* is a combination of score and source music that the characters can hear and that also underscores the emotion of a scene. The purpose of scource music is to segue from one scene to another. Sometimes it is created, blended, or manufactured by the score composer or music editor.
- *Songs* created specifically for sync are different than hit songs, in that they were written to enhance the emotion of a scene, not necessarily for pure listening enjoyment. Songs are sometimes used in place of an instrumental score, but the lyrics do not tell the story. In some cases there is dialog over the singing, and in other cases the dialog is interspersed between the singing.
- *Instrumental cues* are used in TV shows, movies, video games, commercials, and many other types of media. Of all the music that gets synced, instrumental cues are used most often. Instrumental cues are also called *beds, tracks*, or *underscore*, but it is important to note that simply taking out or muting the lead notes (melody) and vocals from a song with lyrics is not the same thing as writing an instrumental cue. More on this below.

GENRES REIGN SUPREME WHEN WRITING MUSIC FOR SYNC

One of the most important early decisions you need to make is the genre in which you will work. *Genre* means the type of music or songs that fit in a specific category. For example, some mainstream genres include pop, country, jazz, folk, rock, or hip hop. Some rock subgenres are classic rock, yacht rock, progressive rock, blues rock, and rockabilly (see the list of "Sync Music Genres and Subgenres" in appendix D).

When writing music for sync, it is important to know your intended target: What is your song or cue's main genre? What is the subgenre, if there is one? This is critical information when describing your music. Music supervisors and editors need to have a starting point when first selecting music, and the genre is one of the most important clues they get before they even listen to the first note.

Though new hybrid genres and subgenres are created constantly, it's beneficial to keep a reference list handy. To improve your chances of getting placements, you will find this list helpful in aiding you as a music creator—and listener—in deciphering how music is categorized. If you are not sure what the subgenre is, do an Internet search for in-depth descriptions and offshoot genres. Listen to the referenced artists, and study the subtle differences. Nothing irritates the music user more than receiving music that does not match its description exactly. Another plus: Your list of genres may spark creativity and lead you to experiment writing in other styles. Perhaps you will find—or create—a new genre, subgenre, or hybrid genre.

THE SEARCH IS OVER

Some songwriters and composers are not comfortable writing music in a specific genre because they feel their music is being put in a box. It's important to realize that, when someone is searching through a massive music catalog or database, one of the categories they'll enter is the genre and even the subgenre. If your music doesn't have an identifiable genre, it's unlikely to show up in a music search and probably won't get licensed.

1A FILM 2

If your music doesn't have an identifiable genre, it's unlikely to show up in a music search and probably won't get licensed.

JV 3

If you're lucky, the styles of music that you like writing and producing will happen to be needed in the music marketplace. If you're like the rest of us, you'll have to figure out where the overlap is between genres you're good at composing and what's licensable.

At times you will hear, "No one is good at every genre." While there is a lot of truth to this statement, most of us are good at writing for more than one genre. When we started, we focused on new age and smooth jazz. Then we realized that these two genres don't get licensed as much as others. As we did our research, we discovered that other familiar styles, like rock, were actually licensable, so we produced some rock cues.

Next, we tried different licensable genres with which we had no experience, such as Caribbean music. It turns out we really enjoyed writing and producing this genre, and the cues got placed frequently. We learned that genres we hadn't even known existed were being asked for constantly by publishers—and they were used so much that it was worth studying.

One example was dramedy (the word being a combination of "drama" and "comedy"). *Dramedy* is a style of music that gets licensed in TV shows, film trailers, commercials, and just about every type of media. Generally, it has a "sneaky" feel to it, using light orchestral instruments. Dramedy has evolved to include hip hop beats and contemporary elements, known as hip hop dramedy.

A PLACE FOR US: FINDING YOUR BEST FIT

For us, it was important to try different aspects of media music to see if anything would stick. It turns out, we're really not that good at movie trailer music. However, that's okay, because we found our successful genres, and we stick with those, although we'll try something new occasionally. It's like finding a pair of comfortable shoes; it feels right.

Many times, we get requests for *hybrid music*. This is where elements from two or more different genres are incorporated into one cue. For instance, orchestral hip hop gets used a lot; this hybrid features the slower tempo and drums of hip hop combined with strings and other orchestral elements. It's important to understand the elements of each respective style *independently* in order to be successful writing hybrid music.

Keep in mind that sync music is not just a matter of the composition and instrumentation. Mixing techniques are also inherent in many genres. Usually hip hop drums are mixed very hot, so this needs to happen with hip hop hybrids as well. Similarly, rock guitars need to be mixed to sound huge in rock hybrids.

YOU'RE AN ORIGINAL

A common practice in the music business is to ask a composer or songwriter to create a cue or song that sounds like another musical artist's style. Oftentimes you will receive a *reference song* or *track* to emulate. This music is *never to be copied—ever*! The purpose of the request is to give the composer or songwriter an idea of the musical ballpark in which their music should be.

Under no circumstances should you use *any* portion of the reference music, including lyrics, melody, intro, and other aspects. Be original! There is room for creativity within the parameters outlined in the reference music. Choosing to write *soundalikes* or *knockoffs* may lead to legal problems, and no one wants that.

WHO ARE YOU? FINDING YOUR VOICE

Not only should your music sound authentic, it should sound like *you*. Your music should reflect you and the music to which you've listened and that you've played throughout your life. At times, this influence happens very consciously, and at other times it's very subconscious. One of the things that took us the longest to do was to "find our voice." We used to think that was a strange phrase, but now we realize how important it is. It applies to the creative side of composing, songwriting, lyric writing, producing, and mixing.

As music creators, your voice is like a painter's palette, but instead of using paints, pigments, and colors to express yourself, you use instruments, interesting sounds, beats, rhythms, lyrics, melodies, and mixing techniques. Your musical voice is what makes you unique in the music business.

To find your voice, ask yourself these questions:

- *As a composer.* What kinds of films do you enjoy watching? Which genres move you? What types of instruments do you like to use?
- *As a songwriter or lyricist.* Do you get emotional listening to a heartfelt song? Are you comfortable putting your feelings in your lyrics and music?

- *As a musician.* Do you like to play different instruments? Have you tried unusual tunings on your guitar?
- *As a producer.* Do you notice interesting arrangements? Do you experiment with different recording techniques?
- *As a mixer.* Can you hear when the drums in a recording are "in the listener's face"? Can you bring out the feeling in a vocal performance? Do you like the challenge of trying to get a unique bass sound?

IS BEING A CHAMELEON A GOOD THING?

Being good at one thing is great. Being good at several things can be beneficial. Being good at everything is considered unlikely in the music industry. It is often said in the sync world, "No one is good at *everything*."

Music industry people don't believe anyone who claims to be good at all types of music. They would prefer to know you as the person who writes ______________________________ (fill in the blank with one or two genres). Over and over again, you'll be asked to "Send us *only* the type of music you do best."

YOU'RE THE ONE THAT I WANT: BEING THE GO-TO PERSON

We joined the Los Angeles chapter of the SCL—the Society of Composers and Lyricists—and attend screenings of Oscar®-worthy films. Customarily, at the end of the screening there is a question-and-answer session with the composer. Time after time, we hear the composer say the director would go to them because they write using their own unique voice, such as quirky or ethnic-infused scores (think: Mychael Danna). Or they write sweeping, memorable melodies with big, grand orchestrations (think: John Williams). Or they write dark, brooding, pulsating beats blended with vintage keyboards and cutting-edge sounds (think: Trent Reznor). Or they write hybrids using electronic elements mixed with traditional symphonic instruments, and they're a fun hang (think: Hans Zimmer).

HEY! READ THIS!

One composer known for scoring many hit comedy films said he has no problem with being the go-to composer for this genre and becoming pigeon-holed. He quipped, "Show me the hole; I'm your pigeon."

WHY CAN'T I JUST LICENSE THE MUSIC I WROTE FIVE YEARS AGO?

Licensable music has many qualities that are very specific. It's possible that music written for another purpose may happen to be licensable—or it may not. Something as simple as a fade at the end of a perfectly good song can disqualify it from consideration. A song titled "Pat Was the Love of My Life" may be a perfectly crafted gem of a song, but if this song were to be used in a TV show, people would wonder, "Who's Pat?" Even if there was a character in the show named Pat, it would be too on the nose.

This guide is intended to help you know what will make your music licensable. Once you know the process, then write new music or look at any back catalog you may have to see if any of it is licensable as it is or if it can be made licensable with some tweaks.

WAIT—BEFORE YOU BEGIN WRITING, DO SOME DETECTIVE WORK

Since there are many books about songwriting and composing, we're assuming you already know how to write and put together a song or instrumental cue in general. *The purpose of this book is to illustrate, in particular, how to write music for placement—or sync.* This is a tough, competitive business, so your music has to be *great*. Finished. Polished. Perfect. Always. Here are some tips to help you move ahead of the pack.

As a music creator, you have to know what's getting placed. Do research. Then do more research. Yes, that sounds boring and clinical, but doing research is one of the major keys to success. What type of research is needed?

SECRET AGENT MAN OR WOMAN: CRACKING THE CODE

This is very basic advice, but watch—and understand—the medium for which you'd like to write, such as film, TV, commercials, games, etc. If you want to write music for video games, then you must play video games. If you want to write music for reality TV, you'll need to know current genres and use edgy production techniques. If you want to write songs for film trailers, you'll need to know how to make your song over-the-top dramatic and *trailerized*, as one music supervisor likes to say. Here are some tips:

- Research the type of music that's placed in the particular medium and how it's being used. Some questions to ask: What genre is it? Is it fresh and cutting-edge? Are there a lot of short 2- to 10-second cues being used (as is the case in many reality TV shows)? Is there an "arc" with various styles of music used throughout (as in many film trailers)? Are songs with vocals being used (as in many prime time network shows)? Is the music being *looped* (using the same two to eight bars over and over again, as is common in video games)?
- Determine which company got the placement. This can be challenging, but the information is out there. Some sources we use include IMDbPro, Wikipedia, Tunefind, iSpot.tv, and doing Internet searches. For example, search the name of the show, followed by the words "music by," and you'll probably find some clues. However, one of the best pieces of advice is to watch the end credits of a TV show or film. The end credits will usually include the companies that provided the music.
- Reverse engineer the process by researching the composer for the show. This may lead to the music publishers. In fact, some composers create their own music libraries, so their music goes directly into the show. Keep in mind, these composers occasionally need additional composers to help them. This strategy worked well for a friend of ours. Our friend met a TV composer who was speaking on a panel at a music convention. After the panel, our friend bravely approached the composer, told him he was a big fan of his music, and handed him a copy of his CD. A short time later, the composer was so impressed with our friend's music that he contacted him. Our friend ended up writing additional cues for several reality TV shows whenever the composer needed assistance.

HEY! READ THIS!
Watch a TV show, paying close attention to the music. What's happening? How is the music being used? What catches your attention? Can you tell what is going on in the scene just by hearing the music?

LISTEN TO THE MUSIC: ADDITIONAL RESEARCH TIPS

Go to the websites of production music libraries and sync agencies, and listen to the music. There is a wealth of information: What genres do they have? What instruments are being used in those genres? What scales and chords are being used? How is each song or instrumental structured? How are they arranged, produced, and mixed? How long is the music—a minute? Two minutes? More? What types of alternate mixes are there for each song?

Listen to genres with which you're familiar, but also listen to genres that aren't familiar to you. You might find genres you never knew existed, or you might find something new that you want to learn more about and try.

YOU GOTTA HAVE HEART: GREAT MUSIC NEVER GOES OUT OF STYLE

Some of our less-than-great pieces of music that we wrote early on certainly showed room for improvement, but they are still getting used today. We cringe when we hear the cheesy sample libraries, the bad edits, the out-of-time instruments, and the questionably mixed tracks. However, many of the compositions were good. The titles were enticing. The melodies were catchy. The vibe was right. The cues had heart.

You're going to make mistakes like we did. You might have time or financial limitations. You may not have connections in the music business. Or perhaps you have no idea where to start. To that we say, to begin, just begin.

Some additional solutions? Continue to learn. Take classes. Read books and blogs. Sign up for informative music email lists. Get feedback. Have an open mind. Join professional music organizations. Go to a music conference and meet collaborators and mentors. If this is something you really want to do, make it a priority. "Treat this as a profession, not a hobby," a friend told us many years ago. You'll get better.

PRO TIPS . . . About the World of Sync

The best music for sync has both genre clarity and mood clarity. The audience needs to understand exactly what type of music they are hearing as well as the mood it is expressing. Music only becomes a valuable storytelling tool for filmmakers or advertisers if it can be understood.

—**John Houlihan**, Music Supervisor

Listening to—and analyzing—what is working is probably the best way to learn what to aim for. These songs and cues must have done something right. Use the tools and techniques that are proving to be successful, but add your own spin to them.

—**Jason Blume**, Emmy®-winning Hit Songwriter and Author

When writing for sync, the music and lyrics should support the visual and reinforce the storyline without overpowering it. Your music should be broadcast ready, well crafted and well performed, with lyrics that have sync-friendly, universal themes. The biggest deal breakers in sync include music that is sonically distracting from the dialog and lyrics that are too specific for the script.

—**Brian Thomas Curtin**, Composer and Songwriter, Eaglestone Music

The most important thing to keep in mind is that in a sync setting your music typically won't be "the star." Depending on the exact application, it could be a costar, but more often it is a supporting actor. Knowing this going in should help with writing, pitching (e.g., dealing with rejection), and, ultimately, managing expectations.

—**Matt Hirt**, Composer, Songwriter, and Producer, and Co-owner of Catapult Music

As soon as you get your music licensed and used in something, you'll know you're doing it right. There is a learning curve that everyone must experience to get it right. Be patient.

—**Steve Barden**, Composer and Author

CHAPTER 2

Writing Instrumentals for Sync

HIT ME WITH YOUR BEST SHOT: THE INSTRUMENTATION MUST BE SPOT ON

What makes a genre a genre? The most obvious element is the instrumentation: Rock music has distorted guitars and powerful drums. Latin music has characteristic percussion instruments, like bongos, congas, and timbales. Hip hop is all about the electronic drums. Is it possible to write and record a rock cue without distorted guitars? Yes, it is, but why would you want to work that hard? Most genres embrace instruments that are inherent to that style of music.

The listener should know within *seconds* of the start of the cue what kind of music it is, primarily due to the instrumentation. A 2-second Dobro slide tells you you're in the southern United States. A koto strum tells you you're somewhere in Japan or perhaps an Asian restaurant. A church organ tells you you're, you guessed it, in a church or chapel.

HEY! LISTEN TO THIS!
"Ancient Chinese Secret"

Notice how you can identify this cue as having an Asian flavor in the first few seconds because of the instrumentation. It also uses a five-note or *pentatonic* scale, common in Asian music. This is a good example of simplicity, as it only has two stringed instruments and a gong. To help keep it interesting, the melody changes octaves.

Non-musicians who hear a rock cue might not be able to identify whether that sound is a Les Paul played through a cranked-up Marshall amp or a Stratocaster played through a Vox amp or even that it's a guitar at all, but they know it's a rock sound. Don't be afraid to use obvious instrumentation. It gets the message across.

HEY! LISTEN TO THIS! "Bad Attitude"

This is about as obvious as it gets. When it starts with the distorted guitar, the listener knows right away this is a head-banging rock cue. Notice there is no full melody; instead, there is a chord riff and lead guitar *motif*.

As musicians, identifying instruments in a music recording should be one of the easier things you do. However, there are genres that use instruments with which you may not be familiar. Does that Latin cue have a shaker or a maraca? Or both? Or some other unique percussion instrument that's not as recognizable? Thankfully, you live in the Internet age, and these things can be researched. Depending on how authentic you need to be, you might find that some Latin styles always use a shaker and *never* a maraca, or the other way around. Use the resources that are available to you to learn which instruments are typically used in various genres of music, especially ethnic styles.

A constant in instrumental cues is the use of orchestral strings and other orchestral elements. They are found in many cues, sometimes in pure orchestral form but often in combination with instruments from other genres (even hip hop). Strings are combined frequently with synths and *pads*, which are synthesized sounds that fade in slowly and sustain. Keep your ears open.

FOR ALL WE KNOW

An in-depth knowledge of music theory is not necessary for you to be a skilled composer or songwriter, but it certainly helps broaden your musical palette. There are some who are very successful but have an incomplete understanding of the intricacies of music and its terminology. However, the goal here is to shed light on the subjects involved in creating and marketing your music for sync and illuminate your path to success. In addition to aiding in the composing and songwriting process, understanding the language of music is very helpful when communicating with other musicians, producers, and engineers. This knowledge is also beneficial when encountering musical terminology in recording equipment and software.

You are encouraged to learn more about how the beautiful sounds of music come together to create an emotional response in a listener.

HERE IT IS IN BLACK AND WHITE

Music theory makes sense when it is expressed in terms of looking at the notes on a piano keyboard. It is not necessary to be a keyboardist, but knowing visually how the notes are laid out is advantageous.

In the music production world, an electronic keyboard is more convenient than an actual piano, for many reasons:

- It will work with the recording software.
- It never goes out of tune.
- You may use several different sounds rather than only a piano sound.
- It makes editing much easier.

If you need more background on reading music and playing keyboards (or guitar), you can reference the "Recommended Reading" list in appendix H.

IF IT'S MAJOR, IT MUST BE IMPORTANT

A *scale* is a sequential series of (usually seven) notes arranged in ascending and descending order. For instance, the eight notes from C to C on the keyboard make up the C major scale. C is known as the *tonic* (or *root note* or *keynote*) of this scale, and it gives the scale its name, as well as being the note that makes the scale sound finished and resolved. In sync music, a major scale is associated with sounding happy, bright, and positive.

When a song uses the notes from the C major scale, that song is in the *key* of C major, abbreviated as "the key of C." Play around with the notes in the C major scale. Try some of these suggestions to write a simple melody:

- Play a few notes up the scale, then down (for example, C–D–E–F–G–F–E–D–C).
- Play the same notes, but change the timing (C–D–E [hold E] F–G–F [hold F] E–D–C [hold C]).
- Then, skip notes to bring interest to your melody (C–E–G–F–G–E–C).

- The same note can be repeated (E–G–G–G, F–A–A–A, D–E).
- Repeat phrases of three or four notes (F–A–A, F–A–A, G–B–B, C).
- To create a feeling of expectation, go up the scale from C to B (C–D–E, F–G–A, G–A–B . . .). What note could follow B? Most listeners will want to hear C—the resolution (tonic) note.
- The opposite can be done as well, coming down the scale.

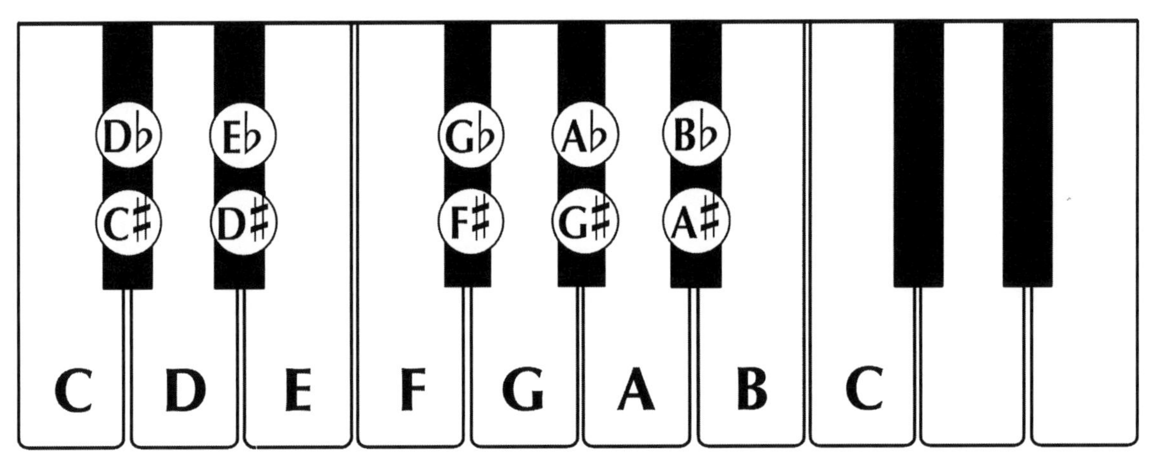

Figure 2.1. *A piano keyboard with the note names of the white and black keys.*

A series of notes can have a different effect or impact on the listener. Notice how various sequences and timings of notes sometimes imply what could come next. The crucial part of this exercise is to listen while you play. There are endless possibilities to create melodies using the major scale, but to hear them you must pay close attention.

Notice that you do not have to physically write a melody using pen and paper or music notation software. You can create music with a keyboard, guitar, voice, or any other instrument and simply record it on your phone. Creating music should not be a difficult chore!

HEY! LISTEN TO THIS! "Island Pleasure"

This Caribbean track, "Island Pleasure," uses the C major scale. Our goal was to capture the carefree feeling of being on vacation in a tropical location. In combination with the instrumentation and the rhythms, the major scale contributes greatly to achieving this result.

BACK HOME AGAIN

During the melody-writing process, it is important to consider the power of the tonic note. It has the simple quality of making a melody sound finished (resolved). If resolution is the desired effect, the tonic can be used at the end of a phrase or melody. However, not every composition ends with the tonic note. A melody that does not conclude with the tonic can have a discomforting, unresolved effect, if that is what is needed. Consider the emotional goal of your music, and let this knowledge guide you.

While it is customary to use only the notes in one key, interesting results can be achieved by including some notes, called *accidentals*, that are not in the current key. It is important to establish the key, to be aware of the notes in that key, and to be sure that the use of any notes not in the key is intentional. Feel free to experiment.

HIGH (AND LOW) STEPPIN'

The distance between two musical notes is referred to as an *interval.* The notes C and D are an interval of a *whole step* apart. On a keyboard, in between them is a black key, referred to as "C sharp," and notated as C♯. A "sharp" means a note is a *half step* interval higher than another.

Conversely, a "flat" indicates a note that is a half step interval lower than another. The C# note is also referred to as a "D flat," notated as D♭, since it is a half step below the D note. The other sharp and flat notes played on the black keys are similarly named based on the adjacent white key notes. The notes on the white keys are also known as *natural notes.* (For guitars or most other fretted stringed instruments, each fret is equal to a half step, and two frets are a whole step.) A whole step is also known as a *whole tone*, and a half step is sometimes referred to as a *semitone.*

Most pairs of consecutive natural notes have a sharp or flat note between them. The exceptions are B and C, and E and F. Notice that there are no black keys between these pairs of notes. The notes B and C are a half step apart, as are E and F.

THE WHOLE TRUTH ABOUT THE MAJOR SCALE (IF YOU "HALF" TO KNOW)

The intervals between the consecutive notes in the major scale are in a pattern of whole and half steps, as clearly illustrated by the piano keyboard:

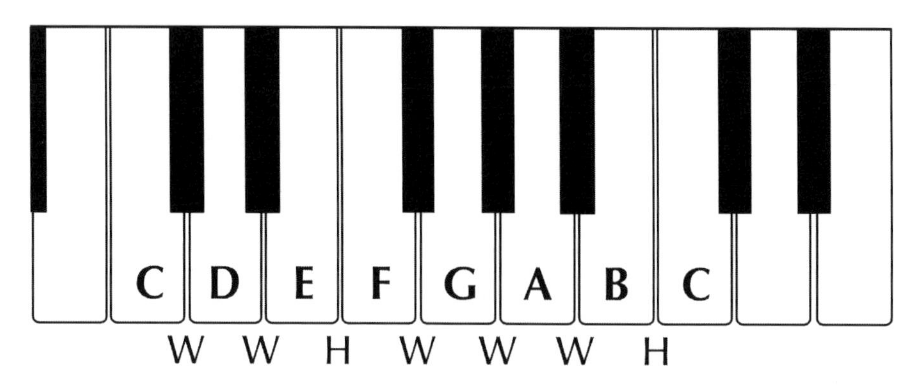

Figure 2.2. *Whole and half steps in a C major scale. W means "whole step," and H means "half step."*

Every major scale has the same interval pattern of whole and half steps. This pattern of whole step/half step intervals determines the notes of a key, starting from the note for which the key is named. Other scales follow different patterns, yielding different sounds.

A common variation of the C major scale omits the F and B notes, leaving five notes: C, D, E, G, and A. This is referred to as a *major pentatonic scale.* Removing the F and B notes eliminates the half step intervals. Major pentatonic scales are often heard in pop and traditional folk music.

There are eleven other major scales and keys, each starting with one of the other eleven notes. For instance, consider the D major scale. If you start on the D and go up a whole step, that takes you to E. The next note should be a whole step higher than E, but F is only a half step higher, as there is no black key between them. For this reason, the next note in the D major scale is an F♯.

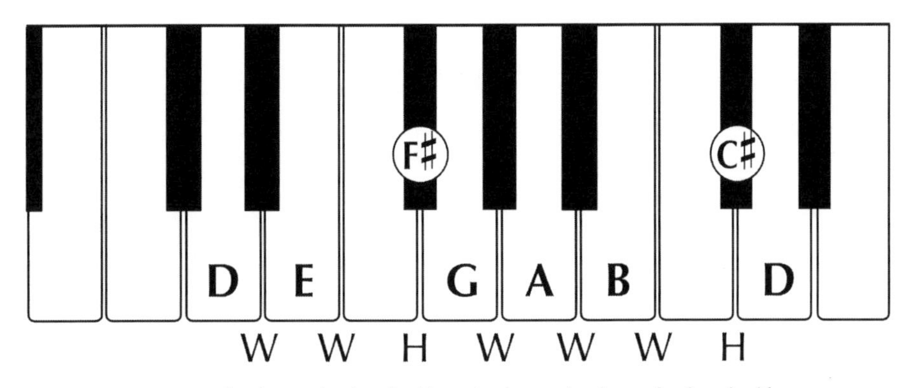

Figure 2.3. *Whole and half steps in a D major scale.*

LOOK SHARP!

As a result of following the pattern of steps in a major scale, starting on the root note of each of the keys yields a unique *key signature*. Some of these involve certain notes being sharp, while others require notes being flat. Ideally, composers and songwriters should be familiar with the notes and key signature of the music they are creating.

Key Signatures - Sharps

G: F♯
D: F♯, C♯
A: F♯, C♯, G♯
E: F♯, C♯, G♯, D♯
B: F♯, C♯, G♯, D♯, A♯
F♯: F♯, C♯, G♯, D♯, A♯, E♯

Key Signatures - Flats

F: B♭
B♭: B♭, E♭
E♭: B♭, E♭, A♭
A♭: B♭, E♭, A♭, D♭
D♭: B♭, E♭, A♭, D♭, G♭
G♭: B♭, E♭, A♭, D♭, G♭, C♭

Figure 2.4. *Key signatures.*

VARIATIONS À LA MODE

By using the notes from the C major scale and starting on a different note, a *mode* is created. A popular mode/scale derived from the notes in the C major scale is A minor, abbreviated as "Am." By starting on a note other than C, a new pattern of steps is established. For minor keys, this pattern is illustrated by the piano keyboard:

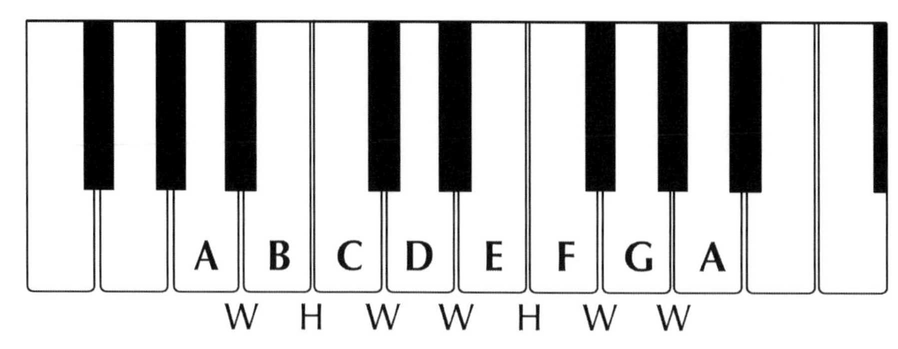

whole • half • whole • whole • half • whole • whole

Figure 2.5. *Whole and half steps in an A minor scale.*

Since the A *minor scale* uses the same notes as C major, it is called the *relative minor key* of C major. Similarly, C major is the *relative major key* of A minor.

Unlike the happy-sounding quality associated with major scales, minor scales in sync music have a dramatic, melancholy, or emotional feel. The quality of minor scales often makes them more effective in highlighting the emotion in scenes.

Like the major scale, the minor scale also has a variation called a *minor pentatonic scale.* As in C major, the A minor pentatonic removes the half step intervals by taking out the B and F, leaving A, C, D, E, and G. Minor pentatonic scales are found in blues, traditional folk, world, and rock music.

In addition to the two modes discussed, there are five other modes that are found by starting on any of the other notes of the major scale. These modes can sound different, which is perfect for the times you are asked to write music "that's unique or edgy." They each have their own sound and should be explored.

Here is a list of the seven modes using the C major scale as an example. (The number indicates the starting note from the major scale.)

1. Ionian C–D–E–F–G–A–B
2. Dorian D–E–F–G–A–B–C

3. Phrygian E–F–G–A–B–C–D
4. Lydian F–G–A–B–C–D–E
5. Mixolydian G–A–B–C–D–E–F
6. Aeolian A–B–C–D–E–F–G
7. Locrian B–C–D–E–F–G–A

Because listeners are unaccustomed to hearing some of these modes, compositions should emphasize the tonic of their mode. For example, if a piece of music is using the D Dorian mode, starting and ending phrases with the D note and playing it more than the others is a way of convincing the listener that the D is the tonic.

The combination of twelve different keys and seven different modes for each of them gives you many options for composition. After writing music for a while, your new compositions may have a tendency to sound similar to previous ones. Selecting a key and mode you've not used previously is a great way to break out of a composing rut.

HEY! LISTEN TO THIS!
"Cowabunga"
Most surf rock uses minor scales, while others, like "Cowabunga," use the Phrygian mode. It has a similar feel to a minor scale while sounding a bit exotic.

UNTANGLING CHORDS

Although two notes played simultaneously create harmony, they are not a chord. *Chords* are made up of three or more notes.

When two consecutive notes from the C major scale are played together—for instance, C and D—the *harmony* that is created sounds odd and somewhat unpleasant. This is referred to as sounding *dissonant*. If you instead play the C and E together, the sound is much more harmonious. This is a *consonant* sound. In order to create a chord, a third note is needed. Since a combination of nonsequential notes leads to a consonant sound, adding a G results in C, E, and G; this is a C major chord, also simply called a C chord. Three notes played together are called a *triad*.

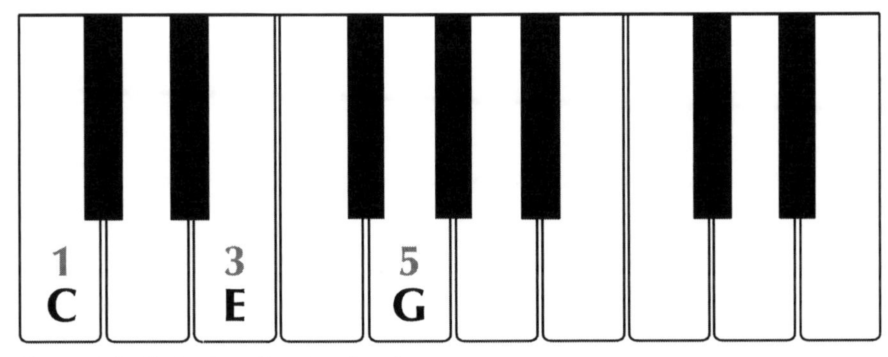

Figure 2.6. *Notes in a C major chord.*

C, E, and G are the first, third, and fifth notes of the C major scale. Therefore the *chord formula* for a major chord is 1–3–5. Because all chord formulas are expressed in terms of the order of the notes in a major scale, become familiar with thinking about *all* scales this way. It's easier to understand the chord formulas in all keys if you know how the notes in a major scale are numbered.

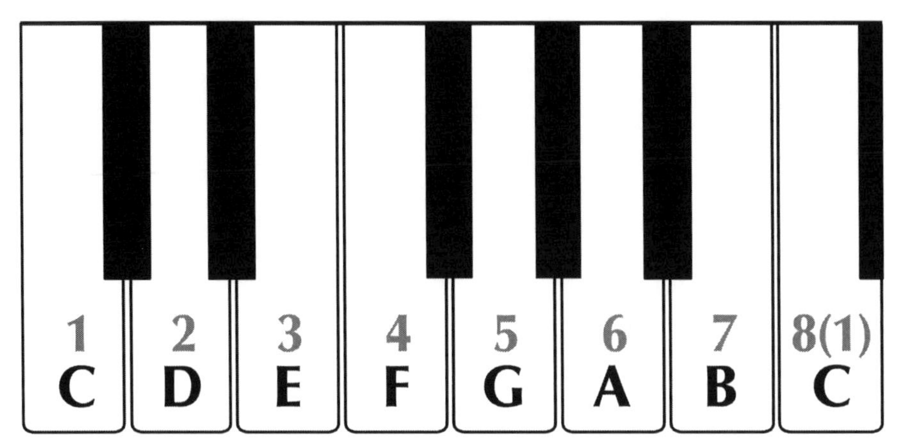

Figure 2.7. *Note names and numbers in a C major scale.*

Another common chord is the *minor chord*. Its formula is 1–♭3–5. The notes in a C minor chord are C, E♭, and G (abbreviated as Cm). The 1 and 5 are the same as the major chord; the difference is the flat 3. The 3 is the note that determines whether the tonality of the chord is major or minor. Because of the E♭, the Cm chord does not occur naturally in the key of C major.

The harmony created with only the 1 and 5 is ambiguous and uncommitted, as it sounds neither major nor minor. Though not technically a chord, this *open fifth* harmony can be very effective in writing instrumentals for sync, because it has a vague, uncertain, or inconclusive quality.

HEY! LISTEN TO THIS! "Doing It My Way"

The piano part plays only two notes at a time. It starts with an open fifth (G and D). While the G remains the same, the D moves to an E♭, then a C. The string motif includes a quick B♭, which briefly creates a G minor chord (G–B♭–D). Though the piano never commits to a G minor chord, its harmony is implied when combined with the notes played by other instruments.

UPSIDE DOWN: EXPLORING INVERTED CHORDS

The notes in a chord need not adhere strictly to the order outlined in the initial 1–3–5 chord formula. For example, a C major chord with the formula of 1–3–5 indicates that the notes are C, E, and G. This order of notes is known as *root position*, as the lowest note is the root. However, the C major chord may be played, low to high, as E–G–C or G–C–E. These are known as *inversions*.

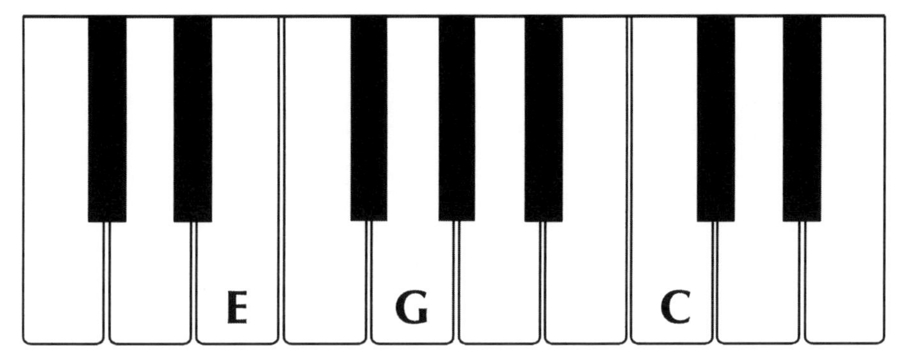

Figure 2.8a. *First inversion of a C major chord.*

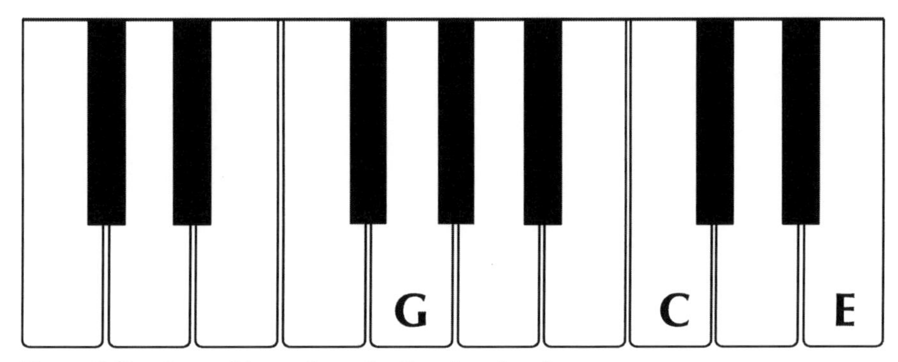

Figure 2.8b. *Second inversion of a C major chord.*

Chords are not limited to only three notes; many contain four or more notes. For instance, the addition of the higher octaves of the notes in a chord creates a fuller sound, such as C, G, C, E, G or C, G, E, C (on piano, you'll need two hands for these). These are called alternate *voicings* of the chord. There are many voicings possible on a piano and guitar, but even more are possible when the notes in a chord are spread over several instruments or voices in a band, orchestra, or choir.

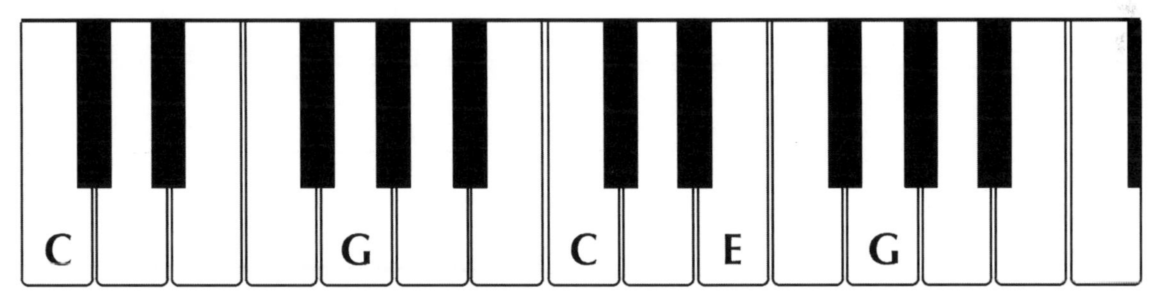

Figure 2.9a. *Alternate voicing of a C major chord.*

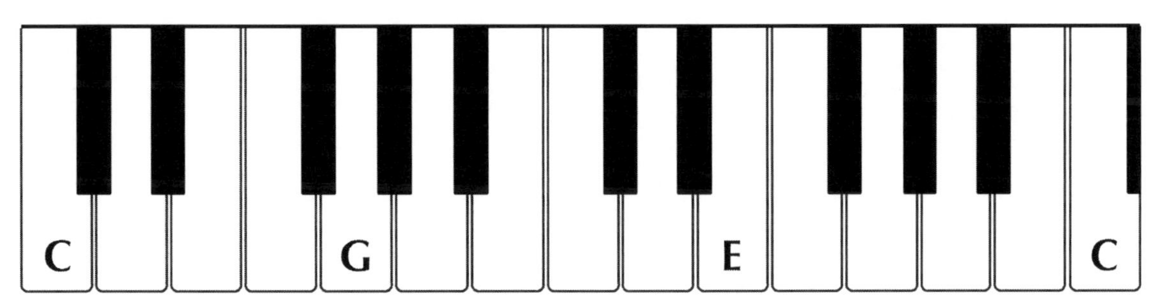

Figure 2.9b. *Wide voicing of a C major chord.*

COUNT ON ME

Since the C major chord has the first note from the C major scale as its root, it is referred to as the I (one) chord. Uppercase Roman numerals are used to indicate major chords and lowercase Roman numerals for minor chords. The seven chords in the key of C major are:

1. I	(major)	C
2. ii	(minor)	Dm
3. iii	(minor)	Em
4. IV	(major)	F
5. V	(major)	G
6. vi	(minor)	Am
7. vii°	(diminished)	Bdim

As chords are built on the notes of the major scale, they can be used to create compatible accompaniment for melodies containing notes from the scale. The major chords, the I, IV, and V, are used in countless pop and traditional songs. If a minor chord is added, such as the vi, the overall sound is still major. One of the most enduring chord progressions in pop music is I,–V–vi–IV. For example, in the key of C, this would be C–G–Am–F. Experiment with the sequence and duration of chords in progressions, and listen for familiar ones in addition to finding new ones that are not as recognizable.

In the same way that the tonic note of a scale brings a sense of resolution, the I chord, which is the *tonic* chord, makes a chord progression sound completed. Though the tonic chord appears frequently at the end of a piece of music, it is not required if the desired effect is to leave the listener feeling unsettled. When this information is used to make decisions about chords and melodies, it becomes a powerful tool in controlling the emotion of your music.

HEY! LISTEN TO THIS! "Breakout"

Rock music often makes use of chords based on minor pentatonic scales. However, our cue "Breakout" uses chords based on the major scale. In the key of G, it uses the I, IV, vi, and V chords, which are G, C, Em, and D. While the distorted guitars make it sound like rock, the major key and up-tempo groove give it a positive feel.

THIS IS NO ORDINARY CHORD

There are more chord formulas than can be listed here; however, below are some of the more common ones.

• major	(M)	1–3–5
• minor	(m)	1–♭3–5
• suspended 2nd	(sus2)	1–2–5
• suspended 4th	(sus4)	1–4–5
• augmented	(aug)	1–3–♯5
• diminished	(dim)	1–♭3–♭5
• major 6th	(6)	1–3–5–6
• minor 6th	(m6)	1–♭3–5–6
• major 7th	(maj7)	1–3–5–7
• minor 7th	(m7)	1–♭3–5–♭7
• dominant 7th	(7)	1–3–5–♭7

- dominant 7th sharp 5 (7♯5) 1–3–♯5–♭7
- minor 7th flat 5 (m7♭5) 1–♭3–♭5–♭7
- diminished 7th (dim7) 1–♭3–♭5–♭♭7
- added 9th (add9) 1–3–5–9
- major 9th (maj9) 1–3–5–7–9
- minor 9th (m9) 1–♭3–5–♭7–9
- dominant 9th (9) 1–3–5–♭7–9

Some chord names and formulas contain numbers higher than 7, which is more than the number of notes in a major scale. An easy way to find the number to which it refers is to subtract seven. For example, when the number 9 is used in chord names and formulas, it refers to the 2 from a major scale.

HEY! LISTEN TO THIS! "Golden Lotus"

The first chord strum on "Golden Lotus" is a G major 6th chord, and the second chord is a C major 6th. While sounding uplifting, as expected of a major chord, the added 6th note gives it a wistful and thoughtful flavor.

THE OUTSIDERS: CREATING CHORD INTRIGUE

The quest for interesting chords to use does not necessarily need to include complex chords containing four or more notes. Using chords that include notes outside of the major scale can produce intriguing possibilities using only triads.

One approach is to change the major or minor tonality of one of the six common chords in a major key. The ii chord, which is minor, can be changed to a major chord. Likewise, the IV chord, which is normally major, can be changed to a minor chord.

Another strategy is to choose a root note that is not in the major scale. The root of the vii° chord may be lowered a half step to create a ♭VII major chord. In the key of C, this would be a B♭ major chord. One of the reasons that this variation is not very disturbing is that the other two notes in the B♭ major chord, D and F, appear in the C major scale. In this example, a B♭ note may be a better fit in the melody than a B.

It's not necessary to limit yourself to "coloring within the lines" by using only notes and chords from the major scale. To the contrary, adding interest to your music by being aware of some of these concepts and applying them to your composing process is highly encouraged.

HEY! LISTEN TO THIS! "Puka Shells"

Here is an interesting cue to study because, in spite of containing only two ukulele tracks, it has been licensed hundreds of times. It is in the key of C major, though the melody quickly uses a few notes that are not in the C major scale. Most of the chords, however, are found in the key of C. The exceptions are the C7 (usually C major) at the end of the A section, the D7 (usually Dm) near the end of the B section, and the A7 (usually Am) and D7 near the end of the piece.

THE BLANK CANVAS AND SELECTING YOUR MUSICAL PALETTE

Like a painter who has chosen the colors on their palette, once you know what instruments to use, the next step is to focus on the music itself. Does music in the genre you are writing use major scales? Minor scales? Pentatonic scales? Modes? What about the chords? Majors? Minors? Open fifths? Or perhaps no clearly defined chords but notes and harmonies that imply chords? You could try to write a jazz cue with only major and minor chords and scales, but it won't sound very authentic. The complexity of the chords and scales in jazz make it sound *jazzy*. It's very important to compose your music to sound like the genre in which you're writing.

How are the instrumentation and music put together to create a vibe? A rock band made up of drums, bass, and two electric guitars playing open fifth chords and minor pentatonic scales can create different vibes. A fast tempo, with everybody pounding on their instruments, can create an exciting or frenetic vibe, while the same band at a slower tempo with a shuffle groove, and everybody playing fewer notes at a lower volume, can create a more subdued or laid-back vibe. Tempo and intensity are important things to consider in creating a feel.

Attitude is another thing to think about. Music that is played or sung off pitch or out of time has an effect on the listener. In this digital recording world you may have a tendency to "fix" everything you record. However, leaving the raw performance as it was recorded may actually give you the vibe for which you're looking. Some scenes call for music that will make the viewer uncomfortable, and this is one way to achieve that result.

HEY! LISTEN TO THIS! "Island Pleasure"

This cue features a catchy, syncopated major scale and a steel drum melody with marimba counterpoint. In each four-phrase A section, the melody starts with the same five notes except for the third phrase. However, all four phrases finish differently. It also features a lot of Latin percussion, a B section, and a breakdown section where only the percussion and melody are playing. This gives the music editor options.

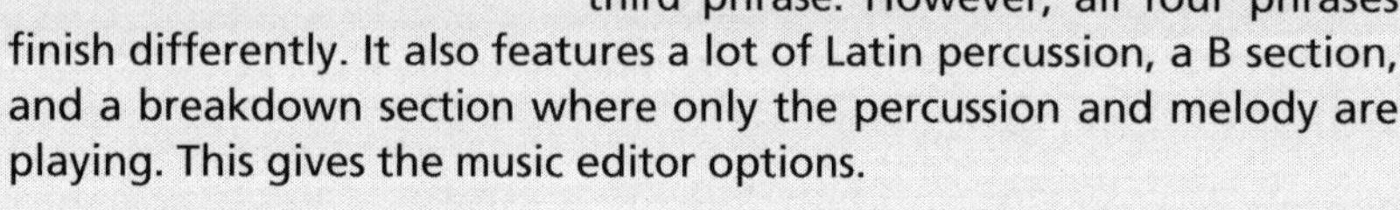

MELODIES, RIFFS, AND MOTIFS—OH, MY!

As is often the case with any artistic endeavor, there's no one rule to follow when writing melodies for sync music instrumentals. The nature of melodies is frequently genre-dependent. Some genres use melodies that are very similar to songs, while others use short musical *motifs* instead of melodies. This is another thing to note when researching a genre.

For instance, Caribbean music features, characteristically, a prominent steel drum melody. In addition to using major scales, the melodies in this genre use syncopated rhythms and are very hooky. They may start with an eight-note melody, repeat it with a variation, contrast with three long notes, and then repeat the first melody, ending on a tonic note. Later in the piece, a steel drum harmony in thirds may be added, as this is commonplace in this style.

TAKE IT EASY: SIMPLE IS EFFECTIVE

Suspense and tension cues are a bit different. They don't have long melodies but instead favor short three- or four-note phrases or motifs. In these types of cues, space and simplicity can be very effective. As the cue unfolds, those spaces can be filled with other instruments or sounds. You can make the task of adding instruments easier for yourself if, early on, you leave some room in your cue. Create the space; then fill the space.

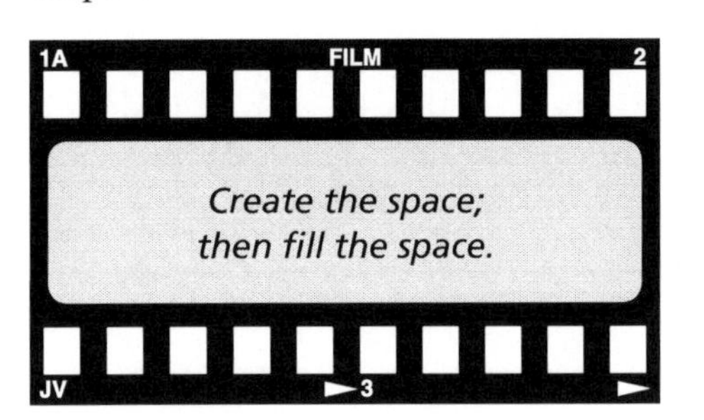

Often these short motifs may repeat exactly the same way each time, or with variations. Don't be afraid of repetition. It's good to have a certain degree of predictability in sync music. Instead, accept the challenge of making a repeating motif interesting by using arrangement techniques (more about this later).

HEY! LISTEN TO THIS! "Secrets and Lies"

This cue starts with a marimba playing a four-note motif, followed by a similar four-note motif. Then the first motif is repeated, followed by a different motif. Notice how the entire cue goes back and forth between two implied chords. The bass fills the space between some of the motifs. More instruments enter as the cue unfolds, leading to the last note.

THIRSTING FOR THE TONIC

Speaking of predictability, of all the notes that affect the listener's expectation, the tonic note is one of the most powerful. This is not to say that you should always end your phrases and melodies on a tonic. Instead, in a tension cue, avoiding the tonic to make the listener uncomfortable can be a useful tool in your composition. However, going back to the Caribbean cue example, always end the section on the tonic, because you want the listener's expectation to be met. (Who wants to go to the Caribbean and be stressed out?)

Chords and harmony are very powerful tools to use to create a *feel* in a cue. For example, a simple three-note motif evokes a different vibe when a minor chord is substituted for a major chord.

TRUE COLORS

There are so many other kinds of colorful chords you can use besides the major and minor ones. Though not technically a chord, an open fifth works very well in some kinds of cues, as it sounds undecided, neutral, non-committal, and ambiguous. This is because it does not have a third, which determines whether a chord is major or minor.

Sus2 and sus4 chords are good for creating a little bit of tension that can be resolved or left unresolved. Augmented and diminished chords can be very dramatic or humorous. In addition to the kinds of chords your cue may have, consider the combination of chords you use and whether or not they're in the same key.

The technique of alternating between two chords is used considerably in tension and suspense cues. Much like repeating a short motif, it becomes more important to use your arrangement skills to help the cue evolve.

Again, the tonic chord is critical and powerful in melodies and motifs. Finishing a section or cue with a tonic chord has a satisfying effect.

HEY! LISTEN TO THIS! "Can't Feel the Love"

This cue goes back and forth between two chords. Notice how the first chord is not the tonic chord. It's in the key of Cm but starts with an Fm. It also features a hooky piano motif. More instruments enter, building up to the last note.

STRIKING THE RIGHT CHORDS

Using differing chords under a repeating motif is a good way to keep the repetition from getting too monotonous. A riff with the notes A, B, and C can start with an A minor chord under it, then be repeated with an F major chord under it, creating the illusion that the notes changed, even though they didn't.

In many genres, chords are played rhythmically by keyboards or strummed instruments. A nice variation is to have the chords played as held-out whole notes that change with the chords. Modifying the rhythm from whole notes to quarter notes or eighth notes makes it sound busier, depending on what else is happening with the cue at that time.

TIMING IS . . . EVERYTHING

Play around with the timing of the chord changes. Having each chord held for the same number of beats is a comforting and predictable way to do it, if it fits the feel of your cue. But changing the timing can create some interest or tension, if that's what is called for. Instead of holding each chord for four beats, try the first one for six beats and the second one for two beats—or the first one for three and a half beats and the second one for one and a half beats.

There are times when chords are not played by one multinote instrument but instead by several single-note instruments, like strings or voices. This allows chord changes to be more fluid and less rigid. It also increases the likelihood of finding chords whose names you may not know but that sound cool. The vibe is what matters. If you want to play a game of "Name That Chord," feel free, but when your cue is finished, what matters is the feeling it evokes.

REPEAT AFTER ME: REPEAT. REPEAT. CHANGE. REPEAT.

In general, songs for sync have verses and choruses. Instrumentals for sync have A sections and B sections (and occasionally C sections). As a rule, the A section starts and ends the piece and is the main part. Some pieces have only A sections. The A section is commonly four, eight, or sixteen bars long, but this length can vary. The A section may repeat a time or two and then go to a B section. The B section should contrast musically, sometimes with different chords, melodies, or motifs, but it should retain the same feel or vibe as the A section. The piece then returns usually to the A section. However, it may also return to the B section a second time before finishing with a final A section.

To be clear, these sections are not just copied and pasted to fill out two minutes of a cue. Though some instruments play the same part on every A section of a cue, other instruments should enter, leave, or change what they're playing to contribute to a variation in the intensity level of each section and to help the cue evolve.

Some cues are through-composed and have no apparent structure but have a consistent feel that helps support some scenes. *Through-composed* means there are few or no repeating sections. It's a technique used more in the scoring world than in sync music. Overall, cues with a defined structure tend to get placed more frequently than through-composed cues, because they're easier to work with.

THE FIRST CUT IS THE DEEPEST: HEY! THEY CHOPPED UP MY MUSIC!

Very rarely does a piece of music get synced in its entirety from start to finish. In fact, many placements are twenty to forty seconds long, with some being as short as two seconds. (Yes, really—two seconds.) Most cues are written at one and a half to two and a half minutes in length, but they usually end up being edited. A 20-second placement is not necessarily twenty *consecutive* seconds from the original piece of music. It could be the first five seconds of the piece, ten seconds from the middle, then five seconds from the end. In fact, this is a common occurrence: the beginning of the piece, a little or a lot from the middle, then the end.

This is very important: Ideally, instrumental cues are written and arranged so they can be cut up and put back together—as seamlessly as possible.

HEY! LISTEN TO THIS! "Little Schemer"

Notice how "Little Schemer" has orchestral strings combined with a light hip hop beat. It's also a good example of short silences, or *edit points*. You can imagine how an alternate mix of this cue would be useful with the drums removed, leaving only the strings.

STILL THE SAME: SCORING POINTS WITH THE MUSIC EDITOR

A good rule in sync music is to always keep tempo and key consistent, with no changes throughout. It's also a good idea to have clear delineations between the sections of the piece. These are called edit points and will occasionally include a very short silence to make it easier for the music editor to work with your music.

A *music editor* puts (syncs) your music together with the video of a show. Anything you can do to make the music editor's job easier will increase your placement opportunities. Why? Because the music editors are often the ones making the final decision about which piece of music is used. Regarding instrumentals,

- Use the same key throughout the instrumental piece.
- Keep the tempo and groove consistent throughout the piece so the sections sound cohesive.
- Don't change the overall vibe.
- Bring instruments in or out, making sure their entrances are not jolting.
- Avoid drastic changes within a piece.

COME TOGETHER: ARRANGING 101

It's a good idea to map out an overall arc for your cue. Depending on the genre, it might start small and grow. Or it could start big, quiet down, then build again. The challenge is to keep the piece interesting by using subtle changes while maintaining the same vibe throughout the cue and varying the intensity.

HEY! LISTEN TO THIS!
"The Cover Up"
This cue has many layers and breaks that create tension. Music editors like cues with spaces and surprises.

To help understand how arranging works in instrumentals for sync, consider the cue "The Cover Up." It's based on an eight-note motif made up of a four-note motif followed by silence. The four-note motif is then repeated with different notes but the same timing, followed by more silence. Eight seconds into the cue, you've heard all the composition. The rest is arranged to keep it interesting and create different levels of instrumentation and intensity. The motif is repeated eleven times throughout the cue. Here is how the cue progresses:

- A1 Eight-note motif.
- A2 Percussion enters.
- A3 No change; short break at the end.
- A4 Motif goes up an octave, more percussion enters, single mandolin strum on downbeat, and bass fills the space between the four-note motifs.
- A5 No change.
- A6 All instruments exit except motif, back down to starting octave, and single mandolin strum and minimal percussion that is different than percussion in A2.
- A7 More percussion enters.
- A8 Motif goes up an octave, mandolin strums low string as sixteenth notes, and more percussion enters.
- A9 Bass enters but starts at the same time as the motif (not in the space), and more percussion enters.
- A10 Second mandolin enters, strumming all strings as sixteenth notes, and bass plays more notes.
- A11 No change.
- End The piece finishes with a buildup to the last note.

In the preceding example, there was neither a lot of musical complexity nor virtuosity going on. It was all about the arrangement and instruments coming in, going out, and changing what they're playing to keep the cue interesting without changing too drastically. The same vibe was kept throughout the piece, but the intensity changed: it became more intense, less intense, and more intense again at the end. Many cues have a big buildup to the last note; music editors love that. Most licensable music has a hard ending and doesn't fade out.

In today's world of digital recording, the way a cue like this is approached is to figure out which instruments to use and then record all the parts for an A section. Then copy the A section as many times as needed to reach about two minutes, and add a marker for the beginning of each A section (A1, A2, etc.). Recording software allows the user to place markers that can be named along the time line of a piece of music and can be very helpful in finding a section of the song quickly. Mute all the tracks, and unmute the ones with which you want to start; hit "play," and keep unmuting and muting until you find an arrangement that works.

You can also try changing octaves or the timing of some of the instruments and perhaps double some of the parts with other instruments to thicken them up. Then delete or mute the notes you don't need. At times this is when you may realize a B section is needed.

DON'T GO OVERBOARD WHEN WRITING CUES

Many years ago, a music publisher emphatically told us, "You guys are writing too much! There's no need to overwrite. Ever!" This was career-changing advice for us; he had thrown us a musical life preserver.

The takeaway? We learned that a two-minute piece of music did not require composing two actual minutes of music! What?? "That's right," the publisher said. "Write less, arrange more." We took his advice and started writing eight-bar A sections and then repeated the A sections with interesting arrangement variations. We were amazed how seemingly simple but challenging this technique was—yet very effective in the end.

A NOTE WALKS INTO A BAR . . .

Many sections in a cue have an even number of bars—often a multiple of four. However, depending on the genre, this is not always the case. To be a bit edgy, try a five- or seven-bar section. Be *really* edgy and throw a half bar in there. This is another subtle way of creating tension and instability and an element of surprise, if that's what the style of your cue calls for.

And speaking of edgy, who says you always have to have four beats in every bar? The timing 6/8 has a lilting feel, but 5/4 and 7/8 can be very unsettling. Just *try* to dance to them.

HEY! READ THIS!

So, how long does it take to write a two-minute instrumental cue? *Longer than two minutes.* When we started writing music for sync, it took us three weeks to finish a two-minute cue. Really. Of course, we had a lot to learn about composing, arranging, recording, producing, and mixing. Now it takes us about six to eight hours to finish one in a genre with which we are familiar. If it's a new style for us, or if we're using new software, it takes longer. Composers each work at their own pace. Streamlining the process and being familiar with your tools is essential. The important thing is that the final product must be top-notch and usable.

I'LL TAKE "MUSIC GENRES" FOR $500, PLEASE

People are accustomed to thinking about music in terms of its genre, such as hip hop, rock, country, blues, soul, pop, or jazz. In the world of sync music, in addition to genre, think about how the music will be *placed.* Songs and instrumentals of these genres are used in films and TV shows. However, composers and songwriters of sync music frequently consider the end use of their music while it is being created. These uses include music for commercials, movie trailers, sports, news, dramas, video games, reality cable TV shows, and music that identifies geographic locations. Music written for these purposes may incorporate elements of the genres mentioned above, but they are handled differently. Here are some typical characteristics of music written for these uses:

- *Commercials.* Music written specifically for commercials is likely to be happy, upbeat, and in a major key, with positive, optimistic song lyrics and themes.

- *Movie trailers.* Trailers consistently follow a three-part visual formula—an intro, a buildup, and a climax—so the music that is composed must follow the same formula: intro, buildup, and climax.
    - The finished trailer may contain one cue from start to finish, or a different cue may be used for each of the three sections.
    - In many cases, bits and pieces from dozens of cues may be included in the final version.
    - The composition should not be complicated. Simple music that is not highly melodic is best; the challenge lies in the production and mixing, which must be top-level.
    - This is not to say that trailer cues are easy to write. The goal is to make simple music sound interesting for two to three minutes while following the formula and incorporating acoustic and electronic sounds. A common request for music in trailers is that it sound "epic."
- *Sports.* Viewers of sports programming expect high-energy, intense music that fits the competitive attitude of their games. Aggressive styles, such as rock, hip hop, orchestral, or a combination of these, are standard in accompanying sports. This music is not for the timid.
- *News.* Music for news is typically a combination of electronic and orchestral elements. Brass and strings make it sound very important and serious. Mid- to up-tempo cues bring the urgency required.
- *Tension.* This is a very broad category. It frequently combines elements of electronic, orchestral, hip hop, and rock. It's often in a minor key and creates tension via dissonant harmonies and pulsing beats.
- *Video games.* Most of the music in video games is written by a composer. However, depending on the subject and length of the game, the rest may be licensed. As with many dramatic movies and TV shows, the score composer for a video game does not usually write songs with lyrics for the project.
    - Because of the varying lengths of the scenes in video games, the music is written specifically so that it can be looped: the end of the cue should seamlessly lead back to the beginning. This way, the same music can accompany a short scene or a long scene. If you write music for video games, it is imperative that you actually play video games.
- *Scene-setter or location music.* When a story moves to a new location, a change in the music and images lets the viewer know that the characters are in a different place. This is known as *scene-setter music.* Using instrumentation that is commonly associated with the geographic location, as well as musical scales, harmonies, and rhythms that are characteristic in music from the region are important factors in composing effective music.

PRO TIPS . . . About Writing Instrumentals for Sync

I mostly compose the underscore for various projects. When I write tracks for a production music library, the two most helpful tips have been on two levels: First, regarding the structure of my composition, I use song form A–A–B–A, where I compose the A theme and two more fleshed-out variations, then a contrasting B theme. Second, I keep the music focused on one emotion/tone (each track needs to focus on *one emotion* and develop it over two minutes). The B theme needs to be in the same overall vein but not too different.

—**Penka Kouneva**, Composer for film, TV, and video games

For me personally, the impact of getting sync licensing for my music has been immense. I have always been an artist before anything, so ultimately licensing has just helped put more of a light on my art, and it has financially enabled me to have the flexibility and fuel to keep making and releasing that art independently.

—**Katie Herzig**, Artist, Songwriter, and Producer

The most important criterion for music to be considered for sync, in my opinion, is sticking to a singular emotion for a cue. Make it easier for a music editor to fit it into a scene. Music should be functional and not self-serving. Your job is to support the scene and define the emotion. It should never be, "Hey! Look at me!"

—**Steve Barden**, Composer and Author

Don't send reality TV underscore tracks to a boutique trailer library, and don't send music for commercials to a reality TV library, and so on. A lot of the really successful writers in production music write music with a specific intent and purpose and can tell you immediately what that was.

—**Derek Jones**, Director of Creative Services at Megatrax Production Music

CHAPTER 3

Writing Songs for Sync

LET'S START AT THE VERY BEGINNING . . .

You've learned about the overall basics needed to write instrumental music, many of which also apply to writing songs for sync. Here are some additional fundamental guidelines for songs.

Songs are made up of sections: The most common are the *chorus* and *verse*. The chorus has the same melody and lyrics usually each time it appears. The verses have their own melody but different lyrics each time they occur. The lyrics in the verses explain and point to the title of the song, often without containing the title. The title of the song is found typically in the chorus, where it may repeat (more about *hooks* below).

Like the sections in an instrumental, choruses and verses should contrast each other musically. A popular way of achieving this is by using higher-pitched notes in the chorus melody than in the verse melody. Another option is to use notes of different lengths in each section. If the verse melody has long, slow notes, the chorus melody can have short, fast notes, and vice versa; the crucial aspect is *contrast*.

Here are some optional song sections:

- *Pre-chorus.* Also known as a *lift* or a *climb*, the pre-chorus leads up to the chorus melody. It is situated between the verse and chorus, and it may occur once or twice. If it recurs, it may or may not have the same lyrics. It is customarily shorter than the verse or chorus.
- *Bridge.* This happens later in the song and occurs once. The lyrics in the bridge contain new information, and the music contrasts strongly that of the rest of the song. The bridge can reveal something important.
- *Post-chorus.* This is especially useful in songs for sync. It appears after a chorus, and its lyrics contain the title or other lyrics from the chorus, repeated in a catchy way. A post-chorus may contain no lyrics at all and instead use nonsense words, also known as *vocalises*, such as, "la, la, la," "doo, doo, doo," or "whoa-oh-oh." This section works well in commercials and other placements where a scene needs music with vocals that are not distracting.

OUR HOUSE: BUILDING A FOUNDATION WITH SYNC MUSIC STRUCTURES

Structure is the sequence of sections that create the form of a piece of music. In general, songs for sync have the same structures as pop songs, such as the tried-and-true verse–chorus–verse–chorus–bridge–chorus. And, like pop songs, the chorus lyrics don't usually add any new information, instead, focusing on a single idea or emotion, sometimes repeating a phrase.

In many instances, it's the choruses of songs that are placed in shows, so some songs for sync contain only a repeated chorus. Then why bother writing verses if they're not going to be used? Because the verses *do* get used.

The music users (music supervisors, music editors) like to know that the song is complete and legitimate—that it's not an unfinished song. If this song gets placed in a TV show, then the viewer may search for the song and listen to it in its entirety. Also, because there is now some *traction*, the song may get used in other media. This would make it a hit song in the sync music world!

Like instrumentals, it's very important for the arrangements of licensable songs to have defined sections that evolve and change in intensity as the song unfolds. Add a second guitar and a vocal harmony on the second verse. Let the drums kick in on the second chorus. Bring in the choir or background vocal harmonies and handclaps for that big last chorus. Or take some instruments out in some sections. Lay the foundation and experiment with different song structures, and you'll give the music editor some options from which to choose.

YOU PICKED A FINE TIME TO . . . RHYME

Listeners enjoy hearing song lyrics when the last words of some of the lines rhyme. The use of rhymes follows a pattern referred to as a *rhyme scheme.* Though sections may also contain a different number of lines, many verses and choruses contain four lines, so that will be used as an example. There are other rhyme schemes, but these are the most common:

- *AABB.* The last words of the first and second lines rhyme, and the last words of the third and fourth lines rhyme:

  I love the moon
  In the month of June
  Glowing in the night
  A beautiful sight

- *ABAB.* The last words of the first and third lines rhyme, and the last words of the second and fourth lines rhyme.

  I love the moon
  Glowing in the night
  In the month of June
  A beautiful sight

- *ABCB.* The last words of the second and fourth lines rhyme, while the last words of the first and third lines do *not* rhyme.

  I love the moon
  Glowing in the night
  In the month of May
  A beautiful sight

The rhyme schemes of the verses often remain consistent. For example, if the first verse is ABAB, the second verse is CDCD. The rhyme scheme of the chorus typically contrasts that of the verses. In this example, a chorus with a rhyme scheme of AABB would be appropriate.

There are two main kinds of rhyme: perfect and near. In *perfect rhyme,* the vowel sound and the last consonant of the words are exactly the same:

- Book, look, took
- Red, said, fed
- Day, weigh, stay

In *near rhyme* (also known as *close, imperfect, false,* or *lazy rhyme*), the vowel sound is the same, or very close, but the last consonant is different:

- Me, need, sweet
- Dive, wide, night
- Tough, love, cut

Some songwriters use only perfect rhyme, while others prefer the additional possibilities available with near rhyme. Like many other songwriting decisions, it is up to you.

Rhymes of one syllable are easier to find and are therefore more common. Words that rhyme two or more syllables are a challenge but are very satisfying to hear. Examples of double rhyme include:

- Going, knowing, showing
- Station, nation, vacation
- Better, letter, go-getter

There are additional rhyming techniques other than perfect and near rhymes: Some lyricists use *slant rhyme*, also known as *half rhyme*. Sonically, the words sound similar, like "form" and "foam," "eyes" and "ours," or "yours" and "years."

YOU SAY "POTATO," AND I SAY "AVOCADO"

Another option is to make up your own, original rhyme. This is called a *mangled* or *stretched rhyme*. Because the artist's words are intentionally twisted in a contemporary or unusual way to make them work in the song, the listener understands what is being communicated and gets it.

Examples are "know me" and "lovely," "feels" and "hills," "more" and "sure," "his" and "yours," and "rain" and "again." Find more examples by doing an Internet search for "types of rhymes."

If you have difficulty finding words that rhyme, consult a rhyming dictionary. These are available online or in printed form. They can be very helpful. If you keep rhyming the same words over and over, use a rhyming dictionary to break out of your rut.

INVERT YOUR WORDS, DO NOT

It can be a challenge to have your lyrics say what you want them to say while rhyming. To facilitate this, some writers change the order of the words to make the rhyming word fall at the end of the line. The problem is that the lyrics sound forced and unnatural, making it hard for the listener to understand what they mean. For example, a lyric may be

Walking through the snow, hand in hand we'll go.

Though grammatically correct, most people would not say it that way in a conversation. They would likely say

We'll go walking hand in hand through the snow.

Yes, it's more difficult to convey a message clearly using words in what seems like a contrived way, but that's what great songwriters do. You can do it too. Don't settle. Dig deeper.

GETTING IN TOUCH WITH YOUR INNER RHYME

Though rhymes usually occur at the end of a line, they can also fall in the middle of a line, creating *inner rhyme*. An example would be:

I *know* that things will *go* my way
I'm *back* on *track* again today

The obvious rhymes at the end of each line are "way" and "today," with the more subtle inner rhymes being "know" and "go," as well as "back" and "track." The inner rhymes can occur anywhere throughout a line. This technique can be challenging for songwriters, but the payoff for the listener is worth the time and effort.

SAY WHAT YOU NEED TO SAY

Songwriters and lyricists know that establishing a rhyme scheme is gratifying for the listener. However, there are times when the song's message is obscured or it no longer makes sense because a rhyme has been forced. When this happens, the song does not flow well.

The most important goal when writing lyrics for sync is to communicate a feeling. If a gratuitous rhyme is getting in the way of the listener understanding that feeling, there are a few workarounds you can try: use different words with the same meaning but a different sound, or change the rhyme scheme altogether. This will prevent the listener from being distracted or confused.

THIS SOUNDS LIKE SOMETHING STUPENDOUSLY SENSATIONAL

Another useful tool in writing lyrics is *alliteration*. This is a device in which words within a phrase contain the same consonant sound, usually at the beginning of a word or stressed syllable. Alliteration creates sonic patterns that are pleasing to the listener:

- Ball, bat, above
- First, photo, before
- This, that, although

Alliteration can also be used anywhere within a line or song section. When combined with rhyme, alliteration makes certain words sound satisfying.

DON'T BORE US—CREATE A SURPRISE FOR US

The last thing any songwriter wants to do is write a boring song. To avoid this, put surprises in your songs. A surprise is when the listener expects one thing and instead another thing happens. That unexpected thing could be a surprise word, rhyme, melody note, or chord. Alternatively, the song may deliver something expected, but it may occur a little earlier or later than the listener thought it would.

How do you get the listener to expect something? You can achieve this by having a degree of predictability in your songs. When a song establishes a pattern, the listener expects this pattern to continue. This pattern may include:

- Pitches of the melody
- Timing of the melody
- When the rhymes occur
- Lengths of lines
- Chord changes

Once a pattern has been established, any deviation from that pattern creates a surprise. If a song has no recognizable pattern, there is no expectation and therefore no surprise. Ironically, this leads to an uninteresting song, which disengages the listener.

Yet when a song is completely predictable, this is boring too. If the listener can anticipate what lyrics or melody notes are coming, the song seems lifeless and dull.

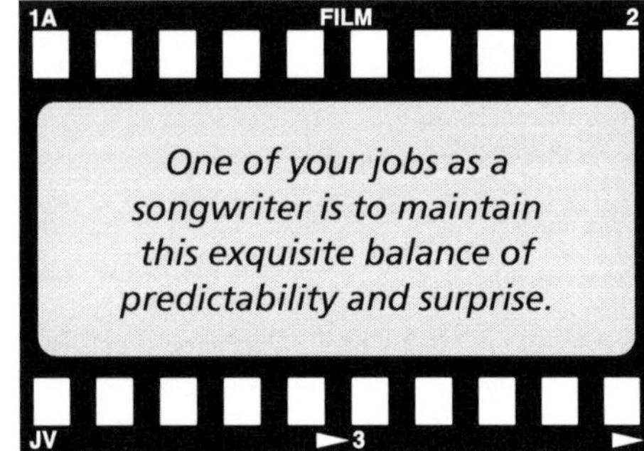

One of your jobs as a songwriter is to maintain this exquisite balance of predictability and surprise. It is among the hallmarks of a well-written and -crafted song. Think about some of your favorite songs: How predictable are they? Are there surprises? When you listen to a new song for the first time, do you have any expectations? How do you feel when the song does exactly what you think it's going to do? How about when it does something you didn't think it was going to do? The odds are, the songs you enjoy the most are the ones that maintain a balance between predictability and surprise.

The length of each line in a song can be varied to keep it interesting. If every line contains the same number of syllables and is sung with the same timing, the song is not as appealing as it could be. Though lines of the same length can be used for effect in a song about monotony, it does not make for a captivating song. A more compelling sequence of line lengths in a verse would be seven syllables followed by five, seven, and five. Or three, six, three, and eight. Preferably, the pattern established in the first verse of a song should continue in the other verses, unless there is an intentional surprise. Also, having a different pattern of line lengths in the chorus is an effective way to contrast it with the verses.

WE HEREBY GRANT YOU PERMISSION

What makes many songs likable is that they contain *hooks*. A hook is a memorable part of a song that repeats, usually in the chorus. Most of the time, the hook contains the title of the song. When people hear catchy songs, they often like to sing along with the hook. It is short, simple, and easy to remember.

Although it is good to have variety in a song, listeners want to sing along with the part that repeats. They cannot do this if you do not write some repetition into your songs. So, by the powers vested in us by the songwriting universe, we hereby grant you permission to repeat hooks in your songs. Go forth and be hooky.

Keep in mind that hooks do not have to repeat in the exact same way each time. Here are some possible variations:

- The chords that accompany a repeated hook can change.
- A hook can be repeated with one or more of the notes changed to a different pitch.
- The melody of the hook can be repeated with different lyrics.
- In one of the repetitions, the melody of the hook can be raised or lowered while keeping the same timing. For example, a hook melody with the pitches C–E–C can be changed to E–G–E. It can also be changed to D–F–D, if it fits well with the chords. The important thing is that the shape of the melody remains the same.
- One or two of the words in the hook can be removed when the hook is repeated either at the beginning or at the end. For example, "We're having a good time, a good time." (The words "We're having" are removed.) Or "I love you, girl, I love, love, love you, girl."
- A word or nonsense word (whoa, ooh, hey) can be added, usually at the end.
- A hook can start on a different beat in the next measure.
- Any combination of these.
- If a hook is repeated four times, one or two of the repetitions can contain some of the variations suggested here while the other two or three remain the same.

TIGHTROPE: HOW TO MAINTAIN A DELICATE BALANCE

Repeating a pattern is good. However, there is such a thing as too much repetition. This is another kind of balance to consider having in your songs. One of the most frustrating things for songwriters is that they never get to hear their songs for the first time. It is difficult to listen to them with objectivity. This is especially true of a song you have been working on for a few hours or a song you are performing yourself.

If possible, make a rough recording of your song, and listen to it the next day. With some distance, you are more likely to make objective observations about your song. In addition to whether or not there is too much or too little repetition, you may notice if your song conveys the message and emotion you intended.

It is also helpful to have a trusted circle of music-loving friends or family on whom you can rely to be honest with you and can consult about whether your songs achieve your goals. Do not ask them specifically about any aspect of your song; see what stands out to them.

ALL TOGETHER NOW

A successful songwriter was once asked, "Which comes first, the lyrics or the music?" The response was, "The phone call." Others may reply, "A burst of inspiration." There really is no standard answer to this question, as every songwriter has their own process. Some songwriters write the lyrics first, while others start with the music. Others are able to write both simultaneously. There's no doubt that when it all comes together, it will sound right, perhaps even exciting, like seeing a colorful display of fireworks.

If you start by writing lyrics and have difficulty putting them to music, try writing the music first. If you start with music and your lyrics sound forced, try writing the lyrics first. A different start frequently yields a different result.

If you have not written with another songwriter previously, try co-writing. The ideal collaborator is someone who has strengths where you have weaknesses, and vice versa. In addition to complementary skill sets, the best co-writers share goals and levels of professionalism. However, some songwriters are not interested in writing songs for licensing and may not be appropriate writing partners for sync. Choose your co-writers wisely.

KISMET: MEANT TO BE

Regardless of which is written first, when the lyrics and melody are combined, they need to work together in a way that sounds natural, as though the song was inevitable. The lyrics and melody should sound like they were conceived in complete and final form, even though a lot of editing and crafting has actually taken place. The song is finished when there are no distractions or deal breakers and everything about the song makes sense.

The accents of the words should align with accents of the melody. In cases where these accents are inconsistent, small adjustments can be made to the timing of the melody. If large changes are necessary, the lyrics may need to be altered. If any of these changes is being made to a verse, keep in mind the goal of maintaining the same melody, line lengths, and rhyme schemes in the other verses. Adding another five notes to the melody of the second line in the second verse to accommodate the lyrics will make it difficult to maintain melodic consistency with the second line of the first verse unless the same change is made.

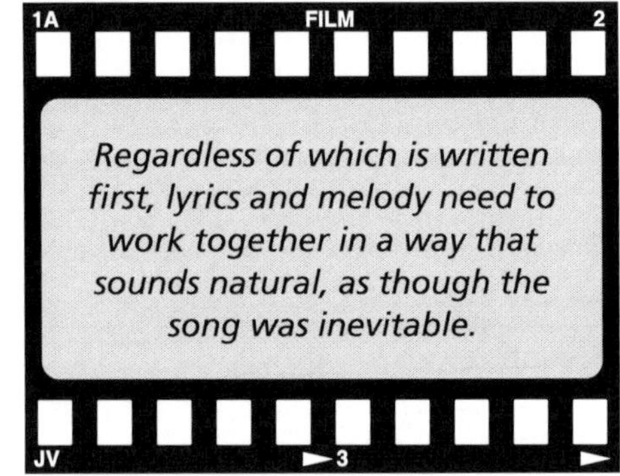

ACCENTUATE THE POSITIVE

There are some styles of music where accenting a syllable in a word that is normally unaccented is acceptable. For example, the word "writing" might be accented on the second syllable to rhyme with "sing." If this technique is commonplace in the genre of your song, you are encouraged to do it. Be sure that it is intentional and not accidental.

A common songwriter solution to the problem of mismatched lyric and melody timing is to jam a cluster of words into a short amount of time. This will sound forced, and the lyrics are likely to be difficult to enunciate and understand. Try changing the order of the words or using a thesaurus (online or in printed form) to find different words to convey the same idea. Often one word can be found to replace multiple words. Some synonyms may have a different number of syllables than the original word. They also may rhyme with different words, which creates new options. Sometimes switching lines around in a verse solves the problem.

I NEED ANOTHER WORD FOR "SYNONYM"

At this stage of the process, part of a songwriter's job is to be a puzzle solver and master of wordplay. What word has two syllables, rhymes with "sleeve," and can replace the word "trust"? "Believe" would be a good candidate. Songwriters need to answer these kinds of questions many times in the crafting of the lyrics of a song.

Keep the crafting part of the process separate from the inspiration and conception part. Write what needs to be said, and then go back and edit and craft what you have written. Crafting a song is known as "digging deeper," and it means finding a unique way to express what has been said in past songs. By doing so, you'll also avoid clichés. Though there are exceptions, very few great song ideas came to life fully formed. The crafting can be done by you, the originator of the idea, or by a trusted collaborator.

When bringing together lyrics and melody, consider which vowel sounds are held, especially if the last word of a phrase is long. Vowel sounds like the ones found in the words "stay," "go," "free," and "you" are excellent ones to hold out because these are open- or long-vowel sounds. Vocalists love singing these vowels and listeners love hearing them. However, closed- or short-vowel sounds in words such as "him," "met," "rub," "that," and "her" are not pleasant to hear on long notes. This provides you with yet another piece in your songwriting puzzle. (If it were easy, everyone would be doing it.)

HEY! WHO SAID THAT?

The best lyrics in songs intended for sync are engaging and allow the listener to feel what the singer is feeling. The perspective of the lyrics has a big influence on this and is an important decision a songwriter has to make. There are three perspectives used in songs:

- First person (singular is "I," and plural is "we")
- Second person (singular is "you," and plural is "you")
- Third person (singular is "he," "she," and plural is "they")

The most effective and, therefore, most-often-used perspective found in licensable songs is *first person*. This is the point of view of the singer and uses the words "I" and "me": "I am the luckiest guy in the world," or "Why does this always happen to me?" are two examples. Most listeners are drawn to the experiences, observations, and feelings of the person right in front of them. It feels intimate and personal and gets the viewer into the head and heart of an on-screen character.

Another perspective is *second person*. This is when the singer is speaking directly to the listener and brings them into the song by using the word "you." For instance, "You are the luckiest guy in the world," or "Why does this always happen to you?" This point of view is also intimate and personal, as the singer and the listener (*me* and *you*) are often in the same space at the same time. It can be very compelling when good things are being said about "you." However, if the "you" in the lyric does not sound like a nice person, the listener may feel defensive. Be careful with this perspective. Fortunately for film and TV songwriters, the "you" in the lyrics is assumed to be a character on the screen.

Third person lyrics are told from the perspective of people who are not immediately present or are not a part of the conversation. This point of view uses the words "he," "him," "she," her," "they," and "them," as in, "He is the luckiest guy in the world," and "Why does this always happen to her?" With the third person perspective, it's easier for the listener or viewer to assume the lyrics are talking about an on-screen character. There is more distance with this point of view, which may be appropriate in songs about being apart (physically and emotionally) or feeling isolated from someone.

RIGHT HERE, RIGHT NOW

There are two other aspects of a song's perspective that affect how the listener perceives it—time and place. The lyrics in a song may reference events that happen in the past, present, or future. They may also convey how someone in the song feels now about what has already happened or what may happen, or how their feelings in the past have now changed.

In songs for sync, any reference to when events occur should be nonspecific. It is important that no exact dates or times be given. As always, there are exceptions. Songs about Christmas, the summer, or

Valentine's Day need to make those references to be effective. Relative time can be mentioned, like "yesterday," "tomorrow," "minutes ago," "days ago," "weeks from now," or "years in the future." Experiment with each of these perspectives to find which one helps your song communicate its message.

Where the singer or other people in the song are located can impact the listener's perception. Like time, the place should not be mentioned specifically. It may instead be ambiguously referenced as "here," "there," "at home," "far away," or "right next to me." However, few or no specific descriptions, such as color or size, can be revealed about the place where the song is happening.

Nonspecific information can be presented in lyrics, such as "cold room," "fast car," or "dark hall." Where appropriate, each of these adjectives provides emotional information without giving details that are too specific that may conflict with the images on the screen. The room may have been "cold," but the lyrics don't have to indicate the precise temperature. Likewise, the car may have been "fast," but the lyrics don't have to mention the exact speed. No song will be a good fit for every scene, but you can stack the odds in your favor by using lyrics that are ambiguous about details but clear about the emotion.

ASK AND ANSWER: WHO? WHEN? WHERE?

In combination, these three perspectives—who, when, and where—provide the setting for the lyrics of your song and should be considered before the song is written. Many songs for sync are written from the point of view of "me, right here, right now." This represents the most immediate of each of the perspectives and is preferred over "him, way over there, long ago." For example, "My heart is being broken here and now" is more engaging than "His heart was broken in another country years ago." There are songs where changing one or more of the perspectives may make the song stronger.

Before a song is written, consider which of these perspectives will be applied:

- *Who.* First, second, or third person
- *When.* Past, present, or future tense
- *Where.* Here, there, indoors, outdoors, in private, or in public

In some instances with sync, any of these can be changed after the song is finished. However, some of the wording and rhymes may also need to be changed. Before your song is finalized, try each of the three perspectives to decide which will best suit your song. After you have chosen one, stick with it throughout your song. If the perspectives keep changing, it is difficult for the listener to keep track of what is happening.

HEY! READ THIS!

A critical part of the process of writing songs for sync is watching TV shows and movies and paying attention to the songs and how they are used. Typically the lyrics in these songs are perceived to be the thoughts and feelings of one of the characters in the story. Similar characters appear in several different shows. Take note of these characters and the situations in which they find themselves. They may break hearts or have their hearts broken, always win or always lose, feel confident or insecure, be motivated or lazy, be optimistic or pessimistic, think only of themselves or be considerate of others, or (here's a classic) be good or be evil. Observe the traits of the characters in the shows that interest you, and write songs from their perspective. Do not tell a story featuring these characters. Instead, write about how they feel when they exhibit their typical behavior, how they feel about the way they are, or how other people feel about them and their behavior.

There are other techniques worth considering at the start of the writing process: One is to begin by selecting a title. This gives the lyrics more focus and makes it harder to drift away from the central idea. Another is to have a singer in mind. This will affect the language, tone, and attitude of the song.

Songs may be inspired by real events in the life of the songwriter or someone they know. This can help to ensure that the feelings expressed in the lyrics are real, relatable, and likely to be reflected in the story of a TV show or movie. It is best to focus on one emotion and not offer any specific details. Though the real-life experience may have been a more involved story and taken many twists and turns, the lyrics should remain concentrated on a single idea. Do not let the truth get in the way of a good song.

YOUR MUSIC'S GOT ME FEELING EMOTIONS

Lyrics in licensable songs are universal and most often about a feeling, such as: looking for love, being in love, falling out of love, loneliness, having fun hanging out with friends or partying, belonging, exploring or discovering life, feeling like an outsider, feeling inadequate, feeling empowered, feeling lost, and other emotions or situations.

Lyrics in licensable songs are universal and most often about a feeling.

It's important to not simply use the words "happy" or "sad" to talk about these emotions but, instead, to describe and write about the physical manifestations of these emotions—such as, "a big smile with a gleam in her eye" or "looking away as tears rolled down his cheek."

Engage the senses by describing what can be seen, heard, or felt when someone is experiencing an emotion. Describe their facial expression, body posture, or movements.

METAPHOR OR SIMILE: SO, LIKE, WHAT'S THE DIFFERENCE?

Instead of using literal terms, another way to spice up your lyrics, when making a comparison, is to use a simile or a metaphor.

A *simile* compares two things using the words "as" or "like." For example, "Her eyes were as dark *as* midnight" or "His voice was *like* gravel."

Instead of comparing, a *metaphor* says one thing *is* another. For example, "Love *is* a fuzzy blanket" or "You *are* my sunshine."

Similes and metaphors can help move the story along and heighten what the characters are experiencing. This will engage the viewer more. The song should focus on one emotion, and the emotion should be evident very early in the song. If the scene changes and has a different feel, they'll use a different song.

WHY MIXED METAPHORS ARE POSITIVELY A NO-NO

Songwriters need to be careful about mixing metaphors, or putting lyrics together that don't make sense.

For an extreme example, a beginning singer-songwriter's lyrics in verse one are about "walking all alone in the cold, freezing rain"; then in verse two, his lyrics are about how his new love makes him feel like he's "flying to the moon and back." Next, he writes in the bridge that he is "driving down the highway in the blazing summer sun with a carload of friends." This song would be considered a hot mess.

If the song is about loneliness, keep it sad, and use appropriate metaphors and similes pertaining to these feelings. If the song is happy and upbeat, then this is your chance to use all of the sunshine metaphors you want.

Remember, if the song takes the viewer out of the story because something about it is distracting, it might not make the final cut. The song functions like the scenery, and the clothes and makeup the actors are wearing.

NOW, LET US TELL YOU WHAT WE THINK YOU SHOULD DO

Songwriters have a tendency to speak from the perspective of knowing all the answers to life's questions. Their lyrics may come across as preachy as they tell the listener what they should do or think. Some listeners bristle when the singer takes a position of authority and ultimate knowledge. You may have felt offended when you read the title of this section. Though this was done for an intentional effect, it should not be done on a regular basis. Nobody likes a know-it-all.

The exact opposite approach is warmer and perceived differently. Lyrics that express uncertainty, doubts, or confusion can be more appropriate for roles portrayed in TV shows and movies. Having the singer ask questions and seek answers is more common for characters in storylines. This viewpoint makes the song more relatable and less off-putting for the listener.

JUST THE WAY YOU ARE: GENRE PURITY AND THE USE OF LANGUAGE

Each genre of music has its own language. Be as true to the genre as you can be. Hip hop songs use different language than folk songs. Rock songs use different language than jazz songs. And be authentic. Most music listeners can spot an imposter a mile away. Consider who will be singing your song, and ask yourself if your lyric sounds like something the singer would actually say in your song's genre.

TELL IT LIKE IT IS: USE UNIVERSAL, SIMPLE LYRICS

Just as important as what the lyrics are about is what they are not about. Ideally, licensable lyrics do not have specific references to names of people or places, dates, times, colors, exact sizes, car models, styles of clothes, or other such specifics. At times, general references work, such as "in the city," "in the country," "late at night," "tall," "short," "dressed up." Often, when writing lyrics for songs intended for listening, songwriters describe in great detail what can be seen, known as, "putting furniture in the room." This does not work well in songs for licensing.

As always, there are exceptions: Despite not following these guidelines, hit songs are licensed frequently. That's because they are hit songs and are used so the viewer recognizes the song and has an association or familiarity with it.

There are times when some specificity is acceptable. For instance, many stories take place in major cities, such as Los Angeles or New York, so music supervisors may look for songs with those place-names in the lyrics. However, it is a good idea to target as many potential placements as possible, so use your judgment.

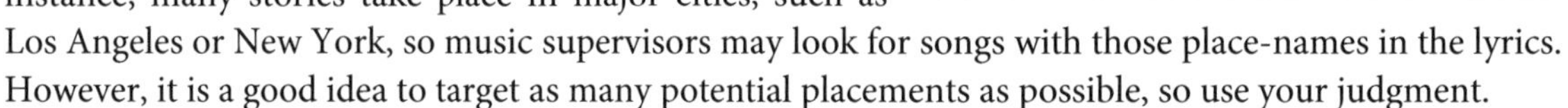

At times, songs are used as *source music*, or music that the characters hear, such as in a restaurant or in a bar coming from a jukebox. Specificity is not much of a problem here, but, again, if you want to further stack the odds in your favor, make your lyrics more general and universal.

WE GO TOGETHER: DEFINING PROSODY

Prosody is important whether or not songs are written for licensing. In the songwriting world, *prosody* (pronounced *PRAHZ-a-dee*) is the marriage of the music with the lyrics and how appropriate they are with each other. If a song has a light, up-tempo beat in a major key and the lyrics are about being sad and miserable, this is an example of bad prosody. It is like sighing and dejectedly saying, "I'm having a great day." The listener is confused and wonders if the speaker is being sarcastic or ironic. Think of prosody as the singer's tone of voice if the lyrics were being spoken. The message is sent and received more clearly if the content of the lyrics matches the delivery.

A basic way to address this in sync songwriting is to use this time-tested technique: major keys and chords are happy; minor keys and chords are sad. However, there is more to it than that. The previous analogy of comparing someone singing with someone speaking is a good starting point: If a person is so excited that they cannot contain themself, they are likely to speak very quickly and probably would not stop to take a breath. In a song being sung from the standpoint of this thrilled person, the melody, phrasing, tonality, and tempo should reflect this.

Listen to your song as if you did not understand the language in which it is written. What emotion is being conveyed? How do the music and the vocalist's delivery make you feel? If it feels different than what you had intended, make some changes to the lyrics, the music, or both.

ONCE UPON A TIME . . . WHY LYRICS WITH STORIES WON'T WORK FOR SYNC

Lyrics that contain a story can be problematic in sync because the storyline of the show may not be the same as the one in the song and confuse the viewer. If the storylines are the same, that can be too on the nose. However, a song about a single scene from a story, and the emotions in that scene, can find success.

Some people think the music licensing world is a place to dump their poorly written songs. We disagree wholeheartedly. Writing music for sync is not easier or harder than writing other types of songs; it's just different. Although there is some overlap with other styles, the goals are not the same. Most other songs are self-contained and don't rely on any accompanying video to get their message across. Ordinarily, songs for sync don't tell a complete story but, rather, convey an emotion that can engage a viewer watching a scene. And yet the song can be enjoyable to listen to apart from the show in which it's been placed.

Songwriting for sync uses good songwriting techniques. Use all the skills you may have already learned. Listeners still like to hear rhymes, alliteration, interesting phrasing and melodies, a cool groove, and a fresh perspective. They also love contrast, and that's what makes a song more interesting. Add an emotive singer and expert producing and mixing, and your chances for success will increase even more. Above all, the listeners and viewers want to *feel* something.

ALL BY MYSELF

There are some self-contained solo composers and songwriters who are able to do just about everything on their own. We can do most things on our own, but not all. Then there are those who either prefer or need to work with others. They collaborate, especially if they have some weaknesses in certain areas. This is known as having a team.

There are advantages and disadvantages of working solo versus working as a team. We've done both, and this is what we've learned over the years:

- *Pros of working solo.* You get to call the shots. You can keep your copyright or sell it. You can work on whatever projects you want, whenever you want. There's no one to argue with you.
- *Cons of working solo.* It can be lonely! You can be limited when it comes to ideas. It's tough to do a collection of ten to twenty songs or instrumentals all by yourself without the music becoming repetitive. It can take a lot longer to finish a project. If you can't work for a few days, nothing gets done.
- *Pros of working on a team.* You can get a lot of fresh ideas. Others can pick up the slack. There is a deeper pool of knowledge, experience, skills, and talent from which to draw. You can get instant objective feedback on ideas.
- *Cons of working on a team.* There can be indecisiveness and too many opinions. If you don't do songwriter split agreements beforehand (more about this in part 3), it could come back to bite you. If there is no clear goal, the music may languish unsigned for years. You will depend on others, and they may not take deadlines or quality as seriously as you do.

THESE ARE MY PEOPLE

Who should be on your musical team? The ideal team would consist of people who do what you can't do as well or what you can't do at all, such as singers, artists, musicians, recording engineers, or mixers. Perhaps you're strong writing music, but you need someone who is stronger with lyrics.

You can see how quickly things get arduous with all of these people involved in the writing and recording of a song. There is a lot to keep track of, not only regarding the music itself, but with the music business aspects as well, so organizational skills are essential. Either do these tasks yourself and do them well, or find someone with these skills to do them for you.

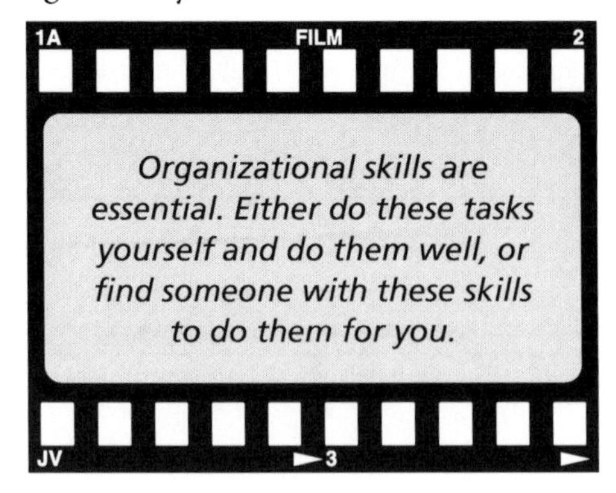

In some cases, it might be practical to barter services with someone. A vocalist could sing on a producer's track, and the producer could record the vocalist's next project. In other cases, paying people for their services is a good option.

In all cases, make absolutely certain you have signed work-for-hire agreements and a songwriter split sheet (see appendix B).

FACE THE MUSIC

One of our friends is a fantastic bass player who gigged professionally for many years. Yet he admits he couldn't hold a candle to an amazing slap bass player who recorded on his funk compositions. Yes, you have to be honest with yourself.

Where can you find people to be on your team? It might be time to start going to music conventions. Or join and support songwriting organizations in your area. You can also find people on various music forums. (See appendix I for more suggestions.)

Some people are okay working with strangers. However, it's better to work with people you have known for a while. You want to be as sure as you can that your personalities, musical abilities, and levels of professionalism are compatible. Referrals from friends can be helpful. It's important to know how to work with people on your team; communication and diplomacy are essential.

Now that you know the basics of how to put your song together and you've found some collaborators, here are some tips about making your musical creations stand out from the crowd.

HEY! THAT'S A GREAT TITLE! HOW TO GET THE MUSIC USER'S ATTENTION

Think of your titles as headlines that will grab the attention of the music editor or music supervisor, because these music users will decide whether or not to place your music. Here are a few tips about titles to keep in mind:

- Two- to three-word titles are great because there's less typing involved. Music users don't have the time or patience to deal with weird, long, or complex titles.
- Try not to use special characters (!, #, $, quotes, etc.)—such as "Hey! This Is a Cue!" or "$how Me the Money" or "Ain't It Good?"—because they can make registering your songs difficult.
- Instrumental titles matter just as much as song titles.
- If it's a song title, the title should be in the chorus. Obscure titles are great for songs by artists and bands, but titles that are too abstract won't be found and used—or remembered.
- Be original.
- Be creative.
- Indicate the vibe of the music.

- Avoid clichés. Instead, create a unique variation, such as "Slick and Twisted" or "Reckoning Crew."
- Use titles that do not reference existing artists or their songs to avoid any potential legal entanglements.

The title can pair the genre with an action verb and/or an adjective. Here are some examples of our music that have been placed over and over again, and the titles may have helped:

- "Carnival Lights" (circus music)
- "Ancient Chinese Secret" (Asian track)
- "Top Hat Rag" (ragtime solo piano)
- "Rainbow Shave Ice" (ukulele music)
- "Mean and Nasty" (epic rock track)
- "Viva Sevilla" (Latin track)
- "Always Welcome" (uplifting, positive song)
- "Waiting in the Dark" (anticipation, ominous, mysterious, unsettled)
- "Pick Up the Funk" (swagger, upbeat, confident)

A VERITABLE "TITLE" WAVE

Where do you find great titles? Once you start thinking about titles, you'll probably find them everywhere. Here are some helpful resources:

- News sources, such as newspaper and magazine headlines; websites such as Wikipedia. Browse through "personality-type" magazines, and you'll find a wealth of titles.
- Blogs, podcasts, and social media posts. Follow songwriters, artists, authors, and music supervisors, because they tend to make pithy or interesting comments and observations.
- Billboard ads, bumper stickers, roadside signs, street names, and car license plates.
- T-shirts with slogans in department stores, catalogs, e-commerce craft websites; or do an Internet search for "T-shirts with funny sayings."
- Décor and home goods–type stores and online handmade crafts and gift sites that have posters, banners, and signs. You'll find endless quirky or funny titles at places that sell greeting cards, collectibles, or tchotchkes.
- Paint chip samples in home improvement stores are useful if you need a moody or colorful song title. Or do an Internet search for "color charts."
- Retail drugstores have a treasure trove of potential song titles in nearly every aisle. In the beauty section, for instance, there are nail polish names with some interesting twists. (One polish was called "Lover," and another was "Natural," which happen to be titles of two hit songs.)
- Funny texts, quotes, or conversations with friends or family; listen to people talking in restaurants or out in public. Some great songs were written as a result of eavesdropping. Hit songwriters Diane Warren and Liz Rose admit using this technique.
- TV shows, especially reality shows; listen (between bleeps) to some of the dialog, and you'll get title ideas.
- Book or movie titles.
- Online dictionary, thesaurus, and synonym finders.
- Alternative dictionaries online (but be warned the slang can be "salty" and may not work for sync).

Other great resources include *MasterWriter*, *Roget's Thesaurus*, Thesaurus.com, Dictionary.com, and *The Synonym Finder* by J. I. Rodale.

HEY! READ THIS!
Here's an easy exercise for coming up with titles. For instance, let's say you've composed ten dramedy tracks and need ten titles.

1. Start with the word "sneaky."
2. Now add another word before or after this word: Acting Sneaky, Sneaky Eyes, Sneaky Feet, Sneaky Peek, Quiet and Sneaky, Slick and Sneaky, Sneaky to a Fault.
3. Now change the word "sneaky" a bit: Sneaking Around, Sneaked Away, Sneaks About, Sneak Around the Corner.
4. Now find some synonyms for "sneaky," such as "deceitful," "shifty," "sketchy," "double-dealer," "slinky," "prowling," and "tiptoeing," and follow the first few steps above.

INSTRUMENTAL TITLES VERSUS SONG TITLES

We prefer to write titles for our instrumentals after they are completely written, produced, and mixed. When the cue is finished, it's easier to come up with a good title that fits the mood.

However, regarding song titles, we do the complete opposite. It's important to think of the concept and title first, and then write the song so it points to the title. The title is almost always in the chorus, so it has to be memorable. It helps keeps us on track.

Keep in mind that the music editor or music supervisor is often on a crazy deadline, frantically looking for just the right song. When you select an enticing title that fits your well-crafted music, everybody wins.

PD (PUBLIC DOMAIN) IS FREE FOR THE TAKING

Do you want to record music but can't think of anything original? Here's a solution: arrange and produce a song or instrumental that is in the *public domain*, also known as *PD*. PD means the copyright has expired and the song now belongs to all of us, or the public. Anyone can do a recording of a public domain song. However, it's essential to do research on every PD song you would like to record, because every country has a different copyright term. When we were first learning how to record and do production, we played and arranged nursery rhymes and simple PD Christmas songs. Some of these recordings still get licensed. It was an interesting project because we didn't have to think about writing a song, just recording and arranging it.

There have been many versions recorded of most PD songs, so why do another one? If you have a different or contemporary interpretation of a PD song, you may have good luck with it. We've had a lot of success with a hip hop version of "O Christmas Tree." It's been placed in dozens of TV shows and commercials. In addition to using hip hop beats, we also changed the time signature from 3/4 to 4/4 and added syncopation to the melody to make it more contemporary and different than many other versions.

"FREE BIRD" IS NOT FREE: RESEARCH IS ESSENTIAL WHEN USING PD SONGS

Caution: Make sure the song you choose is truly in the public domain. The hymn "Amazing Grace" is PD; however, the hymn "How Great Thou Art" is not. The winter song "Jingle Bells" is PD; however, "Sleigh Ride" is not. There are many classical pieces that are PD; however, there are some classical pieces that, although they were written a century ago, still retain their international copyright.

Even though the song "There Is Love (Wedding Song)" was written in 1971 by Noel Paul Stookey (of Peter, Paul and Mary) for Peter Yarrow's wedding, it is in the public domain. This is because Stookey generously gifted the song to the world.

Do research to make absolutely sure a song or piece of music is definitely PD, not only in the United States but in the rest of the world as well.

HEY! LISTEN TO THIS! "Jingle Bells"
We did a version of this carol featuring two ukuleles and a few other instruments. Once again, simplicity is key. Notice how the timing of the melody was syncopated to make it more contemporary-sounding.

MUSIC JAIL

It is permissible to arrange and record public domain music. However, it is *not* permissible to incorporate any part of any composition or recording of another party's copyrighted work into your own that is not in the public domain. Even the shortest snippet of a recording (*sampling*) of someone else's music used in your recording will land you in "music jail."

Okay, there's no such thing as music jail, but the sync music industry's equivalent is that if a songwriter or composer commits this egregious act, no music supervisor or music placement company of any kind will work with that person ever again. There is potentially too much money at stake in fines and legal fees, not to mention the time involved in dealing with this situation. Industry people talk to each other, and this is precisely the kind of thing they talk about. Do not be the person they're speaking about.

COVER ME: PUTTING YOUR OWN SPIN ON A WELL-KNOWN SONG

You can create your own recordings of *cover* songs. Covers are reinterpretations of preexisting (typically well-known hit) songs that reflect the style of the artist. These reimagined, remade songs are transformed in a way that brings fresh and contemporary elements. Many times, after getting placed, these songs go on to become popular—or even hits—again.

Although permission is not required to record a cover song and release it, permission is required to *license* a cover song for sync. Start by doing an Internet search to find out who the songwriters and publishers are for the song you want to cover, and obtain permission. The owners of these valuable copyrights are very particular about how their music is used and are closely involved in the licensing process.

Though licensing fees are typically split evenly, with 50% for the songwriter/publisher and 50% for the artist/master recording owner, the songwriter/publisher may likely take more than 50%. There have been cases where the song's copyright is so valuable that the artist doing the remake received only a small fraction of the licensing fee.

ARC OF A DIVER: HOW DEEP IS YOUR SONG?

A common request from music supervisors is a *trailerized* version of a familiar song. As mentioned earlier, this is usually an epic, over-the-top, moody, or dramatic treatment of a song and may include edgy sound throughout. Conversely, the song could be a stripped-down version with haunting vocals, eerie synth pads, and in a minor key. Perhaps it could be an arrangement done in a completely different genre. Interesting spins on a song include taking a rock song and turning it into a simple ukulele track or taking a simple folk song and making it a punk rock anthem. The possibilities are endless.

Before recording a cover song—or trailerizing it—find out all you can about the song and the people who created it. What's the song's story? This is known as doing a "deeper dive," and it can affect how you interpret the song, bringing it to another level.

To begin diving into the song, watch and read interviews, search the Internet, find background information, and discover all you can about the song's history:

- How did the song come to be, and why?
- Who wrote and produced it?

- How did the artist's (or band's) style and musicianship affect the song?
- What was happening locally, or in the world, that may have affected the song's creation?
- Were the songwriters going through a life-changing event that inspired them to write the song?
- Which other artists and bands have covered the song? (Many established and up-and-coming artists post their covers on streaming platforms.)
- After doing research, why do you think this song resonates with artists—and, more importantly, the listeners?
- Does this song get sync placements and if so, in which media, typically?
- How will you put your own spin on the melody, chords, arrangement, and production, and will these elements bring a new meaning or a different emotional quality to the song? (This separates a good rendition of a song from an amazing one.)

Because publishers know unique, well-done covers can create additional revenue, many make lists of coverable songs available in their catalog and encourage artists to record them. These publishers may sign and then exploit the new recording and seek to get it placed.

PRO TIPS . . . About Writing Songs for Sync

Choose an attention-grabbing title. My most successful sync song, "Show Me the Honey," written to a track by Sharron March, has gotten more than twenty major placements, including *Scrubs*, *Friday Night Lights*, *Kickin' It Old Skool*, and *Assassination Games*. I have no doubt that the unique title played a big role in that song's success.

—**Jason Blume**, Emmy®-winning Hit Songwriter and Author

I go to a beautiful place and make up songs into my iPhone video. That is the "El Blurto" phase. Then I look at them later with coffee and a yellow pad.

—**Jack Tempchin**, Writer of "Peaceful Easy Feeling,"
Member of the Songwriters Hall of Fame

Songs in media only have a few seconds to establish themselves so the viewer understands what feeling the music is contributing to a scene. If you are making songs for media, be sure that within five seconds it expresses a specific vibe: Female Pop, Indie Rock, Retro Funk, Dirt Road Blues, etc. And then nail that vibe with authenticity.

—**John Houlihan**, Music Supervisor

Write what you know. If you've never been on a "Freight Train to Nowhere," don't write about it.

—**Steve Dorff**, 2018 Inductee to the Songwriters Hall of Fame

Songwriting has really helped me be both be flexible and stubborn! You've got to be willing to pivot, change, and rearrange ideas like a puzzle—and also wait and protect those magical moments or hooks that are undeniably moving or good. It's a balance between the two. As someone who is very stream-of-consciousness in the way I create, capturing a good idea is half the trick.

—**Katie Herzig**, Artist, Songwriter, and Producer

Lyrically, let the story and the imagery be provided by the filmmaker, not the songwriter. Specifics belong to the emotional impact, not to the visuals. But a nifty way around this is the metaphorical, symbolic use of imagery. Play with the "shape" of melodies, and vary them in chunks of melody (motifs). I love making games or experiments out of the writing process. Try out the phrase "What if?" Throw in a surprise. A tip I got from Steve Dorff about melody writing was, make a pattern, get the ear ready for repetition, and then change the pattern. Once.

—**Lisa Aschmann**, Songwriter and Author, Nashville Geographic

There are always more things to learn. If I ever had a "light bulb moment," it would've been realizing that there is a place for almost any type/genre of quality music in the music for media space.

—**Matt Hirt**, Composer, Songwriter, and Producer, and Co-owner of Catapult Music

I make sure a *song* for sync is the best it can be—and that the melody is heard. I think of a song as a beat and a vocal; those two things drive the song. They make your foot tap, your head nod, and you want to sing along. These are some of the building blocks when approaching a mix. Mixing needs a great balance that works for the song.

—**Brian Scheuble**, Mixer

CHAPTER 4

Getting the Most from Feedback

TELL ME SOMETHING GOOD: HOW FEEDBACK CAN BE HELPFUL

Feedback, schmeedback. Who needs it? We all do. Song *feedback* is a reaction and advice that comes from a knowledgeable and experienced music industry professional. The most effective feedback indicates what's working with a song and what can be done to improve its quality.

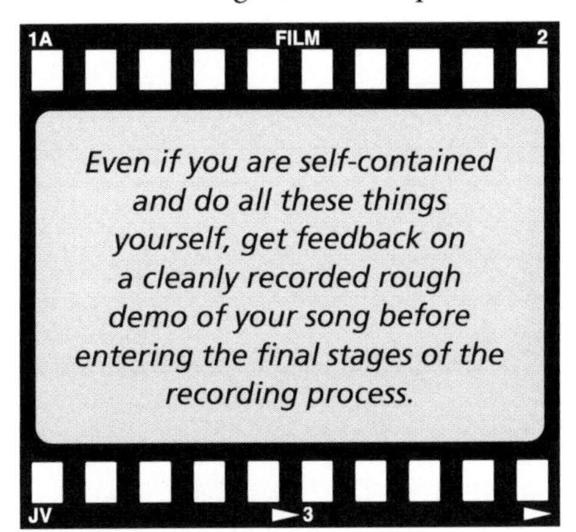

Before getting your music out there, especially if you are new to the writing-for-sync process, find trusted sources to listen to your music. This is vital: Get feedback on the writing of your song *before* you start spending time and money on quality recordings. Even if you are self-contained and do all these things yourself, get feedback on a cleanly recorded rough demo of your song before entering the final stages of the recording process.

We've heard amazingly performed, recorded, mixed, and mastered songs and instrumentals that needed just one lyric change or a simple music tweak to turn them into very licensable songs; however, the project was completed, and it would have been difficult, if not impossible, to make any changes. Missed it by that much!

EVERYONE'S A CRITIC

There are free music forums that offer feedback. At times the critiques can be helpful, but often they're either too kind—or too harsh. A word of caution: some organizations that give song feedback on hit songs may or may not understand the nuances of writing for sync, which is problematic.

What is most useful is constructive feedback. This means that the feedback is based on facts rather than opinions. Constructive feedback should be focused and helpful: "The vocals are out of tune." "The rhythm guitar is off time and needs to be quantized." "The ending fades out, but for sync purposes, it should have a hard button ending." "The lyrics don't convey a consistent feeling."

GIMME SOME TRUTH

Finding someone who can give you honest and effective feedback on your songs is difficult but not impossible. There are qualified music industry professionals who provide in-depth feedback for a fee. It can be worth the price—if the feedback is valid. Before hiring a consultant, find out a few things first:

- What is their musical background?
- Is their expertise in songwriting, composing, production, or mixing?
- Do they have experience regarding music for sync?
- How much is the fee (per song or per hour)?
- What kind of reviews have they received from past clients?

When receiving professional feedback, have an open mind, and try not to defend your song. Graciously accept comments, whether or not you agree with them. If you think the suggested changes make your music stronger, take them into consideration. It's always nice to get positive comments on your music.

However, if you hear the same comments more than two or three times, it's time for a reality check and a look at what the commonalities are. You might be missing something obvious. Any one person can be incorrect or off the mark, but several music industry experts are unlikely to be wrong about the same problem in a song.

HEY! READ THIS!

One publisher offered this advice for songwriters: "Remember *QTIP*, an acronym for Quit Taking It Personally. Uncomfortable feedback can be upsetting, but it stings less when you remember not to take it to heart."

SHAKE IT OFF

Unfavorable reviews have always caused many songwriters, composers, artists, and bands to hang it up. It's important to realize this is just part of the process. There is some comfort knowing just about all of us in the music business have experienced not-so-positive feedback at some point in our careers.

Even though the critiques we received early on led to disappointment, and, at times, heartache, we survived the tears and the more than occasional threats to "quit the business." Eventually, your skin will thicken too.

PRO TIPS . . . About Getting the Most from Feedback

Think of a professional critique as a way of learning the craft of songwriting from someone who has already had proven commercial success. This doesn't mean you have to agree with everything you're told, but, at the very least, understand that there are certain commercial conventions out there. Then, if you decide to disagree with them, you can do so in an informed way.

—**Cliff Goldmacher**, award-winning Songwriter and Producer, and Songwriting Consultant

Getting professional feedback on your song is a reality check for what is otherwise a very isolated profession. You need to be competitive, and it's very hard to have the right perspective alone. Feedback is someone holding the mirror so you can see your song from all angles. Remember, people give you feedback to pull you up. When presenting a song, if you already think it's great and you are purely looking for validation, it's a waste of time—and usually disheartening. Bring songs you know aren't really working but you can't put your finger on it. Use the pros to improve.

—**Suzan Koç**, Publisher and Songwriting Mentor

Embarking on a career in music means you will face countless rejections that sometimes are hard to not take personally. But you have to believe completely in what you do—and have those rejections become the fuel for you to move forward instead of retreat backward.

—**Michael Eames**, President of PEN Music Group, Inc.

CHAPTER 5

Performing and Recording of Live and Virtual Instruments

THE EVOLUTION OF THE RECORDING PROCESS

In the early days of professional audio recording, musicians would gather in a room and work out the parts they were going to play for a previously written song. Then the recording engineer would set up the microphones, check the levels, and hit the record button on the tape machine, and the musicians would expertly perform the song. The recording of music was a collaborative effort between many talented people.

This process has changed. For many music creators, the writing and recording process is now often a solitary endeavor. The main benefit is that one person can choose to work on a music project as long as they want, whenever they want, however they want, and they don't need to consult with anyone. The major shortcoming is that, without other people involved in this artistic process, a creator does not have access to input from those people and their unique ideas.

It can be difficult to wear more than one hat at a time during the recording process. A common challenge is recording yourself singing or playing an instrument. When a recording engineer is involved, the performer doesn't have to worry about proper microphone placement for the best sound or keeping an eye on recording levels. A performer should not be focused on anything but their performance. If you have the luxury of having quality assistance in the studio, take advantage of it. However, in the interest of time, money, and convenience, compromises are made by many of us working in the sync music business as we work alone.

THE NOT-SO-GOOD OLD DAYS

Most of us no longer record to tape or use studios full of large, expensive equipment. In fact, much of the music we hear has been recorded digitally with a computer, usually a laptop. These computers and the recording software they contain are referred to as *digital audio workstations* or *DAWs*. This process is sometimes called "working in the box"—the box being a computer.

There are many advantages to recording digitally: A computer with all the bells and whistles and the latest recording software is more affordable than old-school mixing consoles, hardware compressors, and equalizers. Digital recording is much more flexible and easier to edit. It is also more convenient to recall an old project and the settings that were used last.

One of the common critiques of music recorded digitally is that it does not have the warmth of analog hardware and tape. While this may be true, most of our ears have become accustomed to the sound of digital recording. Some audiophiles can hear the difference between analog and digital recordings right away, while the average listener can hear no difference at all.

Common DAW recording software includes Avid Pro Tools, Steinberg Cubase, and Apple Logic, among others (and always more appearing on the market). Music software is sometimes purchased as a perpetual license and other times rented as a subscription. It is always advisable, no matter which purchase plan you choose, that you are certain you can receive regular updates to your software.

Though different kinds of recording software perform the same functions, the ways of accessing these functions vary from one to another. None of them is easier than the others—just different. Learn how to use your chosen software as thoroughly as you can. There are many classes and online tutorial videos available.

TAKE THE LONG WAY HOME—OR USE A SHORTCUT

We recommend learning as many computer keyboard (sometimes referred to as a *QWERTY keyboard*) shortcuts as you can, especially for your most-repeated commands. It takes a while to become comfortable with them, but keyboard shortcuts can accelerate your workflow greatly. For example, if you do a lot of audio or MIDI editing and your computer is a Mac, pressing *command-C* on your keyboard is a faster way to copy than selecting the copy function from a drop-down menu.

Since there are many shortcuts to memorize, there are QWERTY keyboard covers (also called *skins* or *overlays*) available that show shortcuts for common DAW commands. For a little more money, there are keyboards with these shortcuts imprinted on them.

Figure 5.1. *A QWERTY keyboard with shortcuts. (*Source: *LogicKeyboard)*

Recording software comes with most of what is needed to record and mix your music. However, most producers want more options, so there are third-party software developers who sell plug-ins. Despite the name, you don't actually "plug in" anything. Instead, *plug-ins* work within the recording software, allowing you access to more sounds and processing effects. Many of these emulate classic old-school recording hardware and have become very close to being indiscernible from the originals.

WHOA! NOW YOU'RE GETTING TECHNICAL!

Most plug-ins are available in three common formats. Each DAW is compatible with at least one of them: Pro Tools works with AAX plug-ins, Cubase with VST, and Logic with AU. Though AAX plug-ins are only supported by Pro Tools, VST and AU work with additional DAWs. Typically, when the plug-in is purchased, all three formats are included.

When you are considering buying plug-ins, be sure they are compatible with the current version of your DAW, your computer hardware, and its operating system. Keeping all of these elements up-to-date so they work with each other can be a juggling act. If it is not managed carefully, the result may be money poorly spent or an inefficient system that does not meet its potential.

I'VE GOT THE POWER

Your computer is the foundation of your recording system. Like the rest of the necessary equipment, purchase the best computer you can afford. Newer computers are more powerful than older ones and will remain compatible with your software longer.

A problem that occurs with computers that are not powerful enough is *latency*. This is when there is an audible delay between when a sound is performed while recording and when it can be heard through the headphones or speakers. It is very hard for any musician to provide a good performance with this delay.

In some cases, computer settings, such as the buffer size, can be adjusted to minimize latency. Turning off some of the plug-ins can be helpful. The makers of some plug-ins and recording software also make

DSP (digital signal processing) hardware to assist in providing extra power for their products. Have a powerful enough computer for the number of tracks you record simultaneously and the number of plug-ins you use to mix. Be sure to optimize the computer's system settings according to recommendations from the maker of your DAW.

IT'S A GAS—BUT IT SHOULDN'T BE

When most music producers are starting their careers, their first goal is to obtain the hardware and software tools necessary to do their job. Then they realize that there are more tools available to them that professionals use or that can make their job easier, so they purchase more. This fuels a phenomenon known as Gear Acquisition Syndrome—GAS—the belief that in order to improve the quality of the work you do you need more gear.

While it is recommended that you have the best tools at your fingertips, do not buy into the myth that because the professionals use certain equipment you must necessarily have the same equipment to get the same results. Learn to use the equipment you have before skipping the rent or remortgaging your house to buy more.

SHH! WE'RE RECORDING IN HERE!

With digital recording, it is relatively easy to record a clean take of any acoustic instrument. Recording is commonly referred to as *tracking*. It is essential to avoid having unintended sounds or noise on your recordings. In home studios, these noises may include vehicle traffic, air traffic, rowdy neighbors, noisy pets, birds and other wildlife, air conditioners, heaters, and the fan on a computer or on other recording hardware, to name a few.

Many self-contained producers track themselves in the same room where they mix, while others use a separate room. Whichever you choose, consider any unwanted noises, as well as how the room will affect the sound of your recording. If you are fortunate, your home/office/studio is insulated well and keeping doors and windows closed may be enough to keep these interferences to a minimum. If not, you may have to wait a few moments for the problem to pass. If you experience frequent interruptions and you record a lot of audio, you might consider reconfiguring your recording space or looking for a different one.

CAN YOU HEAR ME?

A common misconception is that treating a room with acoustic foam will make it soundproof. It won't. Instead, acoustic treatment reduces *reflections*, the term for sound bouncing off the walls, floor, and ceiling. In rooms where recording and mixing take place, some acoustic treatment can be helpful but is not always necessary. It is not advisable to cover every square foot of a room with foam or other acoustic treatment; a little goes a long way. Hanging heavy cloth, rugs, or curtains on the walls and windows is an alternative approach that can also dampen unwanted sounds and reflections effectively. (More on acoustic treatment in chapter 7.)

In a highly reflective room with hard floors, empty walls, and little or nothing to absorb sound, there may be too much of a *reverb* or echo effect picked up on the recording. There are times when this is desirable. However, when the sound of a recording with no reflections or reverb is wanted (known as being *dry*), it can be difficult or impossible to remove the reverb sound from a recording in a room with a lot of reflections. Because it is easy to add reverb to a dry recording, many home recordists utilize some acoustic treatment while recording to minimize the sound of the room. They then add the desired amount of reverb in their DAW.

Manufacturers of music equipment are always inventing ways to assist you. There are several companies that make *microphone isolation shields*, sometimes called *reflection shields*. These products form an acoustically absorbent semicircle around the back of a microphone and reduce the sound of the room on the recording. The advantages are that they are portable and more affordable than putting up acoustic treatment in the studio.

Figure 5.2. *A microphone reflection shield.* (Source: *sE Electronics*)

MINDING YOUR P'S AND Q'S (NOT REALLY THE Q'S)

On the subject of useful recording accessories, when recording vocalists it's worth considering using a *pop filter*. These are circular screens that usually attach to the mic stand and are positioned between the singer and the microphone to reduce the effect of *plosives*. Plosives are sounds that result from a sudden release of breath that overwhelms the mic and distorts the signal.

Though there are other letters whose sounds create this phenomenon, the most common is the sound of the letter P. If this happens on the perfect vocal take, it is possible to fix, but it requires editing on a surgical level. So use a pop filter to minimize this problem. (Proper singing and mic technique will prevent this, too.)

DON'T DROP THE MIC!

The three common types of microphones used in professional recording are dynamic, condenser, and ribbon microphones. Here are some basics:

- *Dynamic mics* are more affordable and durable than the others, and, though used in studios, they also work very well in live settings. They do not require a power source and are usually used on drums, electric guitars, and other loud sound sources.
- *Condenser mics* have a higher cost and are more fragile than dynamic mics. They require a power source that is available on the interfaces into which they are plugged. They have a better response to high frequencies than dynamic mics, making them good for use with vocals, acoustic guitars, and any other sound source where detail is important.
- *Ribbon mics* are priced similarly to condenser mics but are even more delicate. Most of them do not require external power and are used typically on vocals, electric guitar amps, and strings.

Microphones are available with a small or large *diaphragm*—a capsule within the mic that converts sound waves into an electrical signal. Here are some common applications of microphones with small or large diaphragms:

- High frequencies, like those associated with hi-hats, cymbals, and small percussion, are usually recorded with small-diaphragm mics.
- Low frequency instruments, such as basses and kick drums, work well with large-diaphragm mics.
- Vocals and acoustic guitars are recorded with either small or large-diaphragm microphones.

Figure 5.3. *Microphones.* (Source: *sE Electronics)*

These are customary usages, but when the situation allows, experimentation during the recording process is encouraged.

Microphones have various *polar patterns* that affect the directions in which they are sensitive to sound. Here are some of the common polar patterns:

- Mics with a *cardioid* polar pattern pick up sound coming from the front but reject sound from the back and sides. These are ideal when the sound of the room is not wanted. They are used commonly on vocals.
- *Supercardioid* mics have a narrower area of sensitivity in the front and a small amount of sensitivity in the back.
- *Bidirectional* or *figure 8* mics pick up sound from the front and back but reject sound coming from the sides.
- *Omnidirectional* mics pick up sound from the front, back, and sides and are intended for use when the sound of the room is desired on the recording.
- Some microphones are switchable and offer several patterns, therefore providing more flexibility. These may be priced higher.

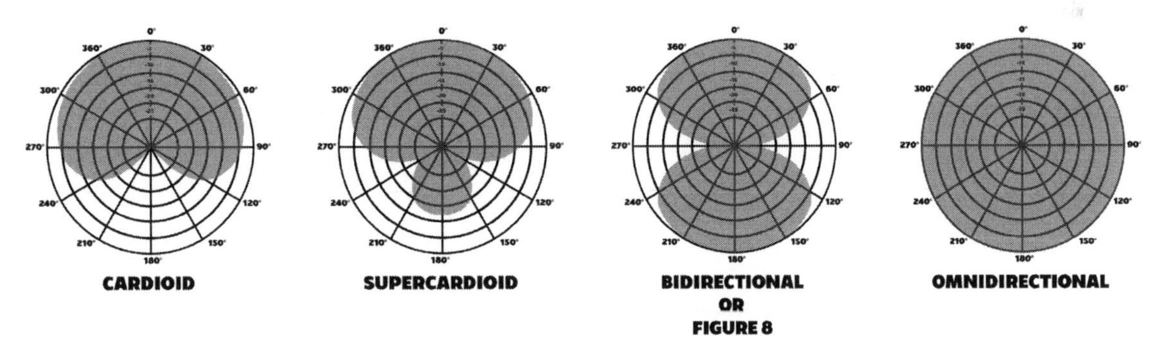

Figure 5.4. *Microphone polar patterns. The front of the microphone is represented by the top of each diagram.* (Source: *PreSonus)*

A feature available on some microphones is a *pad* or *attenuation* switch that reduces the output signal of the mic, if the sound source is too loud. (Drummers, we're talking to you.) A *low cut filter* switch is an option that will remove the low frequencies from the output. Some sound sources, like vocals, may not need these low frequencies and can be recorded more clearly and efficiently without them.

Many professional studios have all the above microphones available in a variety of sizes and polar patterns, which can come in handy at times but are not always necessary. If you have one decent dynamic mic and a good condenser mic, and one is small and the other is large, you have more than enough to get you started. You can always buy more microphones when your licensing money starts rolling in.

The above-referenced microphones are intended for pro audio use, meaning there are opportunities available to alter the audio signal as the person recording sees fit.

USB mics are affordable and convenient but not ideal for broadcast quality recordings. A USB mic plugs directly into a USB port on your computer and is powered by the USB connection. This type of mic is intended for podcast use and may have reduced control and sound quality. It is not recommended for recording music that will be licensed.

SENDING SIGNALS

There are four levels of audio signals that flow through cables:

1. *Mic level* is the weakest and, no surprise, is the signal that comes out of a microphone. To be usable, this signal requires a boost by a *preamp* (preamplifier).
2. *Instrument level* is a bit stronger but still requires preamplification. This is the signal that comes from electric guitars and basses.
3. The strengthened signal that comes out of the preamp is *line level*. This is the one that is most common to and compatible in audio systems.
4. *Speaker level* is the high-level signal that comes out of an amplifier and is sent to the speakers.

Signals are important to understand, because improperly plugging in devices can result in possible damage to equipment. Most crucially, do not plug an amplified signal into anything but speakers.

HELLO—IS THIS THING ON?

After a microphone has been selected, the next step is to plug it into something. In many studios, the mic is connected first to a preamp to raise the signal level. As the signal level is increased, some preamps color the sound and give it a touch of the analog warmth that may be missing in the digital realm. Preamps are available with one or more channels. If you are recording one instrument or voice at a time, one channel will suffice. If you plan on recording more than one sound source at a time, or a stereo source, consider a multichannel preamp. Remember that this means more microphones, stands, and cables.

Figure 5.5. *Preamp. (*Source: *Universal Audio)*

Most preamps have the option of supplying the power needed for condenser microphones. This is called *phantom power* and is sometimes indicated as 48V—or forty-eight volts.

The signal that comes out of some dynamic and ribbon microphones needs to be strengthened before entering the preamp. Without this level increase, the preamp input gain needs to be turned up to a level that introduces noise. *Mic signal boosters* are available for this task. These may also require phantom power.

LET'S BE DIRECT

Preamps are not only used to record an audio signal from a microphone; many preamps also offer the ability to record via *direct input*, known as *DI* (sometimes called *direct injection*). As the name implies, an instrument can be plugged directly into a preamp. These instruments include electric guitars and basses, which deliver weak instrument level signals.

While preamps have controls that allow the signal level to be adjusted, be careful with these adjustments. Since performers sometimes get louder suddenly, it is best to set these controls conservatively. Many times that louder performance is one of the better ones. If your levels are set too high and the signal distorts, you cannot fix it—and the performance is lost.

In digital recording, the next step in the signal path is an *A/D converter*. This converts the analog signal from the microphone and preamp to a digital signal that the computer can understand. Converters are available with one or more channels. Most converters are also *D/A* converters that convert the digital signal from the computer to an analog signal that is sent to the speakers.

KEEP PLUGGING ALONG

The digital signal from the converter is then sent to an *audio interface*. This needs to have enough inputs to accommodate the number of outputs from your preamp and converter. For most people starting out, two channels will be adequate. The audio interface and converter need to be compatible with your recording software, and its specifications should be compatible with the desired audio quality. (Audio quality and file formats are discussed in chapter 6.) The audio interface also controls the sound going to the speakers.

The final destination for the audio signal is the computer, where it will be recorded. The same connectivity needs to exist between the audio interface and the computer. This is typically via USB or Thunderbolt. These connection protocols are constantly updated. Try to get the latest and fastest one you can. The DAW controls the recorded signal from there. However, there is another option . . .

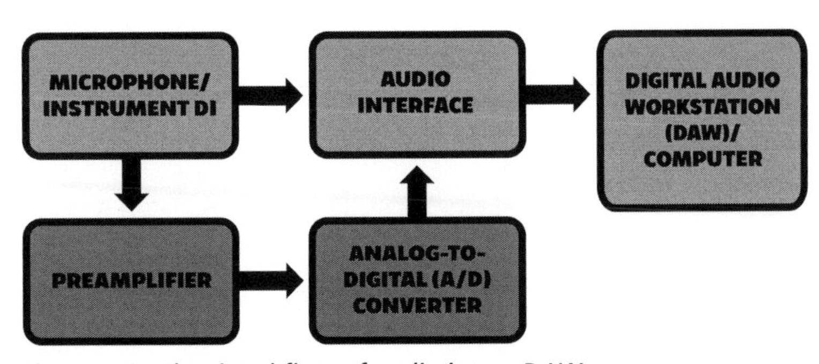

Figure 5.6. *The signal flow of audio into a DAW.*

IT'S COMPLICATED . . . BUT IT DOESN'T HAVE TO BE

Modern digital recording systems can be as simple or complex as you desire. When starting out, keep it simple. There are some audio interfaces that function as a preamp, converter, and interface all in one device. Most of the time these have phantom power for condenser microphones and mic signal boosters. If you are setting up your first home recording studio and are on a budget, this is the recommended approach.

Figure 5.7. *An audio interface.* (Source: *Focusrite)*

FINDING THE SWEET SPOT

Using the best microphone to record the greatest performer in a high-quality studio is not always enough to get an amazing recording. The position of the mic has a significant impact on the character of the recorded sound.

If your recording room is a large one, try different locations within the room. It is better to maintain distance from walls, especially if they are not treated acoustically. When your speakers are in the same room where you are recording, turn them off and use headphones so that nothing but the intended instrument is recorded.

There is not a "correct" part of the instrument toward which to point the microphone, nor is there a "correct" distance for the sound source to be from a microphone. Different instruments have different sweet spots that work for certain songs, while aiming the mic toward another part of the instrument may work better for other songs. Intimate music occasionally calls for the mic to be close to the strings of an acoustic guitar, while an up-tempo song that will have many other instruments added could call for the mic to be further away and pointed toward a different part of the guitar. Angling toward the twelfth fret, or where the neck meets the body, is a good starting point for acoustic guitars and most fretted stringed instruments.

TO THE LEFT, TO THE LEFT. NOW, MOVE IT TO THE RIGHT. UP A LITTLE. THAT'S IT!

When recording another musician, place the mic where the sound comes out of the instrument, and listen through headphones as the performer plays. The headphones will let you hear what is being recorded instead of what is heard in the room. Experiment with moving the mic closer or further away, or with pointing it at a different part of the instrument. Change the mic position until you find a sound you like. Though it can be changed later within your DAW, it is best to get the sound you want while recording.

The process is a little different if you record yourself. Find a good starting position for the mic, and record ten to twenty seconds. Listen to the playback on headphones, and keep experimenting until you are happy with the results.

When a microphone is close to a sound source, it will pick up more low frequencies. This is known as the *proximity effect*. The converse is also true: When the mic is farther away from the sound source, the low frequencies get softer. This information can be useful. For instance, if a group of singers is being recorded and a gang vocal effect is desired, place the mic several feet away from them.

LET'S GO!

To record music for licensing, you do not have to be a virtuoso. In fact, flashy piano runs and showy guitar solos can get in the way. Some of the most successful composers keep it on the simple side. However, quality instrumental performances do require at least two things: a quality player and a quality instrument.

The ideal circumstance is when you are a good enough musician to play on your own recordings. If this is not the case, consider finding an experienced, skilled musician to collaborate with (or to pay).

Quality musicians own quality instruments and are most comfortable playing them. Make sure the instrument being recorded has been maintained properly. Some songs may lend themselves to dull, ten-year-old guitar strings, while most do not. If higher or lower notes played on the instrument go out of tune, change the part it plays, or find another instrument. The instrument needs to have a nice tone with no extraneous noises, and, above all else, *it must be in tune*. There are rare exceptions to this rule, such as songs that require performances that are intentionally loose in pitch and timing for a specific effect; but for the most part, being in tune is critical.

THE MUSICIAN WHISPERER

Detailed communication with your musicians is crucial. Some musicians read music notation; some do not. For the readers, provide a copy of the part you want on your recording. For those who don't read music, figure out how to best tell them the part you would like them to perform. Additionally, a chord chart is very useful.

It is essential to give the performers a rough recording of the song before they show up to record. Some musicians are comfortable making up their own parts, while others are fine with being told exactly what to play. Communicate clearly with them before the recording session so everybody knows what is expected.

MOVING IN STEREO

Pianos and acoustic guitars are instruments that can be recorded in stereo by using two microphones and panning the audio recorded by each mic to opposite sides. Be cautious when recording with more than one microphone. If each mic is not the same distance from the sound source, there may be *phase cancellation*. This is when the sound waves recorded from two microphones are out of phase, causing some of the frequencies to be weakened.

The best way to tell if this is occurring is to listen to both tracks in mono by panning them both to the center. If the overall sound level is softer or thinner, or if some of the frequencies are missing, then phase cancellation may be happening. This can be fixed by repositioning the microphones so that they are the exact same distance from the instrument. Before recording several takes, check to see if this is occurring. Although it is better to solve this problem during the recording process, it can be addressed after recording by inverting the polarity of one of the recorded tracks in your DAW.

WE DON'T NEED NO STINKING AMPS!

When recording electric guitars and electric bass guitars, many producers place a microphone in front of the amplifier. This is the classic sound you have grown accustomed to hearing on many recordings.

However, there is another option: By utilizing direct input (DI), an electric guitar or bass can be plugged directly into a preamp or audio interface instead of plugging it into an amplifier. The sound of a DI electric bass, combined frequently with the signal from the mic in front of the amp, works very well in a recording. However, the sound of a DI electric guitar is very unpleasant and unmusical. This can be remedied with amp modeling plug-ins.

Amp modeling is the process of emulating a physical guitar or bass amplifier. One of the reasons this approach is preferred by some producers is that the sound of the amp can be changed after the recording is finished. It can be switched to a different tone or to a dirtier or cleaner sound or can be changed to a completely different amp. Most popular guitar amps have been modeled, as well as bass amps.

Another benefit is that, because the instrument is plugged in directly—even in a noisy environment—no unwanted sounds are recorded. In fact, it can be done with headphones so no one else will hear it being recorded.

Once again, some audio enthusiasts think this approach is not ideal, but the improving quality of amp modeling plug-ins is making it hard to tell the difference.

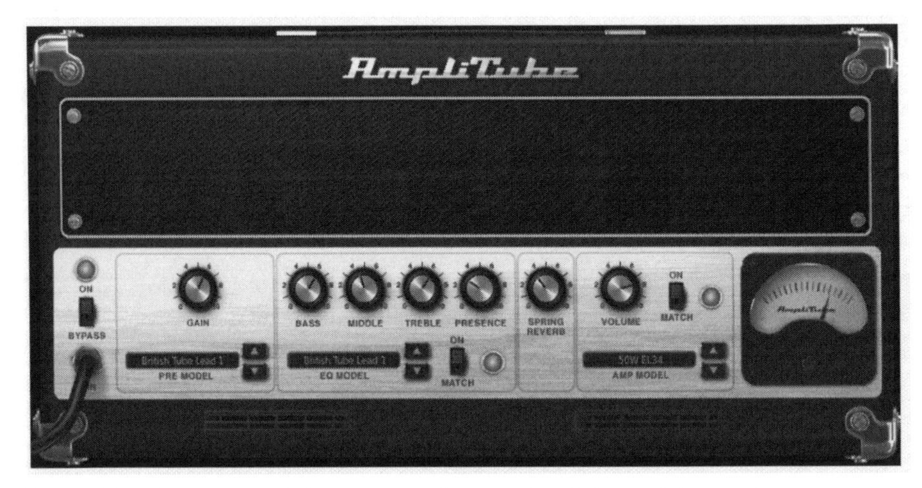

Figure 5.8. *An amp modeling plug-in.* (Source: *IK Multimedia*)

GET IT RIGHT

When recording vocals or acoustic instruments, it is important to get the best results possible. Being proficient or adept with the musical instrument or singing well is essential. Audio can be edited, but the entire process is smoother if you start with a good performance.

On recordings of music intended for licensing, vocal and instrumental performances that are flashy or showing off distract from the original emotional intent of the music. The greatest musicians and singers are the ones who contribute exactly what the song needs—no more, no less. Taste and restraint are indispensable.

The greatest musicians and singers are the ones who contribute exactly what the song needs—no more, no less. Taste and restraint are indispensable.

When recording sources like vocals or acoustic guitars, the rule of thumb is that you must get it right *at least once.* Some aspects of audio can be manipulated, like pitch and timing. However, if a vocalist sings the wrong word, or if a guitarist plays the wrong chord, it can be very difficult, if not impossible, to fix it. If the vocal phrase or guitar part happens somewhere else in the song, that part can be copied and pasted onto the problem area. It is imperative that you have all the takes you need before the performer leaves.

Be sure the performer holds out the last note long enough on an instrument part. It is easier to shorten the recording of a note that is too long than it is to lengthen one that is too short.

LOOP DE LOOP

If you are recording yourself singing or playing an instrument, DAWs have a function called *loop record* that allows you to record a section of the song over and over; the section can be of any length.

This is very helpful if you perform away from your recording controls and find a rhythm but don't want to keep stopping to hit the record button again.

Another function called *punching in* allows you to record a short piece of audio in the middle of a good take to replace a small mistake. This saves you from having to rerecord a large section because of a small problem.

Using up-to-date recording software, it is easy to record multiple takes of a vocal or live instrument part. You can record five to ten takes of a performance and comp together the best pieces of each take. In the digital recording world, *comp* is short for "compile" or "compilation"—a critical part of the process of making sure the best performance of each part ends up on the final recording of a song.

When the recording is done,

- Look for a take that has the fewest issues, and then copy and paste it with other takes to create a smooth comp that best serves the song.
- Make sure none of the edits can be heard by adjusting the location of the edit to find the sweet spot.
- Always apply a *crossfade* at each edit to reduce the likelihood of any pops or clicks. This will fade out the level of the end of the first piece of audio while simultaneously fading in the level of the start of the next segment of audio.
- Confirm that the singer's breaths sound natural.
- To make the comping process easier, it is essential for the recording levels of each take to be consistent.
- Also focus on the intensity of the performance so that it is steady. It is hard to edit seamlessly a quiet, low-intensity word in the middle of a loud phrase.

HEY! READ THIS!

If the singer knows the song very well, we record the song from start to finish a few times. In other cases, because the song has just been written, and the singer may not be familiar with it yet, we record several takes of the first verse. Then we record several takes of the chorus, followed by several takes of the second verse, until the entire song has been recorded, section by section. We pay special attention to the emotional arc and prosody of the song. If the song starts with a low level of intensity and then builds, we advise the singer before each take where the emotional depth and energy should be.

SING A SONG

Technically, the human voice is a musical instrument—one with no equal. It conveys emotion more effectively than any other instrument, especially when there are lyrics. When there is a lead voice on a recording, it instantly becomes the most important sound on that recording. Listeners' ears are immediately drawn to it, and all other instruments must stay out of its way.

Choosing who will sing your song is one of the most critical decisions you will make about your team. Your singer must have a voice and a level of singing ability that fits the feel of your song. If you think your own vocal talents are up to the task, sing your song yourself. However, if you have access to a singer who can help your song better connect with a listener by speaking to their heart and reaching into their soul, work with that singer. You may even wish to involve them in the songwriting and split some of the income with them. Be very honest with yourself when making this decision. We have heard many well-written songs that did not reach their potential because the vocalist was not the best fit.

HONESTY: THE IMPORTANCE OF THE SINGER'S AUTHENTICITY

Keep the lyrics in mind when selecting a singer. It does not make sense to have a young vocalist singing about having been in love for fifty years or being a grandparent or to have an older vocalist singing about being kissed for the first time.

Every singer has their own singing style in which they can give a comfortable and believable performance. Some vocalists can stretch a bit and sing in varied styles and deliver an effective performance. However, it is best to "cast" singers according to their realm of familiarity and experience. Some singers simply cannot sound authentically happy; others make you laugh or smile after the first note, when they are not even trying. Unless the goal is for your recording to be ironic, it is not advisable to have a vocalist with a sad vibe singing about dancing in the sunshine. Listeners will hear through it right away.

Some singers have an "artistic" voice that is more than the voice that comes out of their mouth. Their passions and dislikes come through with every word and note they sing. An artist may be an animal lover and may not have the right vibe to sing a jingle for a burger joint. Another artist could be shy and may not be convincing singing about being the life of the party. Take the singer's personality into account when looking for a vocalist. Find a vocalist who can convey the message and emotion of the lyrics of your song authentically.

TELL ME ABOUT IT

Once you have found the appropriate vocalist for your song, it is necessary that you set them up to succeed during their recording session. If they are not having a good day or are stressed out about something, it is the job of whomever is running the session to manage the situation.

There are times when a singer is not into performing that day and their vibe will be audible on the recording. Depending on the circumstances and the personalities involved, it may be possible to loosen up the vocalist by talking with them about their problem. Another good solution is talking about something else to take their mind off their troubles. Perhaps take a walk or pause to stretch and breathe. Or, you may consider rescheduling the session.

To get the desired performance, a good *vocal producer* knows exactly what to say to the singer. While recording, the vocal producer may coach and give guidance to the singer about delivery, diction, emotion, phrasing, breathing, tone, pitch, volume, or other vocal-performance details. The singer may also need gentle reminders about technique or their position in front of the microphone. Avoid filling the singer's head with too much to think about, and instead point out what the vocalist is doing well and make suggestions to fix any areas that need attention.

HUMBLE AND KIND

Above all, it is important that the musicians and vocalists you are working with feel comfortable and confident. Create a welcoming environment:

- Make sure the space in which they record has enough light and the temperature is suitable.
- Check that the microphone is positioned in a natural place for them.
- Customize their headphone mix by removing any instruments that are distracting so they can better hear what they prefer.
- Add a little reverb to their voice or instrument so it doesn't sound so bare.
- After a few takes, check with them to see if they would like to take a break or get some water.

Being considerate and understanding are appreciated. Not only will you be more likely to get a great performance from them, they will be more inclined to want to work with you again.

HEY! READ THIS!
We write and record many happy songs. When the singer comes in to record, we try to get them laughing between takes. No joke is too corny. Their light-heartedness comes across in their singing.

SETTING THE (GAIN) STAGE

Every sound that makes its way to the final version of your recording has a starting point and an ending point. It is important as the audio signal passes from one place to another that you give careful thought to the strength of the signal. This is known as *gain staging*.

For live audio, this starts at the microphone. Usually, the audio signal proceeds to a preamp. The signal level before the preamp input is controlled by the attenuation switch on the mic, as well as the performer and the distance they are from the mic. The input of the preamp should be at an optimal "Goldilocks" level: not too much, not too little, but just right—which means medium. Signals that are too strong may distort, and decreasing them later will not remove this distortion. Signals that are too weak will need to be increased later, and this could add unwanted noise. If you are unsure, in the digital recording realm, it is better to err on the side of being too soft.

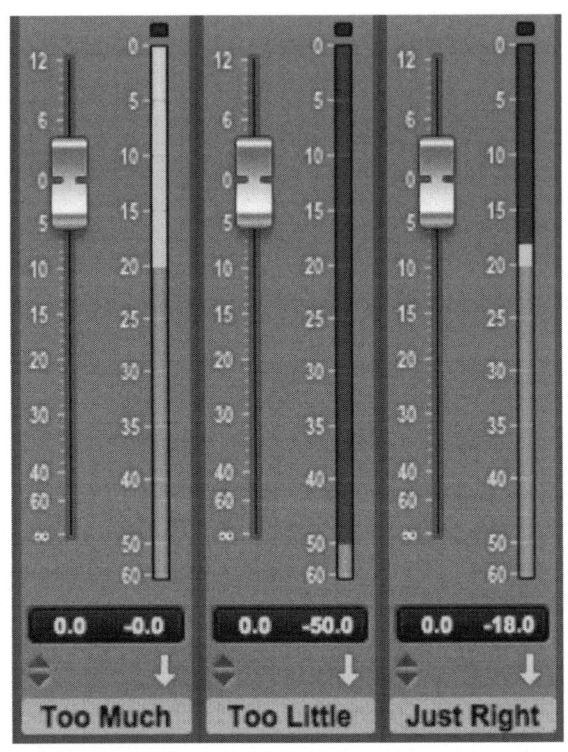

Figure 5.9. *Meters showing various signal levels.* (Source: *Avid)*

The same is true throughout the audio signal path as it continues out of the preamp. The output of the preamp should have a moderate setting. The signal then continues to the converter, the audio interface, the computer, and finally to a track in the DAW. Several of these have input and output settings that need to be adjusted.

Finding these in-between levels should be done with your eyes and not your ears. You will need to look at the meters. Reducing the volume of your speakers or headphones does not affect the audio signal level as it passes from one stage to another. Each device the signal passes through should have a meter indicating signal strength. The ideal setting should not be at either extreme but be somewhere in the middle. If a change is made early in the path, adjustments may need to be made later in the path.

ACOUSTIC OR SYNTHETIC?

Some genres of music primarily use electronic instruments. These include hip hop, electronic dance music (EDM), and modern pop. Other genres feature acoustic instruments—blues, folk, and classic country are examples. Commonly, electronic and acoustic instruments are combined.

It is fairly easy to get electronic instruments to sound electronic; they come out of the box that way. In a lot of electronic music, tracks are recorded generally as short one-, two- or four-bar loops that are repeated throughout the song. This requires some knowledge of music and how to program the instruments but does not require much musical virtuosity. Whatever is programmed can be edited to fix unwanted notes and bad timing. This is true of many electronic drum and synthesizer parts. EDM drum parts are recorded in perfect time, right on the *grid.*

GOT TO BE REAL (WELL, MOST OF THE TIME)

Instruments such as synthesizers and electronic drums are supposed to sound electronic, as acoustic instruments are supposed to sound acoustic. However, with the quality of available software, it is possible for electronic instruments to sound like real acoustic instruments. Software plug-ins that create electronic or acoustic instrument sounds are called *virtual instruments.*

In some cases, it is hard to tell the difference between the sound of virtual and real instruments. Certain instruments lend themselves very well to being recorded as virtual instruments; drums, percussion, and piano are included in this group. Since few people have a full orchestra at their disposal, and also because of the popularity of orchestral music, a lot of effort has gone into creating very real-sounding orchestral software.

MAKING IT VIRTUALLY IMPOSSIBLE TO HEAR THE DIFFERENCE

Virtual instruments are used often because producers sometimes need an instrument they do not own, do not know how to play, or cannot find someone to play it for them. Using virtual instruments can be more convenient and cost-effective.

Virtual instruments use *samples,* which are pre-recorded sounds or notes. Here's a description of the process:

- When creating a sample library for a virtual instrument, the manufacturer records a real musician playing one note at a time on the instrument at different volumes, intensities, and articulations.
- This procedure is continued for every pitch in the playable range of the instrument.
- The pitches are mapped out across a MIDI keyboard, which resembles a piano keyboard.

MIDI—or *Musical Instrument Digital Interface*—is the language that digital devices use to communicate with each other. These digital devices include computers, synthesizers, and other digital music instruments. The primary information that is conveyed via MIDI is the pitch, length, and intensity of music notes on a specific instrument.

Figure 5.10. *A virtual instrument plug-in. (*Source: *IK Multimedia)*

TAKING CONTROL

The most common way to enter MIDI data into a DAW is with a MIDI keyboard. Synthesizers contain their own banks of sounds and samples that can be recorded into a DAW. They can be used to play MIDI notes into a DAW to trigger samples from a virtual instrument. There are MIDI keyboards (sometimes known as MIDI *controllers*) that have no built-in sounds, and these can also be used to enter MIDI data. This is one of the reasons basic familiarity with where the notes are on a piano keyboard is important for every producer. Proficiency is not required.

Figure 5.11. *A MIDI controller keyboard (*Source: *IK Multimedia)*

Accessing the variations of the characteristics of each note is different for each virtual instrument. *Velocity*, or how hard the key is struck, triggers a louder or softer sample. Most MIDI keyboards have a *modulation wheel* (or *mod wheel*) that can be used to transition smoothly from one sample to another or to add expression and dynamics to musical phrases. There are some virtual instruments that use *key switches* to change to a sample with a different articulation. This is where a MIDI key outside of the playable range of the instrument is used to switch to a different sample.

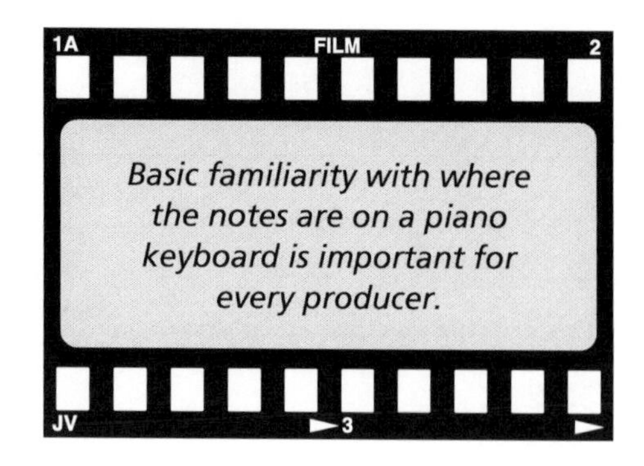

ROCKIN' (ROUND) ROBIN

In order to create a real-sounding performance, some virtual instruments feature *round-robin samples.* This is where two or more samples are assigned to the same MIDI note. When the same MIDI note is repeated, a different performance of the same sound is heard each time. These sounds may be drum hits or a pitched instrument playing the same pitch each time. The more samples assigned to a MIDI note, the less often the same sample is heard. Use of round-robin samples adds to the realism of the overall performance.

Some virtual instruments, especially ones that emulate drums and percussion, include MIDI performances. Many are preprogrammed by real musicians. Look for a drum sound in the virtual instrument you like, and then listen to some MIDI performances contained in the plug-in. If a drumbeat pattern (also known as a *drum groove*) is not exactly the one you want for your song, find one that is close to what you have in mind and make changes to it. This frequently results in a better-sounding drum part than what you would have programmed yourself and may include some ideas you might not have considered.

Drummers are not machines; every hit is not played with the same intensity. They play some notes louder and others softer. Nor is every note played in perfect time. The same can be said of all musicians. These slight imperfections and inconsistencies are a big part of what makes their performances sound alive and vibrant.

JUST BREATHE

Many virtual instruments sound very convincing, but what makes them sound more realistic is *how they are programmed.* If the intent is to make a virtual instrument sound like a real one, it is very important to think about how a real musician would play their part.

For instance, brass and woodwind players need a breath every few measures. Having their virtual instrument performance go for two minutes without a pause for a breath is a dead giveaway that it is not a real instrument. Take these ideas into account when programming your virtual instrument parts.

A CUSTOM FIT

Most virtual instruments default to having effects, like reverb and delay, turned on. However, *default* settings can be turned off. Sometimes these effects are of decent quality; other times they fall short of others that are available. Depending on the circumstance, we generally turn these off and use the same effects as we use on our other tracks.

The better virtual instruments allow a great degree of control of many of the parameters of the samples and how they behave. The available parameters can be seen on the *Graphical User Interface* (GUI) of the plug-in. There are many helpful online video tutorials that show you clearly how the settings can be adjusted or tweaked. Remember that if you bought a virtual instrument, other producers bought the same one. Tweaking the settings will not only make the sound fit your song better, it will also make them sound slightly different than the same instrument being used by others. Experimenting may also lead to finding your unique voice, as mentioned earlier.

SOME CONSTRUCTIVE ADVICE

Speaking of sounding different than other writers and producers, be careful with *construction kits*. These are virtual instruments that in addition to containing instrument samples also contain instrumental pieces of a song, such as a verse, chorus, and bridge. These song pieces were written by the maker of the plug-in. The chords, motifs, and structure are all there. If used as they are, the result will likely be the same as another customer who bought and used the same product. However, construction kits can be useful. If the order of notes or chords that is being played by some of the instruments is changed, shorter sections are repeated, or instrument parts are mixed and matched with other construction kits or your own original ideas, there may be a fresh outcome. They can also be used as a starting point for a new composition.

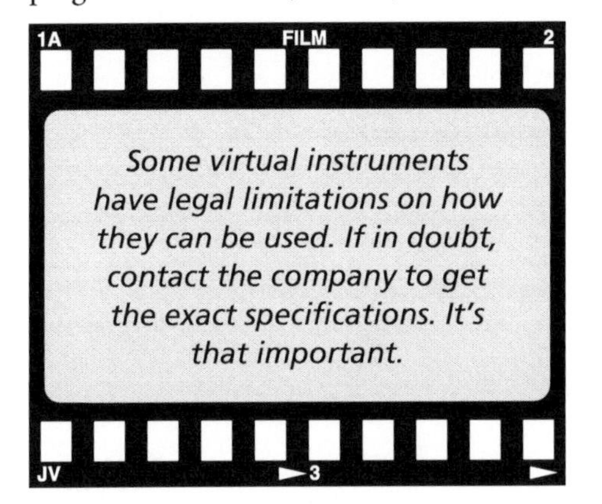

Some virtual instruments, especially ones with MIDI performances and construction kits, have legal limitations on how they can be used. In some cases, using the composition that you create with the virtual instrument cannot be licensed for film and TV placements. Check the agreement included with your software. If in doubt, contact the company to get the exact specifications. It's that important.

On the subject of software agreements, many virtual drum or percussion instruments prohibit the user from leaving the drum or percussion loop exposed with no accompaniment in a production. This is primarily so the loop cannot be captured for free and used by another producer in another song. Be sure there is at least one other instrument playing along with loops, unless it is a loop you created yourself.

THE VELOCITIES THEY ARE A-CHANGIN'

DAWs allow control of the intensity of every MIDI note recorded. Like all aspects of MIDI notes, the velocities can be edited after being recorded. Good sample libraries not only change the volume of the samples as the velocity changes, but they change the intensity of the samples too. When a key is struck very forcefully on a real piano, not only is the note loud, it may also sound a little out of tune or have a different sound quality than when struck more softly. If you bring down the volume of a recording of a vocalist, it does not sound like a whisper, because a whisper has a completely different sound, tone, and timbre than a voice at regular volume. If you turn it up, it does not sound like shouting for the same reasons. The better sample libraries take these concepts into account when designing their software. To maximize your results, vary the intensities of your MIDI notes by playing and editing them so they have different velocities.

In the figure below, the horizontal lines represent MIDI notes that trigger piano samples. The first eight notes are perfectly on the grid with the same velocities, shown with vertical lines below the MIDI notes. The playback sounds very stiff and unnatural. The second eight notes are close to the grid but not right on it. The velocities vary, as they would when played by a live musician, creating a more realistic-sounding performance.

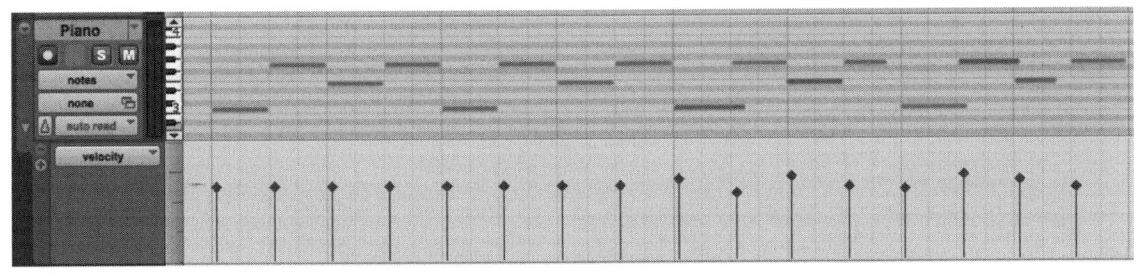

Figure 5.12. *MIDI notes with varying velocities.* (Source: *Avid*)

When programming virtual instrument parts that are intended to sound like they were played by a real musician, resist the temptation to *quantize*, or correct, the timing of each note to make the performance perfect. Quantization has its place in certain electronic genres but not in others. DAWs have a function that allows the timing of notes to be corrected perfectly but also to be just short of perfect. This function is sometimes called *humanize*. If a perfect performance is considered corrected 100%, try 90% or 95% to hear if the performance sounds less stiff but still falls into a groove. If it is too imperfect, it could be distracting. If it is too perfect, it could sound too artificial. Find the balance in between.

HEY! READ THIS!
One of the secrets to our success is to use real instruments whenever possible. Although many virtual instruments and sample libraries have come a long way in recent years, there is still a cheesy quality if they are not used correctly or tweaked in some ways.

AIN'T NOTHING LIKE THE REAL THING

Even though technology and software developers have made great strides in creating virtual instruments that sound like the real thing, some are not quite as convincing. These include many strummed string instruments, such as guitar, ukulele, mandolin, and banjo. Solo brass instruments, like a trumpet or a trombone, and solo woodwinds, like a saxophone or a clarinet, are also hard to simulate with plug-ins. In fact, most solo orchestral instruments do not lend themselves to the virtual treatment.

If you write music that features some of these instruments, consider layering solo parts from different virtual instruments to create a section. This is a small compromise, especially if the arrangement really calls for a solo violin. However, it is better to make this compromise and have three or more violins that sound convincing than to have a solo violin that is distracting because it does not sound real. Write and arrange to the quality, strengths, and weaknesses of your virtual instruments.

It can also be very convincing to layer a real instrument with virtual instruments. Adding a live violin to a virtual violin section can create the sound of a group of actual musicians. If a real trumpet is combined with a virtual trombone and a virtual saxophone, the result can be a more realistic-sounding horn line. The listener can be fooled into perceiving three real instruments.

Occasionally it might be worthwhile assigning a part to a different instrument for which you have a better virtual instrument or perhaps a live instrument you can play. This may turn out better than the original instrument you had in mind.

Try to find a musician to play the part for you. There are some who would gladly play on your recording for pay or for your assistance with their future recordings.

MORE THAN A FEELING

When the recording is done, keep in mind that what matters most is the vibe and emotion that the music evokes. Do not let technology or the lack of proficiency with it get in the way of your ability to make the listener feel something.

PRO TIPS . . . About Performing and Recording

If you are using virtual instruments, you need to treat them as the instruments they are. That means careful attention to color, attack, dynamics, articulation, vibrato, etc. Even all-electronic tracks should evolve and transform. Beware of "cut-and-paste" disease! Nature never does the same thing exactly the same way, and neither should you.

—**Michael A. Levine**, Curator, Mpath

A common mistake is focusing on making improvements in the *later* stages of production. The priorities should always be in the *early* stages. Improving a performance or arrangement is far more important to the success of a production than anything you can do at the mix stage.

—**Ronan Chris Murphy**, Producer and Engineer, Veneto West

For me, collaboration can be fantastic. Personally, I enjoy the idea of working with someone I trust to ensure that the music being made is as good as it can be. We may not agree on everything, and we'll almost certainly butt heads, but we can—and should—keep each other honest and objective. Also, it's almost impossible *not* to learn something when working with a collaborator. Big or small, that's a plus.

—**Jason T. Miller**, Composer, Producer, and Songwriter

I have found that collaborating with others has really nourished what I create when I am alone. Kinda like when you go see a great concert and all you want to do is go home and make your own music, I have the same feeling when I get home from a co-write or do an assignment for sync. My best case scenario is when a song I write for myself as an artist is found and used for film or TV. But I do love getting to put music to a piece of film as well.

—**Katie Herzig**, Artist, Songwriter, and Producer

When collaborating, listen and empathize. Learn something from your co-writer. Communicate. Err on the side of generosity. Don't settle when co-writing; only arrive at a consensus for when the song is ready (to pitch or showcase). Regarding co-writing, my motto is, Dare to be stupid! Co-writing can be free and fun, playful, intimate, and goofy. It ain't rocket surgery.

—**Lisa Aschmann**, Songwriter and Author, Nashville Geographic

Find a team of people who you can have fun with, and be ready to honor the emotion that enters the room, because that's where you'll find the real gems.

—**Nitanee Paris**, Award-Winning Songwriter,
and Partner and Director of A&R, ArtistMax

It's helpful to be able to play some live instruments yourself, as well as to collaborate with somebody who plays instruments you don't. This allows you to use at least one or two live instruments more often. Even one or two live instruments mixed in with a virtual ensemble can make a huge difference.

—**Matt Hirt**, Composer, Songwriter, and Producer, and Co-owner of Catapult Music

Having fun gear is great, but it may lead to overtweaking a song. This might result in a song that's too fatiguing, harsh, off-balance, or noncompeting.

—**Brian Scheuble,** Mixer

Deciding on when to use live versus virtual instruments mainly depends on the style of music and instrumentation required, the project deadline, and the budget. I use live musicians whenever possible. Although the quality of virtual instruments is incredible and keeps improving, even just one or two live instruments added to the mix creates that extra magic of authenticity. Also, with Internet-based remote-recording capabilities that are available, you can collaborate with skilled musicians from all over the world.

—**Brian Thomas Curtin,** Composer and Songwriter, Eaglestone Music

As an orchestral composer, I rarely hire live musicians. It's mostly "in the box." But for smaller ensembles where some instruments might be real (like a guitar), using inferior sampled instruments might tarnish an otherwise great piece of music. If money is an issue, try trading services in order to get a live player on your cue.

—**Steve Barden,** Composer and Author

CHAPTER 6

Producing and Arranging

WAIT, WHICH HAT AM I WEARING?

Due to the revolution of digital recording, and the effect it has had on the way music is created, the lines have blurred between the processes of writing, arranging, and producing. It has become hard to tell where one ends and another begins. In chapter 2, on composing, you also learned some basic arranging concepts, because it is difficult to separate the two processes. (There is more on arranging later in this chapter.) Now for some background on production.

YOU'RE THE TOP(LINER)

In pop music, it is common for a producer to assemble and, perhaps, create a track that includes the chords, structure, and arrangement of a song, along with recordings of all the instrumental parts except the vocals. Then a collaborator writes the *topline*—the lyrics and melody—of the song. There are some who believe lyrics and melody *are* the song, but this definition is changing. The producer may get songwriting credit if the lyrics and melody were inspired by their track; without the track, the topline would likely have been written differently. This practice also occurs in writing songs for sync and is an example of the unclear distinction between producing and songwriting. When one person handles all of these tasks, it can be very difficult to tell which hat is being worn. Instead of being several separate processes, it starts to be one big process.

THE EVOLVING ROLE OF THE PRODUCER

The music producer used to be defined as the person who oversaw the creation of a recording by an artist . . . from the writing or selecting of the songs to deciding on the musicians who performed on the recording . . . to arranging the music to booking the studio and equipment that was to be used . . . to the mixing and mastering of the music. Plus, there was usually a *recording engineer* who set up and plugged in the microphones, adjusted the levels, and handled all of the technical details. Some recording projects are still done this way in the world of writing for sync, but due to the coordination involved, time constraints, and the added expense, many are not.

OH, I'M WEARING *ALL* THE HATS

Here is today's definition of a producer: The person who owns or has access to recording equipment and knows how to use it. This includes a computer, recording software, audio interfaces, microphones, mic stands, and a room for the recording to take place. In many cases, the producer is also the person who wrote or co-wrote the music, the recording engineer, the mixer, and the one who masters the music after it is recorded.

Becoming comfortable and proficient in the various recording jobs will benefit you greatly in your music career. Otherwise, find someone who excels at the tasks that are not your strengths.

HEY! WHAT'S "BROADCAST QUALITY," AND WHY IS IT SO IMPORTANT?

Broadcast quality means several things, but it is basically well-recorded music. This means it is a crystal-line song or track with excellent singing, interesting arrangements, and great musicianship. There are no unintentional pops, cracks, or outside noises, like dogs barking or planes flying overhead. The mix is clear, well balanced, and appropriate for the genre; it was recorded to be broadcast, and there is nothing about it that will distract the viewer or listener.

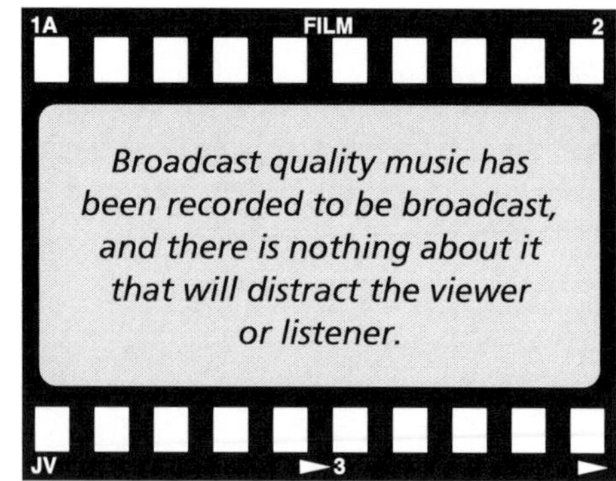

There are some companies that want music recorded from a certain time period or era or want music that sounds like it was recorded during that era, so they expect the audio quality to match. The musicianship has to be clean and perfect unless there is a reason for sloppiness.

There is no such thing as a "demo" anymore regarding music for sync. You must deliver the finished, perfect, unblemished product.

ONLY THE BEGINNING

When a producer creates a new session to record a song in their DAW, they need to select the appropriate audio quality. This is determined by the file format, sample rate, and bit depth.

- *File format.* There are two common high-resolution (hi-res) file formats: *AIFF* (*Audio Interchange File Format*) files have a file extension of .aif or .aiff. *WAV files* (*Waveform Audio File Format*) have a file extension of .wav. These are both lossless, uncompressed files. *Lossless* means that no audio quality got lost during the process of recording or converting. *Uncompressed* means that the files have not been made smaller. To accommodate the quality of the audio, these hi-res files are large. There is no noticeable difference between the audio quality of AIFF and WAV files, and they are often the same size. The only difference is that, while it is possible to embed *metadata* or information (more on metadata in chapter 17) in a WAV file, it is easier with an AIFF file.
- *Sample rate.* The sample rate of an audio file affects its quality and size. Music on compact disc has a sample rate of 44.1 kHz. However, most music for sync is delivered at a sample rate of 48 kHz, which is better quality, but the files are bigger. Once again, many cannot hear the difference between 44.1 and 48 kHz, but audio professionals can. Sample rates of 88.2, 96, and 192 kHz exist but are not usually used in sync music.
- *Bit depth.* The other specification of audio files to consider is bit depth. Music on compact discs has a bit depth of 16. Many music supervisors, sync agencies, and production music libraries accept this, while others prefer 24-bit. Like the sample rate, the higher the bit depth, the higher the audio quality and file size. Though not common, 32-bit float is available.

In music intended for sync, *stereo*—or two channels of audio—is still the standard. Individual tracks, like a vocal or a guitar, are recorded traditionally in *mono*—or one channel of audio—but will be part of a full stereo mix. Certain individual instruments are recorded in stereo, like drum kits, synthesizers, and electric pianos. Though some score composers prefer to record and mix in 5.1 or 7.1 surround sound, licensed music is in stereo.

When a new session is created in a DAW, all of these parameters need to be outlined. All of the audio for that session is recorded in the same file format with the same sample rate and bit depth. When the project is complete, an audio file of the full mix can be exported. This file can be of a different format and a lower sample rate and bit depth but should never be higher. Though it is possible, converting up to these specifications after the original recording was done at a lower setting does not improve the audio quality. Companies that license music explicitly advise against this practice.

Before you create your session and start recording, make sure you know what audio quality the company with which you are working requires. There is software that converts exported AIFF files and WAV files of different sample rates and bit depths to other kinds of files. This is helpful when there is a need to deliver files in a different format than was originally intended. A 48-kHz, 24-bit AIFF file can be converted to a 48-kHz, 16-bit WAV file. Once again, it is advised not to convert upward. Because file conversion is a one-way street downward, it is best to record all audio at the highest rates allowed by your DAW, A/D converter, and audio interface. Keep this in mind when purchasing equipment. You will end up with many large audio files on your hard drive, so get the biggest drive you can.

HEY! READ THIS!
We always record 48-kHz, 24-bit WAV files and have never had a request for anything higher. If requested, we convert to a different file format and lower resolution.

DO YOU HAVE THIS IN A SMALLER SIZE?

It is not always convenient to deal with large hi-res audio files. Companies interested in signing your music may want you to send recordings of your work for consideration or review. When smaller files are preferred, MP3s are the customary solution. Depending on the parameters, MP3s are about one-tenth the size of AIFF and WAV files. An *MP3* (*MPEG-1 Audio Layer 3*) is a lossy-compressed file, meaning that as a result of being made smaller, the quality of the audio has been decreased. Like hi-res files, MP3s can have sample rates of 44.1 or 48 kHz. Instead of bit depth, MP3s have bit rates of 128,160, 192, 224, 256, and 320 Kbps (kilobits per second). Lower bit rates are available but with a noticeable deterioration in audio quality. It is almost unheard of to be asked for an MP3 with a bit rate lower than 128 Kbps.

Unlike hi-res files, it is easy to embed metadata into MP3s. The software to do this is readily available.

A FILE WITH NO NAME

When initiating a session in your DAW, it is advisable to consider carefully how the session file is named. In addition to the name of the song or instrumental, include the date, the key in which the song is to be recorded, and the tempo of the song. When you are writing several songs or instrumentals for a project, be sure that there are few, if any, in the same key or at the same tempo. Putting this information in the file name makes it easier to access it and to have variety within the collection without having to open up each session file to check for this information. There are times when the key and tempo end up being different than intended originally; in these instances, simply close the session file and rename it.

When naming a session file or folder, it is best to use numbers, letters, hyphens (-), or an underscore line (_). Avoid using special characters because in some instances the session may not function properly if these are used. Also, when you use a file-sending service, odd characters may affect how your files are sent or transmitted. We learned this the hard way on a deadline project.

HEY! READ THIS!
Here is an example of how to name your file in your DAW session: TITLE-TEMPO-KEY-DATE. It could look like this: "The Cover Up 124 Am 6-8-18." This makes it easy to identify the tempo and key of each cue, preventing a cookie-cutter approach within a collection.

It is also beneficial to organize folder structure in ways that make it easier to find files. For instance, if you are writing ten instrumentals for a music library, they can all go in a folder with the following information specified:

- Name or initials of the music library or sync agency
- Genre
- Date of creation or date it is due

"APM Americana 01-20-25" is a sample.

Create a folder system that makes sense to you.

THE BEAT GOES ON

Music may be flowing, loose, *rubato*, and without a tempo or have a tempo to which it does not strictly adhere. However, most music is recorded to a *click track*, which acts like a metronome. It is to keep the tempo or speed of a song steady. Tempo is measured in *beats per minute* (*bpm*). For easy reference, think of ticking seconds on a clock as 60 bpm; double that, and you have 120 bpm. The steady click or pulse can be heard while recording but can be turned off during playback.

Take some time to acclimate yourself and your musicians to recording with a click track—it may feel unforgiving and unnatural initially. Make sure there is preparation and practice ahead of the recording session.

After creating a session file, use your best judgment when selecting a tempo. As long as virtual instruments are the first things recorded or programmed, it is easy to change the tempo to a speed that better suits the song. Although it is possible to change the tempo of audio after it has been recorded, it can be challenging.

Some producers and composers may use a fractional tempo, like 83.5 or 119.7 bpm. However, most everyone prefers that their music have a tempo with a whole-number value, such as 90 or 128 bpm. There are times when no tempo is given for a piece of music, and it has to be determined later. A fractional tempo is difficult to calculate—and it can present a problem when entering the amount on a spreadsheet. When possible, assign a whole-number tempo marking.

There are many advantages to working on, editing, and mixing a song that has been recorded to a click track:

- It is much simpler to copy and paste performances from one part of the song to another.
- Tempo-based effects in the mixing process are easier to adjust.
- When your composition is signed, many sync agencies and music libraries need to know the tempo.
- With a click track, accurate tempo information is readily available.

NAMES, NOTES, AND PRETTY COLORS

Because many sync music producers and composers write and record a large volume of music, organizational skills are essential. Some producers work on songs that have dozens of tracks, each containing performances of different instruments. The nature of certain genres of music requires this. In big recording sessions, it is critical to know which tracks contain which instruments. A good way to deal with this is naming your tracks in a deliberate way. Naming a track "Vocal" is good, but "Lead Vocal" or "BG Vocal" (for a background vocal) is better. If there are several background vocals, one of them could be labeled "BG Vocal 1" or "BG Vocal Hi," if it is a high part. If there are several singers recording individually, their initials can be used. Some producers prefer to use the instrument name first, followed by the role that it is playing, such as "Guitar Lead" or "Guitar Rhythm."

SHORT AND SWEET: MAKE IT BRIEF

Since there is a limit on the number of characters that are visible in a track name, abbreviations are more efficient. Here are some common examples:

- "Vocal" becomes "Vox"
- "Harmony" becomes "Hrm"
- "Guitar" becomes "Gtr"
- "Strings" becomes "Str"
- "Percussion" becomes "Perc"

Feel free to develop your own shorthand. Unless you are going to pass it off to someone else for mixing or more production, it only needs to make sense to you.

For future use, it is practical to keep notes regarding the recording of a track. Each track in a DAW has a space for this purpose. These notes can include which microphone was used, how it was placed in front of the instrument or vocalist, preamp settings, where the track was recorded, which instrument was used, and who performed the part. If there is a guitar or other stringed instrument involved, notes could include whether an alternate tuning or a capo were used.

This information can be useful later if you need to record additional parts and you'd like to match what has already been recorded. It can also be handy if you like the way an instrument was recorded and want to use the same process on an upcoming recording.

Additionally, the comments or notes field can include information about the sample patch you are using and how you may have tweaked it, in case you want to use those settings on a different recording.

COLOR MY WORLD

Most DAWs allow the color coding of tracks. This is very helpful in keeping your session organized and makes it easier to find individual tracks or groups of tracks. For instance, you may have all of your drum tracks in brown, your guitar tracks in green, and your vocal tracks in blue.

Developing a consistent color scheme that you use for every song makes it easier to navigate around your sessions. There is no accepted standard, so the colors you choose to assign to different instruments are up to you.

TEMPLATE LOVE

If you are really familiar with your DAW, when creating a new session you can add tracks you need fairly quickly. However, it is sometimes more efficient to use a template.

Your DAW may have *templates* available, with tracks already created that can serve as a good starting point for a new session file. You may want to create your own customized templates, which works well for us. Include track names and colors in your templates to save time in creating new sessions from them.

HEY! READ THIS!

For songs, we create a template for a session that includes vocals, keyboards, guitars, bass, and drums. For electronic tension instrumentals, we set up another template that has tracks for synths, pads, electronic drums, and percussion. We also load the virtual instruments on the appropriate tracks. We prefer to have too many tracks in our templates, because it is easier to delete unwanted tracks than it is to create new ones. If you want to be more efficient, make using templates a part of your workflow.

IMAGINE—HOW TO USE REFERENCE SONGS AND TRACKS

When a music supervisor needs music for a scene, they don't always look for something completely original in style or form. They search by describing what they need in terms of preexisting music. It can be difficult to characterize or define music any other way. Citing genres and subgenres can be helpful but still incomplete.

The preexisting music used to express what fits their project often translates into reference tracks and songs for the people who assist them with their searches. Reference music helps the people who create or represent music know what to provide to the music supervisor or music user. A publisher once advised, "Imagine your song on the same playlist as the reference song." The reason for these requests is that some TV shows have a constant need for certain styles of music. The benefit is that it gives songwriters, composers, and publishers some direction in which to go, especially when putting together a collection of several tracks.

There is a lot of information to be gleaned from listening to reference tracks and songs:

- Determine characteristics such as the genre and time period, although this information is usually provided in the music user's request (known as *specs*—short for "specifications").
- Identify the instrumentation. Some pieces of music contain acoustic instruments, some consist of electronic instruments, and yet others utilize a combination of both. The specific acoustic instruments used contribute greatly to the vibe of the music.
- Another good observation to make is the nature of the music. Notice the scales, chords, groove, and tempo.
- What is the overall mood? Is it hopeful or hopeless? Is it aggressive or passive?
- While listening to a reference song, also consider the kind of lyrics and who is singing them. Does the request ask for male or female vocals specifically? Is the language new and contemporary or more traditional?

Always make broad, general observations, and incorporate them into your own, original music. One of our composer friends calls this "distilling the essence" of the reference tracks.

A strong word of caution: *Never* take any specific musical or lyrical ideas from the reference tracks. This is plagiarism, and it is illegal. Reference tracks and songs are not intended to be knockoffs or soundalikes. Those are considered rip-offs and can land a composer or songwriter in hot water. Using reference songs is also different than modeling songs, a practice frowned upon in the music business because it involves taking a preexisting song and rewriting lyrics or a melody over the original.

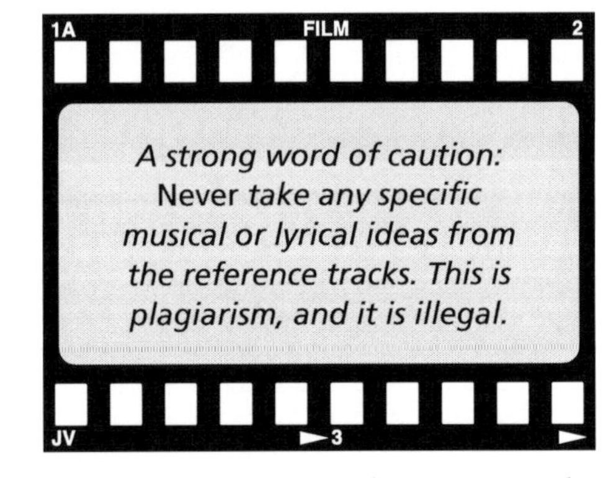

A strong word of caution: Never *take any specific musical or lyrical ideas from the reference tracks. This is plagiarism, and it is illegal.*

Choose instead to create new music that is similar to the vibe and feel of the reference tracks while putting your own musical personality into it. Music supervisors and the companies that represent music do not want to be involved in lawsuits. Just as importantly, they and their colleagues don't want to work with anyone who is known to have committed such an unethical act.

WHEN THE BONES ARE GOOD: USING AN OUTLINE

Everyone has a different process when composing, arranging, and producing. Many turn on the computer and start playing whatever comes to mind. Some begin by writing music notation or creating a chart or lead sheet. Others start with an interesting drum groove or chord progression. Some experiment with a new sample library.

We have created music using all of the above methods, but before we start recording our favorite tip is to create an *outline*—a road map of where the song or cue starts, where it goes, and how it ends. This framework is especially helpful when composing a collection of five or more songs. Usually we have a few reference tracks that were provided to us by a music placement company.

Here is a process for creating an outline:

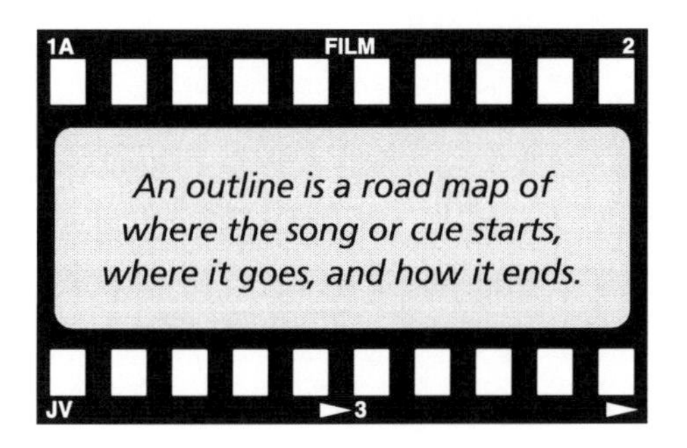

1. Listen to the reference tracks, and make notes about instrumentation, groove, tempo, arrangement, and production elements.
2. Create an outline by sketching a four- to eight-bar chord pattern.
3. Compose a motif (a simple melody) for the A part and for the B part, if needed.
4. Create a recording session, and use all of your original ideas.
5. Record rough takes of the MIDI tracks; then make sure everything makes sense and it all fits the project.
6. After the tracks are recorded, tighten everything up. Make sure all the production elements are there, which means:

    - The instruments are in tune
    - Everything is rhythmically correct and quantized or humanized
    - There are harmony and counterpoint (if necessary)

BUILDING A MYSTERY: USING A MIDI MOCK-UP

After creating an outline, the next step is creating a MIDI mock-up. Using your song template, play and record the parts initially with virtual instruments to hear how the song and the arrangement work. The song in a mock-up might sound a little mechanical at first. However, it'll give you an idea of how the music is unfolding, and you'll learn to hear past the stiffness. Here is one approach:

- If you have a rough phone recording of your vocal or guitar, import it into a template in your DAW. If you don't have a rough phone recording, record a *guide track* into your session. This is a basic, unpolished vocal recording, sometimes accompanied by a guitar or piano. You can then listen to it while recording the instruments and vocals. The guide track, also known as a *scratch track*, is removed after everything else has been recorded.
- Instead of using a click track, use a *drum loop*. This is a one- to four-bar recording of an acoustic or electronic drum performance. Extend the drum loop through the expected length of the song. This can be inspiring because it feels more like playing with a real musician. This loop can remain in the final version after being tweaked.
- One of the biggest advantages of a MIDI mock-up is that, when working with artists, you can make adjustments on the fly before recording audio. This means

    - The key can be raised or lowered to accommodate the artist's vocal range.
    - If the tempo is too fast and the vocalist has difficulty singing the words clearly, the bpm can be made slower.
    - If the tempo is too slow and lacks energy, making the phrases too long for the singer to take breaths, the bpm can be increased.
    - The melody notes can still be tweaked if they are not suitable for the singer.
    - Sections of the song, such as the verse, pre-chorus, chorus, bridge, and post-chorus, can be switched around completely, omitted, elongated, shortened, or changed in any way.

Once everything is in place within the MIDI mock-up, it is easy to get an overall feel for the flow of the song. After recording the vocals, the virtual instruments can be replaced by recording live, acoustic ones, such as guitar, bass, and others.

Now it is time for the fun part—arranging the song. To be licensable and get the attention of a music supervisor, your music needs to be well-written and arranged with varying levels of interest and intensity.

YES, THIS IS REALLY HOW MANY MUSIC SUPERVISORS LISTEN TO A SONG THE FIRST TIME

Music supervisors, like many other people in the sync music business, are very busy. Listening to music is a big part of their job, although it is not the only thing they do. Because they deal with a lot of music, they do not listen to every song submitted from start to finish. This is not what music creators want to hear—but it's true.

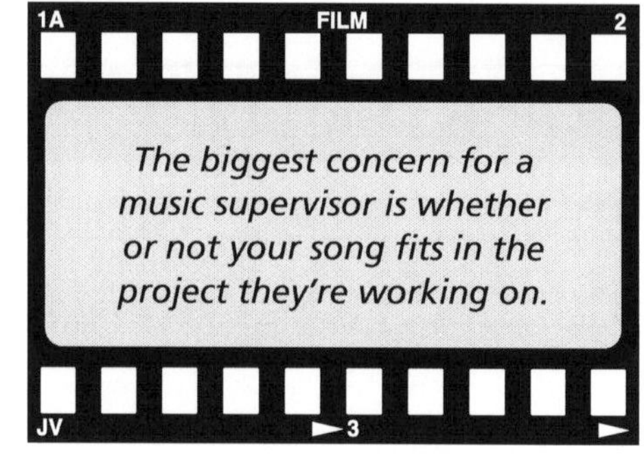

If there is a waveform (more on this later) of the song available to them, they will look at it first to see where it gets bigger (louder) and smaller (softer). If it is a song, and a lyric sheet is available, they will look at that too. Then they will listen to the first ten to fifteen seconds of the song, skip to about the one-minute mark or wherever there is a visible change in volume in the waveform where the chorus might be, and listen for another ten to fifteen seconds. They proceed to around the halfway point for a few seconds, the three-quarter mark for another few seconds, and then the last ten to fifteen seconds. This process takes less than a minute. They then know whether or not the song will work for their current project or possible future projects. And, you know what? Most of the time, they get it right.

If a music supervisor ends up not selecting your song, it is not necessarily because your song is not good enough or wasn't well written. The biggest concern for a music supervisor is whether or not your song fits in the project they're working on.

Once they have determined that a song is viable, they will go back and listen to the whole song all the way through. They need to find music for their projects, or they won't stay employed. It is your job to make their job easier.

YOU NEED TO CALM DOWN

Have you regained your composure yet? If so, what can you learn from reviewing a music supervisor's listening process? You can gain some insight into how to arrange a song or instrumental.

Start by looking at graphic representations of music—*waveforms*. A stereo waveform shows the left channel on the top and the right channel on the bottom. The beginning of the piece of music is on the left end of the waveform, and the end is on the right. Here are the important takeaways: When the music is quiet, the waveforms for both channels are small; when the music is loud, the waveforms are big. It's easy to see without listening to a recording whether the music maintains the same volume level throughout the song or has variations in volume.

HEY! READ THIS!

Not only does your music need to *sound* right, it needs to *look* right, too. Waveforms need to have variations in level. Many times the music supervisor or other music user will scroll through a track, checking for dynamics and different intensities.

SEEING IS BELIEVING

Here is the waveform for our cue, "Waiting in the Dark." Listen to the audio as you look at the waveform.

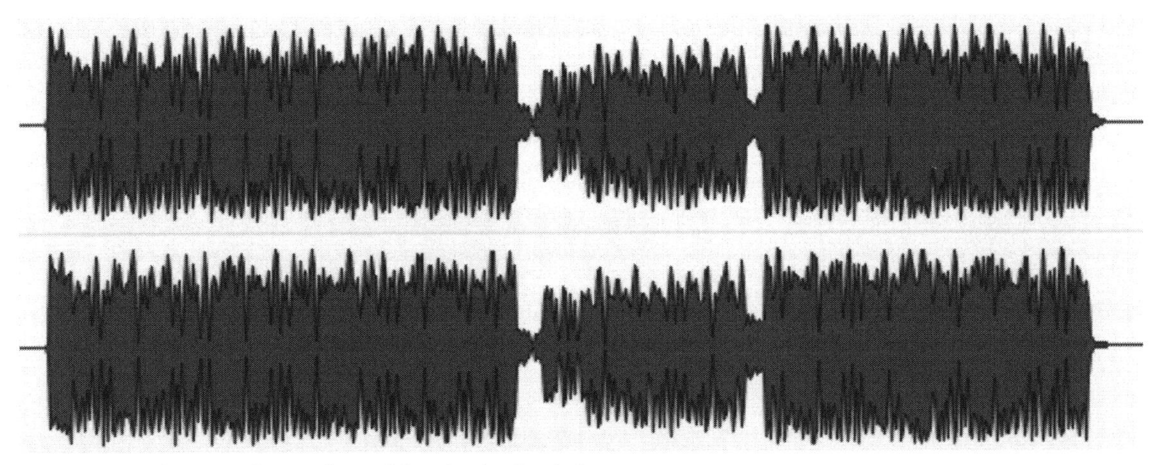

Figure 6.1. *The waveform of "Waiting in the Dark."*

HEY! LISTEN TO THIS! "Waiting in the Dark"

You can see that the cue starts out fairly loud, has a visible edit point where it gets softer, then another where it gets louder again, and has a hard ending. The music editor has the option of starting the cue from the beginning or from either of the edit points. The cue was composed and arranged to facilitate those kinds of decisions and to make them easy for the music editor to execute.

The waveforms for some songs look like a brick. They start as loud as they can, stay loud, and finish loud. Look at the waveform for our rock cue "Basher," and listen to the audio.

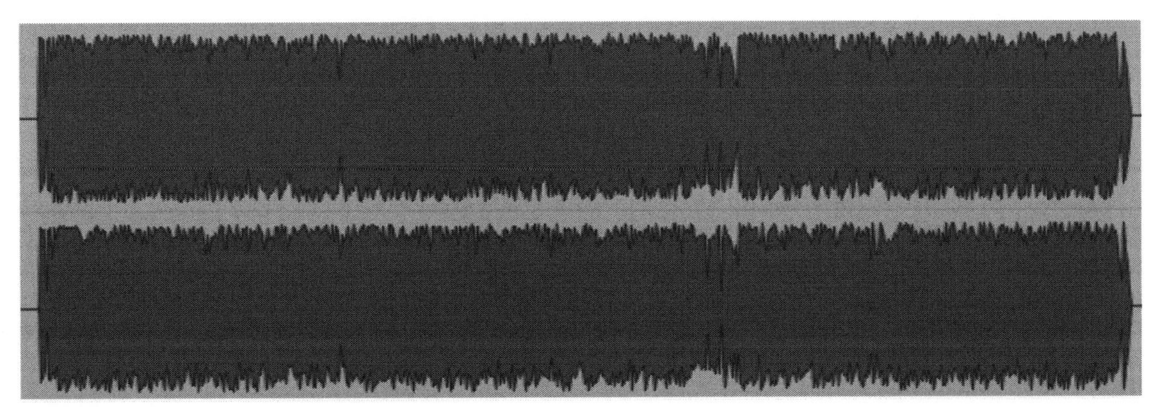

Figure 6.2. *The waveform of "Basher."*

HEY! LISTEN TO THIS! "Basher"

Though there is a visible edit point about two-thirds of the way through, "Basher" never really lets up and maintains high intensity from start to finish. If different levels are desired, this is not the right cue. However, sports programming uses a lot of music like this.

Other cues start very quietly and stay that way to the end. Neither one of these is preferable. Music with these waveforms can get licensed but not as frequently as music with more interesting arrangements.

When music supervisors and music editors view a waveform, this is what they notice:

- *Whether or not the piece of music has different levels of volume.* These different levels can be useful in scenes where the emotional intensity grows or subsides.
- *If those variations in volume are sudden or gradual.* It can be advantageous to have both, depending on the emotional pacing of a scene.
- *If there are any breaks or silences in the middle of the song.* These are very helpful and easy-to-find edit points.
- *How the song starts and ends.* They want a piece of music that elicits a distinct mood or feeling quickly without meandering. Most of the time, they do not want a piece of music that gets quieter gradually at the end. They prefer a dramatic buildup to a big last note.

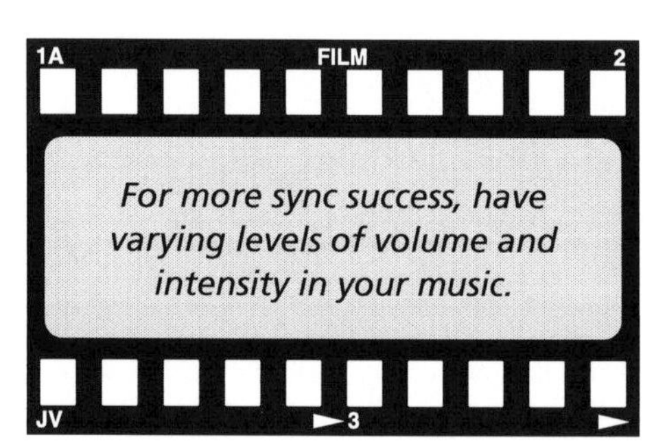

And they make all of these observations before even listening to the music! So, think about how the waveform of your song or instrumental will look, while you are arranging it. To summarize: for more sync success, have varying levels of volume and intensity in your music.

FROM THE TOP

Not every song or instrumental needs an intro. Many start simply at the beginning of the A section, verse, or chorus. Some of those have a drumbeat or two, a percussion hit, a cymbal swoosh, or a short signature sound right before the music starts or a combination of these. Not using an intro or using a very short one is highly recommended. This way the listener knows right away that the music is getting down to business with no delay.

Other songs or instrumentals have a two- or four-bar intro that sets up the music to follow. These short intros do not differ from the rest of the music but instead clearly indicate the feel, genre, and instrumentation of the piece. When the piece actually starts, there should not be sudden changes in tempo, key, or vibe. If there is a contrast here, it should be in intensity.

HEY! READ THIS!

Some pop songs include sound effects in their recordings, which can help put the listener in a desired setting. However, in music written and recorded for licensing, the setting is determined by the parameters of the *visual scene*. If the music includes sound effects, the viewer will be confused about their source. Do the characters hear them? This is a deal breaker for placement opportunities, so save your recording of a car engine revving or people cheering, for another project.

SPOTLIGHT: MAKING THE MAIN FOCUS CLEAR

Most music has a primary focus: If there is a lead vocal, that should be the spotlight throughout that piece of music. In instrumentals, this focal part can be played by any instrument associated with your cue's particular genre. It is essential that there is a clear center around which the rest of the arrangement is built. There are times when the focus shifts to another instrument playing the same or different part, but there is one main focus at a time.

What the main part does has been determined during the writing or composing phase of the process. What the rest of the instruments do is determined by arranging.

THE DIFFERENCE BETWEEN ARRANGING AND ORCHESTRATING

Arranging and *orchestrating* are terms that composers and musicians may use interchangeably, mistakenly believing them to be the same thing.

Orchestration is the art and craft of assigning notes to specific instruments in an orchestra or other music group to play. It offers less flexibility than arranging, as it leaves the original composition unchanged. Careful consideration is given to the range and tone of the instruments.

Arranging is the art and craft of adapting and developing an existing musical composition. This process frequently involves selecting which instruments will be a part of the arrangement and assigning parts to them. Although the core composition remains intact, there is greater freedom in arranging to change harmonies, timings, and structure.

IMAGINATION + ORCHESTRATION = SYNTHESTRATION

Each of these processes is an integral part of bringing a composition to life. If any one is not executed well, the composition may not realize its full potential for emotional connection with a listener.

Another term to become familiar with is *synthestration*—creating a session using all virtual instruments and then adding, blending, or substituting the real instruments later into the mix, if necessary. Many composers, especially those who work in the TV field, have gotten so good at finessing virtual instrument sounds quickly that it is difficult to hear what is real and what is fake. In addition, high-quality sample libraries have improved their user-friendly and humanly intuitive qualities. Several music schools offer courses in synthestration, and these can be found by doing an Internet search for "virtual MIDI symphonic orchestration classes."

THE REST OF IT

Once again, the genre often dictates which instruments are accompanying the lead instrument. The parts those instruments play are also influenced frequently by the genre. For instance, the kick drum in electronic dance music usually plays steady quarter notes. If it does something drastically different, it won't sound like authentic EDM.

Most importantly, music arrangement is largely about instruments coming in and going out. It also concerns instruments changing the parts they play. A common arranging mistake is having every instrument in a piece of music play the same part from the beginning to the end, without stopping or doing something different. No matter how good the main part is, it won't sound as interesting as it can if the arrangement is unimaginative.

THE THREE ELEMENTS OF MUSIC

After writing or composing, but before recording, think about which instruments will be in your music and what parts they should be playing. To better understand these parts and the roles they fulfill in an arrangement, here are some basics.

Music consists of three elements:

1. Melody
2. Harmony
3. Rhythm

In most cases, the melody will be sung by a vocalist in a song. In an instrumental, a designated instrument or group of instruments plays a melody or a simpler motif or theme. In either case, this part should be created during the writing or composing process.

WHAT'S THE POINT IN HAVING COUNTERPOINT?

Some melodies are very busy and leave no space between phrases. Other melodies and motifs leave plenty of room for counterpoint. Sometimes referred to as *countermelody*, *counterpoint* is a secondary melody that fits in the spaces of the main melody. Since the available space is often small, counterpoint is frequently made up of short two- or three-note phrases. If the available space in the main melody is larger, the counterpoint can be longer and more developed.

HEY! LISTEN TO THIS! "Golden Lotus"

This cue starts with a pipa (a Chinese stringed instrument) playing a melody with spaces between the phrases. When the second A section starts, a shakuhachi flute enters, playing long notes while the

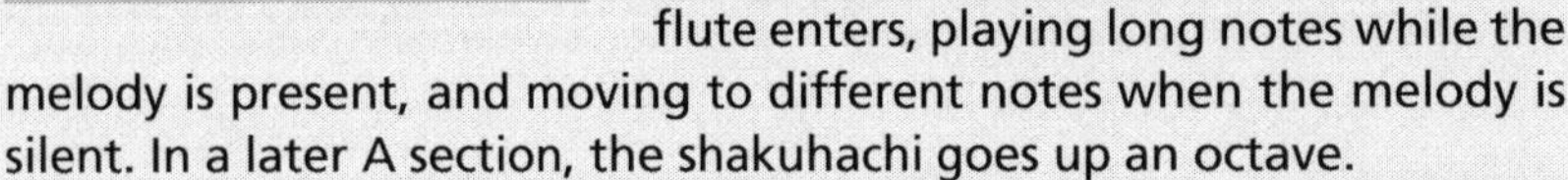

melody is present, and moving to different notes when the melody is silent. In a later A section, the shakuhachi goes up an octave.

Counterpoint complements the melody without imitating it. If the melody is very static—hovering primarily on one or two notes—the counterpoint can involve several different pitches. Conversely, if the melody uses varying pitches, the counterpoint can move between just two or three pitches.

The timing of the counterpoint can contrast that of the melody as well. If one is fast with a lot of eighth and sixteenth notes, the other can be sparse with quarter and half notes. Once again, counterpoint can complement and contrast the melody.

HEY! READ THIS!
Here is an arrangement technique tip: Midway through the piece of music, have the melody exit, leaving the counterpoint, after which the melody comes back. In other cases, the melody exits, then the counterpoint enters, followed by the return of the melody, and they "magically" fit together.

IN PERFECT HARMONY

The basic harmony for a piece of music is generally determined during the writing process. Although the chords have already been established, selecting which instruments play them and how they will be played is part of the arrangement process.

To create harmony—the second element of music—there are three primary options:

1. The more obvious is to have chords played by a multinote instrument like a piano or a guitar (or another strummed stringed instrument).
2. The other option is to have several single-note instruments play individual notes that create chords.
3. Use a combination of these two techniques.

There are countless possibilities and variations for how chords can be played on a guitar or piano. The notes themselves can be low, medium, or high in pitch. (See *inversions* in chapter 2.) Most fretted stringed instruments can be played with a capo to raise the pitch, or the tuning can be changed to lower the pitch. Piano players can simply reach for higher or lower notes.

> 1A FILM 2
>
> *Though it may not be a complete chord with three or more notes, playing two notes at a time can be effective by leaving the harmony ambiguous.*
>
> JV ►3 ►

If there are other instruments on the recording, the piano or guitar chords can have fewer notes. Though it may not be a complete chord with three or more notes, playing two notes at a time can be effective by leaving the harmony ambiguous.

A very common example of this is the open fifth chord, consisting of the root and fifth notes from a major scale. Whether the overall harmony is major or minor can be determined by notes being played by other instruments, including the melody instrument, or it can be left vague and uncertain for effect. Pairs of notes creating harmonies in intervals of thirds or sixths that commit to the tonality of the chord also work well.

CUE THE PIANO

Be cautious when arranging piano parts. The nature of the piano allows the pianist to play melody, chords, and a bass part simultaneously. There are some cases where this is desirable, especially in a sparse arrangement. In busier arrangements, it is best to keep the piano part simple unless it is corresponding with what the other instruments are playing, such as the guitar and bass.

Some piano parts work very well with smooth, connected—or *legato*—phrasing. At other times, some separation of the notes is a better fit, especially with short, rhythmic notes, known as *staccato*. If you are programming virtual piano, be mindful of the sustain pedal and how it affects these two modes of playing. Virtual piano instruments allow for control of the sustain pedal after the notes have been recorded. Make sure the notes are not sustaining through chord changes, unless this is the desired effect.

HEY! LISTEN TO THIS! "Waiting in the Dark"

Listen again to "Waiting in the Dark." The piano is a virtual instrument recorded with the sustain pedal down for two measures at a time. This highlights the dissonance of the notes and creates a haunting vibe. It would sound very different if the sustain pedal were up.

THE BEAT OF YOUR OWN STRUM

Once the harmony notes have been chosen, decide on the timing of those notes. They can be:

- Long notes that are held out
- Short notes with space between them
- Notes that play a rhythmic pattern
- Or a combination of these

For example, a steady quarter note pulse has a different effect than a busy eighth- or sixteenth-note rhythm.

It is possible to add variety by playing chords higher or lower and playing them with different rhythms. Plus, more than one multinote instrument can be used.

An arrangement may include a piano playing triads in the midrange as quarter notes and a guitar with a capo strumming high chords as sixteenth notes. Or a guitar with no capo strumming lower eighth note chords and a mandolin strumming high whole note chords. There are many possibilities. Make sure there is consistency and agreement on the chords between the instruments.

PLAYING NICELY TOGETHER

When combining instruments, find combinations that will complement each other, instead of clashing with each other in the same *frequency range*—the span or spectrum of sound between two specified audio frequencies. Have one instrument playing higher than the other. The person who mixes the music will appreciate this later.

Single-note instruments function in the same way as multinote instruments. The main difference is that every instrument does not have to be playing the same rhythm. A low-pitched instrument can play an E as quarter notes while a midrange instrument plays a G as eighth notes. Then a high instrument can enter on a B whole note and change back and forth to a C whole note. The implied harmonies are then E minor and C major chords, but they have more harmonic and rhythmic interest than if they were strummed on a guitar.

When a multinote instrument or several single-note instruments are playing, another single-note instrument can be added to fill up the mix in a subtle way. This single-note instrument can also add motion by changing to different notes in the chord in an upward or downward direction. To create tension, it can also play notes that are not in the chord. Another possibility is for an instrument to enter playing a note and stay on that note. The tonic note works well for this purpose. This is demonstrated in the cue "Can't Feel the Love."

HEY! LISTEN TO THIS! "Can't Feel the Love"

At ten seconds into this song, a high string section enters on the tonic note. At forty seconds, a lower string section enters playing a different note with each chord change, creating a moving harmony with the sustaining high note. This lower string part moves in a downward direction primarily, adding a somber vibe to the cue. A lower pulsing string part enters on a lower tonic note at the one-minute mark to add more tension.

ARRANGING PARTS FOR SINGLE-NOTE VIRTUAL INSTRUMENTS

To create the illusion of a real orchestra or choir, take care when creating chords with virtual strings or voices. A novice composer's tendency is to open an orchestral or choral virtual instrument and begin recording all parts on one track. With this approach, the music may sound unnatural or inauthentic.

Instead, for a realistic effect, the track containing all the parts should be broken down into individual parts. So, create a separate track for each string section or voice part. Here are some examples:

- For an orchestra, each individual track may contain:
  - Violins
  - Violas
  - Cellos
  - Double Basses
- For a choir, each individual track may contain:
  - Sopranos
  - Altos
  - Tenors
  - Basses

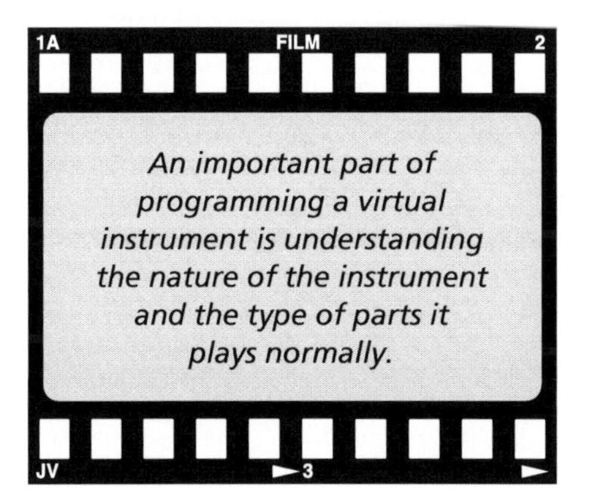

An important part of programming a virtual instrument is understanding the nature of the instrument and the type of parts it plays normally.

Think of chords and harmony as being a vertical view of music, and always keep that in mind. But also think horizontally about what each instrument or voice is playing individually so it also makes musical sense from that perspective. This is known as *voice leading.*

It is neither comfortable nor characteristic for violinists and violists to play a series of wide, odd intervals. Instead, they move traditionally in a scalewise fashion, with the occasional jump in interval. Again, there are no hard rules, just guidelines that lead to a desired outcome. An important part of programming a virtual instrument is understanding the nature of the instrument and the type of parts it plays normally.

GIVE ME A BEAT!

The third element of music is *rhythm*. Chords played in rhythm is a good way to cover both the harmonic and rhythmic elements with one instrument, but this will not have the same impact that a solid groove created by good drum and percussion parts can have.

If the genre you are producing features live drums and you have access to a quality drummer, the ability to record them, and the knowledge of how to best mix drums, then, by all means, record live drums.

However, not everyone has access to these resources. Also, not all genres require real-sounding drums. In such cases, there are several virtual drum and percussion instruments available. They can be found with genre-specific sounds and MIDI grooves. Use the ones that best fit your project. Obviously a virtual instrument with rock drum sounds and grooves works very well in a rock song. On the other hand, one intended for country music can work well in a pop song. Do not limit your use of these and other virtual instruments to their intended purpose. Creative experimentation is highly encouraged.

ALL ABOUT THAT BASS DRUM

Many genres are impossible to replicate without drums or percussion, such as hip hop, EDM, and funk. These instruments aren't as central to other genres of music but make a great contribution to them. Tension instrumentals might not seem like they need drums or percussion, but we use them in many of our tension cues.

Exactly how drums and percussion are played is dependent upon the genre. Listen closely to reference tracks. When doing this kind of critical listening, tune out all of the other instruments, and focus your attention on the drums and percussion. You will notice things you did not notice previously.

The main instruments in a drum part are the snare and kick drums. These are very prominent in most mixes and should be relatively easy to figure out. The snare is generally on the second and fourth beat of the measure, but not always. Sometimes there are softer snare hits between the louder ones. In some genres the kick can be very simple or can get complex. The kick plays an important role in a groove, so be sure to get this one right. Both parts will repeat probably every one, two, or four measures, with occasional deviations.

Remember not to copy the drum parts exactly from the reference track. Other than the snare playing on the two and the four beats, find ways to emulate their rhythms without duplicating them. If the kick part is straightforward, make yours simple in another way; if it is intricate, find a different way to make it complex.

Listen closely to what the rest of the drum kit is doing:

- The hi-hat can be a little more difficult to hear, but it usually plays steady eighth notes with some accents. Then there are times when it does nothing.
- Next, pay attention to the toms. Though they are used generally to play fills going into a new section, they are also used frequently as a crucial part of the groove.
- Last, analyze the percussion. Shakers and tambourines play an important but understated role in many songs.

If you have difficulty hearing what is being played by any instrument on a reference track, especially the higher frequency ones, try listening with headphones.

HEY! LISTEN TO THIS! "Expecting Bad News"

Listen to the drums on "Expecting Bad News," a hybrid cue. It starts with the kick and claps. As this is a hip hop–influenced drum part, the kick plays on the first beat of each measure and is syncopated for the rest of the measure. The claps are on the second and fourth beats. At 23 seconds, the hi-hat enters playing eighth notes with a fast roll added, which is common in hip hop and trap music. The snare enters at 46 seconds, creating tension by playing a syncopated pattern. It changes to a long, extended fill at 1:29, creating more tension. It speeds up just before the last note, rising in pitch, which is also a part of this style.

GET WITH THE PROGRAM

An essential thing to remember about programming drums is that the entire kit does not have to be played at all times. Sometimes just the kick drum works well for a section of a song. At other times the hi-hat alone is a good way to imply that the rest of the drum kit is coming in later. Bringing in one piece of the drum kit at a time is a good way to make subtle entrances. At other times it works better to bring the whole kit in at once.

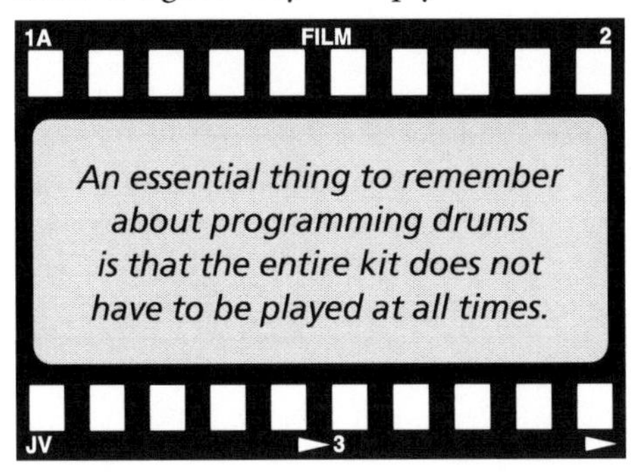

These individual instruments do not have to play the same part alone that they play when the rest of the kit is playing. The kick drum may play quarter notes when the full drum groove starts, but it may play only on the first beat of each measure when the rest of the kit is silent. The hi-hat may play eighth notes during the full drum groove but play only on the second and fourth beats of each measure on its own.

When programming drum parts intended to sound like they were played by a real drummer, remember to "think like a drummer." They have two hands and two feet, so they cannot play sixteenth notes on the hi-hat, kick, ride cymbal, snare, toms, and cowbell simultaneously. Also, the hi-hat stops usually during a drum fill and a cymbal crash.

WHEN IT'S TIME TO ARRANGE, YOU'VE GOT TO REARRANGE

Now that you are familiar with the three elements of music, how should you use this information to arrange your music?

1. For starters, when listening to reference tracks, take note of which instrument or instruments are playing the melody or motif and pay attention to the instrumentation of any counterpoint.
2. Then notice how the harmony is being played. Is it a guitar or piano? Or is it a small orchestral ensemble?
3. Finally, listen to the rhythmic elements:
   - Is there a full drum kit?
   - Are there shakers, handclaps, or other percussion instruments?

For all three of these elements, pay attention to how each instrument is performing its role.

A SERVING SUGGESTION

There are many approaches to fleshing out a musical arrangement. If you have some ideas, start recording them. If you are not sure where to start, make a list of the instruments you can hear playing each of the three elements in a reference track. It could look like this:

- The melody is sung by a female vocalist.
- The harmony is played by a ukulele, piano, vocals, and bass.
- The rhythm is played by drums, shaker, and handclaps.

If the song you wrote is going to start with a quiet chorus, here is an arrangement suggestion:

1. Pick two elements for the beginning. It could be the melody vocal and ukulele.
2. Halfway through the chorus, add a rhythmic element, like a shaker. This will give you one of each of the three elements.
3. On the verse, add the piano for more harmony.
4. For the second chorus, the drums, bass, and some harmony vocals can enter to add more rhythm and harmony.
5. Continue adding and subtracting instruments of each element, assuring that there is always at least one instrument from at least two elements.

Sometimes it's possible to have only one element represented—but only for a few measures.

A CHANGE IS GONNA COME: KEEPING IT INTERESTING

Having all three elements represented is a genre-dependent concept. There are some styles where all the instruments are drums and percussion. There are others that feature only *a cappella* vocals. These are special cases, but most other styles benefit from having all three elements. These ideas are not hard-and-fast rules that can never be broken, because there are always exceptions. Instead, they are offered as guidelines and suggestions.

By covering at least two elements at a time, the arrangement should remain interesting. To provide more options to a music editor, have a different combination of instruments in each repeated section. For instance, in the above arrangement suggestion, one of the later choruses could include only vocal melody, vocal harmony, and handclaps. This way each of the three choruses in this song would have a different texture and feel. If the song has two or more verses, make the instrumentation slightly different on each one.

In addition to considering the element and the role that each instrument in your arrangement plays, keep in mind its frequency range. A piece of music consisting of only high frequency instruments, like a glockenspiel, shaker, flute, and triangle, will not cover much of the available frequency spectrum. It is better to have some instruments of high, mid, and low frequencies for a fuller and more interesting sound. If this is kept in balance, the task of mixing the music will be easier. All of these frequencies do not need to be present at all times; however, having them all during high-intensity sections is recommended.

TWO HEARTS ARE BETTER THAN ONE

Like a strumming guitar, synths can be used to provide harmony and rhythm simultaneously. In genres in which electronic instruments are appropriate, synths that *pulse* on one or more notes can bring energy to a song. An arpeggiator works in a similar way. Instead of remaining on a single note, an *arpeggiator* plays one note in a chord at a time, often in ascending order, though other orders are also possible.

With pulses and arpeggiators, one or more MIDI notes are held out on the MIDI keyboard, and then eighth note, sixteenth note, or other rhythmic patterns are created in time with the tempo of the song. The timing and other behavior of the notes are determined within the hardware, synth, or virtual instrument plug-in. While these parts can be played manually, the sound of the notes being generated by the synth has a mechanical feel that works well in many genres.

I WANT CANDY

Earlier we noted that when you add surprises to your music, it keeps the listener engaged. One way to do this in your arrangement is by using unexpected, subtle textures called *ear candy*. They can be synthetic in nature, or they can be audio clips that have been processed using special effects. Ear candy can be created by tweaking sounds in virtual instruments or by manipulating your original audio, such as a vocal or guitar riff. They can have pitch or not. However, it is best to use them sparingly—that is, one to three at most. They are surprises, after all.

Do not confuse ear candy with using sound effects. Sound effects are sounds that are easily identifiable, such as ocean waves, a train whistle, or an audience applauding.

An effective way to use a piece of ear candy is to add it to your introduction so it stands out and then use it again later in the song or at the end. If you give the ear candy some space, the music editor will thank you.

Note: Once we started adding ear candy to our arrangements, we noticed an increase in placements.

HEY! READ THIS!

One piece of feedback that really helped us with our instrumental cues was to add other surprises in addition to the ear candy. These can be created by:

- Inserting a break or stop at the end of a measure
- Adding a countermelody
- Changing a 4/4 measure to a 2/4 measure
- Moving the lead instrument's octave up or down
- Doubling the lead instrument with a second lead instrument or vocal
- Or adding a simple harmony to the lead instrument or vocal

READY FOR THE STAND-IN

If you don't have the ability to play or record the same instruments as the ones on the reference tracks provided by a library or a client, instruments that are similar and play comparable parts can be substituted:

- An acoustic stringed instrument can replace another. For instance, a strumming mandolin can replace a strumming dulcimer or ukulele.
- Instruments played with mallets can be exchanged. A marimba can replace vibes, and a celeste can replace a glockenspiel. (Though it is not played with mallets, a celeste has a similar sound to a glockenspiel.)
- Percussion instruments can be interchangeable, like maracas and shakers, bongos and congas, clave and cowbell, taiko drums and toms, and handclaps and snaps.
- In certain roles, a trumpet can replace a saxophone, and a clarinet can replace a flute.
- Depending on the part and role being played, an acoustic guitar and a piano can take each other's place.
- An accordion can fill in for an organ.
- A synth pad can serve as sustaining strings.

SUBTLE SUBSTITUTES

What makes these substitutions work is that the replacement instruments have a similar frequency range. The suggested alternative instruments are also played the same way, as they are either strummed, shaken, struck with mallets or hands, or have a stream of air blown into them. The nature of the instruments is similar as well, such as their predisposition to produce long notes or short notes.

The goal is not to try to convince the listener that one instrument is another or that it has the same stylistic nuance. Instead, the goal is to have the substitute instrument serve a comparable purpose, play a similar role, and function as the same musical element as the other instrument.

LOWDOWN

Low frequencies deserve special attention. There is not a lot of room in the low frequency range, so it is strongly advised to limit the number of instruments playing there. In many mixes, a low-pitched instrument, like a bass guitar or bass synth, and a low percussion instrument, like a kick drum, do an excellent job of occupying the lower end of the sound spectrum. The mix can get muddy if other low frequency instruments are added.

The bass plays a unique role in music. Although it is referred to as being a part of the rhythm section, it can also be thought of as a harmony instrument. However, it contributes to the harmony by supplying the lowest note in the chords while simultaneously working with the kick drum to support the low end of the rhythm. Pay special attention to the bass parts you hear in reference tracks and the ones you arrange. Notice whether the bass stays on the tonic note of the chord or it deviates.

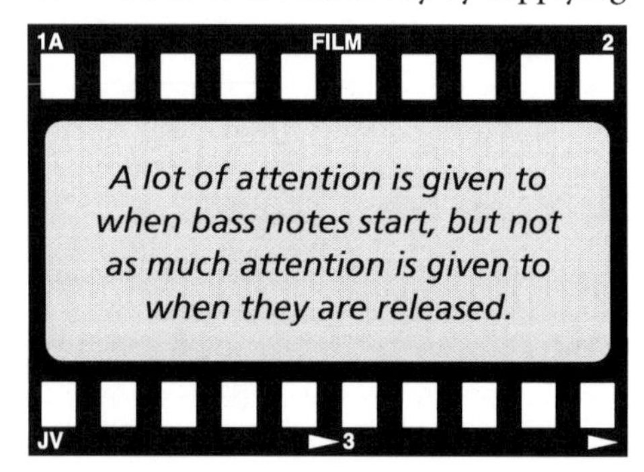

Listen to the timing of the notes relative to the kick drum and how short or long the notes may be. A lot of attention is given to when bass notes start, but not as much attention is given to when they are released (as with all stringed instruments). The length of the notes has an effect on the groove. Bass parts are not as noticeable as other parts, but they carry a lot of weight and have a significant impact on the feel and vibe of a piece of music.

VOICES CARRY

When arranging songs, take advantage of one of the most impactful tools you have available: *background vocals*. These can add a flavor and vibe like no other instrument. Vocal harmonies that run parallel to the melody or background vocals that are independent of the melody bring a unique texture to a song. They can also be used as counterpoint.

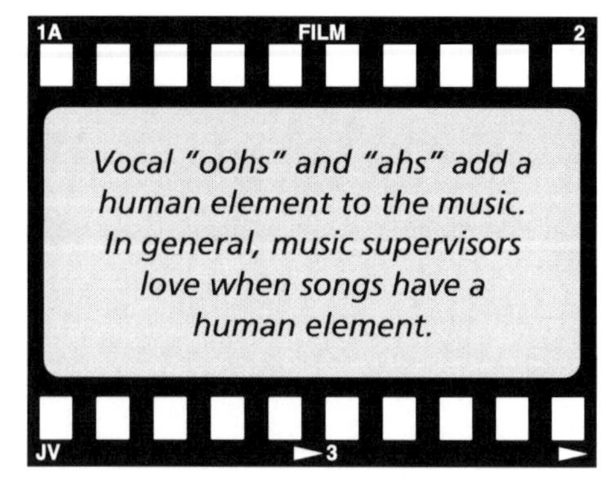

Background vocals that are not in time with the melody may contain the same lyrics as the melody, but they can also have different lyrics or no lyrics at all. "Oohs" and "ahs" add a human element to the music and can substitute for sustained strings and synth pads. In general, music supervisors love when songs have a human element.

Synth pads can be used to fill in space, if that is what the mix needs. These are sounds played on a synthesizer or virtual instrument. They play individual notes or chords typically that are sustained. If arranged and mixed well, they can make the music sound full and rich. Some pads play more than one pitch when one MIDI note is played. There are times when this is desirable, other times not. Be cautious with pads, because if they are not handled properly they can overwhelm a mix.

REMEMBER PROSODY? HERE'S AN ADDITIONAL WAY TO USE IT

In chapter 3, we covered how a song with good prosody has lyrics and music that work together to convey a common message and vibe. In the sync world, prosody also includes how production and arrangement elements contribute to getting these ideas across.

We also discussed the importance of having the appropriate vocalist sing your song. The subject and mood of the lyrics of a song should influence any decisions about additional vocals. Lyrics about being lonely sometimes work better with a solo voice with no extra vocals. Songs about an empowered group of people speaking out call for a lot of vocals. The mood of the lyrics should affect the delivery of the background vocals. They can range from quiet and somber "oohs" to gang vocals intended to excite a crowd. If you listen closely, the song will tell you what it needs. Most of the time an idea that does not work makes itself obvious immediately.

Although the genre affects the instrumentation choices to be made, the exact instruments from that genre to be used in your song depend on the nature of the message and vibe your music requires. Like singers, instruments have voices that can be light and airy like a flute or big and heavy like a distorted electric guitar. Consider the size of the role each instrument will play. Sometimes a full piano part is the best fit, and other times a few piano notes sprinkled here and there get the job done.

The number of instruments and how they are played also contribute to the end result. Some songs have a proclamatory message that calls for a full production with many instruments playing with maximum enthusiasm, while others work better with a small-ensemble approach with plenty of space. Taste, judgment, and a strong musical sense are your main tools.

Experimentation is important here, so start with intuitive and logical ideas that make sense to you. What matters most is the emotion in your music.

OVER THE RAINBOW: CREATING MUSICAL ARCS

Another essential feature to listen for in reference tracks is the *arc* of the arrangement. Some instrumentals start quietly with few instruments and gradually increase in intensity through the last note. Others start loudly with several instruments, get quiet, and grow again. A common successful outline starts small, grows, gets small again with a different combination of instruments, and then grows again with yet another different combination of instruments. By changing the order in which the instruments enter and exit, and adding some new ones, you add variety and give the music editor options.

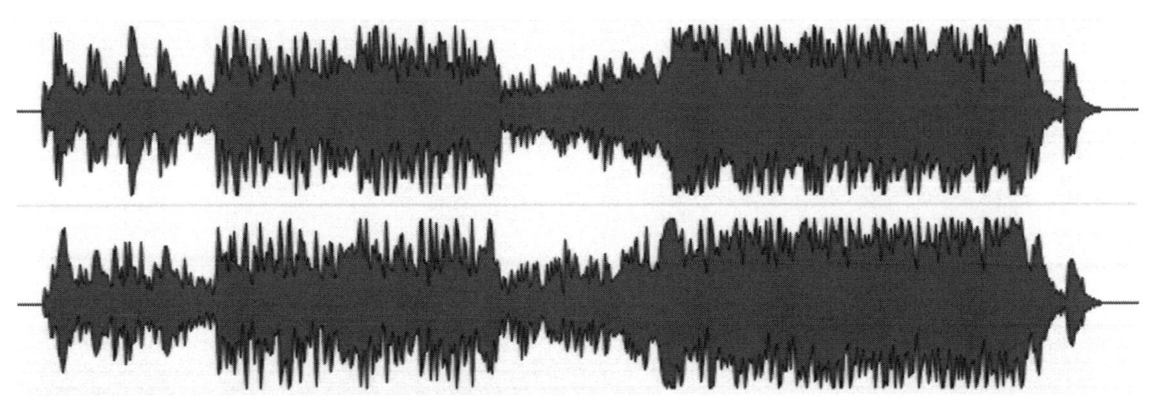

Figure 6.3 The waveform of "Undercover."

HEY! LISTEN TO THIS!
"Undercover"
In this example, the music grows, then gets smaller, then grows again. Its outline can be seen in the above waveform.

UP-DOWN. IN-OUT: CONTRAST MEANS MAKING A DISTINCT DIFFERENCE

The sections in songs with vocals and lyrics should be well defined and contrasted in the writing process and differentiated further in the arranging process. Depending on the reference tracks, a song may start with a quiet verse and develop into a full chorus. Another song may start with a mid-level verse, followed by a stripped-down chorus. Yet another song may start with a full chorus, followed by a quiet verse, and then a mid-level chorus.

If your song's arrangement does not result in choruses with various instrumentation, make changes so each chorus contrasts the others. Since the chorus is often the most-licensed section of a song, choruses of varying intensities and instrumental textures are desirable. Having differently arranged choruses throughout the song provides several options for the music editor. Be sure to keep the transitions from section to section natural and musical-sounding.

> 1A FILM 2
>
> *Since the chorus is often the most-licensed section of a song, choruses of varying intensities and instrumental textures are desirable.*
>
> JV 3

Changes in instrumentation may happen at the beginning of a new section, but not always. There are times when instruments enter or exit in the middle of a section. This is an interesting approach because it is unexpected. When using this technique, be sure that the beginning and end of each section are still clear and defined.

FEELING STRONGER EVERY DAY: ADDING INTENSITY

In some cases, when a new section of a song or instrumental begins, there is a noticeable change in instrumentation to delineate one section from another. Certain genres have ways of ending a section that lead obviously and dramatically into the next section.

When the beginning of the next section arrives, often there is a drastic change in the intensity. This may be achieved by having a cymbal crash or a big hit on the downbeat of the section. However, at times the opposite approach is used; a new section can start with a lower level of intensity, with most instruments dropping out on the downbeat. Though transitioning into a quiet section this way may seem counterintuitive, the result can be dramatic. Surprises in music can be very compelling and powerful.

Segueing to a new section of music may involve changing the parts that the instruments are playing so that they play more notes as the beginning of the next section nears. A common use of this technique is the drum fill. During the measure or two before the next section, the snare may shift from playing on the second and fourth beats of each measure to playing eighth notes or sixteenth notes and then, perhaps adding the toms. This creates tension and a buildup to the beginning of the next section. Similarly, other instruments can play more notes or higher notes, or they can change what they have been playing to contribute to this effect.

THE BIG BUILDUP

Another way of moving forward to the next section is to use the opposite approach: Remove some of the rhythmic elements and the low frequency instruments during the measure or two prior to the next section, leaving the high frequency instruments. The result is a feeling of anticipation that seems like the music is "falling" into the next section.

Both of these approaches can be accompanied by two other techniques: The first is a *riser*, which, as the name implies, is a rise in pitch of a synthesized or acoustic sound that reaches its peak as the new section begins. The other, just as aptly named, is a reverse. Often a preset virtual instrument sound, a *reverse* simulates an acoustic instrument whose recorded audio has been digitally reversed. To achieve this, cymbals are used frequently as well as other instruments. This results in a buildup of sound that goes from quiet to loud and reaches its climax on the downbeat of the upcoming section. Another way of achieving this effect is having some or all of the instruments *crescendo* (gradually grow louder).

Because there are many different ways of transitioning from one section to another, listen carefully to how this is accomplished in reference tracks to find an approach that best fits your song or instrumental.

HEY! LISTEN TO THIS! "Expecting Bad News"

Listen to "Expecting Bad News" again. Notice how the short reverse cymbal at 20 seconds moves the cue forward to the next section. At 1:30, a riser starts and elevates the cue to the last note, with the help of the long snare drum fill that starts at the same time and another short reverse cymbal near the end.

TOO MUCH OF A GOOD THING?

If you are asking yourself if your arrangement is too full, chances are it is. Digital recording allows you to have dozens of tracks in a song or instrumental. Just because you have many tracks available does not mean you have to use them all. One of our most-licensed instrumentals consists of two ukulele tracks. Sometimes less is more licensing potential.

Professional producers may have over a hundred tracks in a song. However, if you look and listen closely you will notice that all the tracks are not playing at the same time. Some may play four notes during the entire song. Others play for one or two sections. If you decide to add more instruments to an arrangement, check to see if an instrument that is already playing can exit, especially if it is of the same musical element as the one being added.

If you suspect your arrangement is too full, try listening to it with one or more of the instruments muted. You may find that the instrument is not adding anything useful and may even be getting in the way of one of the more important instruments. For instruments that do not play well with others in your mix, try having them play in the song for only a section or two or not having them in the mix at all.

DRESS IN LAYERS

In many professional productions with a lot of tracks, some parts are doubled or tripled. *Layering* is a useful tool. Combining two or more instruments that play the same notes can create unique and interesting textures. Many times we layer an instrument such as a glockenspiel with a piano because the glockenspiel alone does not have enough presence. Layering it with a piano thickens it up and makes the pitch easier to recognize. These two instruments complement each other. Sometimes we layer low piano notes over bass parts to define the pitches being played.

Be sure to find a good octave placement for the instruments you are layering. If the octaves of the two instruments are too far apart, they may not blend well. If the instruments are in the same octave, they might cancel each other, or one of them may not be audible. Select one as the primary instrument, and find an octave that sounds good with the other instruments in the mix. Combine the secondary instrument playing the same part, and move it to different octaves to see which one works best.

I CAN HEAR CLEARLY NOW

Be mindful of having instruments stay out of each other's way. Instruments also need to stay out of the way of two other critical components: The first important element in an arrangement that should not be obstructed is the melody. One way to achieve this is to avoid having any other instruments playing busy parts while the melody is playing. Simplify accompanying instruments' parts, and play something uncluttered and predictable under the melody. Some instruments can drop out altogether. This deserves serious consideration if an instrument is in the same frequency range as the vocalist. (Remember that male and female vocalists are usually in different frequency ranges and an instrument can be in the way of one but not the other.)

There are too many examples of instruments that do not fit well together to list here, especially since the parts they are playing should also be taken into consideration. Again, a very important tool to help determine if there is a conflict is the mute button. If you think an instrument in your arrangement is in the way of the melody, mute the suspect instrument. If the melody suddenly stands out more, you have solved your dilemma.

At times the problem is not the instrument itself but the part it is playing. Change the octave in which the instrument is playing, or simplify its rhythm. When an instrument plays a consistent and predictable part, the listener tends to ignore it and instead focus on the instrument playing a more interesting part. Occasionally some of these problems can be addressed during the mixing phase, but they are best addressed during the arranging phase.

KEEP IT DOWN! WE'RE TALKING!

The second component to steer clear of is harder to deal with because it is not in your recording. Music intended for licensing must stay out of the way of the dialog of the scenes where they are to be placed. This is difficult if not impossible with a vocal song, because dialog will likely be in the same frequency range of the singer.

However, this issue can be managed with an instrumental. Limit the number of midrange instruments. Do not eliminate them altogether, but do not have too many of them either. Conversely, be sure to have instruments from higher and lower frequencies to represent a broader spectrum. Simplify the parts they play.

A FINAL WORD ON PRODUCING AND ARRANGING

Much has been written about composing and songwriting. Likewise, there is a great deal of information available about mixing and mastering music; however, producing and arranging music are not discussed as frequently.

Do not take this to mean that they are not important topics to study, especially in music intended for licensing. If the early creative steps of composing or songwriting and the final polishing steps of mixing and mastering are all executed well but the producing and arranging are lacking in imagination and quality, there is less chance that the music will be synced.

Interesting and thought-out production and arranging make up the secret sauce to many cues and songs, especially those that get licensed repeatedly. Taking the time to listen, analyze, and understand these essential parts of the process will help put the odds in your favor.

PRO TIPS . . . About Producing and Arranging

If the arrangement is wrong, the music doesn't get placed.

—**Ken Jacobsen**, Composer and Producer

The most important thing is to find a producer who respects you and your music. Before working together, the artist and the producer should have open and honest discussions about what each party can bring to the work. Some producers will engineer and play on the sessions and help you rewrite your songs. Other producers will barely be in the studio when the work is being done. The producer should have a clear understanding of the artist's goals, resources, and expectations for the work. The producer's job is a combination of creative director and project manager, and the more information the producer has, the more they can help the artist.

—**Ronan Chris Murphy**, Producer and Engineer, Veneto West

To keep my arrangements interesting, I analyze a lot of music of my colleagues and my favorite soundtracks. I improve my arrangement and orchestration chops by learning from the masters. On the other hand, I always strive for innovation and use new sample libraries to keep my arrangements current.

—**Penka Kouneva**, Composer for film, TV, and video games

The most common mistake I see from inexperienced music producers is that they put *way too much* into a production—too many tracks, too many competing parts, too many effects, and too many flashy plug-ins (that aren't used correctly)—when what they really should be doing is hitting the mute button often, turning things down, taking things out, and keeping everything clean and simple.

—**Fett**, Producer, Engineer, Author, Teacher, and Coach

Regarding producing and arranging, listen to your competition. You need to be better than them. Put in the work to become better at whatever you need to become better at. That's the harsh reality. Put in the work.

—**Steve Barden**, Composer and Author

Stripping down an arrangement is often more successful than overloading it with instrumentation, especially if that instrumentation doesn't sound on point. When producing and arranging, less is often more.

—**Matt Hirt**, Composer, Songwriter, and Producer, and Co-owner of Catapult Music

CHAPTER 7

Setting Up a Home Studio and Working with Digital Audio

WORTH IT: WHEN TO DIY AND WHEN TO PAY A PRO

Remember, the recording that you submit for any sync usage has to be *absolutely professional quality*. It's a plus if you can afford to pay mixing and, especially, mastering engineers. Many people who are successful in the sync business are prolific and put out a high volume of music to increase their odds of success and income.

Paying for professional mixing and mastering services can become costly. There is great financial advantage to being able to perform these tasks yourself, but not at the expense of quality. This is one of many important decisions you must make while establishing yourself in the sync music business. If you have not already perfected the skills of mixing and mastering but you'd like to learn them, immerse yourself in educational classes until you can achieve competitive results. Assuming that you have a home studio, read and study this information carefully, and seek further knowledge from reputable sources.

YOU MEAN AFTER ALL THIS, MY MUSIC ISN'T FINISHED YET?

No, your music isn't finished yet, but it's close. Even music that is written, performed, arranged, and recorded very well needs to be mixed. Audio *mixing* is combining and blending multiple recorded tracks together to create a unified, cohesive, balanced, and focused final recorded product that sounds good when played back on any sound system.

IF YOU CAN'T HEAR IT WELL, YOU CAN'T MIX IT WELL

The first priority of mixing is being able to hear your music well in your mixing environment.

Most of the popular music recorded and mixed in the last several decades was done by experts with professional equipment in first-class studios. Your job is to duplicate their results, armed with knowledge and modern recording tools in your home studio. If you have access to a high-quality studio where you can do your mixing or can create one in your home, then that is your best option.

It is difficult to create the ideal mixing environment in a room in your home. Most professional studios are not only larger than a bedroom, but they also have different dimensions and proportions and were designed for the specific purpose of recording and mixing. The ideal mixing room has walls and a ceiling of different dimensions, with none of them parallel. (A perfect square is highly undesirable.) In addition, none of the dimensions should be a multiple of another. If one wall is twelve feet long and another is twenty-four feet long, that can be an acoustic obstacle.

IN MY ROOM

Obviously it can be tricky to find the perfect room for mixing. In most homes, acoustically perfect rooms are non-existent, because they do not meet the above criteria. However, there are two ways of mitigating your room's shortcomings.

The first way to minimize the flaws of your mixing room is by positioning your desk and speakers in an advantageous manner. Accept that most of the walls in your room are going to be parallel. If you are fortunate enough to have a rectangular room, center the desk along one of the shorter walls so the longer walls are at your sides. Do not place the desk against the wall. Ideally the desk should be positioned so that, while seated, your head is 38% of the distance from the wall you are facing. If the side wall is ten feet long, the desk position should allow you to sit 3.8 feet, or 45.6 inches, from the front wall. If you cannot place the desk to allow this precise position, it isn't a big problem; this is just an optimal target. Get as close as you can. However, be sure to avoid sitting in the center of the room. In a room with a side wall ten feet in length, if your head is five feet from the front wall, you will have difficulty hearing the bass frequencies accurately.

SOUND ADVICE ABOUT SPEAKERS

Speakers should not be placed near or against the wall in front of you, because this will distort your perception of low frequencies. In addition, the position of the speakers relative to your ears is important. Your ears should be the same distance from each speaker as the speakers are from each other. The two speakers and your head should form an equilateral triangle. For example, when seated in the listening position, if the speakers are 52 inches apart, you should be 52 inches from each speaker. The small speakers in each speaker cabinet should be the same height as your ears. Because the vibration from the speakers can be transferred to the desk, it is advisable to have isolation pads below them to absorb the sound.

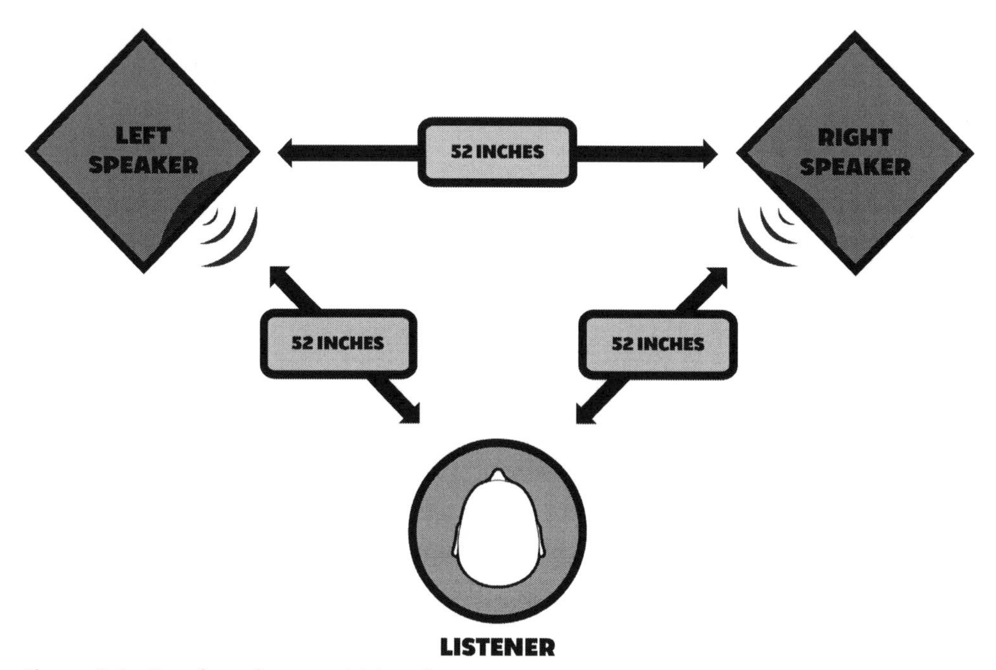

Figure 7.1. *Speaker-placement triangle.*

The other way to decrease the effects of your room's imperfections is by using acoustic treatment. As mentioned earlier, *acoustic treatment* does not soundproof a room; rather, it minimizes sound reflections and reduces the effect that the sound bouncing off the walls, ceiling, floor, and other hard surfaces can have on your perception of the frequencies in your music. Just because you do not hear any low frequencies in your song does not mean they are not there. Bad acoustics in a room mask what you hear playing back through your speakers. You may hear more, less, or none of certain frequencies than actually make it onto your recording. If you do not hear certain frequencies and boost them until you do, a listener in another acoustic environment may hear too much of these frequencies in your song. You may have a similar result if you hear too much of certain frequencies and you turn them down. Your goal is to hear frequencies as accurately as you can so you can adjust them appropriately.

It can be complicated when treating a room acoustically. Most acoustic treatment companies offer comprehensive information on their websites, so you can start there.

HEY! READ THIS!
Software developers create room correction software. They measure and calculate the acoustics of your room and compensate for any weaknesses. It is still recommended that you situate your room as well as you can before using these products. They are not intended as a substitute but as a supplement to setting up your mix room strategically.

SPEAKING OF SPEAKERS . . .

Mixing audio is such a specialized endeavor that there are speakers made specifically for this purpose. Sometimes referred to as *studio monitors*, *reference monitors*, or *monitor speakers*, the ideal pair provides a flat, uncolored, transparent, detailed, and accurate representation of how a recording sounds. They provide minimal distortion and do not emphasize any frequencies at any volume. Note that monitor speakers are different from consumer home stereo speakers, which are known to sweeten the audio and make it hard to hear the original, unaltered signal.

In home studios, producers use *nearfield monitors*, as they listen in close proximity to their speakers. These are intended to be placed three to five feet from the listener to reduce the effect of the room's acoustics. There are also *midfield monitors* that are larger, more expensive, and not commonly used in home studios.

Some monitor speaker cabinets are sealed or closed. Others have an opening or port on the front or the back to enhance reproduction of lower frequencies. Rear ported monitors placed against a wall will distort your perception of low frequencies even more. If there is no way to avoid having your speakers against a wall, use a pair that is closed or front ported.

Regarding how they are powered, there are two types of monitor speakers: *Passive speakers* are unpowered and require a signal from an external amplifier. *Active speakers* contain built-in amplifiers and are more common in home studios, as they are more affordable and take less space than passive speakers and the amps that they require. Active speakers also have the advantage of having amps that match the speakers, which provides optimal sound.

Figure 7.2. *Studio-monitor speaker.* (Source: *PreSonus)*

WOOFERS AND TWEETERS ARE SERIOUS BUSINESS

A monitor speaker is a speaker cabinet or enclosure that contains more than one speaker. Often there are two speakers, or *drivers*, inside the enclosure. A small speaker, or *tweeter*, carries the high frequencies, and a larger speaker, or *woofer*, handles the midrange and low frequencies. If it is an active speaker, it is likely *bi-amped*, meaning there is one amp for the tweeter and another amp for the woofer. The power of monitor speakers is measured in watts. They are available in a wide range, but anywhere between 50 and 150 watts is suitable for home studios. This number is a measure of total power for the monitor. A bi-amped speaker may have a 40-watt amp for the tweeter and a 60-watt amp for the woofer, which provides a total of 100 watts of power.

The size of the monitor refers to the size of the woofer. Generally these range from five to eight inches. The larger the woofer, the better it will reproduce low frequencies.

Subwoofers, which handle very low frequencies, are available but are not used commonly in home studios, because low frequencies may already be a problem. You might consider having a subwoofer *if* you have an ideal mixing setup—or close to it. They can be useful when mixing low-end genres like EDM and hip hop. Because low frequencies are not very directional, you may need only one subwoofer.

GIMME ME A BREAK

If you write, perform, arrange, produce, and record your own music, your ears may lose objectivity when it is time to mix. When the schedule allows, consider completing the aforementioned tasks and setting an official start to the mixing process. This can be accomplished by waiting to start mixing until after a break of a few hours or until a new day. Then you will have fresh ears and won't be distracted by other facets of the music, and you can better trust what you hear.

A key part of mixing involves comparing one sound to another and assessing whether any processing you are doing makes the audio sound better, worse, or no different. During these comparisons, a common mistake is to believe that the louder option sounds better. Loudness may be appealing to your ears; however, the best way to compare two sounds is at the same volume. For this reason, it is a good idea to mix at moderate volumes. This gives you a clearer perception of what you are hearing and helps minimize ear fatigue, which happens after mixing at high volume for too long.

Even while listening to the highest-quality monitor speakers in the most acoustically desirable room, also listen to the mix on different speakers in a different room or setting. Checking your mix by moving to a different part of the room can reveal details not audible in the listening position.

HEAR IN MY CAR

For many, the mix is not finished until they hear it in the car. The sound systems and acoustic environments in cars reveal frequencies and sound characteristics that you won't hear in the studio. As a reminder, an important aspect of a great mix is that it sound good on *any* sound system. (You don't even have to drive anywhere.)

Listening in the car has another major advantage: since you may listen to a lot of music there, you know how a good mix is supposed to sound. You can use this back in the studio by taking songs you know well and using them as reference tracks to compare with your mixes. This process works best if the reference track is the same genre as the track you are mixing. If your mix of an EDM song that you wrote, recorded, and mixed does not have the low-end thump of a professionally mixed EDM song, you have some work left to do.

UP CLOSE AND PERSONAL

Another way to evaluate your mix is by using headphones. One of the advantages of headphones is that they take the acoustics of the room out of the equation. However, this is not the same as listening to studio monitors, because sound from the right speaker is heard by the left ear and vice versa. With headphones, each ear hears only the audio from its respective ear cup, which can impact the listener's perspective of the stereo field. Frequencies are also perceived differently with headphones; high and low frequencies sound different than on monitor speakers. The use of headphones in mixing is not intended as a substitute for studio monitors but as a supplement.

Like consumer speakers, consumer headphones are neither flat nor accurate enough for pro audio mixing. There are different kinds of pro audio headphones available: *Circumaural* headphones are used most commonly in home studios. These have ear cups that cover the ears, as opposed to *supra-aural* headphones with ear cups that rest on the ears, without completely enclosing them. Supra-aural headphones are popular with consumers because of their portability, but they are not well suited for mixing, because they do not isolate your ears completely from the environment.

There are different kinds of circumaural headphones used in pro audio: *Closed-back* headphones have ear cups that seal around the ears so no sound leaks in or out. These are often used when recording vocals and acoustic instruments. Due to the maximum sound isolation they offer, no audio bleeds from the backing track in the headphones into the microphone.

Figure 7.3. *Studio headphones.* (Source: *PreSonus)*

Closed-back headphones are not recommended for mixing, because sound reflection in the ear cups impairs your perception of low frequencies. *Open-back* headphones are better suited to mixing, as they allow airflow through the ear cups to release sound pressure. This results in a more natural sound and more accurate frequency balance.

It would be ideal to have both of these kinds of headphones available for their intended purposes in your studio. If you can only buy one pair because of budget, semi-open-back headphones are worth considering. Though they involve a compromise, they can serve the purposes of both recording and mixing adequately.

RIGHT BACK WHERE WE STARTED FROM

In chapter 5 you followed the audio signal from the microphone to the computer. The signal path from the computer to the speakers follows a similar path, but in reverse. When a sophisticated setup is involved, the audio signal:

1. Leaves the computer.
2. Enters the audio interface.
3. Goes to the D/A converter (now performing a digital-to-analog conversion).
4. And then goes on to a *studio monitor controller*, which routes the audio signal to one or more pairs of speakers, as well as to headphones. It allows the volume of each of these destinations to be adjusted individually. It can be helpful when switching to different pairs of speakers when evaluating a mix.

In a simpler setup, the audio signal leaves the computer and enters the audio interface, which may control the routing and signal level without the need of a studio monitor controller. If the monitor speakers are active, the audio signal leaves the studio monitor controller or audio interface and goes directly to the speakers. If the speakers are passive, the signal must first go to an amplifier before going to the speakers.

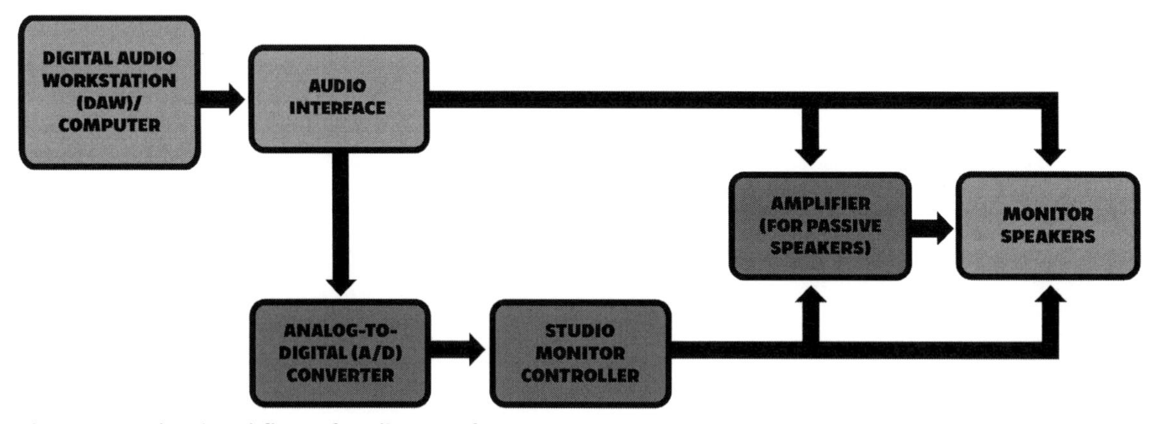

Figure 7.4. *The signal flow of audio out of a DAW.*

FADERS! SLIDERS! BUTTONS! AND KNOBS!

Now that your music has been routed from the computer to the speakers, which have been properly placed in your acoustically optimized studio, allowing you to hear clearly how your music sounds, you can move on to mixing.

Controlling track volume levels is a basic step in the mixing process and the best place to start. The visual representation in your DAW, the terms used, and the whole process of adjusting the volume of each track is based on the way mixing was done originally with analog hardware.

The central tool used in the physical world is the *mixing console*. The virtual version of this resembles the hardware, though the specifics vary from one DAW to another. The diagrams and references that follow will reflect how Pro Tools is laid out, as it is a commonly used DAW. The following descriptions of the controls may vary a little in your DAW but should be similar enough for the purposes of understanding how they are organized and how they function.

The mix window in each DAW contains several *channel strips*, or *tracks*, each of which offers control of the audio signal passing through it. There are five different kinds of tracks, most of which can be mono or stereo:

1. An *audio track* contains audio recorded from a microphone or DI instrument source and played back.
2. An *instrument track* is used to host a virtual instrument plug-in. MIDI information is recorded into an instrument track and audio is played out of it.

3. A *MIDI track* is recorded MIDI information used to trigger samples from a virtual instrument or hardware synthesizer. Most DAWs do not use MIDI tracks anymore and instead use instrument tracks. A MIDI track is neither mono nor stereo.
4. An *aux* or *bus track* contains no audio of its own, but audio from other sources is routed through it for processing.
5. A *master bus* or *master fader* is the final destination for audio within the DAW before it is sent out to the audio interface and speakers.

LOVELY RITA . . . METER READER

Each track has a *meter* to indicate the strength of the audio signal passing through it. The numbers on each meter indicate the level of audio, which is measured in *decibels* (*dB*).

Looking at the meters is the easiest way to see if a track is mono or stereo. Mono tracks have a single meter, while stereo tracks have two meters, side by side. Most meters show lower levels as green and higher levels as yellow. Preferably the level on most tracks should be around the range where the color changes from green to yellow. If the meter is barely moving, the signal is too weak. If it goes to the top and stays there, the signal is too strong and in danger of distorting.

It is helpful to put the name of each track at the bottom of each channel strip. Though sometimes controlled with a rotating knob, volume is most often controlled with a volume *fader* or *slider*. When pushed up, the slider increases the volume level; when pulled down, the volume is reduced.

In the vicinity of the volume fader are three buttons, usually labeled with an R, an S, and an M.

- The R button is the *record enable* button and is usually red. When activated, new audio or MIDI is recorded to the corresponding track during the recording process.
- The S stands for *solo* and is used to hear the selected channel alone or with any other tracks whose solo buttons have been activated.
- The M button is used to *mute* the channel to hear the mix without the selected track. Several channels can be muted at one time.

Figure 7.5. *Pro Tools mix channels.* (Source: *Avid*)

Each track has a has a knob or slider that allows you to *pan* audio. The panning control directs the audio to the left speaker, right speaker, or somewhere in between. If the same level of audio is sent to both speakers, it is perceived as being in the center.

BUS STOP

Routing of the audio signal is a very important part of the recording and mixing process. The *input* of each track determines the source of audio to be recorded to or routed through the selected track. This is usually a signal from an audio interface, which receives a signal from a converter, preamp, instrument, or microphone. Likewise, the output routes the audio to its next destination, which is likely the master bus.

The audio from a channel is not limited to being routed to the master bus. Audio can be sent to an aux bus instead, which receives audio from several tracks to be processed together. For example, drum kits ordinarily contain audio from more than one microphone, and, after being processed individually, the combined audio can be routed to an aux track to be managed in one place. This makes it easier to control the overall volume of the drums with one fader or knob on the aux bus.

INSERT PLUG-INS HERE

One or more plug-ins can be placed on the *inserts* of every kind of track except a MIDI track. Some plug-in makers have created rack-style plug-ins that can host several of their plug-ins on one insert. Others produce individual channel strip plug-ins that provide the functions of several different plug-ins. A virtual instrument plug-in can be placed on the insert of an instrument track. Effects plug-ins can be placed on any track except a MIDI track. The order in which the plug-ins are inserted determines the order in which the audio will be processed. Changing their order may yield different results. After going through the plug-ins, the audio passes through to the output of the channel. (*Sends*, shown in the figure below, are discussed in chapter 8.)

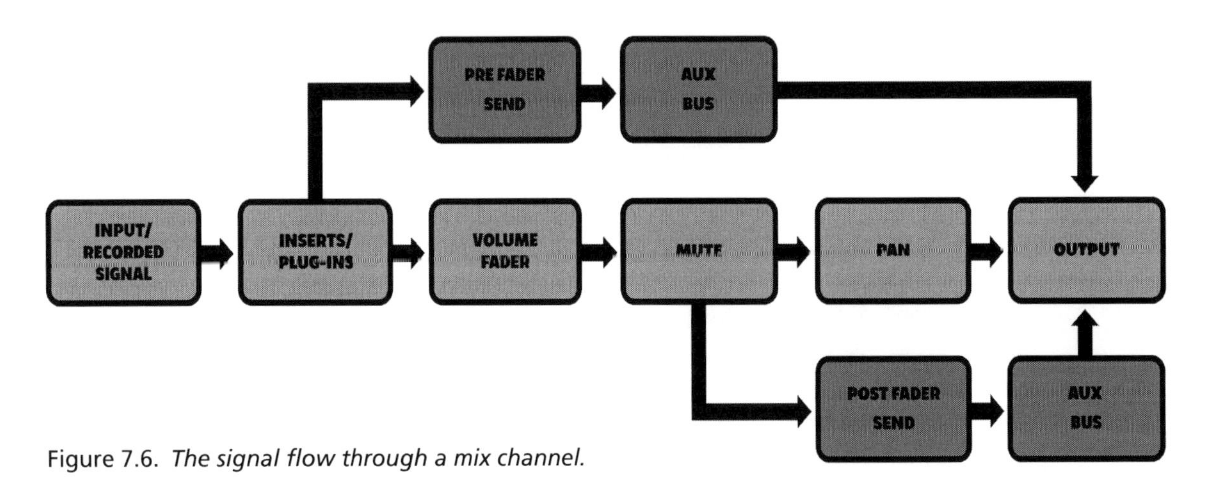

Figure 7.6. *The signal flow through a mix channel.*

AUTOMATED FOR THE PEOPLE

Many plug-in parameters remain the same from the beginning of a song to its end. However, some parameters change throughout the course of a song. These parameters can be *automated* digitally within your DAW.

Automation can turn mutes or plug-ins on or off. It can also control changes in volume and panning. Plug-ins also have parameters that can be varied throughout a song with automation to keep it interesting. This is a very powerful tool.

PRO TIPS . . . About Setting up a Home Studio

Just keep your project clean. No need to process tracks in advance; that's my job, and anything you do to it might be hard for me to undo if needed. Do learn how to edit cleanly, and don't send confusing outtakes or alternates (unless you want help editing or tuning, which I can do). Keep your track titles short and sweet (I can accommodate any DAW, and this will help). And, on your singing mic, please use a pop filter.

—**Les Brockmann**, Recording Engineer, Mixer, and Score Mixer

If *air* can leak under a door or through a vent, then *sound* can too. Soundproofing a room not originally designed to be soundproof can be difficult and expensive. A "flutter echo" that arises when sound bounces between parallel walls without acoustic treatment can be fixed by treating one of the walls acoustically.

—**Dr. Jonathan Rathsam**, Acoustician

You can get phenomenal recordings at home with the proper use of acoustic treatments. Even the room tuning software for your speakers only really works well if you've already done acoustic treatment. It can't remove flutter echoes and the acoustic smearing that occurs from untreated walls. Acoustic treatments are the most important part! There is no plug-in or piece of gear that can undo bad acoustics.

—**Derek Jones,** Director of Creative Services at Megatrax Production Music

My advice for getting *any* music production up to a broadcast quality level is to do *less*!

—**Fett**, Producer, Engineer, Author, Teacher, and Coach

Obtain the best equipment and software you can, and continually hone your skills. Compare your recordings with others in the marketplace, and be sure that they are competitive. If you need some audio engineering guidance, ask a knowledgeable friend for help, or hire an experienced professional.

—**Brian Thomas Curtin**, Composer and Songwriter, Eaglestone Music

CHAPTER 8

Mixing Basics and Techniques

MIX IT UP

Keep in mind that mixing is combining and blending multiple recorded tracks together to create a unified, cohesive, balanced, and focused final recorded product that sounds good when played back on *any* sound system. Making sure your recording has *focus* means ensuring there is an element that remains clear and unobstructed. In most cases, this is the vocal or instrumental melody or motif. If you have arranged your song well, keeping the focus on the melody or motif requires some effort but should not be difficult.

The concept of *balance* is critical. The instruments in an audio recording should be balanced in three different ways:

1. Left and right (horizontal)
2. Up and down (vertical)
3. Front and back (depth)

Horizontal balance is achieved by panning instruments to the left or right. Vertical balance is addressed by adjusting frequencies with *equalization* or *EQ*. Balanced depth is attained by controlling the *ambience* with reverb or delay.

A good way to visualize this concept is to picture musicians performing on a stage:

- *Horizontal.* If all of them were on the left side of the stage and none on the right, it would look and sound odd and unbalanced.
- *Vertical.* If there were a high ceiling with the stage all on one level with no raised platforms and no video screens, the top would look like a waste of space.
- *Depth.* If all the musicians were at the back of the stage, if would be difficult to hear the melody clearly and identify the distinct characteristics of each instrument.

When mixing music, your job is to fill the stage in a balanced way by placing each instrument in an appropriate place in this three-dimensional space.

RATTLE THOSE POTS: PANNING

Horizontal balance is the easiest of the three dimensions to understand: some instruments are panned to the left, others are panned to the right, and some are in the center. But which instruments should go where, and how much should they be panned? The short answer: Wherever and however you want, as long as the sound level on the left side equals the sound level on the right and at least one instrument, preferably the main melody instrument, is in the center. The better answer has to do with how you are accustomed to hearing instruments and sounds panned on recordings that you have heard for years, as well as on reference tracks.

For the last several decades in recorded and professionally mixed music, you have gotten used to hearing the melody (often sung by a vocalist), snare, kick, and bass in the center. Having the melody in the middle makes sense because it is the focal point of the mix. The human ear does not always perceive the lower frequencies of the kick and bass as coming from any direction, so they are usually in the center. The snare is also in the center, because that is where the kick is, and they are expected to be parts of the same drum kit.

These are the accepted standards, though you are free to experiment. The frequently discussed reference tracks continue to be of utmost importance during the mixing process. If your reference track is a '60s rock song and features the drums panned to one side, that is what must be done to achieve the same effect in your mix. Let your ears be your guide.

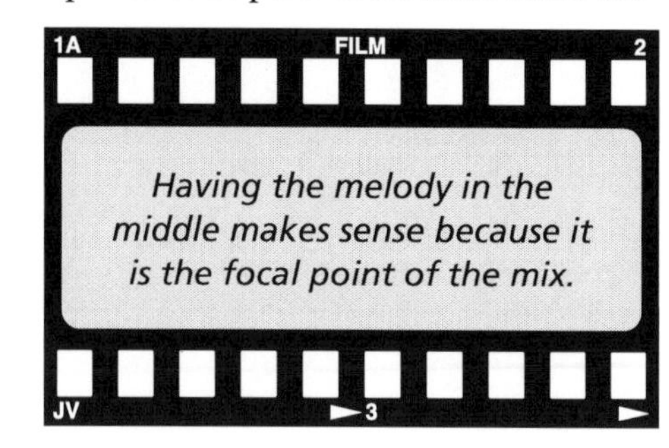

There is no standardization for the panning of the other instruments in the mix. Because the goal is balance, a common strategy involves finding pairs of instruments that are in the same frequency range that play similar roles and panning one to the left and the other to the right. These pairs might include a shaker and a tambourine, a ukulele and a mandolin, a trumpet and a saxophone, a violin and a viola, or a harp and a piano.

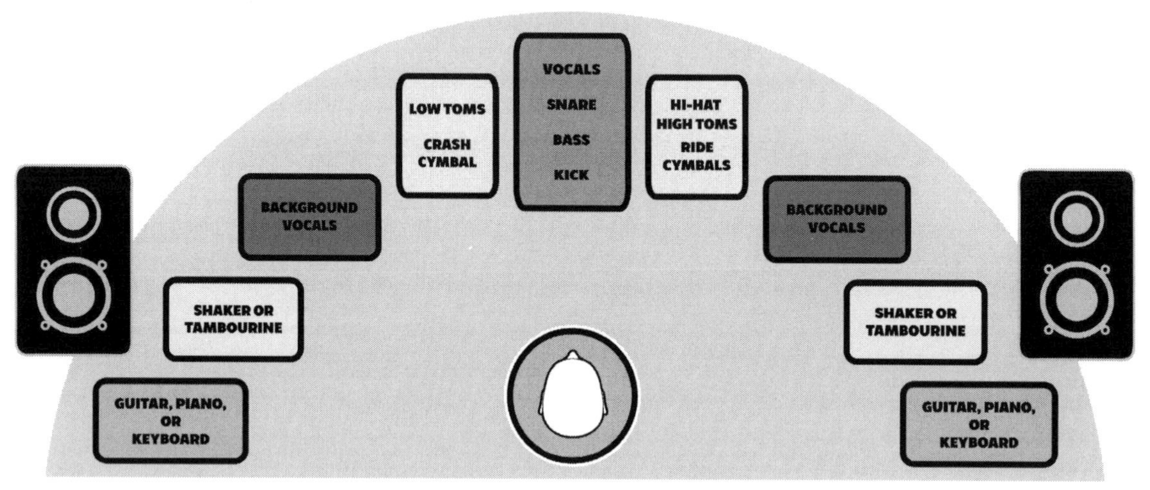

Figure 8.1. *A stereo panning example.*

Another pair of instruments to pan to opposite sides is two of the same instruments playing the same part. This is done often with acoustic guitars or electric guitars, frequently playing rhythm parts. Mixers like this technique because it makes the guitars sound big and leaves room in the center for other instruments. The effect works better if the two instruments and the performances are slightly different from each other. In the case of acoustic guitars, this difference can be achieved by using two different guitars, two different microphones, two different players, or any combination of these three. If everything is exactly the same, the listener will not be able to distinguish between the two guitars.

Recording a single instrument in stereo can be challenging; however, the resulting track can have a full sound that works well with a sparsely arranged song. In broader mixes with more instruments, the effect of a single piano or acoustic guitar in stereo has less impact. Though the two tracks can be panned left and right, they can also be panned to the same place and used to blend and sculpt the sound of the instrument by changing the level of each one. There is a lot of flexibility here, so try different options.

BANG THE DRUM ALL DAY

Drums are most commonly recorded in stereo. Though the kick and snare are often panned to the center, the other pieces of the drum kit are normally panned to the sides. There are two perspectives: that of the drummer and that of the audience. Assuming that the drummer is right-handed, in the audience's perspective the hi-hat is on the right, the toms from high to low go from right to left, the ride cymbal is on the left, and the crash cymbals are spread between the two sides. There are variations to this setup, but this one is typical. The drummer's perspective, of course, is the exact opposite.

MORE WAYS TO HANDLE PANNING

Like writing, performing, arranging, and recording music, there are varied philosophies of mixing that professional mixers adhere to. One such philosophy is *LCR panning*—or *left, center, right panning*. In this concept, there are three options for panning each instrument: all the way to the left, in the center, or all the way to the right. This is an interesting technique to experiment with. It certainly cuts down on the number of decisions that need to be made. A variation of this concept is to add two more panning options: half left and half right. This offers more flexibility.

There are many degrees of panning available, allowing you to place instruments exactly where you want them from left to right across the spectrum. Going back to the analogy of a group of musicians on a stage, imagine three background singers standing next to each other on the right side of the stage. If your panning controls go from zero being in the center to 100 being hard right, one of the singers could be panned to 50, another to 60, and the third one to 70. They would all be panned to the right, but not in the exact same space. Thinking ahead, there would be instruments ideally on the left side of the mix in a similar approximate position to balance your singers on the right side of the mix. These are very subtle and barely audible nuances. However, mixing is all about many small decisions that when taken together dramatically impact and improve the sound of the original, unmixed recording.

THE HIGHS, THE LOWS, AND THE IN-BETWEENS: EQUALIZATION

The second way your mixes should be balanced can be envisioned vertically: sound should be distributed as evenly as possible among low, mid, and high frequencies. *Equalization* (*EQ*) is the tool used for this purpose. EQ is the process of increasing or decreasing the level of different frequencies within a sound. Striking a balance can be achieved rather simply by not having a group of frequencies in the same range in your mix. The challenging part is realizing that instruments contain frequencies you may not associate with them.

For instance, a kick drum and an electric bass guitar are understood correctly to contain a lot of low frequency sounds. However, both of these instruments also contain high frequencies that give them definition and character. Similarly, the sound of an acoustic guitar has a bright quality with high frequencies. However, in sparse arrangements without other low frequency instruments, accenting the low end of the guitar can result in a fuller-sounding mix. This is the reason you should not use the same equalizer settings on an acoustic guitar in every mix. How to EQ a guitar or any other instrument depends on what role it is playing—and what other instruments are present within the mix.

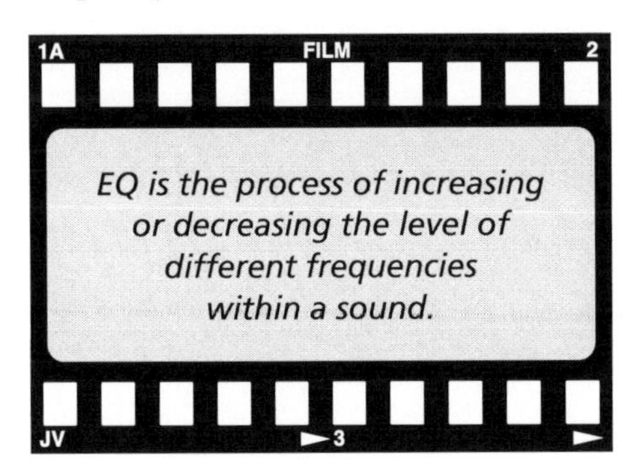

Frequency, or the speed of sound vibration, determines the pitch of the sound and is measured in cycles per second. Slow vibrations create sounds that are low in pitch, and faster vibrations create sounds that are high in pitch. The frequency of 50 cycles per second, or CPS, is more commonly referred to as 50 *hertz*, or 50 *Hz*; 1000 Hz is also known as 1 *kilohertz*, or 1 *kHz*.

The accepted range of human hearing is from 20 Hz to 20 kHz. There are many differing viewpoints among professional mixers on how to subdivide this range, but here is one way to think of it:

- *Low range*. 20 Hz–200 Hz
- *Low midrange*. 200 Hz–600 Hz

- *Midrange.* 600 Hz–2 kHz
- *High midrange.* 2 kHz–6 kHz
- *High range.* 6 kHz–20 kHz

Here is another way to think of frequency ranges in more descriptive terms:

- *Boominess.* 20 Hz–100 Hz
- *Muddiness.* 100 Hz–300 Hz
- *Boxiness.* 300 Hz–500 Hz
- *Nasal and honkiness.* 800 Hz–2 kHz
- *Presence, brilliance, and clarity.* 3 kHz–6 kHz
- *Sibilance (harsh consonants).* 6 kHz–8 kHz
- *Air, breath, and sparkle.* 10 kHz–20 kHz

These terms can be positive or negative, depending on the instrument being referenced. For example, "honkiness" may be a frequency range to be increased in a saxophone but reduced in a female vocal.

If the sound of each instrument contained its own frequency range and none of the ranges overlapped, the EQing part of the mixing process would be easy. In reality, the frequency ranges of most instruments overlap. In order to get them to play nicely together, certain frequencies from some of the instruments need to be increased, or *boosted*, while other frequencies need to be decreased, or *cut*. The challenge lies in figuring out which frequencies to boost or cut—and to what degree.

THIS IS A MUTE POINT

Your solo and mute buttons should get a real workout during the mixing process. A track played by itself can sound amazing alone and yet not be a good fit with the other tracks in the mix. How the full mix sounds is much more important than how a single track sounds by itself. In order to make the full mix work, an individual instrument that may sound odd on its own can make a vital contribution to the combined sound of all the instruments together.

There are different strategies and techniques to consider when beginning to mix a song: Some mixers start with the vocals, while others start with the drums. There is no right or wrong approach, so experiment to find which method works best for you. Remember the two main concepts from the mixing definition—focus and balance. Be sure the instrument or group of instruments playing the melody or other focal part can be heard clearly. At certain frequencies, some key instruments may need to be given priority. Also, be vigilant that frequencies do not get crowded into a particular range. The mute button provides you with a lot of insight and can reveal where these buildups may be happening. Muting an unnecessary track can open up an otherwise cluttered mix.

IF I HAD A HAMMER: USING THE TOOLS OF THE TRADE

In order to better understand how to manage frequencies, your main tool is the equalizer. It is recommended to start out using EQ plug-ins that contain a graphic display allowing you to see how the frequencies of audio are being manipulated.

A commonly used EQ is the bell EQ, which boosts or cuts around a central frequency. When viewed on a graphic display, the result creates a *bell curve*, so named because it resembles a bell. The diagram below shows a boost of 8 dB at 1000 Hz, or 1 kHz. The amount of boost is indicated by the numbers on the left side and is controlled by the *gain* knob, shown on the right. A *boost* is indicated by a dot and curve above the zero line, whereas a *cut* would be shown as a dot and curve below the zero line and a negative gain value. (Cutting frequencies is also known as *attenuation.*) The frequency at which the boost is taking place is indicated by the numbers at the bottom and is selected by the frequency ("freq") knob.

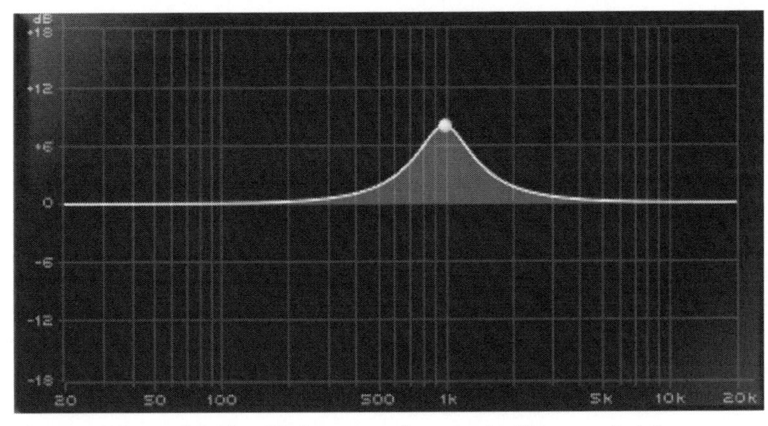

Figures 8.2a and 8.2b. *EQ boost and controls.* (Source: *Avid)*

The third knob on the top controls the *quality factor*, often referred to as the Q. This affects the shape of the EQ curve and its *bandwidth*, or range of frequencies. Low Q values, such as 1, result in a wider curve, shown below left. High Q values, such as 5, result in a narrower curve, shown below right.

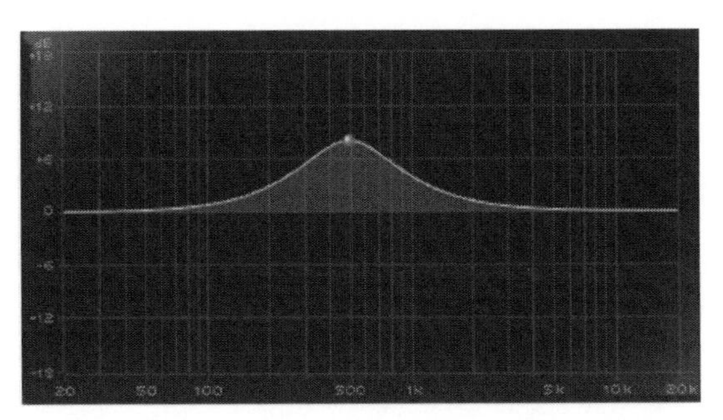

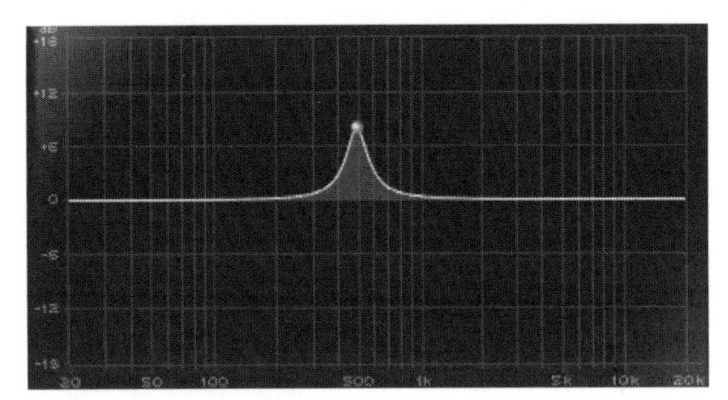

Figures 8.3a and 8.3b. *EQ boost with low Q and high Q.* (Source: *Avid)*

There are times when all of the frequencies below or above a specified frequency need to be adjusted. A *shelving EQ* can be used for this purpose. In the figure below left, all the frequencies at or below 100 Hz are cut by 6 dB with a low shelf. In the figure below right, all the frequencies at or above 6 kHz are boosted 6 dB with a high shelf.

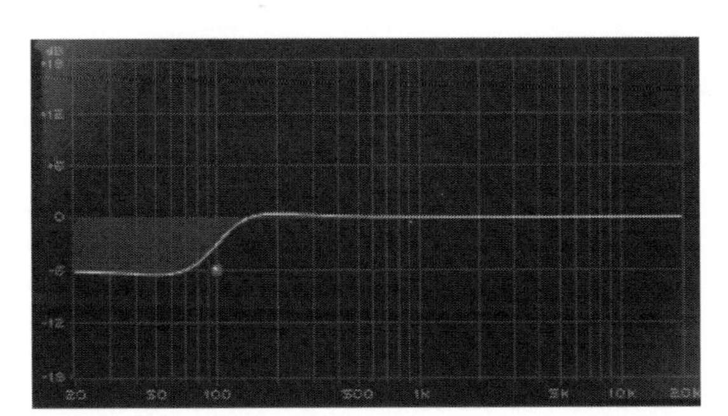

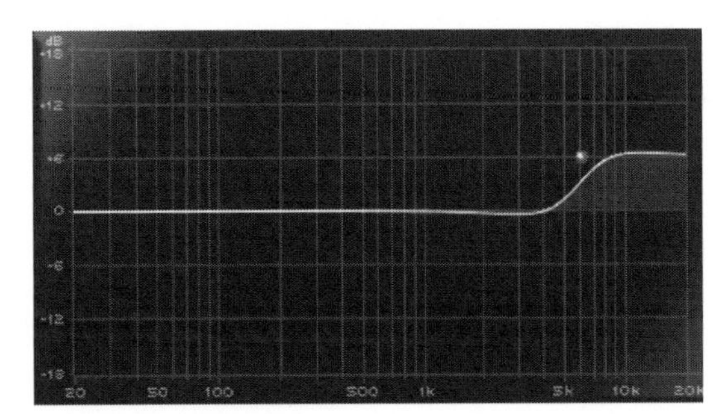

Figures 8.4a and 8.4b. *Low cut shelf and high boost shelf.* (Source: *Avid)*

Like a bell EQ, a shelving EQ can boost or cut. It also has a Q value that determines the shape of the curve.

There are times when high or low frequencies don't just need to be reduced but eliminated altogether. A *filtering EQ* serves this function. A *low cut filter* removes low frequencies. It is also called a *high pass filter*

(*HPF*), as high frequencies are allowed to pass through. Instead of a Q setting, it has a *slope*, measured in decibels per octave. The higher the number, the steeper the slope. The figure below left shows a low cut at 100 Hz with a slope of 6 dB per octave, while the one on the right shows 24 dB per octave at the same frequency.

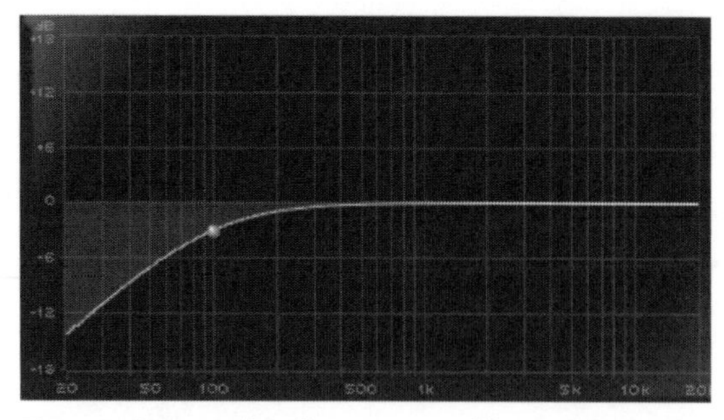

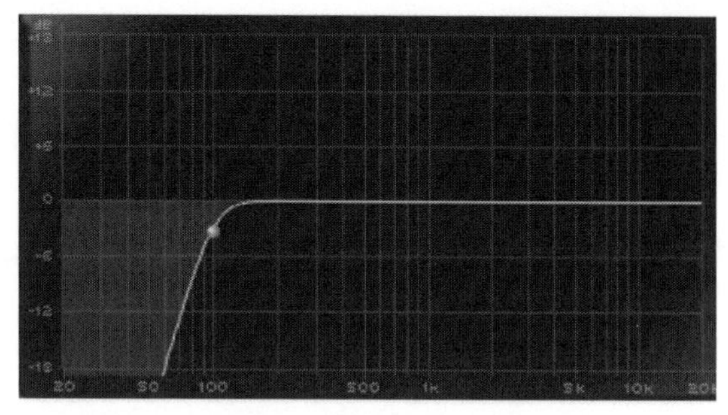

Figures 8.5a and 8.5b. *Low cut filter with moderate slope and low cut filter with steep slope.* (Source: *Avid)*

Similarly, a *high cut* or *low pass filter* (*LPF*) removes high frequencies.

In all of the preceding examples, it is important to note that the boosts, cuts, and filters are affecting more than the targeted frequency. In addition, surrounding frequencies are also altered depending on the Q or slope settings.

READY, PRESET, GO!

EQ plug-ins usually contain *presets*. These are EQ control settings that are created by a professional mixer with the same plug-in for a specific instrument. Most EQ plug-ins contain presets for vocals, guitars, pianos, basses, drums, and many other instruments. Some may get very specific, like "sibilant female vocal" or "bright snare." Find one that is close to what you need, and then make the appropriate changes to it.

Figures 8.6a and 8.6b. *Classic EQ plug-ins.* (Source: *IK Multimedia)*

CIRCLE GAME

Here is one example of how to apply EQ to the tracks in a mix:

- In order to EQ a kick drum, you have to hear how it blends with the bass.
- To get the bass working, check how it sounds with the piano.
- The piano shouldn't conflict with the guitar, so you have to get that straightened out first.
- And the lead vocal? That has to be clear, so the piano and the guitar have to be out of its way.
- Is the hi-hat making it hard to hear the lyrics?
- And you haven't even touched the snare yet! The snare is probably going to interfere with the accents on the guitar.

Welcome to a common dilemma in mixing: *Where do you start?*

In mixing, there is no right or wrong place to begin EQing. It may or may not be a better idea to do panning first. No matter which process or instrument you start with, you will likely need to return to it.

The instruments in a mix are interdependent, and adjustments made to one will probably affect another that has already been EQ-ed.

Start with your best estimate on EQ for an instrument, without fine-tuning your settings too much. Then circle back around through the other instruments. You may find that one pass through is enough, but don't count on it. The second time through, make more precise adjustments, addressing each instrument. It may take a few more times around each instrument to find a satisfactory mix. Until you listen in a different environment, some issues do not make themselves apparent. So be flexible, be patient, and *use your ears.*

Learn your craft to the best of your ability, but don't overthink it. When the EQ of your mix sounds good in different listening environments, the EQing is done. A possible exception to this is when processing (like compression, discussed later in this chapter) takes place after the EQ and results in a change to the frequency response; then EQ readjustments may be necessary.

CAVERN OR CLOSET: CREATING AMBIENCE

The third way to balance a mix is to adjust its perceived depth by controlling *ambience.* A recording that sounds like it was made in a car has a considerably different vibe than one that sounds like it was made in a large concert hall. Once again, let prosody guide your decisions. In this case, "prosody" refers to how the mood of the song's content not only matches the music, chords, and lyrics but also the arrangement, production, and mix.

If the song is about an intimate conversation between two people, it should be treated differently than a proclamation to the world from a mountaintop. Just as importantly, it would be confusing to the listener if one instrument has the ambience of a closet while another instrument in the same mix sounds as if it was recorded in a church or concert hall.

Much like panning and equalization, balancing ambience is about each instrument being in its own place, without having too many of them crowded together. Think of it as all the instruments situated in different areas of the same space. The primary tools used for this purpose are *reverb* (*reverberation*) and *delay.* They are similar in that they reproduce the original audio as *reflections* or repeats and play them back fractions of a second later, resulting in an echo effect. However, the difference is that delays have discernable reflections that are distinct and separate, while the reflections of reverbs have no audible space between them and are hard to distinguish from one another.

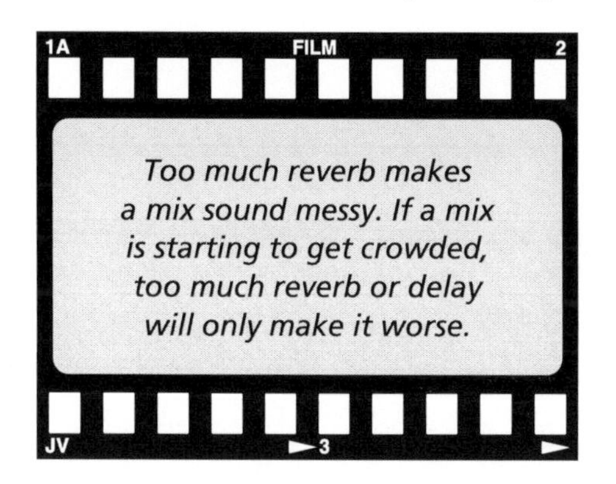

Too much reverb makes a mix sound messy. If a mix is starting to get crowded, too much reverb or delay will only make it worse.

Reverb and delay can have the magical quality of making audio sound better. It's easy to get carried away using them. Inexperienced mixers may feel that if a little reverb is good then a lot must be great. Actually, too much reverb makes a mix sound messy. If a mix is starting to get crowded, too much reverb or delay will only make it worse. Ambience takes up a lot of sonic real estate. Use discretion, and remember that the goal is to make the full mix sound focused and balanced.

Focus is achieved by being judicious and conservative with the overall amount of reverb used, while balance is achieved by applying varying amounts of reverb to each instrument. This will result in some instruments with less reverb sounding like they are close and up-front and others with more reverb sounding like they are farther away and in the back. Still other instruments can be placed between these two extremes.

Think of this like placing musicians on a stage, but not as literal and structured. For example, although the lead vocalist in a live band may have less reverb on their vocal because they are closer to the audience, the lead vocal may have more reverb in a recorded mix. In either case, the vocal will have a different amount of reverb than the drums.

A LITTLE REVERB AND DELAY GO A LONG WAY . . . WAY . . . WAY . . . WAY . . .

A common technique in applying reverb or delay is increasing the amount on an individual track while listening to the full mix until the reverb is audible and then backing it down a little. A frequent and desired outcome of this technique is that the reverb is not *that* noticeable unless it is turned off; then it sounds like something is missing. Listening to the full mix is an important part of this process. What may sound like excessive reverb on an isolated track may sound inadequate when all the instruments are playing along with it. Once again, the sound of the full mix takes priority.

Because reverb and delay add more sound to a mix and can potentially overwhelm it, managing them carefully is essential. A standard way of doing this is removing the low and high frequencies from reverb or delay. Many reverb and delay plug-ins contain the ability to filter these frequencies. For clarity, this concept does not involve altering the EQ of the original audio—just the signal to which reverb or delay has been applied. The reflections will sound smaller than the initial instrument, but the effect will still be present and it won't overload the mix by taking up more bandwidth than necessary.

RETURN TO SENDER

Reverbs and delays, as well as other kinds of plug-ins, can be used in two common ways. The first is as an insert on a channel of audio. In this process, the audio recorded on a track passes directly through the reverb plug-in. It is possible that the effect may be too strong. Fortunately, most reverb and delay plug-ins offer a *mix control* that adjusts how much of the effect is applied. Usually, this control ranges from 0% (*dry*, or no effect) to 100% (*wet*, or full effect).

Many times, as reverb is applied to more than one track, multiple instances of the same plug-in can be used on several tracks with varying amounts. However, using several reverb plug-ins can tax the processing power of many computers. If the only difference is the amount of reverb applied to each track, there is an alternative method that will allow one plug-in to add reverb to several tracks while not using as much computer processing power as multiple reverbs.

Another way plug-ins can be used is by utilizing a *send*:

1. An aux bus is created, and a reverb plug-in is placed there. This is frequently a stereo bus, as reverbs and delays are often stereo, even if the original audio is mono.
2. The reverb plug-in mix setting is usually set to 100%.
3. A send is then created on the track in need of reverb.
4. The output of this send is routed virtually to the input of the aux channel containing the reverb. The output of the send controls the amount of signal sent from the original track to the aux channel, thus determining the amount of reverb the track will receive.
5. The audio with reverb from the aux channel is combined and mixed with the original audio.

This is also known as *parallel processing*, since an affected signal is blended with an unaffected one. This process can be repeated with the sends from more audio tracks being routed to the same aux channel input. In this way, one plug-in can be used to add reverb to multiple tracks. Since each track has its own send level control, they can each be set to different values so that some tracks will have more reverb than others.

There are two kinds of sends: *post fader* and *pre fader* (see figure 7.6 on page 104). When a post fader send is used, the output of the send and the volume fader on the original track affect the level of signal going to the aux bus. This is why it's important to set the volume level of the original track *before* adjusting the send level when using a post fader send. If the track volume is changed drastically, the send level will also change drastically, requiring it to be reset.

A pre fader send is unaffected by the volume fader on the original track. While this may seem advantageous, a problem arises when creating alternate mixes. When an unneeded track with a pre fader send is muted, the signal sent to the aux bus can still be heard, unless the send is also muted. This is why post fader sends are generally preferable to using pre fader sends with reverb and delay when mixing music for sync.

HEY! READ THIS!
Most virtual instruments contain reverb and other effects that default to being turned on when the plug-in is opened. We discussed this earlier, but it bears repeating. If this reverb fits well with the reverb you have chosen for the rest of your mix, leave it on. Experience has shown us that this is not always the case. The quality of the effects in virtual instruments is inconsistent; some are of high quality, while others leave much to be desired. In this case, turn off the reverb in the virtual instrument, and use a separate reverb plug-in to make it easier to blend the reverb of this instrument with the others in your mix.

WHERE *ARE* YOU?

There are two major categories of reverbs: natural and unnatural. *Natural reverbs* are modeled after real spaces, such as concert halls, chambers, churches, recording studios, rooms, and other physical spaces. If your music is intended to sound like it was recorded in a specific kind of real setting, choose from these.

Unnatural reverb—or synthetic reverb—still sounds like reverb, but it is hard to identify exactly what kind of room the performance occurred in. *Plate reverb* is a common unnatural reverb. The name comes from its original physical configuration in which a large metal plate was suspended by springs in an enclosure, giving the audio a somewhat metallic sound. Plate reverb is used often on vocals and drums. *Spring reverb* is the other common synthetic reverb. It uses a small coiled-up piece of metal instead of a large plate, making it more convenient in the analog world. Spring reverb is used frequently in guitar amplifiers but works well on other sound sources.

WITHOUT FURTHER DELAY

While reverb reproduces the sound of acoustic spaces, delay does not. Think of delay as being similar to an unnatural reverb, as the effect that it produces does not occur in any natural setting. Instead of generating reflections, delay produces repeats. Delay's main advantage over reverb is that its repeats are often distinguishable and have audible space between them. This makes delay less likely to make a mix sound too busy.

Many of the same concepts that apply to reverb are helpful in making decisions about delay. Like reverb, it is common practice to filter out the high and low frequencies of the repeats. If a delay plug-in is used as an insert, adjust the mix control to taste. If a delay plug-in is used on a send, set the mix control to 100%, and adjust the amount of delay with the send level.

Varying the amount of delay applied to each instrument is a good way to keep a mix balanced and interesting. Delay plug-ins with different settings can be used on different instruments. However, like reverb, it is best not to use too many different delay plug-ins in the same mix.

Some tracks can use delay, while others use reverb. A mix could contain short and long delays *and* short and long reverbs. Delay and reverb can be used on the same instrument, preferably as sends. If both are used as inserts, you would feed its signal into the other, which might create more ambience than desired; so use discretion.

Consider the order of the plug-ins when using them as inserts. Any plug-ins that follow the delay or reverb will affect the original audio signal as well as the signal with ambience. Having the delay or reverb plug-in inserted last is recommended. This is one of the reasons sends are preferred when using ambience plug-ins. One technique is to route a send from a delay bus to a reverb bus; but set it judiciously.

DYNAMITE VERSUS DYNAMIC: USING COMPRESSION

A big part of experiencing a live musical performance is hearing the variation of volume and intensity among the musicians throughout the piece. The overall sound is dynamic and captivating. However, this same performance can be problematic when recorded, because it causes consistency issues in the mix. Compression to the rescue. This is yet another must-have tool to help achieve balance and focus in mixing.

Some vocalists who know their way around a microphone will back away from it for high, powerful notes; others won't. The best drummers can hit the snare or kick with the same intensity every time when necessary; others can't. When these levels vary throughout a song—even with the best of performers—it can be difficult to perceive balance between two or more instruments. At one moment, an instrument is loud and booming, and the next moment it's whisper-soft. It can also cause distraction from the main spotlighted instrument. Likewise, if the lead vocal becomes inaudible in some places, the focus will be lost.

Your main tool to deal with these fluctuations in volume is *compression*. The basic function of a compressor in audio mixing is to make the loud parts of a performance softer and the soft parts louder. This is also referred to as reducing the audio's *dynamic range*—or the difference between the strongest and weakest audio levels in a recording. However, if overdone, too much compression can squeeze the life out of a performance, so use caution. Here are the common controls on a compressor:

- *Threshold.* The input level at which the compressor starts working.
- *Ratio.* The amount of compression, expressed as a ratio, applied to the incoming signal relative to how much it exceeds the threshold.
- *Attack time.* The time it takes for the compressor to work after the signal reaches the threshold.
- *Release time.* The time it takes for the compressor to stop working after the signal falls below the threshold.
- *Gain reduction meter.* The display showing the amount of compression applied by indicating how much the incoming signal is being reduced.
- *Output:* Controls the amount of signal leaving the compressor.

Depending on the other control settings, the overall level of the incoming audio may be softer or louder than it was before compression. *Makeup gain* allows the output level to be brought back closer to the incoming level, if desired. Some compressors have automatic makeup gain. This can make it easier to compare the compressed signal with the uncompressed signal without being distracted by level changes.

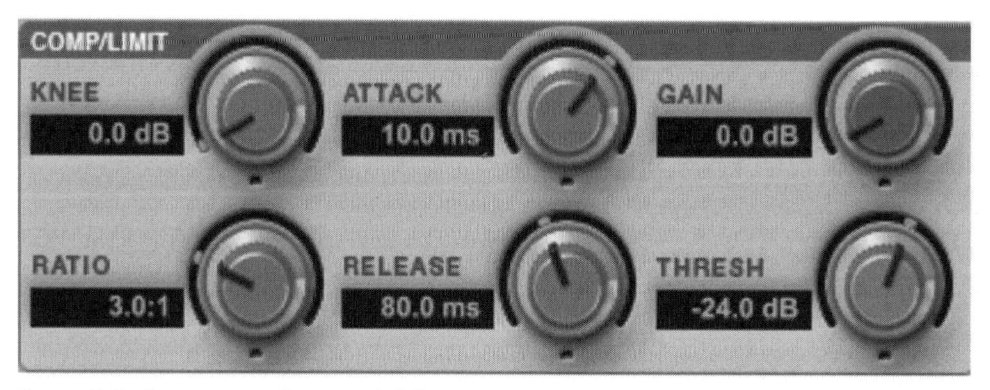

Figure 8.7. *Compressor.* (Source: *Avid)*

HEY! READ THIS!

Many new composers question whether to EQ first or compress first. There is no right or wrong answer. One accepted approach is to cut frequencies with EQ first, then compress, and then boost frequencies with a second EQ. This is done so that the frequencies to be cut do not contribute to overworking the compressor. It also prevents the compressor from reducing the frequencies that are boosted. Always give careful consideration to the order of plug-ins.

MR. CELLOPHANE: KEEPING IT TRANSPARENT

Ideally, compression is transparent and not discernable. So, why should we use compression if no one is going to hear it? The reason to use compression is to decrease the dynamic range of audio so the soft parts are audible and the loud parts are not overwhelming.

Compression can also be used to bring out more detail, to shape audio, or to give it a more aggressive sound. Adjusting attack times and allowing more or less of the initial *transient* through can change the way a drum sounds and make it fit better in a mix. A transient is the *very* first, sudden sound that can be heard at the beginning of a piece of audio. With more extreme compressor settings, an instrument can be made to sound bigger or distorted or otherwise have its character changed.

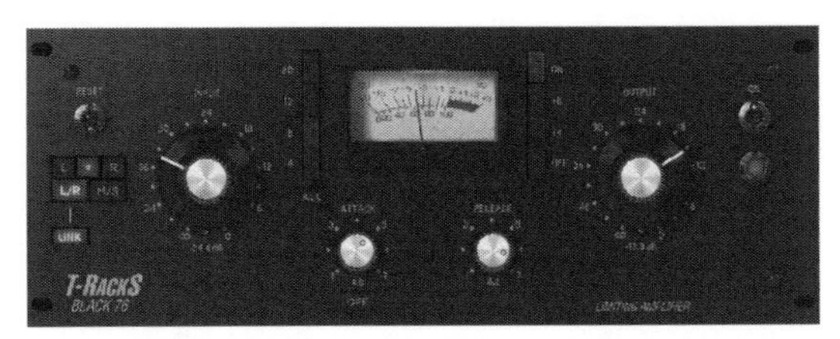

Figures 8.8a and 8.8b. *Classic compressor plug-ins.* (Source: *IK Multimedia*)

Your DAW allows you to make the job of the compressor easier. You can use automation or other forms of level control of audio to increase the volume of soft notes manually and decrease the volume of loud ones. The means of achieving this, and what they are named, vary from one DAW to another, so familiarize yourself with yours. It may involve volume automation. If this step is taken before compression is applied, the compressor will not have to work as hard and is less likely to be audible.

SOS: SILENCE OUR S'S

A *de-esser* is a very specific type of compressor that focuses on the sibilant frequency range of the human voice from about 4 kHz to 10 kHz. A de-esser allows control of the threshold where the compression is triggered, the range of attenuation it provides, and the frequency on which it focuses.

When set properly, a de-esser can significantly reduce the "s" sounds on a vocal track without removing desired frequencies. Other sibilant sounds include "z," "sh," and "ch." Be aware of the order of plug-ins; a compressor used *after* a de-esser may bring the sibilance back.

STOP! HEY! WHAT'S THAT SOUND?

An expander does the opposite of a compressor; it makes loud audio louder and soft audio softer, thus increasing its dynamic range. A *gate* is a more extreme version of an expander, as it completely removes the soft parts of audio.

Expanders and gates have many of the same controls as compressors, such as threshold and attack and release times. They can also be useful in reducing or removing sounds like a singer's breaths or other unwanted noises.

THERE ARE SOME THINGS YOU *CAN* FIX IN THE MIX

Vocalists and producers have a love-hate relationship with *pitch correction* plug-ins. Before their use became commonplace in recordings, singers had to sing in tune if a pitch-perfect performance was required. Some vocalists feel insulted when they discover their vocals have been pitch corrected. Because listeners have come to expect tuned vocals, you are obligated to deliver the best quality recordings you can. Unless audible pitch correction is desired as a special effect, be conservative with the plug-in settings.

There are various noise removal plug-ins available to get rid of clicks, crackles, hums, and other noises in audio. At times these have an audible effect on the quality of the audio, so it is better to record in as quiet an environment as possible to avoid the need for these plug-ins.

HEY! READ THIS!

There are so many tools available for mixing that it may not be easy to know where to start. Here is a suggestion:

1. Begin mixing by setting the relative levels for your tracks.
2. Apply high pass filters on most tracks, except the bass and kick drum.
3. Pan individual tracks to balance the stereo image.
4. Add a moderate amount of reverb or delay, if desired.
5. Listen closely to each individual track in solo and then with the rest of the mix to hear what can be done to make it play well with the other tracks.

This process lets you know if the arrangement is working. You may need to add or subtract some instruments or change the parts they are playing. Revisit each of these steps to determine whether more adjustments may be necessary.

ELIMINATING POTENTIAL DEAL BREAKERS

Perhaps you've written several songs or cues and pitched them but keep getting returns—or even worse, silence. As ridiculous as it may seem, it could be due to one slight flaw. It is not always obvious what's wrong unless a fresh set of ears can hear it. In chapter 4, we discussed getting feedback before presenting your music. However, use this checklist to see—and hear—whether there is a particular issue that needs to be addressed first:

- The cue is rambling or has no edit points or distinct sections.
- An instrument or vocal part is out of tune (sharp or flat).
- A wrong note was played or sung.
- The singer sang a wrong lyric, or the words are unclear.
- The chords don't complement the melody.
- The harmony part conflicts with the melody or the chords.
- An instrument is off time and needs to be quantized; or, conversely, the tracks were quantized too much, and everything sounds rigid.
- The arrangement is boring, and nothing changes for several measures; or the arrangement is distracting by changing too much.

- The virtual instruments are not top quality and sound "cheesy" or unintentionally fake; they were not tweaked or manipulated to have a "humanized" sound.
- The cue is too compressed or not compressed enough.
- There is too much or not enough low end or high end.
- Unwanted background noises are audible.
- Clicks, pops, or distortion can be heard.
- One instrument is too soft or too loud. One of our songs was rejected for a project because the hi-hat in the drum track was too prominent in the mix. This tiny oversight still irritates us to this day, but we learned a tough lesson.

PRO TIPS . . . About Mixing Basics and Techniques

I feel like I could keep mixing a song because there is so much to do! Details keep popping up that require attention. But at some point, after I've focused a lot of time on the mix, I need to step back and *listen*. I'll take a nice break and go for a walk or drive without listening to the song. I'll come back and hear the complete song better, and I'll be able to pinpoint issues that still need more work. I suggest doing this over and over until you're done. It's awesome hearing a song drop the beat, a cool sound that leads into the bridge, or a guitar solo that makes you want to play air guitar! These are some of the reactions I'm hoping for happens once the mix is complete.

—**Brian Scheuble**, Mixer

I listen to tons of different styles of music so I can usually zero in on what you're going for. If there's an example from your library or from another artist that you'd like for me to listen to and to match, don't hesitate to share it with me. Lots of composers have some knowledge of mixing, and tools and gadgets can be fun. But I'd rather not talk about decibels; I sometimes talk about teaspoons and tablespoons, just to stay on the level of more "feel"-based comments. By trying something and sending it to you and then getting your response, I can usually quickly figure out what it's going to take to make it sound good to you.

—**Les Brockmann**, Recording Engineer, Mixer, and Score Mixer

Find a commercially released piece of music that is in a similar style as yours to use as a reference. While mixing, constantly go back and forth and A/B your mix against the reference mix to stay on track. Keep making adjustments until you are satisfied. Listen to your mix on different speakers and electronic devices to make sure it is translating well. If doing it by yourself gets to be too daunting, get some help by hiring someone who is an experienced mixing/mastering engineer.

—**Brian Thomas Curtin**, Composer and Songwriter, Eaglestone Music

Using an A/B comparison plug-in that allows you to switch between your mix and a commercially released production in the same genre is extremely helpful to hear if your mix is in the ballpark. If it's not, ask yourself, "What is different?" Then try to listen in as much detail as possible. This may not allow you to fix your mix immediately if you lack the requisite skills, but it should allow you to seek out relevant information/education.

—**Matt Hirt**, Composer, Songwriter, and Producer, and Co-owner of Catapult Music

CHAPTER 9

Mastering and File Delivery

POLISHING YOUR MUSICAL GEM: ADDING THE FINAL, FINISHED SHEEN

After your music has been mixed, the final step is mastering. This truly should be done by a mastering engineer. However, here are the basics: Using many of the same tools utilized during the mixing process, the goal of *mastering* is to balance the elements of a stereo mix to ensure the sound is optimized for playback on all sound systems. Note that this definition has a lot in common with the definition of mixing.

An important distinction is that even though the same kinds of tools are used, mastering is not simply more mixing. In the same way that the mixing process should be separated from the recording process, mastering should be separated from the mixing process. A mastering engineer works with a stereo recording delivered by the mixing engineer. Thus the person doing the mastering cannot adjust the levels of volume or processing on any of the individual tracks.

1A FILM 2

The goal of mastering is to balance the elements of a stereo mix to ensure the sound is optimized for playback on all sound systems.

JV 3

Equalization, compression, and limiting are used in the mastering process to "glue" the mix together, apply the final polish, and bring the loudness of the music to a competitive level. If a group of songs is involved, mastering should result in all of the songs being at about the same loudness level so that none of them sounds noticeably softer or louder than the others.

There is a great advantage in having a fresh pair of ears working on the final phase of refining your music. If you choose this option, *do not use any plug-ins on the master bus* when bouncing your track for delivery to the mastering engineer. We cannot stress this enough.

Some mixers bounce a stereo file and import it into a new session for mastering. Other mixers keep working in the same session file as the full mix and insert plug-ins on the master bus. Either approach is valid.

LET'S MAKE THIS CRYSTAL CLEAR

Having an excellent listening environment during the mastering process is essential. This is the most focused listening you do during the entire process. Try not to master on garbage pickup day.

Once again, reference tracks are of great assistance when you are mastering your music or if you have someone else master for you. Select a few high-quality, professionally recorded songs or instrumentals that have the style of mix you would like to emulate. Compare the sound of your mix with a few reference tracks in the same genre. This process is referred to as *A/B testing* tracks. Make observations on headphones or different speakers. Before opening any plug-ins and making adjustments, listen objectively for what makes yours sound different, and make note of what you hear:

- Is the main instrument clear sonically all the way through the song?
- Are any of the instruments standing out or obstructing others? If so, at which frequencies?
- Are the low, mid, and high frequencies balanced?
- Does it sound too boomy or muddy? Or is it not full enough?

- Does it sound too brittle or tinny? Or does it sound dull?
- Does each instrument occupy its own space while sounding as though it's in the same room with the others?
- Are there varying levels of intensity and dynamics? Or is it loud from start to finish?

MIXING AND MASTERING ARE SIMILAR BUT DIFFERENT

Once you have a list of adjustments to make, you are ready to open some plug-ins on your master bus. Some people start with equalization, while others start with compression. There are advantages and disadvantages to each approach.

A quality EQ plug-in is recommended for the mastering process. *Linear phase EQs* are ideal for this purpose, as they are very accurate and do not change the phase of the audio. As subtlety is the favored approach, use wide boosts or cuts of no more than 3 dB to any frequencies requiring attention. Usually there is a lot of buildup of low frequencies on a full mix, many of which may not be audible but can cause issues with a compressor or limiter. It is common to use a high pass filter at 20 to 30 Hz to remove these frequencies.

Subtle use of a *bus compressor*—a compressor designed to be used on a group of tracks, like those of a drum kit, but especially useful when mastering—is a fundamental part of the process. A ratio of 2:1 or 3:1 with a slow attack and fast release is recommended. Use caution when adjusting these release settings. If used improperly, the result may be an undesired "pumping" effect, making the music sound unnatural. Most bus compressors have an automatic release option that, if present, can be utilized. Try not to have more than 2 dB of gain reduction.

ANOTHER BRICK IN THE WALL

The final plug-in on the master bus should be a brickwall limiter. A *limiter* is an aggressive compressor with a ratio setting of 10:1 or more. A *brickwall limiter* is an extreme limiter that does not allow any audio signal over the threshold to proceed to the output. Limiters and compressors are in the class of processing called *dynamics*.

A limiter may have a "look-ahead" feature that allows it to detect audio and calculate its reaction before the audio passes through it. This type of limiter is worth considering, as it can be more accurate. Since it is crucial that the brickwall limiter function properly, we have provided a detailed description of its use.

The output ceiling should be set between –0.2 to –0.02 dB. Resist the temptation to set this to 0 dB, as this would not allow enough of a safety net. The goal is to prevent *clipping*, which is when the signal level on the master bus meter goes over 0 dB and distorts. There is a reason most meters indicate this with the color red as it is to be avoided at all costs!

If your brickwall limiter has an attack time control, it should be a fast attack. An automatically controlled release time is preferred. The ratio in most brickwall limiter defaults to infinity to one. (Brickwall limiting is the "extreme sports" of compression.)

On some brickwall limiters, attenuation starts by increasing the input gain; on others, it starts by lowering the threshold. In either case, proceed until the gain reduction meter shows 2 to 4 dB of attenuation. Be sure to listen through the loudest parts of the song. Do not squash the signal by having too much gain reduction and distorting the signal. This setting will determine the perceived loudness of the music, so it is imperative that you do this as flawlessly as possible.

HEY! I THOUGHT YOU SAID TO NEVER FADE!

There are two places in your song that are critical and deserve special attention: the beginning and the end. A marker should be placed in both of these locations. The marker at the beginning should be placed about two-tenths of a second before the first note of the song. Be sure none of the instruments has its entrance or the attack of its first note cut off.

The placement of the end marker is a little more involved. As mentioned earlier, music for licensing does not fade out; it has a final note. Sometimes the note is long or short with reverb that rings out. It may be difficult to hear when the reverb or last note has faded away completely. Listen closely to when the audio is totally gone. Some synthesizers have a tendency to continue sustaining. The track should not end while there is still audio that can be heard. If you are not sure where the audio stops exactly, and even if you are, automation of the volume on the master bus should be used to fade the last note to silence. Be careful where this fade starts and how fast it is. It should not be too sudden or too long. Find what sounds natural. An end marker can be placed about two-tenths of a second after the automation brings the audio to complete silence.

ALTERNATE MIXES: GIVE 'EM WHAT THEY WANT

In the sync world, when the mixing and mastering are completed, the exporting can begin. *Exporting* is also referred to as *bouncing* or *printing*. This is the process of creating the audio files for delivery. If the project was completed for a specific client, confirm the file resolution they require. For many clients, 48-kHz, 24-bit WAV files are common. If there is no specific client, export your files at the sample rate and bit depth of your session. Make sure to export *stereo* files.

In addition to the full mix, clients often ask for *alternate mixes*, or *alt mixes*, which provide more opportunities for your music to be licensed. These may include:

- A no melody mix
- An instrumental melody mix (for music with a vocal melody)
- A no background vocals mix
- A no drums mix
- A no drums and no bass mix
- A drum and bass mix (one of the most-requested types of alt mixes)

If your music is being mastered by someone else, you will need to provide most, if not all, of these types of alternate mixes to the mastering engineer. A "no melody mix" is sometimes referred to as an *instrumental mix*, an *underscore mix*, a *TV mix*, or a *bed mix*. Clients have their own definitions and requirements regarding which instruments to include in these alternate mixes, so ask for direction.

Most of these alternate mixes are created simply by muting tracks in the full mix (yes, it's really that easy). Sometimes these alt mix variations are referred to as *minus mixes*. A notable exception is the *instrumental melody mix* of a song. This requires that a new track be recorded with an instrument playing the same melody as the lead vocal. This new track is then added to the rest of the instruments, and the vocal melody and background vocals are muted. *Do not remix or remaster the song.* This version is not always requested but can be very useful under dialog.

Make sure that each of these alt mixes is musical and usable. Instead of just muting tracks, listen to each alternate mix all the way through. Confirm that there are no long periods of silence. If there are, do not submit that alternate mix. Instead, try to find another combination of tracks to mute that leaves no silence. Do not rearrange the song, and do not change any of the mix settings.

THE DANGERS OF BEING EXPOSED

Confirm that none of your alternate mixes contains an exposed drum loop. If the drum loop is one that you created or tweaked extensively, that's not a problem. If the drum loop was created by the maker of the plug-in or came from some other source, providing an alternate mix of the drum loop—without any other instruments accompanying it—may be in violation of the license agreement between you and the creator of the loop. This "exposed loop," as it's known, can get a composer into trouble. Once again, try a different combination of tracks.

These alternate mixes are licensed frequently. Music editors may use various alt mixes of the same cue within a scene. So, in order to make their job smoother, each of your mixes should start and end in the exact same place and should be the exact same length.

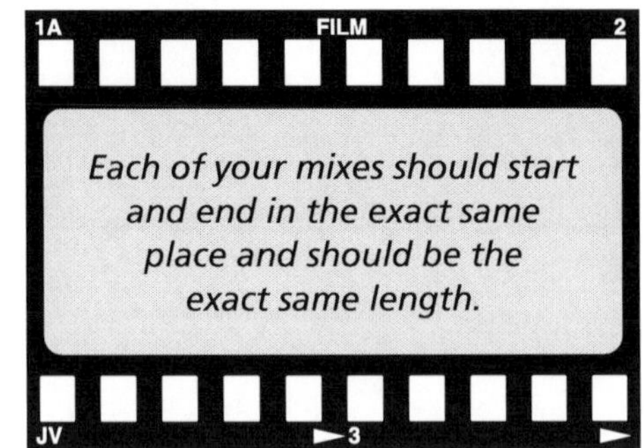

Some companies like to have the *stems* of your music. These are different than alternate mixes. Stems are the individual tracks or groups of tracks from your song. In most cases, they will not want the snare track alone; they'll want the whole drum kit. They will not want each individual background vocal separately; they'll want all the background vocals together. Every track should be included once.

The goal with providing stems is to give a producer or music editor the pieces they need to put your song back together again. This way, they can create their own custom mixes of your music. Like alternate mixes, these stems should all be of the same exact length. However, unlike alternate mixes, even if an instrument does not enter until a minute into the song, leave the silence at the beginning or end to preserve the stem length.

U CAN'T TOUCH THIS

While exporting alternate mixes and stems, do not change *any* of the plug-in settings on the master bus. Even though these plug-ins will respond differently to having fewer instruments, leave them as they were on the full mix.

Label each file clearly with the song title and the mix or stem name. Some clients have a preferred file-naming protocol. It's easier to name them appropriately as you are exporting them. Double-check all mixes and stems. Verify that the no melody mix has no melody and the drums stem has nothing but drums.

GIVE ME JUST A MINUTE

In addition to these alternate mixes, *edits* of different lengths may also be requested. In addition to a shorter version of the full mix, a client may also ask for edits of the alternate mixes. These may include:

- A 60-second edit
- A 30-second edit
- A 15-second edit
- Or a sting

GET TO THE POINT: CREATING EFFECTIVE EDITS AND STINGERS

A *sting* (or *stinger*) is usually the last two to four measures of an instrumental, leading up to the last note. It is customarily six to twelve seconds in length. If full and alternate mixes are used to create multiple stings, they do not each need to be of the same length. Make sure the ending of the stinger rings out for a second or two.

HEY! LISTEN TO THIS!
"Expecting Bad News—Sting" and "Secrets and Lies—Sting"
Here are two examples of stings. Notice how they start and end.

Creating shorter versions of your song increases sync opportunities. Consider creating 60- and 30-second edits for commercial placements, as these are common lengths for ads. The definition of what exactly a 60-second edit is varies from one client to another, so be sure to ask for clarification. It's advisable to provide your clients with edits that are 59.5 seconds or 29.5 seconds long. Some producers edit the stereo mix, while others prefer to edit within the full session, as it offers more flexibility.

The challenge of editing music down to 60 or 30 seconds is keeping the musicality of the piece intact. Copy and paste the sections you need after the full mix ends so that all the track and plug-in settings are retained. The A section (of an instrumental) or chorus (of a song) should always be included. Figure out how many sections you can squeeze in, and occasionally it ends up magically being the correct length. Most of the time you have to strategize by using a quarter, a half, or three-quarters of a section of the song. The edits do not necessarily need to be at the beginning or end. In some cases you can edit together the first A section with the last, creating an edit in the middle. Check each track at the edits to be sure that no notes are cut off in an unnatural way.

Your final versions may be made up of three or four different parts of the song. You may have to shorten, lengthen, remove, or create an intro to make the time constraint work. Frequently you also may have to play with the length of the last note. For example, if a long held-out note occurs at 59 seconds, a quick fade-out would sound forced. Two or three seconds is a good target for the length of the last note. The end must sound natural, and the overall edit cannot sound edited. Do not use audio-stretching plug-ins, and, no matter what, do not change the tempo or pitch of the song. Think of it as solving a puzzle: there is always a solution.

SHIP IT: HOW TO DELIVER FILES

If a client requests high-resolution files of a song, alternate mixes, and stems, the combination of all these files will be large in size. Clients no longer ask for CDs. Files are now delivered online. There are many *online file-delivery services* available. Some are free, while others require a fee. The main advantages of using a paid service are that they usually have a higher capacity for sending files and the files can be stored on their servers for a longer period of time (for a year or sometimes more).

In most cases, these services require you to upload your files to their website. They then send you a download link that can be emailed to the client. Beware of download links that expire after a few weeks. This is one of the features that sets free file-delivery services apart from paid ones. At times clients may take a while before they find the time to download your files. If your download link expires before they have the opportunity to download, they will have to ask you for another. They then have to wait for you to send it to them, and you have just made it harder for them to work with you. This interaction may be one of the first impressions a client will have of your professionalism; make it a good one.

YOUR MOST VALUABLE ASSET

The process of writing, performing, recording, arranging, and producing your music is a long one. It involves much thought, careful planning, heart, soul, blood, sweat, and tears. The final product, in the form of files on your computer, is irreplaceable. If your hard drive fails, your music is gone forever. No one can re-create your songs for you. You can try to re-create them from memory, but they will never be the same.

Your music on your computer is one of your most valuable physical assets. Take care of it by backing it up. No hard drive lasts forever; they all fail at some point. Be more redundant than you think you need to be. Back up your computer data to external hard drives in your studio. Store extra hard drive backups away from your studio, such as in a bank safe-deposit box, with a trusted friend, or at a relative's house. Back up your data to offsite cloud servers. You might not like to think about it, but unforeseeable hazards occur. Long after your music has been delivered, clients may still contact you for an alternate mix, requiring you to reopen old session files. When your precious music is gone, it's gone. Protect your hard work. It is the professional thing to do.

PRO TIPS . . . About Mastering and File Delivery

When submitting music, remember: It has to be master quality. Vocalists have to be on key. No copyright issues.

—**Tanvi Patel**, Owner and CEO of Crucial Music Corporation

When submitting material to a production music library, send one nonexpiring streaming link to no more than ten songs of your strongest material only—no attachments or downloads. The key here is to *make sure the links do not expire*. It can take us up to several months to catch up and listen to everything we receive. By the time we get to them, you'd be surprised how often the files either expired or were taken down. We've even seen some composer's own websites no longer exist.

—**Ron Goldberg**, Vice President of Manhattan Production Music

When writing for sync, make the first few seconds count with a strong start and a clearly defined mood. Construct your music so that it has multiple edit points, and finish with a well-defined ending (not a fade-out). Providing alternate versions of your main mix gives music editors more options and increases your chances for placements. When submitting songs, deliver both the vocal and non-vocal versions.

—**Brian Thomas Curtin**, Composer and Songwriter, Eaglestone Music

Make your music easy to edit. Provide loads of stems (mix options).

—**Lisa Aschmann**, Songwriter and Author, Nashville Geographic

Try to learn how to do mixing and mastering yourself. If you're not there yet, hire a professional. But try to learn something from them so you can one day do this yourself.

—**Steve Barden**, Composer and Author

PART 2: MARKETING

Hey! Who Wants My Music?

Steps to Getting Your Music Out There, Signed, and Placed

CHAPTER 10

Marketing Your Music for Sync

MAKING MARKETABLE MUSIC FOR THE MARKETPLACE

As creatives, you know that making music is fun. It's as natural for you to do as it is to breathe. However, songwriters, composers, artists, and bands are often baffled by the business side of music. Creatives are also not known for their marketing skills, so it's imperative that they acquire these abilities—or find assistance. Everyone needs a way to pay the bills, and it's nice when your music can do that for you.

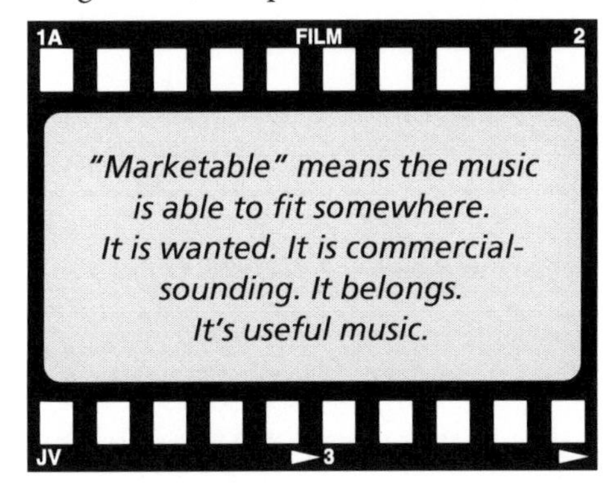

Marketing in the music business world simply means promoting, advertising, and doing research.

In the sync world, the "music marketplace" is another name for the music industry. It includes the companies that get placements for your music. Even though these companies have hundreds of thousands of pieces of music, the good news is, *they always need more.*

When we learned how to write marketable music, it was a game changer. It meant our music was able to fit somewhere. It was wanted. It was commercial-sounding. It belonged. It was potentially profitable. It *would* get placed (eventually). One music publisher told us, "It's useful music."

WHAT THE (SYNC) WORLD NEEDS NOW

Marketable music in the sync world can be:

- Current, progressive, ahead of the curve, and futuristic
- Timeless, retro, and nostalgic, like it was recorded long ago
- Native to a place or region in the world
- Edgy, uneasy, tense, and unpredictable
- Safe, easy, laid-back, and predictable
- Serious, dramatic, and emotional
- Fun, upbeat, and positive
- Sophisticated, elegant, and classy
- Raw and flawed, with glaring imperfections
- Vibey, with a distinct sound
- Generic, nondescript, middle-of-the-road "elevator music"

Is this list puzzling? It was to us at first. Marketable music can be any of the above. It's whatever the market needs—and is getting placed—in various media. Pay attention to what is getting placed, and you will hear the varied music from this list. There are always trends when current, cutting-edge music is desired.

However, there is also a need for retro music, and sometimes that retro music will require a current-sounding production technique, twist, or vibe. This is why it's good to be aware of what is being licensed in all genres.

Sync music is marketable when it creates an emotion. It can be a reflection of what the characters are feeling, or it can provide a clue as to what action is about to take place. Marketable music can also establish where or when a scene is occurring and whether it's here and now or there and then.

THE DREADED PHRASE: "THIS SOUNDS DATED"

Have you ever watched a TV show from the 1960s? The music probably sounds dated. However, at that time it was current and appropriate. If a scene in a new TV show or film is happening in another time or place, there is a need for authentic-sounding music that embodies that time or place. This could mean using scene-setting music that was recorded years or decades ago, or it could mean creating new music that sounds like it came from that period.

The difference between writing music from a specific time period and writing dated music is intent. Many songwriters and composers tend to gravitate toward writing music they loved in high school. This is fine if the goal is to write music that sounds like it came from that era. However, if the goal is to write music that sounds contemporary, but the writer creates music that sounds like the glory days of youth, their music will likely sound dated.

THAT'S JUST THE WAY IT IS

The way music is written, performed, recorded, produced, and mixed can influence whether it sounds dated or contemporary. Trends come and go, so it's important to note characteristics such as:

- *Melody.* Does it tend to repeat the same note several times before changing, or does it move fluidly up and down the scale?
- *Phrasing:* Are the phrase lengths even, or do they vary?
- *Lyrics.* Are they poetic or conversational? Does the song have nonsense words or vocalises? What types of rhymes are used?
- *Structure.* Is there a bridge, pre-chorus, or post-chorus?
- *Vocal delivery.* Is the singer's voice light and breathy, or is there a heavy vibrato?
- *Instrumentation.* Which instruments were selected, and how are they being played? Are they acoustic or electronic?
- *Mixing elements.* To what degree are reverb and delay being used? How are all the instruments panned? How much high end or low end is in the mix?

To avoid writing dated music, experiment using fresh, contemporary beats on the track. Another idea is to use those vintage instruments and classic gear but to mix them using the latest mixing techniques.

However, the most effective remedy is to continually listen to and analyze contemporary music and the music that's getting licensed. That's one of the "insider secrets" in the sync world.

EVERGREEN: THE APPEAL OF WRITING TIMELESS MUSIC

You have been presented with many creative possibilities, and by now you realize the most frequent request is for current-sounding music. Contemporary means *now*. The caveat? Current music today will be dated-sounding music tomorrow. Consider branching out and taking the approach of writing timeless or *evergreen* music. This is music that is not obviously tied to any specific time or place and therefore has an ongoing appeal. This music never fades away, and it is always marketable.

Some examples of timeless-sounding music include a song featuring a solo vocalist with an acoustic guitar or piano, a choir singing Christmas carols, orchestral music, a small cocktail hour jazz trio—the list goes on.

SOMEDAY SOON: WHEN IS MUSIC NEEDED IN THE MARKETPLACE?

Keep in mind that music supervisors, editors, and production companies work on a show three to six months before that show will air. In addition, most companies that market music take weeks or months to process the music submitted to them. For these reasons, music that is intended for specific events, seasons, or times of the year must be written and submitted many months in advance. Here are examples of typical time lines:

- Fall football music should be delivered in the spring.
- Baseball music is needed in the fall or winter.
- Music to be played during international sporting games—like Wimbledon, the Summer or Winter Olympics, America's Cup, World Cup Soccer (FIFA events), or major golf tournaments—should be scheduled several months before the event takes place.
- Thanksgiving and Christmas holiday music is needed in the summer.
- Summer, beach, and vacation music is needed in the winter or early spring.

GOT MUSIC?

Now that you've written marketable music, there are several types of companies to explore to get it signed and placed. These include:

- Production music libraries
- Sync agencies
- Music publishers—major, midsized, and indie

In addition, composers and songwriters may also find themselves dealing directly with music supervisors, music editors, video editors, and film, media, and TV production companies.

WHAT IS MUSIC PUBLISHING?

Starting out in the music business, we had always heard about "music publishing." We assumed incorrectly this meant printing and distributing sheet music. We soon learned music publishing in the sync world (and the real world) is not about actually printing music, although you might find this aspect of the business mentioned in some of your contracts. A music publisher exploits music to find placements, handles administration, and distributes income.

EXPLOIT? THAT SOUNDS SUSPICIOUS!

In the sync world, *exploiting* means getting as many placements or sync opportunities as possible. You will also hear people talking about "exploiting the song's copyright"; an adept music publisher will leave no sync possibility unturned.

IN THE SYNC WORLD, YOUR MUSIC IS NOT FOR SALE

Novice composers often say, "I want to *sell* my songs . . ." Your music in the sync world is for licensing or rent; it is not for sale. There are exceptions, such as a work-made-for-hire or buyout project (see chapter 21), but these are not typical deals, because you may not earn additional income. So, skip the phrases: "I want to *sell* my music," or "I hope someone will *buy* my song," and instead say, "I'd like to *sign* my music and get it *licensed*."

ONE STOP AND GO!

Before signing music with any music company or pitching directly to music supervisors, all songwriters, composers, artists, and bands should become familiar with this important phrase: *one-stop licensing and music clearance*. This means you are prepared with answers to the following questions:

- Who are the songwriters?
- What are the ownership splits for each songwriter? Did each songwriter give consent and sign an agreement, and do you have a copy?
- Who owns the copyrights?
- Who owns the master recording? Is there a signed agreement with the owner(s), and do you have a copy?
- Who performed on the recording? If there was additional talent used, are there signed work-for-hire releases, and do you have a copy?
- Who has permission to pitch the music?
- Who is handling the administration? Administration duties include:
    - Handling the signing of agreements and having copies available.
    - Filling out the metadata, which includes information about the song and the music creators (see chapter 17).
    - Distributing money if necessary.
    - Registering the music with royalty companies and copyright organizations (more about these in part 3).
- Is everyone in agreement with how the music could potentially be placed?
- Is this music completely original?
- Were any portions of a third party's (someone else's) pre-recorded song used?
    - This is known as a *sample*, and permission from the artist, songwriter(s), record label/recording owner, and publisher(s) would need to be obtained before using it.
    - Even something as simple as a drum hit lifted off of another song is a sample, and this would have to be cleared.

If all the criteria from the above list have been met, your lyric sheet, spreadsheet, MP3, and any other materials you provide when pitching your music may include the phrase "one-stop licensing and clearance is available." The music company or music supervisor will know you answered the above questions truthfully and can verify the information is correct. Taking these steps will ensure no one will come back to haunt the music supervisor by asking for more money or disapproving of the use. This is extremely helpful when music supervisors are on a deadline.

ALL I ASK OF YOU: QUESTIONS TO CONSIDER BEFORE MARKETING YOUR MUSIC

Marketing means finding the companies who get you and your music, and you get them. Who values your music? Who is respectful of your time? Who works hard and is honest? Our music is with more than sixty music publishers. About forty of those publishers have never made any money for us. A handful of those publishers send us a check for $10, $50, $100, maybe even $500 now and then. However, about a dozen publishers place our music in media daily around the world. It took years to find some of these companies, but our patience and persistence eventually paid off.

A few years ago, we went to lunch with a composer colleague and compared notes. He had music with many of the same music publishers as we had. We asked him about Company A. This was one of our most successful companies, yet our friend said he'd only made a few hundred dollars in all the years he was with them. Then we asked about Company B, which had only gotten us a few placements in several years. Our friend said he receives hundreds, sometimes thousands, of dollars every quarter from this company. It didn't take us long to realize, each and every company is going to yield completely different results for every composer, songwriter, artist, or band.

It is important to find the right fit for you, and unfortunately you won't know for certain prior to entering into an agreement with a music publisher. Before you hand over your music, it is wise to limit the number of cues or songs you give them until they successfully get you sync placements. There is always some risk involved, and there are no guarantees. Making educated decisions should minimize this risk. The good news is you have several business models from which to choose.

PRO TIPS . . . About Marketing Your Music for Sync

Begin with the end in mind. What is it that you uniquely have to offer? What are your differentiators and high-value qualities (i.e., appreciate your unique voice)? Can you keep your ear to the ground and intuitively understand your special niche and magnificence in a vast ecosystem? Trust that you have something valuable to offer: Trust = Integrity + Competency.

—**Mirette Seireg**, MSc, and President of Mpath Music LLC

At one South by Southwest (SXSW music conference) I stopped going to all the shows and just hung around in the bar of the most expensive hotel in town. That is where all the Record Company people and Publishers were, drinking and talking with each other. In three days, I got a record deal, a producer, some publishing offers . . .

—**Jack Tempchin**, Writer of "Peaceful Easy Feeling,"
Member of the Songwriters Hall of Fame

An important (and often overlooked) thing to consider is understanding the market, because this market is also trend-driven, in much the same way popular music is . . . It's just that the trends are not always the same.

—**Matt Hirt**, Composer, Songwriter, and Producer, and Co-owner of Catapult Music

If you are constantly trying to get better and seeking work, you will get better, quicker, and more efficient over time. As that happens, more people start to find out about you, in part through your own efforts marketing yourself.

—**Derek Jones**, Director of Creative Services at Megatrax Production Music

CHAPTER 11

Production Music Libraries

WHAT ARE PRODUCTION MUSIC LIBRARIES?

As the name suggests, *production music* is exactly that—music that can fit into just about any type of production. *Production music libraries* represent many styles and genres of music that are organized and categorized in a searchable database. If a music supervisor is looking for a specific song for a scene, they can search the library's catalog to find exactly what they need for their project.

You'll hear outdated terms tied to production music, such as "stock music," "canned music," "pre-recorded music," or "library music." The preferred term today is "production music."

Production music libraries represent both copyrights of a musical work: They are *publishers* because they control the written composition on behalf of the songwriter or composer. They are also *record labels* since they control the master recordings of those musical works. Income derived from both of these sources is discussed in part 3.

The beauty of production music is that it is *pre-cleared* and ready to be dropped into a scene or project. This means the composer or songwriter, as well as the producer and owner of the recording, have signed agreements affirming they've written and produced original music to be included in the library. If outside musicians, producers, mixers, and talent were used on the track, those people have already been paid, and they have signed work-for-hire agreements. Quality production music libraries take extreme measures to ensure every piece of music is one-stop, pre-cleared, and licensable. These are among the biggest reasons their clients use production music.

Another advantage is that the music that has been written to be licensed, is of a clearly defined genre, and is "editor-friendly." Editors appreciate production music because there are often intentional and defined sections, breaks, pauses, or even gaps between the musical sections, known as edit points. An editor can easily cut, stretch, copy, and drop the music into a scene.

Production music is also well recorded and has been expertly and professionally mixed and mastered. The endings are "hard endings," which means they do not fade. Most production music libraries will have several alternate mixes of the songs and instrumentals available. As mentioned in chapter 9, these alternate mixes are helpful, especially if there is a scene with dialog and the vocals are not wanted. Production music libraries often have 30- and 60-second versions of each track or song that can be used in commercials, promos, and webisodes.

Production music libraries are also popular because the person needing music may not have the budget to use a well-known song, or the artist may not want their song used in a particular project, but can find an affordable, already-cleared song with a similar vibe in the library.

In addition to being in sync projects, production music also can be used in live music settings, like stage, fashion or industrial shows, and sports games. One of our tracks is used at the Pittsburgh Pirates' baseball games. Production music can also be used in casino games, toys, children's games, greeting cards, and more. Various production music library business models are discussed in chapter 21.

HEY! READ THIS!
"Production music is heard by millions but remembered by none," a music publisher for a daytime talk show once said. If background music is too flashy, melodic, or busy, it often won't work. It shouldn't call attention to itself unless there is a reason for it to do so.

PRE-CLEARED FOR TAKEOFF: WHAT PRODUCTION MUSIC LIBRARIES DO

It is the duty of the music library to market and exploit the music in their catalog. They develop relationships with TV and film production companies, advertising agencies, video game companies, music supervisors, music editors, and other clients. Production music libraries are very aware of their clients' music needs. If clients ask for styles of music not currently in their catalog, the library will send out requests for this music from their writers.

Here are some additional functions and services a production music library may provide:

- The library signs complete, finished, recorded music from composers and songwriters. They do not sign lyrics only, live performance videos, works in progress, demo recordings, or music that has not been mixed and mastered. However, there are some music libraries that master the music themselves.
- Some libraries will send their composers briefs (assignments) or request music for specific projects. If it's a high-profile or lucrative project, the library may be more hands-on, offering some reference music and listening to the composer's rough recording to make sure the composer is on the right track.
- The library takes care of administrative duties, which may include:
  - Sending contracts to songwriters and composers
  - Ensuring that the music has a signed songwriter split sheet
  - Collecting banking information
  - Obtaining the composer's contact information
  - Filling out spreadsheets with the composer's information and updating it
- A library provides a description of each song or track in its catalog and tags it with metadata and keywords so music supervisors can find the music they need when they search the library's database. (See chapter 17 and appendices C through G.)
- A library often designs artwork for the collection (also known as an "album") to pitch to music supervisors. Some libraries request a biography and professional photo of the composer or songwriter to put on their websites. (Always have updated copies of these available.)
- If the library shares licensing fees (see chapter 19), they collect these fees and distribute them to the songwriters and composers.
- A library is in contact with the *Performing Rights Organizations* (PROs) to register the music and to ensure that royalties are being paid properly to the library and its writers. (See chapter 20).

I'VE BEEN SEARCHING: A STRATEGY TIP TO GET THROUGH THE DOOR

Production music libraries do a very good job of anticipating their clients' musical needs. However, there are times when they miss a style of music that hasn't become mainstream yet. Try to be aware of what's happening in the pop music world as well as the music licensing world. If there's an emerging style of music that a library does not have in its catalog yet, you can be the one to provide them with it.

HEY! READ THIS!

To understand the inner workings of production music and the companies that provide this music, do an Internet search for "production music libraries."

- Choose one, and look at how many different genres of music are available.
- Notice:
  - How each track is categorized and described.
  - What types of edits (30-second, 60-second) and alternate mixes are provided.
  - Whether the titles are creative or sound appropriate.
  - The credits for the composers, songwriters, and artists. Some production music libraries show this information, while others do not.
  - The artwork on the albums and the titles of the collections. These are important marketing tools.
- As an exercise to learn how the library's search engine works, imagine that you're a music supervisor looking for music for a project.
  - Search for a genre and feel, along with other descriptions: for example, "Fun, upbeat, pop-rock song with female vocals with edgy rock guitars."
- Take note of the placement credits to see the shows that use that library's music.
- See how many people are on the company's staff—particularly in sales and marketing.
- Check to see if there is contact information for the production staff or the person who accepts music submissions.
- Some libraries list the countries and distributors of their music. This is an indication of how far their marketing reach is.

The information you need to know about a particular production music library is right there on its website.

GO BIG OR GO BOUTIQUE?

There are large production music libraries with hundreds of thousands of songs and instrumental cues in their catalogs. Their music is placed around the world in all types of media.

Then there are the small libraries with a very specific collection of carefully curated music. These are known as *boutique music libraries*. Both of these business models have pros and cons to consider before signing your music.

For years we were tentative about putting our music in large libraries. We thought our music would be lost among the thousands of cues. However, speaking with a music supervisor changed our view. He said when he works on major feature films and network TV shows, he is given names of a few vetted, professional, reliable *large* libraries he can use. He isn't allowed to take music directly from composers who aren't in these *pre-approved vendor* libraries. He explained this was, in part, due to risks and potential lawsuits that have become common in recent years. Plus, boutique libraries have too limited a selection for his needs. On his recommendation, we decided to work with big major libraries, and it's been a great experience for us. However, it can be difficult to get your music into these libraries without a track record.

Another plus for being in a large library is that the company and its staff will promote and exploit the music, take care of the administration, provide artwork, send out emails announcing the release of the album, get worldwide distribution, and find royalties.

LET'S HEAR IT FOR THE LITTLE GUY!

That said, boutique libraries are wonderful as well. Many songwriters and composers like the fact they can interact with the library owner. Often, boutique libraries get specific projects from production companies. They assign these projects to their composers, and the music almost always goes directly into shows.

Here are examples of individual boutique music libraries that have a specialty or have developed a unique brand:

- Sparse music
- Music that was recorded authentically in a certain era or decade, such as music from the 1980s
- Music recorded using authentic instruments, performed by indigenous bands and artists in remote areas of the world
- High-energy, upbeat rock cues for sports programming
- Original, romantic instrumentals and songs for wedding and anniversary videos
- Public domain music in many different styles and genres for Christmas movies
- Over-the-top dramatic music for reality TV shows

These boutique libraries have gained a reputation for being the go-to library for their niche of music. It's somewhat like going to a jewelry store instead of a department store. They know their business because they focus on it and don't include other genres.

There are stand-alone boutique libraries as well as others that are distributed by larger libraries with a greater reach. This can provide more placement opportunities for your music.

EXCLUSIVE VERSUS NON-EXCLUSIVE

If you decide to pitch your music to a production music library, know that there are two types of libraries: those offering *exclusive agreements* to music creators and those offering *non-exclusive agreements*. There are advantages and disadvantages to each.

I'M YOURS, EXCLUSIVELY (NOT REALLY)

The music in an exclusive library is only available from that library; it is unique. Therefore, this music has more value because it can't be licensed anywhere else for a lower price.

An *exclusive agreement* does not mean that you, as a writer, must write only for one company. In the production music library world, you may write for several different exclusive libraries. The music you write is exclusive to each exclusive library. You cannot sign the same song or track to another company, and (usually) you can't pitch those exclusive songs to a music supervisor. If a writer signs music to an exclusive library and then gives the same music to another exclusive library, that would be a big, career-ending no-no. Here are some exclusive library business models:

- *Exclusive with a reversion.* A *reversion clause* allows a writer to regain control of their music after a period of time as specified in their contract. The time period varies, but it is customarily three to five years. After that, the writer is free to renew the contract or sign their music with a different library.
- *Semi-exclusive.* This arrangement is exclusive, but you can also *pitch to a project*. This means that the song will be signed only to this company; however, if, for example, you find your own opportunity with a music supervisor, you would be able to pitch the song.
- *Exclusive in perpetuity.* In this type of deal, the library retains ownership of the copyrights forever. The licensing fees are usually split with the writer; the writer receives their performance royalties. (See part 3.)
- *Work-made-for-hire.* This type of library pays the composer or songwriter an up-front fee to acquire the copyrights to the music in perpetuity. The writer usually retains the writer's share of the performance royalties. Some libraries keep the licensing fees, while others share them with the writer. (See part 3.)

With all of these types of music library scenarios, read through your contract carefully and thoroughly, and then clarify any questionable points with that company and your music attorney.

Exclusive libraries have the ability to distribute their catalogs throughout the world. Many of them have several offices in the United States and relationships with libraries, or sub-publishers, in other countries. *Sub-publishers* market the music of their U.S. partners and handle the administration in their respective territories. This is a major advantage. Foreign markets are a big area of opportunity for your music.

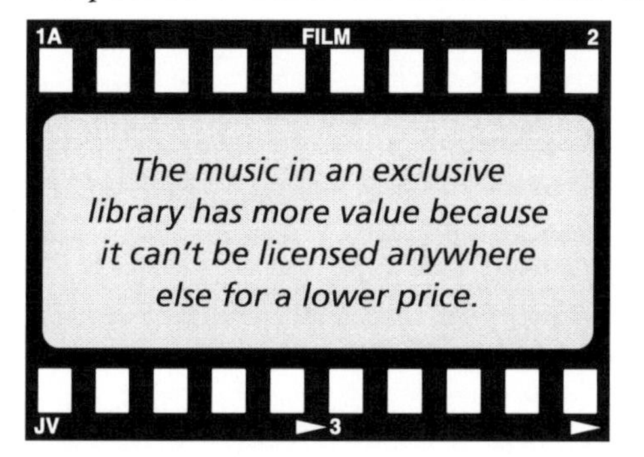

However, if an exclusive library fails to place your music, there's nothing you can do about it—if your deal with them is in perpetuity. This is why some writers prefer agreements that, after a specified time, allow a reversion of their music back to them.

Be very careful about signing the same style of music with many different music libraries. We've found a better strategy: If you are versatile in different styles, provide one library with a collection of ten to twenty tracks in one style, and then write and give a different company ten to twenty tracks in a different style.

One music library owner said he prefers his writers to not write the same style of music and put it in dozens of competing libraries. Another music library VP said it doesn't matter to him if a writer does this. Every company is different!

NON-EXCLUSIVE LIBRARIES: THIS ONE'S FOR YOU. AND YOU. AND YOU . . .

The practice of signing and retitling music with non-exclusive production music libraries is a controversial subject. One exclusive music library owner claims that non-exclusive retitling libraries can "cause confusion in the marketplace." The practice of *retitling* involves composers signing a piece of music with more than one library. This allows the composer to retain ownership of their copyrights.

When the cue is registered with royalty organizations, each library uses a different title. Sometimes this title is selected by the library, other times by the composer. This way, when a library places that piece of music and its title appears on the cue sheet, the library *should* receive their publisher's share of the performance royalties for the placements that library secured. (A *cue sheet* is a list of the songs and instrumentals that were used in a film or TV show; see chapter 20).

This results in the same piece of music being available from more than one source. Even though the proper title is used on the cue sheets, there is sometimes uncertainty among the non-exclusive libraries as to who should receive cue sheet credit. Non-exclusive libraries with some of the same songs in their catalogs often work with the same production companies. When a song that is in two different libraries is placed in a show, the wrong library may receive payment for the placement. If it can't be determined which publisher to pay, this may delay payments to everyone, including the writer.

THE GOOD, THE BAD, AND THE NON-EXCLUSIVE

As mentioned before, some composers prefer using a non-exclusive business model because it allows them to retain and control their copyrights. In addition, it offers the composer more marketing opportunities for their music. Non-exclusive libraries who choose this model do so because it's easier for them to build a large catalog of music quickly.

Non-exclusive libraries have difficulty getting worldwide distribution because most international publishers require that they be the only source for the music they represent in their territory. Therefore this limits the available international opportunities for non-exclusively retitled music to be placed.

Royalty collection societies around the world use audio detection technology services to track music placements (more on these services in chapter 20). If the same piece of music is available from more than one non-exclusive library, these services can't be used to collect royalties effectively. This results in less income for the non-exclusive libraries and their composers.

WHO'S ENTITLED TO THIS TITLE?

Many music supervisors have told stories about their disappointment when a song they thought was fresh and original had been, in fact, retitled and farmed out to various non-exclusive libraries.

The biggest problem with the practice of non-exclusive retitling is how it tends to devalue a composer's or songwriter's music. A music supervisor said he needed songs for a project and found what he was looking for on a non-exclusive library's website. He did more searching on the Internet and found the same songs on a different non-exclusive library's website for a much lower price. Needless to say, he licensed the songs from the cheaper library. If the songs had only been available from the first library, the writer would have made more money.

DECISIONS, DECISIONS, DECISIONS

Here's the best part: You don't have to choose just one route. You can have some music signed with non-exclusive libraries, and you can create more music and sign it exclusively. The choice is yours.

PRO TIPS . . . About Production Music Libraries

You don't need to know everybody, but you need to know *someone*. The music industry, especially the production music business, is incredibly small. The relationships you build truly need to be mutually beneficial, and they need to be authentic. And mutually beneficial doesn't necessarily mean financially beneficial. Find the people that fire up your soul, match your energy, and that you generally feel comfortable being yourself around. They'll be the longest lasting and most impactful for you as you navigate the business.

—**Morgan McKnight**, Executive Director of the Production Music Association

One of my friends calls production music a "get rich slow" plan. If you create enough of a catalog and it is relevant enough to stay in circulation, you can eventually build up a safety-net income that is less dependent on the vicissitudes of Hollywood's "flavor of the month." The biggest plus is that you're never out of work. If you make good quality music, someone will want to license it. If they don't, you probably need to work on your production, arranging, or compositional skills—all of which are invaluable.

—**Michael A. Levine**, Curator, Mpath

Understand the industry. Writing music for sync has specific parameters that can differ from writing for other industries, such as film scoring (writing to picture). It's still music, but it must conform to production music requirements to be used properly and efficiently.

—**Steve Barden**, Composer and Author

This field is called "production music," meaning "production" before "music."

—**Ken Jacobsen**, Composer and Producer

Before submitting your music, know who you are submitting to and how your submission might fit in with that catalog. I talk to composers all the time who say, "I want to get in with this big trailer library because I heard their composers make a lot of money." But the tracks they are submitting aren't trailer cues at all!

—**Derek Jones**, Director of Creative Services at Megatrax Production Music

CHAPTER 12
Sync Agencies

WHAT ARE SYNC AGENCIES?

Sync agencies, also known as *sync licensing companies* or *sync agents*, are companies that operate much like production music libraries: they get placements in all types of media. However, there are differences between the two:

- Sync agencies work with artists and bands. Music libraries work with composers and songwriters, although some libraries have separate artist catalogs. This does not mean sync agents *won't* work with composers and songwriters, but, overall, their business model is to help expose and promote up-and-coming artists and bands and exploit their work.
- Sync agencies will split a sync licensing fee with the artist. Many of these companies let the artist keep all of their writer's share of the PRO royalties and most, if not all, of the publisher's share. (Fees and royalties are discussed in part 3.)
- The deals can be non-exclusive or exclusive, either of which can have a reversion clause.
- The artist or band usually has control of their music to pitch to other projects.
- Sync agencies do not usually take the copyright of the artist's songs, whereas many production music libraries will keep the composer's copyright.

FANS ARE COOL

Sync agents want to see that artists and bands have a strong social media presence with a large following in the thousands. This is appealing because the music placement companies' clients can tap into an artist's fan base to cross-promote shows and products. If the artist gets a placement, they'll announce it to their fans on social media, driving interest further.

The sync agents prefer to sign artists and bands that are touring actively, doing house concerts or online performances, playing regularly in clubs or other venues, posting daily or weekly videos, interacting with fans, and constantly growing their fan base.

Their artists regularly release professionally recorded music. (Some music supervisors still like having artists' CDs.) These artists can provide music to promote and sell to fans and make available to music users. Successful artists and bands should have specific songs in their catalog that can be synced. These are versions that are inoffensive, family-friendly, and without profanity or language not allowed on broadcast TV.

THE ARTIST'S LIFE

If the artist has an interesting life backstory, that's even better. Among some of the stories we've heard: "I lived in my car and was homeless for five months." "I was down to my last ten dollars and couldn't pay my rent, but then I got a call from an indie record label that changed my life." "I sold my car to afford a trip to Nashville." "I ate cat food that I found on sale." "I busked on the boardwalk for three years before a homeless man told me my songs needed 'hooks.' That changed my life."

Some sync agents often like to see—and sometimes even encourage—artists and bands hooking up with a charitable organization or another brand so they can cross-promote or sponsor each other. Of course, this may present benefits as well as challenges on both sides. If an artist aligns with a particular brand, this could boost the artist's presence and be mutually beneficial for both parties. A sponsorship could defray costs on a tour. The artist's song may be used in online promotions or a major ad campaign, which would increase interest in their music.

However, if the brand is involved in a public relations disaster or is somehow damaged in any way, the artist may suffer the consequences and lose fans. Likewise, if the artist is involved in questionable activity or behavior, the brand may no longer want them onboard. It's a team effort, especially when it comes to business.

WHAT'S A "LEGITIMATE, AUTHENTIC" ARTIST OR BAND?

Over the years, we've met people who consider themselves "artists." When we visit their website, or look them up on social media, we take notice of how they are presenting themselves. Many times they have a few bookings at the local coffeehouse, an EP with three or four original songs on it, and a presence on social media with a few hundred followers. However, most also have a full-time, "real" day job; they're not a *full-time* singer-songwriter. Last, their artistic aesthetic is not contemporary, and there is no modern twist to their music.

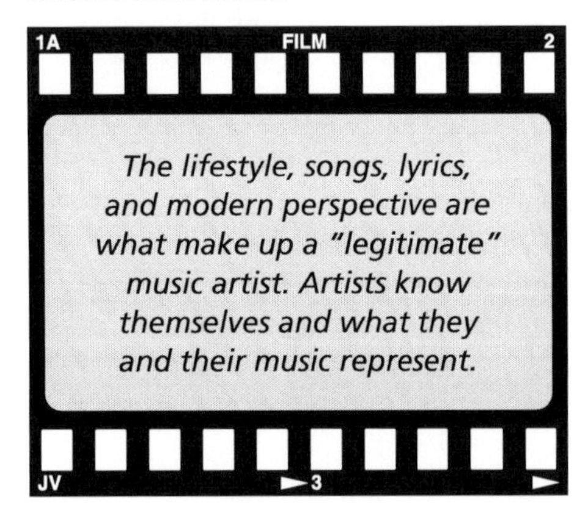

An "artist" can be of any age, as long as their music is either timeless or innovative, the artist is established, or there is a place for the artist's genre in the sync licensing world. The lifestyle, songs, lyrics, and modern perspective are what make up a "legitimate" music artist. Artists know themselves and what they and their music represent. They might have a captivating vocal delivery or write unique, never-before-heard lyrics. These artists are a music supervisor's dream—especially if their music is syncable.

Looking at sync agency websites, it's clear these companies want artists with a voice who have something to say and who present musical concepts in a new and different way. These artists integrate contemporary production techniques and are working with the top music producers in the industry. Perhaps the most obvious observation is that the artists and their music are contemporary and have an instantly recognizable vibe and brand. Any one of a highly vetted sync agency's artists has the potential to cross-sell a product to their fans if their song is featured on a trailer, promo, popular teen TV show, hot video game, new cell phone commercial, or major film. Millions of dollars may be at stake using this artist's music.

GETTING OVER BEING UNDERGROUND

When a favorite unknown, struggling, up-and-coming band or artist gets a high-end sync placement, some die-hard fans consider this "selling out." Years ago, selling out was frowned upon, and fans often took issue with artists and bands that they felt compromised their integrity just to make money or become a household name. This is no longer the case. A high-profile placement can be a turning point in the artist's career—and bring their music to the masses—if that's the direction they'd like to go. Established artists (and many formerly underground bands) see the value of receiving income from sync placements in addition to other music income.

IN THE LONG RUN

Although having a contemporary vibe can be an advantage when working with music placement companies, it is not required. Those composers and songwriters whose careers and track records have endured can collaborate with novice artists and bands, which may result in a desirable combination of broad musical experience mixed with fresh, modern ideas. However, there is a difference between writing songs for sync and writing "synchy" songs.

MUSIC SUPERVISORS CAN SMELL A "SYNCHY" SONG A MILE AWAY

We attended a music supervisor pitch and thought our song would be perfect for a commercial. The music supervisor listened to about thirty seconds, stopped, and said, "I like this, but it's too *synchy* for me." We asked her what she meant. She explained, "The song is trying too hard to sound like a song that was written for sync."

Have you ever had someone try too hard to be your friend even though you don't "connect" with each other? This person is complimenting you, but you don't find their words sincere or believable. That's what "synchy" meant to this music supervisor. It can also mean:

- The concept of the song is pandering and missing an air of authenticity
- The overall emotion of the song isn't real or genuine
- The lyrics have a cheesy, fake quality
- The singer's voice is not convincing, doesn't quite fit, or sounds like a demo singer instead of an artist

Listen to and analyze the songs on the websites of several sync agencies, music publishers, and production music libraries. Take notice of the lyrics and themes, the performance, and the production of the songs. Imagine this music being used in a film, TV show, or commercial. You will find some that sound authentic and others that sound synchy. There is a place in the sync world for both authentic and synchy, but you need to know which term better describes your music.

LET'S MAKE A DEAL

So you're an authentic artist or band and are starting to garner some attention: Your shows are selling out. Your fans can't get enough of your music. You've got the fascinating backstory. You are now prepared and ready for the sync agent to find you. Only . . . it probably won't happen that way. You need to find the right fit for *you*. There are a lot of sync agencies, and some may be following you on social media, but be mindful of some of the deals you may be offered.

Most sync agencies offer what is called an "artist-friendly deal." This type of deal means you will retain ownership of your music while they represent it. You can control what happens to your songs and how they are placed. For example, an artist may have a certain social or political view and doesn't want their song used to support an opposing view. They can demand that their song not be used for those types of media coverage. Another example: an artist just finished going through rehab for an alcohol addiction, and a beer company wants to use their song in a major ad campaign. The artist may feel that this placement might send the wrong message to their fans and declines the offer. This would *not* be possible if their music were in a production music library, in which case, if you sign it, they can use it, and you'll have no say in the matter.

Another part of an artist-friendly deal is that the artist keeps their writer's share and some, or all, of the publisher's share of the PRO royalties. As discussed earlier, this is not a typical deal with production music libraries. In addition, sync agencies do not do *blanket licenses*, as many production music libraries do. This means there is always a licensing fee to split between the sync agency and the artist. (More about blanket licenses in chapter 19.)

Consider the following before signing with a sync agency:

- What types of placements does this company get?
- Do they highlight their placements on their website?
- What do their social media posts look like? Who is following them, and what type of news do they announce?
- Do they work with high-end ad agencies and TV and film production companies?
- Do they get placements in shows or media that are of interest to you and your fans?
- Are there any well-known artists and music producers on their roster, and, if so, what are their credits?

- Would your music be a good fit in their catalog?
- Do they have several staff members who work solely on getting placements (a sales and marketing team), or is it a small company run by one or two people?

Doing research is essential. Something to consider is whether the company has few or no placements listed on their website. This could mean the company is new or not established and may not have the connections it takes to find great sync placements.

However, as with a new production music library, going with a new sync agency can be a great way to get started in the business. They need content, and the artist or composer needs an opportunity. Weigh your options.

THROUGH THE YEARS: REVERSION CLAUSES

A final part of the deal to consider is the all-important reversion clause. This is a specified period of time in which the company will represent your music. It's important to ask yourself, Can you regain control of your music after a reasonable amount of time? What is reasonable—ninety days? One year? Three years? Five? This time period may or may not be negotiable. We also recommend that you work with a qualified music attorney on deal points such as this. We have music signed to one sync agent who asks us in writing whether we'd like to renew our contract each year. Another company will let us remove our songs from their catalog if we give them thirty days' written notice; otherwise, the songs are renewed automatically from month to month. Every company is different.

Just as a reminder: in contrast, many production music library deals are in perpetuity.

MONEY MAKES THE (SYNC) WORLD GO AROUND

There are several tiers of sync agencies, and each has a different business model. The fees vary greatly in the sync world, but the numbers below will give you a rough idea of what to expect. Here are some examples of different tiers:

- Low-tier sync agencies work with reality TV shows, local ad agencies, and social media companies. The licensing fees for these types of placements range from $100 to $1,000, or perhaps a little more. The licensing fee is split between the sync agency and the artist. The artist would still receive their PRO royalties. The lower-tier sync agencies can be a good way for the artist to build up credits while making some extra money. (More about income in part 3.)
- Mid-tier sync agencies often work with network TV shows, commercials, high-end streaming services, indie films, and place music in promos, films, and various other media. Their licensing fees range from $1,000 to $5,000. Again, these fees are split among the artist and the company. The mid-tier companies like artists who have had some type of success or have a steady track record of getting placements, who are serious and starting to get traction, whose fan base is growing, whose songs are on streaming services, and who have a distinct sound.
- High-tier sync agencies work on blockbuster feature films, high-end video games, national commercials, film trailers, major TV networks, and other such media. These fees can range from $5,000 to as much as $100,000 or more, depending on the project, the song, and the artist. These companies sign the crème de la crème: Business-minded, driven, prolific, dedicated, hard-working, touring, breaking artists and bands, as well as those who are well established.

Doing research will offer clues as to what tier a sync agency is. Licensing fee information won't be posted on their websites; however, you can see the kinds of placements they get on their credits page and the types of artists they sign.

PRO TIPS . . . About Sync Agencies

Research the particular catalog and artists/writers that a company represents. Would you and your music be unique and stand out, or would you be redundant to what they already have? Don't compete for opportunities with similar artists on the same roster. You want to be the go-to for your kind of music. Plus, companies want to diversify what they can offer their clients; they don't want to sign more of the same.

—**Marc Caruso**, CEO & Co-founder of Angry Mob Music

Authenticity is what I look for first and foremost in a new artist/writer. A true artist/writer will have their own style, their own vibe. They won't be trying to sound and look like someone else. While others may inspire them, a new artist/writer needs to stand on their own and be true to the creative soul within. I love the discovery of new talent; it gives me hope for the music industry, and it is such a great source of enjoyment for me, personally.

—**Teri Nelson Carpenter**, President and CEO of Reel Muzik Werks, Past President of the AIMP, Executive Vice President of the Independent Music Publishers International Forum

I have direct inbound coming daily from production libraries, placement companies, labels, and publishers. So, I always stress to artists that, while a personal relationship with supervisors could potentially land you a sync, it's rare that we reach out to a single artist. It's much better to be vocal with your sync agent so that you're always on the top of the list when they're sharing with us.

—**Trygge Toven**, Music Supervisor

Regarding some of the most-requested genres or types of music, my company tends to place a lot of contemporary pop, rock, hip hop, and, surprisingly, classical and jazz. Some unusual music genre requests we've received include Norwegian folk songs, vintage klezmer, Dutch folk trio—and that was just this past year!

—**Tanvi Patel**, Owner and CEO of Crucial Music Corporation

As creators of original works, understand who's in the driver's seat; it's a key distinction that drives real opportunity in the music industry. Ultimately, top-tier synch opportunities point to authentic music. Knowing that should be a relief to composers who want to focus on what they do best.

—**Juan Carlos Quintero,** Composer and Producer, Moondo Music LLC

Getting your first sync placement is very exciting, and further validation comes when you see how—and where—your music is being used on your royalty statements. One of my favorite placements is for a song I co-wrote with friend of mine in 1987 that got a placement on a recent Netflix show!

—**Brian Thomas Curtin**, Composer and Songwriter, Eaglestone Music

CHAPTER 13

Music Publishing Companies

PUBLISHING COMPANIES: HOW THEY WORK

The primary function of production music libraries and sync agencies is licensing music. However, this is not true of most music publishing companies. Although they have sync licensing departments, their main goal is representing hit songs and having record label artists record them.

They also sign and develop their writers, exploit songs in their catalog that have the potential to be licensed for sync, and perform administrative tasks associated with collecting and distributing money. Though their focus is on writers who create full songs, they also sign track producers and topliners.

Some publishers have staff members who interact regularly with their writers. They offer feedback on songs and set up co-writing appointments. Other publishers are less involved creatively with their writers.

In addition to the sync department, many music publishers have their own production music library. However, their production music library is often a separately named entity, housed in a different building, operates with its own staff, and has an independent website.

There are three types of music publishers: major, midsized, and independent—more commonly known as "indie."

THE MAJOR ATTRACTION

Major publishing companies have offices in dozens of countries, giving them great reach and marketing ability. They each represent tens of thousands of songwriters and over a million songs. Most of the publishing deals are *co-publishing agreements.* This means the songwriter owns 50% of the copyright and receives 50% of the publisher royalties. There is customarily a 10% administrative fee that the publisher receives.

Some of the iconic copyrights held by major publishing companies are among the best-known songs of all time. In comparison with most music libraries and sync agencies, these companies are huge.

The function of the sync licensing department at the major publishing companies is to find sync placements for the hit songs in their catalogs. Most of these songs are written by established songwriters. Though they may not have been written with the intent of being synced, some of these songs find success by being licensed. These sync licensing departments do not usually look for songwriters to write songs that are intended to be synced. Instead, they go through their catalog to find appropriate and licensable songs to be pitched, and then licensing fees are negotiated. They also respond to requests to license these songs. (That's right—the music supervisors come to *them.*)

DREAM BIG

Because of the clout of the iconic copyrights the major publishers represent, music supervisors know that the licensing fee for a hit song from these catalogs is going to be high. The majors know the value of these coveted songs and that this music is unavailable from any other company, which gives them an advantage in licensing fee negotiations. These major publishing companies are not reluctant to reject any offer they deem to be too small. If a music supervisor's budget for their current project is not large enough, they will need to find a more affordable alternative, which provides opportunities for other music publishers, sync agencies, and production music libraries to offer something with a similar vibe from their catalogs.

The major publishing companies take care of the administrative duties, which can be daunting for most songwriters. The publishers have a large staff whose tasks include:

- Registering the music with the PROs (see chapter 20)
- Pitching, exploiting, and promoting the music
- Collecting and distributing money
- Overseeing rights management (including who owns the copyrights)

WANTED: SINGER-SONGWRITERS

It is advantageous to a major publisher when a songwriter is able and willing to perform the songs they write, because it helps to promote the song. As a result, the record company and concert venue booking companies can also benefit from the songwriter's performances. Publishers want to see that the songwriter has a strong social media presence, because this will propel the song too.

Songwriters signed to a major publisher have a unique advantage of being able to write with other songwriters signed with the company. Many publishers set up writers' camps as a way for songwriters, producers, and artists to interact with one another. A lot of magic comes from these events.

A major publisher will sign a songwriter for an exclusive deal, and this includes writing for sync projects. This arrangement usually incorporates an *advance* payment (against royalties) for a term in the range of two to three years. If a newly signed writer has a proven track record of success, the terms of the deal may be even more favorable.

Unlike when writing for music libraries, the songwriter can only sign with, and write for, *one* major publisher at a time. Once a songwriter signs an exclusive deal with a major publisher, all of the songs they write in the future during the term of their contract will be co-owned and represented by the publisher. However, the writer will retain their writer's share of performance royalties. (More on this in chapter 20.) Most other income will initially go toward recouping the up-front advance payment they received.

The major publishers find songwriters in many ways: on social media, attending concerts, at music conventions and in songwriter groups, and via introductions through managers, attorneys, record producers, PRO representatives, co-writers, and even other artists. They do not respond, however, to *unsolicited* contact.

There are only a handful of major publishing companies, so it's a long shot getting your foot in their door. Your odds are better if you have a hit song, a song that was recorded by a well-known artist (known as a "cut"), significant placement credits, or experience co-writing with established writers or producers.

NOT-SO-BIG IS MAYBE JUST RIGHT

Midsized publishing companies, sometimes referred to as *mini-major publishers* or *major indie publishers*, are what would be expected, given their name: their catalogs are not quite as large as the majors, but their functions are similar. Midsized publishing companies:

- Sign writers exclusively and may offer advances
- Typically co-own the copyrights they represent
- Have a department that handles sync, though they focus on getting songs cut by recording artists
- Often represent iconic hit song copyrights, despite being smaller than the majors
- Usually have offices in foreign territories

Unlike the majors, however, midsized publishing companies:

- Have smaller song catalogs
- Have smaller staffs

Some midsized publishers have administration with major publishers around the world. Many midsized publishers will grow and become harder to distinguish from majors. It is also difficult to sign with midsized publishers, but they may be more approachable than majors.

THE INDEPENDENT'S DAY IS HERE

The *independent publishing companies*, or *indie publishers*, unlike the major and midsized publishers, tend to have smaller song catalogs. However, because of their reduced size, independent publishers can offer more flexibility in terms of their deals. Decisions are made frequently by an individual with authority instead of by a committee. Indies own some of the copyrights they represent but not all. Sometimes they offer a share of the publishing royalties and may or may not offer an advance.

Indies often have valuable, established relationships with music supervisors who like the idea of giving these hidden-gem songs some exposure or breaking the artists who record them with a high-end placement. Usually the licensing fee negotiations are more flexible with independent publishers.

Their independent attitude puts them more within reach for writers; however, a successful track record in the music business is preferable.

HOW WILL I KNOW?

There is a lot of information to digest regarding the types of companies to work with to get your music synced, and there is more than one path available. Here are some factors to consider:

- How do you feel about retaining ownership of your copyrights? Copyrights are valuable assets, especially if some have gotten placements. If you want to keep them, you may not be interested in signing with a work-for-hire music library or a major publisher.
- How do you want to make your money? Some composers and songwriters make a comfortable living having a few tracks or songs signed to a high-end company, while others have hundreds of tracks and songs signed to dozens of companies that get hundreds of placements. Yet over time both may earn about the same amount of money. It can be a *value* or *volume* business.
- Do you primarily write songs or instrumentals? Many publishers and sync agencies do not usually sign purely instrumental composers, but most production music libraries do. (They will, however, sign track producers and beatmakers.)
- Do you produce and record your music? Music libraries often prefer composers and songwriters who can easily deliver finished, broadcast quality recordings.
- How prolific are you? Some companies insist on regular output from the writers they sign.
- Are you an artist? The sync agencies are always interested in artists who also understand writing music for sync.

A CHANGE WOULD DO YOU GOOD

You may become known as the go-to composer for dramedy cues or the songwriter who specializes in upbeat dance music or the artist who is best at creating moody trailer songs. You can be all of the above; that's the beauty of the sync world.

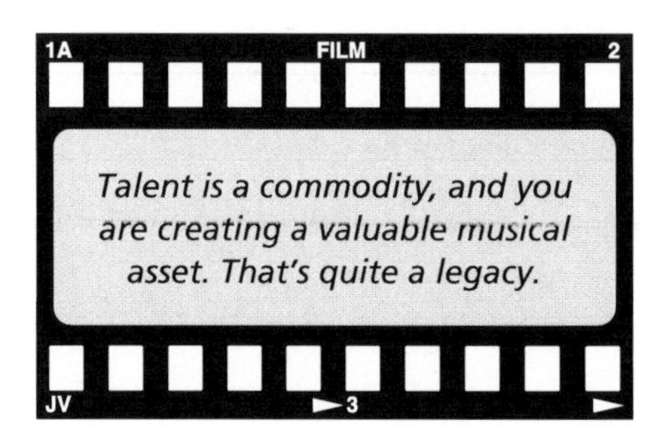

Working with different styles, or with various collaborators, can lead to some great music. It may be beneficial for you to branch out or experiment with other genres. Some artists write and produce under a pseudonym or different creative persona (ever heard of "Eivets Rednow," "Sasha Fierce," "Percy Thrillington," "Nils Sjöberg," or "Chris Gaines"?). Some composers rebrand themselves for a particular project. Some successful songwriters and artists are able to change their style constantly and continue to write hits and get sync for decades.

If you are professional, prolific, and patient, the dividends can pay off, hopefully for the rest of your life—and throughout your heirs' lives too. Talent is a commodity, and you are creating a valuable musical asset. That's quite a legacy.

WHY "UNSOLICITED MUSIC" IS NOT ACCEPTABLE

Perhaps you've seen books and music magazines provide lists of music publishers from around the world. However, you'll see one phrase after most of the entries: "No unsolicited music (or material), please." *Unsolicited* means the music was not requested and it will be either shredded or returned to the sender unopened.

That phrase is frustrating to read, especially for new songwriters. There are reasons companies don't accept unsolicited material—the biggest being the potential of a copyright infringement lawsuit. And no one wants that.

If a publisher later signs or exploits a song in their catalog that resembles an unsolicited song, the songwriter who sent the unsolicited song might file a lawsuit disputing the song's authorship. This potential liability is eliminated if the publisher never received and listened to the unsolicited song in the first place. However, there are some ways around the no-solicitation policy:

- Go on the company's website. Email them to ask permission to send a link to your music. Sometimes it can be as simple as that. We've gotten into several companies this way. You can also try calling the company to ask permission. Get the correct name of the person who handles new songwriter inquiries. Do not send a generic letter addressed "To Whom This May Concern."
- Write a snail mail letter asking permission to send a song or two (but no more than three songs *ever*). This approach is traditional, but some publishers prefer to first receive a brief introductory letter, because it shows a level of respect.
- Do research on social media. Find someone in the company who may have something in common with you, and establish a rapport. After a few email exchanges or phone calls, invite the person for coffee or lunch when you come to their town. *Then* ask permission to send them your music. (Do you see a pattern here? Ask permission, not forgiveness!)
- If the person or company with whom you'd like to work will be at a music convention, do everything in your power to attend. We signed a deal writing for a daytime talk show after attending a music convention, and it was life-changing.
- This tip is more expensive and trickier, but it is beneficial: Find a qualified music attorney (or agent or manager) to represent you for this purpose, and have *them* ask permission. (Plus, the music attorney can help you with negotiating the contract.) Ideally the music attorney would know someone at the company, but sometimes just the mere fact that you have professional representation is impressive enough to help you get your foot in the door.

PRO TIPS . . . About Music Publishing Companies

We as publishers want to commit our time and resources to those who are already 100% committed. When signing a new songwriter, the most important thing for us is a unique and special *musical voice*. It may sound like a cliché, but when you hear and recognize raw talent, it sparks an internal fire that compels you to become involved and do all you can to support and develop that talent. The other important things are drive and determination. We want to work with songwriters who have no choice but to write songs and who show their determination to succeed no matter what comes their way.

—**Michael Eames**, President of PEN Music Group, Inc.

Composers should think like a publisher and have their *administration* in order to offer music users *easy clearances*.

—**Juan Carlos Quintero**, Composer and Producer, Moondo Music LLC

I want to see a sense of drive and purpose in a new artist/writer, along with a willingness to work hard and a creative who is pleasant to work with.

—**Teri Nelson Carpenter**, President and CEO of Reel Muzik Werks, Past President AIMP, Executive Vice President of the Independent Music Publishers International Forum

CHAPTER 14

Pitching Directly to Music Supervisors

WHAT IS A MUSIC SUPERVISOR, AND WHAT DO THEY DO?

In the sync world, *music supervisors* are the people who help find songs and music to place into media projects. However, a music supervisor does much more than listen to and find music. Ideally they must:

- Be passionate about music, and possess a wide range of knowledge about various genres.
- Be familiar with music history by knowing which songs, artists, and styles of music were popular in different eras, including current music trends.
- Find music that works and fits within the confines of the project's budget.
- Use their connections to work directly and communicate with producers, directors, music editors, ad agencies, and production companies.
- Have working relationships with competent, professional songwriters, composers, artists, bands, publishing companies, record labels, sync agencies, and production music libraries.
- Communicate well with all parties at all times (they are the control tower!).
- Be able to clear music. This means:
    - Find who represents the copyrights and obtain the necessary permissions from all parties, including:
        - The owners of the composition (songwriters and publishers).
        - The owner of the master recording.
    - Negotiate a license and a fee with the above owners.
    - Seek approval from the artist and anyone who performed on the recording, dependent on the terms of the recording contract.
    - Make certain that no other composition or sample of another recording was used in creating the music being licensed.
- With absolute certainty, verify whether or not a piece of music is in the public domain *worldwide*.
- Confirm that all loose ends are tied up and contracts are signed (this is when one-stop licensing and clearance is most helpful).
- Follow up to make sure payments are distributed.
- Check that cue sheets are completed properly and filed.

Most music supervisors work independently, either for their own music supervision company or for production companies small and large. If they do not work for the production company, they are paid a lump sum per project. They are fans of music and the people who create it and have your best interests at heart.

Music supervisors are different than music coordinators or music directors. For example, a music coordinator or director at a production music library may assist a client with music selections and know their company's catalog, but they don't have the additional duties that a music supervisor may have.

DESPERATELY SEEKING MUSIC SUPERVISORS

Where can you find these elusive music supervisors? When we started going to events and joined music organizations, we discovered many of them participated on the panels. The more events we attended, the more likely we were to find and meet music supervisors. The lesson? Go where the "supes" go.

One of the great achievements of many music supervisors is to discover or "break" a band or artist. If you are a composer, songwriter, artist, or member of a band, here are some additional ways to research music supervisors and their projects:

- Watch the end credits of TV shows and films.
- Do an Internet search for "movie TV database"; the music supervisors for most projects are listed on these sites.
- Follow them on social media; many will give hints about the types of projects they're working on and even the types of songs they're looking for.
- Join and support the organization for professional music supervisors, and get on their email lists; some have conventions and special events throughout the year, in person or online.

CENTERFIELD: THROWING OUT THE FIRST PITCH

A music supervisor's time is very valuable. Many have established successful working relationships with composers and artists. If you are one of these fortunate people, congratulations! You knocked it out of the park.

If you're not yet connected with a music supervisor but would like to be, here are suggestions to help you hit a home run with them:

- Music that is "vibey" is a music supervisor's dream. This is music that within the first few seconds creates a mood and feeling, even before the singing starts.
- Always send the best representation of your music, which would be sending broadcast quality, complete songs. They must be finished, mixed, and professionally mastered. No roughs, lyrics only, or demos. No exceptions, unless you were requested by the music supervisor to send a rough demo.
- Send a link to one or two songs that are *appropriate for the show or project* on which they are working. Do not send more than this unless you are asked to do so.
- Streamable, downloadable links are always preferred. Make sure the link won't expire—at least for several months (or a year). Whatever you do, *never* attach WAV or AIFF files or MP3s to the email unless you are given permission to do this.

Here are suggestions to avoid striking out with music supervisors:

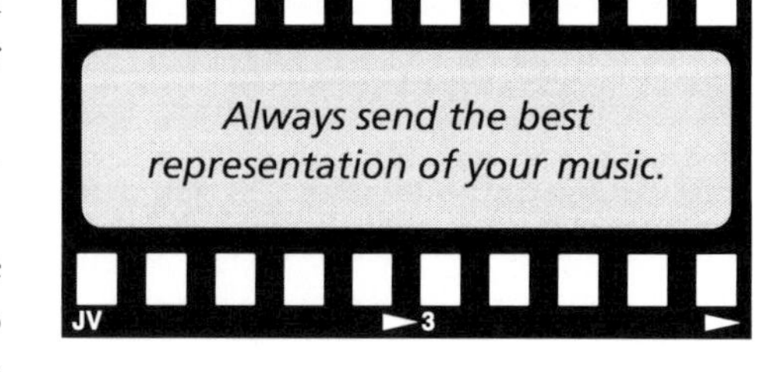

- Do not ask any music supervisor, "What are you working on?" This question is the ultimate instant deal breaker. They expect you to do research and know their current projects.
- Do not pitch music that does not fit the music supervisor's current projects.
- Do not pitch any music for which you do not have signed releases or that you do not have permission to pitch. If you pitch something that doesn't fit or that has entanglements, you risk the chance that the music supervisor won't open emails from you again.
- Do not ask for feedback on your music from the music supervisor, and *never* ask for any materials to be sent back. Often music supervisors keep music for years—decades, even. If they are a fan of your music, it will be forever on their virtual shelf, just waiting for the right opportunity.

HEY! READ THIS!

Music supervisors prefer music that is not too lyrically *on the nose*. That means the song is describing what's literally taking place in the scene, which is not desirable. Rather, the song should be about the feelings or emotions portrayed in the scene. For example, in a scene, rain is falling. A woman sits by the fire and calls her friend, but the phone just rings. A song with lyrics about "rain" or "sitting by the fire" or "hearing the phone ring" would be too on the nose. However, a song about loneliness, rejection, uncertainty, or wondering what happened would likely be selected.

Again, be mindful that you are developing a working relationship with the music supervisor. If your music fits into their current project, they will let you know. If you don't hear from them, don't take it personally. It may mean that your song wasn't quite right for what was needed at that time; perhaps they'll use it later. However, it is a good idea to follow up with a brief, polite email thanking them for the opportunity and their time. Leave it at that and move on. Professionalism and avoiding awkwardness go a long way in the music business.

If your music is selected for a project and you are contacted by the music supervisor, it's now time to move to the next level: talking about money.

EVERYTHING IS NEGOTIABLE (WELL, SOMETIMES)

One thing to keep in mind when negotiating a licensing fee is that you can always ask for more; however, most budgets are inflexible. As much as a music supervisor may *want* to give you more money, their hands may be tied. If you find yourself in this type of situation, it's good to be flexible on the licensing fee. Be mindful that people working on a project usually have a tight deadline and don't have time to go back and forth, haggling over a licensing fee. The music supervisor will appreciate it when the artist plays ball. Then they will (hopefully) remember you in the future, especially if your song was one they wanted to use and you acted professionally. If it's a fair deal and you are likely to get some more sales and gain additional fans of your music, then it's a win-win situation.

GO YOUR OWN WAY

Approaching music supervisors and representing your music yourself is not impossible, but it is not easy to do. We've gotten several opportunities over the years to pitch a song or write a custom song for a music supervisor. Yes, it's a thrill, but it dawned on us: Instead of spending a lot of time writing a specific song and then hoping for *one* opportunity with *one* music supervisor for *one* specific project to pan out, it made a lot more sense for us to write several pieces of music and then put those in high-end production music libraries for multiple placements. It can be fun and challenging to write a song for a specific brief, but if the opportunity doesn't pan out, you're left with a song that may not go anywhere. That's not a good use of time for us.

A successful songwriter we know uses the opposite strategy: She spends six hours a day, five days a week, pitching her catalog of over a thousand songs. Her relentless persistence eventually pays off, and she gets incredible placements, not to mention licensing fees. The upside is that she gets to keep 100% of the income, but she admits it is a lot of hard work. However, she has less time to create new music. Even though she receives briefs and knows many music supervisors, there is still a great deal of rejection, but that doesn't faze her in the least.

HEY! READ THIS!

A music supervisor for a big sports network once invited us to his office and listened to our tracks. After hearing a minute or so of one of our sad, poignant, heartfelt cues, he stopped the music and offered us one of the best pieces of advice we've ever gotten. He said, "You're probably wondering what I'm listening for. I'm imagining this cue being placed in various situations. This track could be used under images of a team that just had an incredible loss. Or it could be used in a scene about a beloved coach who just died. Or it could be used as a marathoner, running in slow motion, is struggling to cross the finish line. It could be used to show a star football player getting a career-ending injury—and so on. This is what you want to write: music that can be placed over and over." To this day, we keep his advice in mind whenever we write a cue. Write highly placeable music that has multiple types of uses, and it will fit into many different scenes. This is one of the hallmarks of writing licensable music.

HELP ME

If you are not comfortable with the business side of music but you'd like to pitch directly to music supervisors, there are *publishing administration* services available that can handle many of the various registration duties with copyright and PROs for you. They generally take a commission of about 15%. Signing an *administration agreement* with a publishing administrator allows a songwriter to retain full ownership of their composition(s) while the publishing administrator oversees the business responsibilities. Sometimes these companies are full-service publishers, and others simply perform the necessary administrative tasks.

Give careful consideration to this decision. Registering your music with domestic royalty organizations involves a small learning curve, after which doing it regularly requires minimal effort. In most cases, domestic royalty organizations also collect international payments for you. Be cognizant of the terms of any agreements you sign, and make sure you are aware of your options.

Understand what is involved in these processes before deciding to handle them yourself or have someone else manage them for you. Then, if any of these tasks seems too cumbersome for you, delegating them might be a good idea.

PRO TIPS . . . About Pitching Directly to Music Supervisors

The songwriters who attend songwriter camps have the ears of the music supervisors who took part and are building relationships with them. They are also continuing to write to the briefs from the camp with the other attendees, so not only do they now have new people to write with and pitch to, they have been given real opportunities to find a home for their music—and to make money from it.

—**Pamela Sheyne**, Songwriter, Singer, and Mentor, and Co-founder of SongWriterCamps

What do I wish artists and bands knew before pitching their music to me? That we're fans first and foremost!

—**Trygge Toven**, Music Supervisor

Always remember it's your job to help the music supervisor, not the other way around. When pitching your song, try to think, "Is this song going to help the supervisor put a strong emotion into the images?" When you help the music supervisor, the music supervisor will help you.

—**Suzan Koç**, Publisher and Songwriting Mentor

People shopping music cannot demand too much feedback. During "crunch time" with a final mix deadline or juggling multiple projects—which seems to be almost all of the time—the music supervisor's time and energy are so strained, they need space. I know it is frustrating to pitch music to hundreds of people and not get much feedback, but that is just the nature of the beast, unfortunately. There is very little time to give feedback about music that was not right for a project. With today's compressed deadlines, especially in television, music supervisors are lucky to have time to complete the business of the songs they are licensing for the project.

—**John Houlihan**, Music Supervisor

When pitching music to music supervisors, *only* pitch *exactly* what is asked for, *immediately*.

—**Tanvi Patel**, Owner and CEO of Crucial Music Corporation

While music supervisors can easily utilize production music services to supply a volume of music, they also know great music can come from any source.

—**Juan Carlos Quintero**, Composer and Producer, Moondo Music LLC

As someone who also pitches music every day, I completely understand how difficult it is for young composers and artists to break through to music supervisors, music libraries, record labels, and publishers. Composers need to understand how busy the people they are pitching to are. I can't speak for the bigger libraries, but in our case, we all wear many hats. Previewing new music is just a small percentage of what we do. Thus getting to the point in all correspondence is crucial.

—**Ron Goldberg**, Vice President of Manhattan Production Music

CHAPTER 15

Networking and Building Relationships

THAT'S WHAT IT'S ALL ABOUT

Being in the music business is not just about writing good music; you'll have to do some networking and marketing as well, especially in the beginning. So, how do you get your music out there? You can put it on social media and streaming sites. You can enter songwriting contests and singing competitions. You can go on tour—or perform at local venues or house concerts. These are all fine, but you probably won't get any *licensing* opportunities. To find those, it takes research and reaching out to music industry people.

WE BUILT THIS CITY

You don't need to live in a major music city to have success marketing your music in the sync world. However, you will need to know people who have connections to the decision-makers. Since a lot of film, advertising, and TV production occurs in Los Angeles, New York, Chicago, and Atlanta, most sync placement companies have offices in these cities.

If you live in or near these cities, find the organizations that cater to the sync music communities, and then join and support them. If you don't live near one of these cities, find opportunities to visit them while music conventions and other industry events are being held. While you don't have to be where the action is, whoever is representing your music should have a presence there and know the music licensing decision-makers. It's up to you to write marketable music *and* make these connections. How do you find these connections?

JUST SHOW UP

One of the best ways is by attending music conferences, either in person or online. There are dozens of events, but the most valuable ones offer panels, workshops, listening sessions, and information pertaining to the sync world. By attending these events, you may:

- Meet music industry people face-to-face and get to know who's who. Many events have mixers and gatherings before or after the event for networking opportunities.
- Find collaborators for your creative and business teams.
- Become aware of other events and professional organizations.
- Play your music at feedback sessions.
- Pitch your music or have one-on-one meetings with publishers and music supervisors.
- Learn about the various aspects of the music business with which you are not familiar.

In-person music conferences can be costly and time-consuming, so do your research to find the best fit for you. Some conferences have thousands of attendees, and this may be overwhelming for first-timers. Other conferences have only a few dozen attendees with personal interactions among the panelists. We've attended hundreds of events over the years, both large and small, and here are some tips:

- Make certain the event has a good reputation and is well organized.
- Have a defined goal as to why you would like to attend this conference.

- Research the panelists and look at photos so you will recognize them if given the chance to speak with them.
- Start a conversation with the person sitting next to you, as you're likely to see them again throughout the event.

HEY! READ THIS!

If you want to catch fish, then "Go where the fish go," says a successful hit songwriter. This phrase means, if you need to find a music collaborator, lyricist, singer, musician, or producer, make it a point to go to music events and talk to people. If you're looking for a music supervisor, music publisher, music attorney, PRO representative, or other music industry professional, then join a music trade organization that has monthly meetings or annual conventions. Industry people attend these events and are on the boards of these organizations. They are approachable, can answer your questions, and appreciate composers and songwriters who support these organizations. You don't have to live in a major music city, but visiting regularly can benefit your career. More about these resources are listed in part 4.

GETTING TO KNOW YOU

Networking is scary . . . uncomfortable . . . difficult . . . Nonsense! Take it from the two shyest people ever to walk the earth: Networking is fun. Networking is a subtle form of marketing that lets people know who you are and what you do. We used to dread it, but after we read several books about it, our perspective changed. Now it's not some distasteful, awkward thing we have to endure. Instead, it's a chance to meet new *friends.* We talk about music and share information. Discover different writing processes. Pass along production tips. Find out what's happening in the music industry. It's all good.

Figure 15.1. *Just a few of the many name badges from conferences and events the Marinos have attended over the years.* (Source: *T. Bannister and M. Weddleton)*

Networking does not mean you have to meet *every* person in the room at *every* event. It may be beneficial getting to know just a few people at a time and having meaningful conversations. We've found this approach works well: quality over quantity. Some people who made a special trip to an event, however, may feel like it's their one shot to meet as many people as possible. Do whatever is comfortable for you.

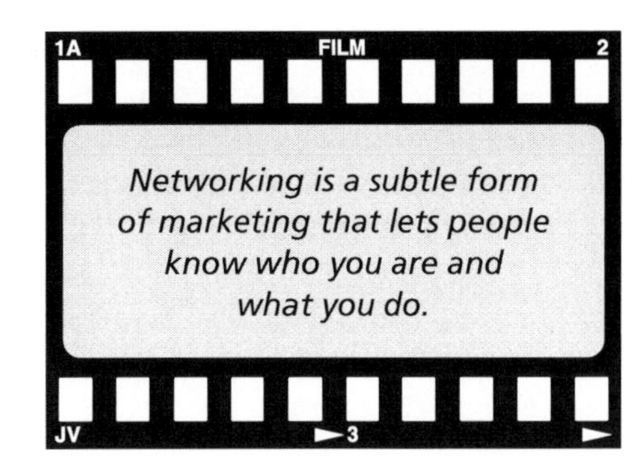

NICE TO MEET YA

One piece of particularly helpful advice is to write, memorize, and practice saying an introduction of yourself. Here is an example of a brief, 10-second introduction when meeting a person for the first time at a music event:

> Hello, I'm Mike Mixer. I write and produce hip hop dramedy cues for reality TV shows. What's your name, and what do you do?

Instantly, we know Mike's name, that he's a composer and producer, the style of music he writes, and where it's getting placed. He's also considerate and asking about you. Now you both have information about each other that you can use to start a conversation.

It's also good to write a longer *elevator speech* for music industry people. This is your 30-second pitch about who you are and what you do. Your pitch doesn't actually have to take place in an elevator; it can be anywhere a planned or chance meeting may occur. (And, yes, we have in fact met many hit songwriters, famous composers, producers, music publishers, and future co-writers in elevators over the years.)

Imagine yourself getting the opportunity to speak to someone who could potentially change your career. What would you say? How would you say it? You have thirty seconds, maybe less, to make an impression. Here's an example:

> Hi, Lizzie Library. It's a pleasure meeting you. I'm a big fan of your production music library. My name is Cameron Composer from Any Town, USA. I write guitar-based tension music with contemporary beats, and I'm interested in submitting my music to you. I visited your company's website and saw you get placements in shows that use this type of music. Mine is a little different, with more edge. Would it be okay to contact you to set up a meeting?

This elevator speech illustrates:

- The composer has done his research. He knows the name of the music library owner and recognized her face. If you do Internet searches, you can find photos of just about anyone, especially if they've been on panels.
- The composer describes the main type of music he writes in an easy-to-understand way. He also describes how his music is distinguished from the music that is already in the library. This is how he stands out from the crowd.
- He knows what type of music the library is placing and realizes there is demand for this style.
- He gets to the point and is direct. He is confident, yet he is respectful of the library owner's time.
- The composer explains why signing his music would be beneficial to the library.
- He proposes the next step to further the relationship.

MEET AND GREET, THEN RETREAT

This is one of the most important pieces of advice that was given to us: *Do not waste anybody's time*, especially in the music business. Here are tips about approaching panelists and music industry people respectfully:

- Smile, introduce yourself, and say your name *clearly*.
- Be polite; thank the panelist for taking the time to be at the event.
- Keep the conversation light. A friend of ours has a great tip: take notes during the panel, and then say to the speaker something like, "I really appreciate the advice you gave about . . ." or "That was a great story you told about . . ."
- Say you are a fan but *only* if you actually are. If you know of their work and have seen their movies or watched their TV shows, then express this. People are flattered when someone knows and appreciates what they have done.
- Let them know, especially if you're familiar with their work, that you write music that would fit in their projects or catalogs.
- You can offer your contact information, but be careful asking for theirs, because this may put them in an awkward position. Some industry people are reluctant to share this information with people they don't know. It's important to grant them this courtesy. If they do invite you to contact them, get in touch with them as soon as you can.
- Do not take more than one minute of their time, especially if you are at a conference and there are people behind you waiting to meet the panelist.
- Refrain from giving them a copy of your CD, a T-shirt, or tickets to your next show. However, if they specifically ask you, then it's okay.
- When first meeting the music industry person, *never* ask them to listen to your music. Avoid putting the person on the spot at all costs. When you get to know them more, then let them ask *you*. If they're interested, they will contact you.

AS TIME GOES BY: FOLLOW UP SOONER THAN LATER

Often music industry panelists talk about building trusted relationships. Inevitably during the question-and-answer time a composer or songwriter will ask, "How do we build trusted relationships with *you*?" The answer is simple: Follow up! Send a *brief* email within the next two days or so thanking the person for being on the panel. Most of the time you *will* get a response, even if it's only a brief thank-you. Business communication is primarily done by email because it is less intrusive and there is a searchable record of the correspondence. When you write emails, *always* include your contact information under your signature line.

If you really want to make a good impression, send a short but sincere handwritten thank-you note. It works very well, and we have personally had a lot of success with this approach. (Thank you, Nancy Moran.)

Perhaps you went to a music conference and met some industry people you'd like to work with. You followed up and thanked them, and they took the time to respond back. It seems like this will be the beginning of a beautiful friendship.

YOU CAN'T HURRY LOVE

Now what do you do? You need to keep going to bring this new relationship to the next level. Here are the crucial steps to take:

1. If you did not do so previously, research them and the projects they're working on, in-depth. Listen to and analyze the styles of music placed in their shows:
    - What are the lyric themes?
    - Is the music edgy or unusual? How?
    - Who is singing?
    - What is the production like?
    - Can you provide this type of music?
2. Now ask yourself, do you write music that would be on the same playlist?
3. Does your music have a similar vibe that would fit the shows?

4. Is your music as polished and of the level of broadcast quality as music placed on the shows?
5. Follow them on social media.
6. See what you may have in common.
7. Politely ask if you can join their music industry groups. If you get no response, try asking again in a few weeks; they are busy and may have missed your request.
8. Does the music industry person attend any conferences or events that you attend or would like to attend? If so, start saving some money, and book a few trips.
9. If you live outside a music business area, write an email inviting them to coffee or lunch (*always* your treat) when you're in their town. Many will gladly accept but only after having had several polite and professional interactions with you.
10. When you have a chance to chat with them—face-to-face, by email or text, or on the phone—and you are *sure* you have the right music for them, *then* ask permission to send them your music.

Remember—you are building a trusted relationship. It takes time. However, if you've followed these steps and have received little or no response, this may be "The Hollywood No,"—a term that means, by silence, the answer is "No," or "I'm not interested right now." Try again later—or move on and try a different person.

YOU'VE GOT A FRIEND

If you go to enough music events and conventions, you'll probably see the same attendees and panelists and begin connecting with them. It's not going to be awkward anymore. You never know who the person you're speaking with may be. They could be a publisher, music attorney, music producer, or potential collaborator.

Start a conversation with, "Hi, I thought I saw you at [pick an event name and insert here]. Was that you?" or "How did you like that event compared with this one?" or "Are there other events you can recommend?" People love to give their opinions. Then add your 10-second introduction: "By the way, my name is Sally Songwriter, and I write pop and country songs. What's your name, and what do you do?" If nothing else, you'll see a familiar face at the next event.

CALL ME MAYBE. OR EMAIL. OR DM. OR TEXT. OR . . .

When meeting people at events, offer to exchange business cards or contact information, as you may want to work together in the future. In private, take a moment to write some quick notes on the back of their card or enter them in your phone. Include the name of the event where you met, the date, and other memorable details. If they were on a panel, jot down some things you learned from them. This will come in handy later when you thank them in a brief email.

It is still customary to have business cards. These cards do not have to be costly or elaborate. Simple is fine, but be sure to include your name, email address, and phone number. It's helpful to also include your website, logo, photo, and a custom-made QR code. *QR* means a "Quick Response," and a QR code reader is available as an app or within the camera function on most smartphones. These codes are free, and they save time when entering contact information. Another time-saver is to take a photo of each other's business card. Tip: when attending events, stash your business cards in your badge holder for easy access.

BADGES? MAYBE WE *DO* NEED BADGES. AND LANYARDS

Most major music conferences provide name badges for attendees and panelists. Make certain your name is visible at all times (and on both sides of the badge), especially if your badge is hanging from a lanyard. Better yet, create a custom-made lanyard, or find something unusual such as a music motif or your artist or band's name. Search online for "custom" or "novelty lanyards," or find colorful lanyards in craft stores. Speaking from experience, something as simple as having an interesting lanyard can get a conversation started.

HEY! READ THIS!
We have a family member who is very personable and outgoing. When he was six years old, he would walk up to another kid on the playground, look the kid straight in the eye, and say, "Hi! My name is Chris. What's your name? Hi, Kelly. Would you like to be my friend?" Instantly, he'd made a friend. It was that simple. He continues this practice today as a young adult and has thousands of social media followers and friends around the world. Sometimes it's up to *you* to take the first step and initiate a conversation. We learned this from Chris (and he's just a kid).

YOU CAN CALL ME "AL"—OR "HAL"

It can be embarrassing forgetting someone's name. However, nearly all of us do it at some point. If you can't remember, it's okay to say something like, "I'm sorry, I'm blanking on your name," or "Hi, I'm Lynn Lyricist. Please tell me your name again." Chances are, they've forgotten your name too. (Tip: Asking for someone's business card and offering them yours can jog everyone's memory.)

When someone tells you *their* name for the first time, a way to remember it is to associate it with something about them—especially if it's a musical reference. For example, if someone's name is Katrina and they're happy and bubbly, the hit song by Katrina and the Waves "Walking on Sunshine" might come to mind and help you remember her name. Using words that rhyme with their name can also be beneficial. Remember Bryan as "Bryan who writes Hawaiian music" or "Lance writes dance music." These are called *mnemonic devices* and are helpful for people who have trouble remembering names.

If you met someone a while ago or you are seeing them again in a different setting, it's better to presume they don't remember your name. Reminding them will prevent an uncomfortable moment. It can be as simple as, "Hi, Susan. I'm Casey Composer. We met at last year's Spring Music Fling." Most people will be polite and say, "Yes, I remember you" (even if they don't!).

It's also okay to politely correct someone if they were close but not correct with your name. It can take *several* times seeing a person before they recognize you and perhaps a few times after that before they remember your name—or what you do.

A LITTLE MORE CONVERSATION

There is an art to talking and listening: Part of being engaged in conversation is to ask questions, pay attention to the answer, and then ask a follow-up question related to that answer. Another tip is if the person asks *you* a question to answer and then ask that person the same question.

SOMETHING TO TALK ABOUT

From years of networking, we've learned that if you want to make an instant friend, find the quietest person in the room—or someone who isn't engaged in a conversation—walk up to them, and introduce yourself. If they seem glad to have someone with whom to talk, start asking questions. Here are some conversation starters:

- *Have you been to this event before?* If you're meeting a first-timer and you've been to this event before, you can perhaps offer tips, such as which panels may be of interest to them. Or introduce the person to some of your friends.
- *What do you do in the music business?* They may be familiar with a part of the music business you're not. Or it may lead to a collaboration.

- *What type of music do you write?* Perhaps the person is working in an interesting genre or can introduce you to something new or unfamiliar.
- *What other music events do you attend?* Or *Are you a member of any groups or professional music organizations?* The person may know about a group that you didn't know existed. We found out about several organizations by asking this question; it was life-changing.
- *Do you have a website?* Or *Where can I hear your music?* People are excited and flattered when someone asks them about their music. Be sure to visit their website, listen to the music, and then follow up with a text or email. You will make a friend in an instant, because not a lot of people take the time to do this.

HOT 'N' COLD

Another helpful tip when engaging in conversation is to "feel the temperature in the room." This means to be aware of social cues, such as the other person's body language, what's being said, how it's being delivered, their facial expressions, and how defensive they are about their "personal space." Some clues that the temperature is "chilly":

- The other person is looking away, getting distracted, backing away from you, or looking at their phone.
- You don't seem to have anything in common; the other person is disinterested, perhaps even bored.
- The conversation is taking a lot of effort and not really going anywhere.

Don't feel as though you need to continue with this interaction, and don't take it personally. Some people are really uncomfortable being around new people or situations. It's good to respect that. Politely tell the person it was nice meeting them, excuse yourself, and find someone else you may have a more positive, educational, or two-sided conversation with.

If the temperature seems "warm," you'll feel it because:

- You are both connecting; there is mutual interest and positive energy.
- You have friends in common or you do similar work; it's easy to talk shop.
- The other person is interested in what you have to say and is asking you questions; you seem to click.

Going to a music event takes time and can be costly. To get the most out of it, make yourself available, and "be present" and approachable. Put away any distractions—especially your phone. Don't be afraid to initiate a conversation, but remember these social cues.

NO PERSON IS A FAILURE WHO HAS FRIENDS

It's important to present yourself effectively with confidence. However, there is a secret to making an even *better* impression on a music industry person: Get a friend to introduce who you are, explain what you do, and sing your praises. In general, people don't like to hear others bragging about themselves; however, if a ringing endorsement comes from someone else—in this case, your friend—that's okay. In fact, it can help.

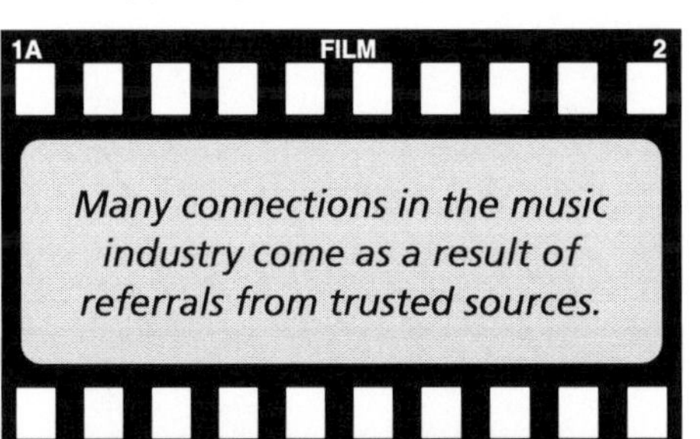

Find a person or business associate who will be your unofficial wingperson—a person who knows and believes in what you do, particularly someone who's a mentor, or a fellow composer, songwriter, or artist.

If this person talks you up and recommends you—in a subtle and genuine way, of course—then it's perceived that you are professional and are good at what you do. Be sure you are able to deliver what's been promised of you. If you don't, it will reflect poorly on both you and the friend who introduced you.

Many connections in the music industry come as a result of referrals from trusted sources. Always keep this in mind, because it is a small, close-knit music world, and you're only as good as your reputation.

A MATTER OF TRUST: BUILDING RELATIONSHIPS

Trusted relationships are the backbone of the music business, and it takes *years* to build them. It is difficult to do quickly. Keep in mind, most people need to see you several times before they remember you.

It is of utmost importance that you are reliable and honest and that you have a good work ethic. Companies and co-creators need to make careful decisions regarding with whom they are going to partner—based on who is serious and who is not. These are crucial qualities successful music creators should have:

- Always meet a deadline.
- Be easy to work with.
- Graciously accept feedback and critiques.
- Deliver what was requested, and provide the best-quality product possible.
- Educate yourself, and read pertinent news that affects the music licensing business.
- Be a responsible and charitable member of the music community. Mentor or give advice on panels, volunteer working at music events, or join and be active with music advocacy groups. Giving back makes a good impression and becomes a big part of how you are perceived. You may also meet valuable contacts, friends, and collaborators.
- Above all, be *professional.*

HEY! READ THIS!
The best things you can bring to a networking event are a pen, business cards, your phone, a smile, breath mints, and your "wingperson" friend. Thank you, Dan Kimpel (author of books about networking in the music business).

SOME THINGS MUST BE EARNED

Our friend is a composer who teaches music business classes. A new student invariably asks our friend if he would share all of his music business contacts with the class. Our friend politely declines and explains that he worked very hard—and for many years—to develop his trusted relationships; he does not share this information with people he doesn't know. He's not being selfish—he's being cautious. Since having put a lot of time, effort, and money earning the respect of his business associates, he does not want to jeopardize their trust in him. Good advice.

PRO TIPS . . . About Networking and Building Relationships

I'd like to think that I've met people over the years due to the shared passion of music, whether it's at a concert, event, or conference. And when that is shared, it's easy to be genuinely interested in another person's life and activities, which keeps the relationship going over the years.

—**Liz Redwing**, Music Management and Consulting

I highly recommend composers and songwriters join and support trade organizations like the Production Music Association (PMA). Their events, like the Production Music Conference, not only provide valuable, up-to-date information, but they offer networking opportunities—and access to music industry decision-makers.

—**Adam Taylor**, President of APM Music, Chairman of the PMA

When attending music conferences, make sure you do your preparation and prioritize the panels and workshops that make the most sense for you and where you are in your career now. Make a list of questions, and write down your goals so you make the most of your day. If you want to make an impression, do your research on the people you are likely to see. Dress the part, take yourself seriously, and stand out from the crowd.

—**Pamela Sheyne**, Songwriter, Singer, and Mentor, and Co-founder of SongWriterCamps

I always tell artists that I'm developing, "Get to know people, and let them get to know you." The best way to find collaborators is to attend music conferences, where you can meet talented songwriters and performers from around the world. There is a sense of camaraderie that happens at these events, and many true friendships are built this way.

—**Nitanee Paris**, award-winning Songwriter, and Partner and Director of A&R, ArtistMax

To make the most of a music conference, come prepared! Conferences can be overwhelming with all of the content and amount of people that attend. It's really important to have a set of goals going into it. Regarding networking at an event, research who will be there, take a look at their work, listen to new music being released, check on any business deals/acquisitions that are happening, and identify who you'd like to meet with.

—**Morgan McKnight**, Executive Director of the Production Music Association

Networking is a vital part of any business, and it takes time to build trusting relationships. Be genuine, polite, and helpful to others. In the music business, deal breakers include interrupting or monopolizing conversations—and failing to follow up. If you go to a conference, have a prioritized plan, but be flexible. Decide on what you want to accomplish, and research the people who you specifically want to meet.

—**Brian Thomas Curtin**, Composer and Songwriter, Eaglestone Music

This is a people business. Get to know people. Go to conferences. You'll go farther when people trust you. Get to know them as people, not just as meal tickets. Don't burn bridges if you can avoid it. It's really a small community. You are not entitled to be successful; you need to earn it. And to earn it, you must prove yourself over and over again.

—**Steve Barden**, Composer and Author

CHAPTER 16

Presenting Yourself and Your Music

BRAND NEW

A brand is a style, and everybody has one, whether it's intentional or not. So, when presenting yourself, it is important that you consider what your "brand" is, because it can make you stand out in a crowd. Depending on how you create your style, you will be more memorable. Many sync agents and publishers value that, because they will know how to market you. However, for others in the music industry, branding matters less; it's only about the music.

Some songwriters, composers, artists, and bands spend a lot of money to bring together their music and their style. Their music includes instrumentation, production, attitude, and what they're communicating in their songs. They have a language and a vibe that speaks and connects to their fans. Their style encompasses clothes, publicity photos, merchandise, their website, even the font they use for their brand name. It's all tied together and reflected in their music.

Consider what your brand is: Are you casual? Formal? Funny? Serious? Is this expressed in your music? If you were to have photos taken of yourself, would the location of the photo be in your studio? At a high-end downtown club? In a field near a train track? In front of a brick wall? Are you smiling? Looking away? Holding your favorite guitar? Are you wearing something interesting? Is there a clue in the photo that illustrates the genre of music you write? It is important that your brand be an authentic representation of you and your music.

WHAT A WONDERFUL WORLD WIDE WEBSITE

Having a website is a necessity, especially when you are making a first impression in the music industry. If you're not adept at setting one up, consider hiring a Web-building professional. However, there are inexpensive, user-friendly online services, and some specifically cater to musicians and music creators. Do an Internet search for phrases like "music Web page design" or "music website templates." It's easy to put up content and upload music onto these platforms. Some are basic; some are customizable. Be sure the Web-building platform allows you to make instant changes, corrections, and updates.

There are many advantages to having a website: You have an all-in-one place to keep your marketing information. This may include photos, your biography, songs (or a link to a music streaming service), video clips, podcasts or interviews, demo reels or montages of your work, news, your list of credits, testimonials from satisfied clients, endorsements from colleagues or fans, tour dates, and—the most important item—your contact information.

Review your website regularly, and note:

- *Overall.* Is the website easy to navigate? Can users find information quickly? Does the site mirror you and your music? Make sure your website looks good on various electronic devices (phone, tablet, computer, laptop, etc.); some websites are easy to read on computers but not on phones. Ask family and friends to look at your site and provide some honest feedback.
- *Pages.* Are they labeled clearly? Does the order in which they appear make sense? Make sure there are no pages that say "Coming soon" or "Under construction." If so, hide these pages from view.

If you have a "Tour Dates" page, make sure it's for *upcoming* dates, not *past* ones. However, you can add the old information to your bio.

- *Copyrights.* Include a copyright notice somewhere on your website—perhaps on the bottom as a footer. In addition, confirm there is no material you may have posted or uploaded that belongs to someone else, which may violate U.S. or international copyright laws. If in doubt, always research or request permission in writing (by letter or email).
- *Readability.* Is the type color, size, and style clear and simple? Double proofread for typos in the text.

MEET THE (ELECTRONIC) PRESS KIT

Artists and composers are often asked for an *EPK—*or *electronic press kit.* It is usually presented as a page on an artist's or composer's website. The EPK may be on a hidden page or viewable by anyone.

Your EPK should include:

- High-quality, high-resolution, 300-plus dpi photos. A headshot is useful, especially if you have been asked to be on a panel or will be interviewed by a journalist or podcaster.
- A bio—both a brief one and a long one. The brief one will be used most often, unless someone requests more details. You can edit the long one to custom fit their request. Include some name-recognizable credits, if you have them. Keep this bio strictly business.
- Links to some audio or video samples of your work.

HEY! READ THIS!

Starting out, we never imagined we would be speaking on panels. However, within a few years of working in the sync music industry, we began to be asked to appear on podcasts and started doing interviews. Fortunately we had our bio, photos, and EPK ready. It's good to think ahead, as you never know when opportunity will knock.

I'LL PLAY FOR YOU: PRESENTING YOUR MUSIC

You've met a music industry person, and they've given you permission to send them some music for review. After doing research, find common ground between the music they need for their projects and the music you do well. Send them one or two songs—three at the most. They don't have time to listen to an album or a large collection of cues or songs. If they let you know what kind of music they need and you have it, pitch only your best. But how should you send it?

- Always ask the music industry person whether they have a preferred method of receiving music. Some want music uploaded to their website or like certain file-transfer services.
- Others may ask for you to send them a link that allows them to stream your music with the option to download it. Frequently this is the case.
  - Some services let you know if the music has been streamed or downloaded.
- Others prefer an email with *one* MP3 attached.
  - Whether downloaded or emailed, the MP3 should be of the highest quality available—320 Kbps, unless they request otherwise.
  - It should be embedded with essential metadata (more on this in chapter 17).

- The most important information to include in the metadata is your *name and contact information*. MP3s frequently end up being separated from emails. Music supervisors have told many stories about finding songs they wanted to license but couldn't because they had no idea how to contact the writers and performers since there was no metadata.

You can choose to embed a picture in your MP3 as well. It can be a picture of you or the cover art from your album or EP. This bit of personalization provides an opportunity to make a memorable visual impression.

Embedding the song's lyrics into the MP3 is another important option. Though they may be available in an email or on a website, having the lyrics easily accessible while the song is playing is most convenient for the listener.

The MP3 that you send is likely for review by the music person. You don't need to include any MP3s of alternate mixes, but you can let the person know the alt mixes are available. (And you *should* have them available.) If they are interested in licensing or representing your music, they will ask you to send high-resolution (WAV or AIFF) files. Since these hi-res files are much larger than MP3s, they should not be attached to emails. Instead, send a download link that doesn't expire—or won't expire for a long time. (Remember, they're busy people and may not get around to downloading your music for a while.)

Then ask which alt mixes they require. Most songs should have a no vocal mix, which is imperative in the sync world. The file names should all be labeled clearly and according to any file name protocol the company may have.

Music placement companies frequently embed metadata into hi-res files themselves, as they may have information and formats they prefer. If you send a hi-res file to a music supervisor, however, embed the metadata yourself.

CONNECTING TO THE CONNECTORS: PITCH SERVICES

Getting started in the sync licensing business can be bewildering, with a lot of hurdles and caveats. Although representatives from music libraries, sync agencies, and music publishers are easier to get in contact with than music supervisors, it can still be a challenge to get their attention. However, you can reach them through the "connectors."

Consider signing up for a music *pitch service*, also known as a music *tip sheet service*. These services offer opportunities to pitch your music, and some offer feedback on your music. These intermediaries can connect you to people in the music industry. Here are some things to look for when researching tip companies:

- How much does the service cost? Some have a monthly or yearly fee. What is included in the price?
- Is there an additional fee to submit a song for a pitch? How much is it? If you submit to many different opportunities, it can add up quickly.
- Do they offer any feedback on your music? Who is providing the feedback? How qualified are they? Do they understand the sync world? Is the feedback free? Some companies charge an additional fee for one-on-one critiques.
- What types of opportunities do they list in their tip sheets? Is it geared toward sync? Many companies will let you see a sample of their clients' requests. Would your music fit any of them?
- Is the service geared toward songs, instrumentals, or both?
- Is this service focused on sync placements or finding songs for hit artists to record?
- Does the service offer additional benefits, such as podcasts, educational videos, conventions, forums, and message boards with peer-to-peer reviews?
- How successful are they? What types of credits do they have?

- Do they take a cut of the income for any placements they get for you? If so, how much?
- Are there reference songs offered in the music requests?
- Do they allow you to directly contact the person requesting the music?

Again, do your research, and read reviews before deciding on a service to use. Ask friends if they've ever tried a pitch service and, if so, which ones they would recommend.

HEY! READ THIS!

After years of working with tip services, we had limited success. However, the biggest advantages were having a *project* and a *deadline*. At first we didn't have any contacts, we weren't with any publishing companies, and we didn't know what to write. We found tip services to be helpful for a few reasons:

- The pitch lists inspired us to experiment with writing in different genres.
- Having specific projects to write for gave us the opportunity to understand how to write licensable music and eventually establish working relationships with music placement companies.
- Having deadlines put us on a regular writing schedule, which was crucial to improving our skills.
- The tip sheets gave us valuable insights into what's being requested by the music industry. We also learned how high the standards are.

BE TRUE TO YOUR SCHOOL

Perhaps you've tried all of the above but are still finding little success. Consider learning more about music composition, songwriting, and recording. Sometimes even the music industry pros need to brush up on certain skills too. Taking in-person or online music and recording classes is a great way to hone your craft, as well as to meet like-minded collaborators and music industry people. You can earn a certificate or degree or just take a course or two.

You can find classes at private music schools, community colleges, and top universities. Many of these schools have extension courses. Take one course to test the waters. Fees can vary from nominal to quite expensive, depending on the reputation of the school and the quality of the education.

If the school is in a music center geographically, the instructors often invite music industry guest speakers for the students. For example, at some colleges in Los Angeles it is not unusual to see famous faces and hit songwriters teaching or even taking the class. One of our friends took classes with a teacher who wrote several hit songs for her favorite music artist and now sits in the front row of every one of this artist's concerts.

Another plus of taking classes is that you will get assignments with a deadline. Completing music projects on a schedule is a good skill to develop. Furthermore, the music you write can become a part of your catalog. Many cues we wrote in our composing classes years ago still get placements frequently.

Be sure to follow up and keep in contact with your instructors and fellow students. This is an opportunity to build trusted relationships. We still see several of our teachers and classmates at various events.

SOMEBODY'S WATCHING ME: WHO'S VETTING WHOM

The music providers are always vetting us songwriters and composers. Part of the vetting process is how well we communicate, follow directions, and act professionally. However, it's good for composers and songwriters to vet *them*. Take notice of a few things in particular:

- How successful are they?
- What types of placements do they get?
- How do they treat their composers?
- Do they split the income evenly?
- What types of deals do they offer?

One friend's advice is to ask the company or publisher how many people they have on their marketing staff. Excellent question!

IF YOU DON'T KNOW ME BY NOW

If your music is not ready, or if you are not sure if it is ready, don't pitch to the more prominent companies. You get only one chance to make a first impression, and it should be a good one. The smaller companies, or the pitch services, may be better places to start. Know your priorities and your comfort zone, and be mindful that you are partnering with people you may not know—nor they you.

Find the right fit—where you "get" them, and the company "gets" you and your music. Sure, they're vetting you, but you need to be vetting them as well. Work with the ones who are excited about you and your music and conversely you're excited to work with.

FOLLOW THE YELLOW BRICK ROAD: YOUR OWN PATH TO SUCCESS

There are several opportunities for success that are available to you. Find which path works for you and your music. In summary:

- If you can get direct access to a music supervisor or editor (which can be a challenge) and your music is ready, you'll be well situated to receive all the income from their placement. But how many opportunities can this one person provide for you?
- It's easier to establish relationships with music libraries, sync agencies, and publishers. There are many different opportunities available from them, but they typically take about half the income.
- Most people start with a pitch or tip sheet service. These can connect you to music supervisors and music placement companies and help you develop your craft and understanding of the music licensing world. However, there is usually a fee involved, and success is not guaranteed.
- Each of these paths to placement of your music is not mutually exclusive. You can use a combination of the above options to see which yields the most success for you.

PRO TIPS . . . About Presenting Yourself and Your Music

As an artist building your brand, simply become a bigger version of yourself. Take your natural qualities, abilities, and talents and blow them up. Accentuate them. Emphasize them. Brand recognition is only important if you want to stand out and be remembered by your audience. And *everyone* wants that!

—**Nancy Moran**, Singer-Songwriter and Artist Development Coach

The most common traits of successful creators are the ability to put themselves out there, knowing the foundations of how the music industry works, having a unique musical voice, and having an openness to take direction. Above all, they are pleasant to work with. If you are someone who enjoys people and has a positive attitude, you will have an advantage.

—**Erin Collins**, Vice President of Film, Television, and Developing Media at SESAC

In our case, the music is all that matters. We don't recommend composers sending long emails, photos, and bios with multiple links. We suggest keeping things as succinct as possible.

—**Ron Goldberg**, Vice President of Manhattan Production Music

Always be prepared, but don't forget to be yourself. You are unique and will have something unique to offer; you just need to make the "right" connection.

—**Liz Redwing**, Music Management and Consulting

Share your knowledge, and ask colleagues for their suggestions. The best resources can sometimes be your fellow songwriters and musicians. Strong interpersonal relationships are the DNA of success in the music business. You achieve nothing if you don't try. So whether it's a creative pursuit, a business idea, or just developing lasting relationships, you have to pick yourself up and constantly push yourself forward.

—**Michael Eames**, President of PEN Music Group, Inc.

To find my unique voice as a composer, I pursued projects in genres I was passionate about (fantasy, science fiction, horror, drama). I watch a lot of films and listen to many soundtracks so I become inspired to search for projects where I feel my music would be a natural fit.

—**Penka Kouneva**, Composer for film, TV, and video games

A unique sound and style of writing songs is always interesting, although some artists/writers can present an old style in a fresh and exciting new way.

—**Teri Nelson Carpenter**, President and CEO of Reel Muzik Werks, Past President AIMP, Executive Vice President of the Independent Music Publishers International Forum

When first starting out, we tend to create music that is inspired by our musical heroes because it resonates with us. As we gain more experience, we learn to listen to our own inner ear to guide us. With increased confidence and determination, we discover and develop our own unique style.

—**Brian Thomas Curtin**, Composer and Songwriter, Eaglestone Music

CHAPTER 17

The Importance of Metadata and Keywords

THE WORDS GET IN THE WAY

We discussed titles in part 1 of this book, but it deserves closer attention.

Some novice composers create a great cue but give it a generic, nondescript title—such as "Sad Drama Cue #1." Would you want to listen to a track with that name? A music supervisor or editor would probably skip over that cue, especially if they are on a deadline or aren't familiar with that composer. The title needs to sell the song *before* the first listen.

Another secret to your song's successful placement is understanding the two most-used terms in the sync music world: metadata (information) and keywords (descriptions). *Metadata* includes the facts about a song or cue, such as who owns the song or who to contact, who wrote it, PRO, timing, and more. *Keywords* list the song's or cue's characteristics, such as tempo, instrumentation, and moods.

Why is metadata important in the music licensing process? Music with no associated metadata probably won't be placed, and you'll see no income.

HEY! WHERE DOES ALL THIS METADATA GO?

You provide metadata to music supervisors and publishers in two ways: in an MP3 or on a spreadsheet. Metadata *must* be embedded in your MP3s. If you do not know how to do this, do an Internet search on "how to embed metadata in MP3s." The metadata should include:

- The title of the song or instrumental
- Your contact information—such as email address, phone number, and website URL
- The legal names of the artists, songwriters, and composers
- The publisher
- The PRO (BMI, ASCAP, SESAC, GMR) of each songwriter, composer or publisher, along with the CAE/IPI numbers (see chapter 20)
- All performers and singers
- The producer
- The composer or songwriter splits
- A copyright notice © with the year and your name
- The lyrics and artwork (optional)
- Keywords—which are detailed descriptions of your music (more about this below):
    - The music genre and subgenre
    - The instrumentation (for example, guitar, female vocals, strings, shakers, hand claps)
    - Production elements (for example, bpm, key, stops and starts, buildup in the middle, structure)
    - The moods, styles, vibes, and emotions

KEYWORDS ARE THE KEYS TO THE (SYNC) KINGDOM

Keywords are the specific words or phrases that describe the music. Like finding the perfect title, finding the right keywords takes some effort and creative thinking. Coming up with suitable keywords under pressure may be daunting. When we were writing music for daytime talk shows, we cultivated a list from many different sources. It was necessary for us to describe each song or cue's mood, vibe, emotion, or feeling so a music supervisor or editor could find the music that matched the scene. Describing music quickly was tough, so to make the search simpler, we came up with an idea to list the words not only in alphabetical order but also in separate columns headed "Positive," "Negative," and "Neutral." (To gain a better understanding and have a reference of keywords, see the very comprehensive list in appendix E). Here are some broad examples of keywords:

- *Positive.* Bright, happy, sunny, upbeat (if your song is up-tempo and optimistic)
- *Negative.* Hopeless, lonely, sad (if your cue is dramatic and slow)
- *Neutral.* Acoustic, flowing, natural (if your piece is mid-tempo, singer-songwriter, indie folk)

WHO WILL BUY THIS WONDERFUL MUSIC? SELLING THE SIZZLE, NOT THE STEAK

Descriptions, when done well, are riveting. Tantalizing. Enticing. Describing yourself and your music is part of the marketing. Doing this effectively can get your foot in the door; if your descriptions are inadequate, your music may be overlooked.

In addition to providing your best, most original music, and in order for your music to be chosen among all the music out there, it is imperative that you use keywords skillfully in your metadata. This is beneficial not only on the music user's end but for you as well. Understanding this is a big deal, or you won't land that big deal.

Take care not to *oversell* yourself and your music. When establishing a brand, a fine balance is struck between blowing your own horn (off-putting) and piquing a music user's interest (inviting). Find keywords that are intriguing.

After your music is signed with a music publisher, production music library, or sync agency, often you will be asked to fill out a spreadsheet using metadata and keywords. This process is a bit tedious, but it is necessary. Familiarize yourself with how spreadsheets work, and the process will get easier with time. Some companies will do this task for you, but always be prepared to offer your own keyword suggestions; no one knows your music like you do.

HEY! READ THIS!

When entering a list of keywords on a spreadsheet or MP3, type in the most important words first and then the rest *alphabetically* so you don't duplicate any. Sometimes a company will chop off the last several words if they think there are too many. Put in words or descriptions that accurately describe the music. Think like a music supervisor or editor, and imagine how you would find your music. Go to a production music library website, and enter keywords, such as "upbeat, island, steel drums" or "heavy metal, epic, trailer," and listen to the results. See which additional keywords are used to describe those tracks.

PRO TIPS . . . About Metadata and Keywords

When I add keywords to my production music cues, I try to put myself in the place of the party that is doing the searching. Often it's a music supervisor or editor who needs to be able to find and audition many cues very quickly. I try to use keywords whose meanings are commonly understood.

—**Abby North**, President of North Music Group

Metadata has become extremely important. Accurate metadata is how composers/songwriters are paid without error. Do not guess when registering a song, and ask if you have any questions when registering your songs. We are here to help. Correct metadata will prevent possible loss or delayed income and headaches down the road. I can't stress this enough.

—**Barbie Quinn**, Senior Director of Administration & Publisher Relations at BMI

Some sync deal breakers: Music that is not broadcast-ready, unimaginative titles, and the lack of essential metadata. To increase your chances for placements, submit high-quality composed music with an evocative title and accurate metadata with relevant keywords. Quality matters!

—**Brian Thomas Curtin**, Composer and Songwriter, Eaglestone Music

Ignoring the business side of the music business in today's market is unacceptable. Information is available, and there are so many opportunities. If you do not have an understanding on how the business works, you are an amateur.

—**Suzan Koç**, Publisher and Songwriting Mentor

PART 3: BUSINESS

Hey! Where's My Money?

Steps to Collecting Your Money and Getting Organized

CHAPTER 18

Taking Care of Business

ORGANIZING YOUR DUCKS

People who work outside of the music business usually have a hard time understanding and relating to how songwriters, composers, and publishers get paid. In many ways, the process is very counterintuitive. Though there are times when money is paid as the music is written, the majority of the money comes months or even years afterward. So if you are looking to get rich quickly, this may not be the business for you.

Not only does the money come later, there is no guarantee you will receive all the money you are due. It is critical that you are aware of what to expect regarding income.

The best way to be assured you get paid appropriately for your work is through knowledge and organization. Having the proper documentation in place is an absolute necessity: signed co-writer agreements, work-for-hire agreements, and contracts should be stored or backed up in a safe place.

Have a list or spreadsheet of the music you have written for licensing that indicates the status of each song or instrumental. This includes:

- The title (and any alternate titles)
- Any co-writer(s) of the music
- How the shares are split among the writers
- The PRO of each co-writer
- Who performed on the recording
- Who owns the master recording
- The company to which the music is signed
- The terms of the deal (exclusive or non-exclusive, etc.)
- The date the music was signed
- If or when the representation of any of your music reverts back to you
- Any work-for-hire contracts that are in place

THE SCIENTIST: ANALYZE THIS

Once you start receiving royalty statements from the various collection organizations, libraries, and publishers, analyzing them is important for two reasons: it reminds you that your music is earning money, and it provides you the opportunity to see which songs are your high earners. If your statement is available in a format that allows sorting by columns, you will be able to sort the data based on the amount each placement earned to see which ones received the most money during that pay period. You can also sort the "song title" column to see which are being placed repeatedly. The name of the publisher who got the placement may not be available on the statement. But take note of the companies that get many placements for you by consulting the spreadsheet you created earlier.

Keep track of this information for each statement to see what trends emerge over time. You may find that some companies are not doing a good job placing your music. Use these observations to help guide your decisions about what kind of music to write and which companies to sign with. If your authentic didgeridoo music is being licensed regularly by a music library, write more cues for them. They are unlikely to turn you down. (And you'll probably have little competition.)

In addition to keeping your data and paperwork organized, the other key to maximizing income is to be sure your music is registered with the proper organizations (see chapter 20). In some cases, the music library or sync agency may handle this for you. Depending on the terms of your deal, registration of your musical works may be *your* responsibility. If you placed your music directly with a music supervisor, you need to register it yourself.

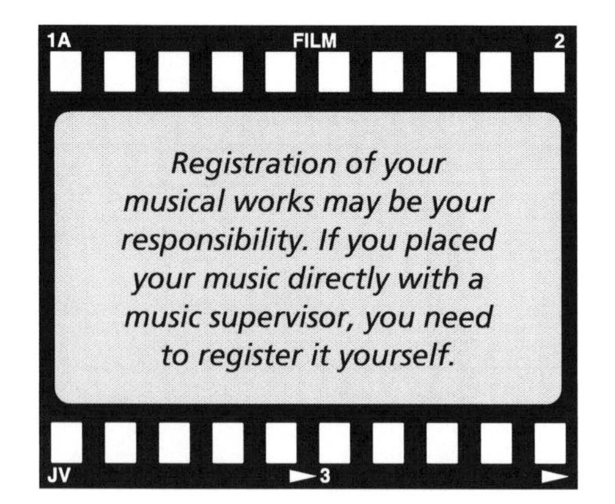

Registration of your musical works may be your responsibility. If you placed your music directly with a music supervisor, you need to register it yourself.

PRO TIPS . . . About Taking Care of Business

Establishing a relationship with a legal professional with expertise in this arena should happen sooner rather than later, especially when your intellectual property is beginning to be presented to the public and/or interested buyers. Working with a knowledgeable legal professional early on can help one avoid pitfalls that could have long-term, negative consequences.

—**Garrett M. Johnson**, Esq., Past President of the California Copyright Conference

Regarding generating income in the global music marketplace, have good and knowledgeable representation. Artists/writers need to create, but they should also understand the business—at least in broad terms.

—**Teri Nelson Carpenter**, President and CEO of Reel Muzik Werks, Past President AIMP, Executive Vice President of the Independent Music Publishers International Forum

Asking fellow songwriters and composers about their experiences, as well as doing online research, can help narrow down the PRO (Performing Rights Organization) choices. Ultimately, it comes down to your relationship with the PRO representatives. Having an advocate makes all the difference. PRO representatives attend a tremendous amount of events, workshops, lectures, and concerts, so meeting one is a matter of introducing yourself and making a connection.

—**Erin Collins**, Vice President of Film, Television, and Developing Media at SESAC

About being professional in the music business: Underpromise, overdeliver.

—**Matt Hirt**, Composer, Songwriter, and Producer, and Co-owner of Catapult Music

It's important to stay as up-to-date as possible regarding licensing trends, especially with the emergence of digital service providers, apps, and streaming services. Find organizations dedicated to educating, and go along with allies, which can help.

—**Morgan McKnight**, Executive Director of the Production Music Association

CHAPTER 19

Licensing Fees

TAKE THE MONEY AND RUN

Now to define sources of income: In the sync music world, the typical sources of income include licensing fees and performance royalties.

YOU NEED A LICENSE FOR THAT

When music is synced in any kind of visual media, a license is required. A *license* is an agreement between the copyright owner and user of the music that permission has been given to use the music in TV shows, streaming shows, movies, online videos, and other forms of visual media. Remember that there are two copyrights involved in music—the written composition and the master or sound recording. A license is needed for *each* of these copyrights.

The written composition requires a *synchronization license* with the publisher of the song. If you write a song yourself and don't assign the publishing rights to anyone, you are the publisher. If you assign your publishing rights to a publishing company, you are subject to the terms of any contract you sign with them.

The master recording requires a *master license* with the owner of the sound recording, which is often a record label. If you record a song yourself, you are the owner of the master recording. If you hire someone to record your song, be sure that there is a written understanding about who owns the recording.

CAN WE AGREE TO AGREE?

When a music supervisor or music user wants to place music in their project, a sync licensing fee should be negotiated with the owners of the two copyrights. This fee is paid once when the music is synced to the show. There should be agreed-upon terms:

- The usage of the music
- How long the show is to be aired, broadcast, or streamed
- On which media platforms
- In which worldwide territories

Each of these terms affects the amount of the licensing fee. If the show is to be aired for a short amount of time in a small area, the licensing fee is likely to be smaller. If the show is to air for decades or all over the world, the licensing fee will be higher.

The owner of each of the two copyrights has the freedom to make whatever type of deal they can. However, in sync licensing the most common split is fifty-fifty between the owner of the composition and the owner of the recording.

For instance, a $1,000 licensing fee would usually have $500 going to the publisher and $500 going to the recording owner. In this example, how much of the $500 goes to the songwriter or composer? That depends on the publishing contract that was signed. Again, this fee is often split fifty-fifty between the publisher and the writer, so $250 each.

There is less of a standard amount for the owner of the sound recording and the recording artist and other performers. The split of that $500 can vary depending upon the terms of the contracts that were signed. In production music, often performers receive a one-time work-for-hire fee when they record the song. They receive no further compensation, no matter how much money the recording generates. There are times when generous songwriters and producers share some of this income with the performers, but they are not required to do so.

ALL OR NOTHING AT ALL?

When publishers have relationships with sub-publishers in different territories, the licensing fees are typically split fifty-fifty between them. Your publisher then splits their 50% with you, giving you 25% of the original fee. This may sound like a poor deal, but 25% of a licensing fee is better than 100% of no fee. Remember, the sync music world outside the United States is a big place.

If a writer performs and records their own music, everything is neater and cleaner, and they also receive a bigger piece of the financial pie.

I'LL HAVE WHAT SHE'S HAVING

During the process of negotiating a licensing fee, the concept of *most favored nations* sometimes arises. This term, abbreviated as *MFN*, refers to one party receiving the same payment as another in a similar situation; it is not always in place in every contract but may be requested. MFN has two applications in licensing fee negotiation.

In the first scenario, the two parties are the owner of the composition and the owner of the recording. If an MFN clause is included in the license of one of these parties, that party is entitled to the same licensing fee as the other party. For example, if the publisher negotiates a $1,000 licensing fee and the deal with the record label is subject to MFN, the label must also receive $1,000. This equal split has become common practice regardless of the existence of MFN.

MFN also applies to the licensing fee paid for two separate pieces of music. If a music library has negotiated a $2,000 licensing fee for the use of a background instrumental in a movie, and a music placement company whose deal is subject to MFN also has a background instrumental in the movie, the music placement company also must receive $2,000.

A LOT OF COOKS IN THE KITCHEN

The sync licensing fee and the master recording licensing fee are sometimes handled by two different companies. This happens often when a popular artist on a major record label or a popular song represented by a major publisher are involved. However, when both copyrights are represented by the same company, like a production music library, the fees are negotiated by that company and are combined into what is called simply a *licensing fee*. This is also known as an *all-in licensing fee* or a *sync fee*.

Because of all the moving parts, you can now understand how difficult it can be for a music supervisor to negotiate a license and a fee with this large group of people. It's so much easier for a music supervisor to go to one company that has their music organized and pre-cleared and to agree on terms and a licensing fee with this one entity (one-stop licensing and music clearance). That's why quality production music libraries are popular with music supervisors and music editors.

I'LL HAVE ONE, PLEASE

A licensing fee paid for the use of a single song is sometimes called a *needle drop license*. The term refers to the needle on a phonograph record player being dropped (gently) onto a vinyl record.

Another common license, a *blanket license*, is a fee paid to license some or all of the tracks in a production music library's catalog for use in an episode or a season of a show or some other project. Depending on their contracts, some libraries share this fee with the songwriters and composers of the music in the catalog. Other libraries don't share this fee due to the difficulty of figuring out how to distribute the money among the writers.

But wait! It gets more interesting. Sometimes there is no fee paid at all for the use of music in a show. This is called a *gratis license*, which has become more common, despite the efforts of many music libraries and advocacy groups.

How does everybody make money? Why do some give music away for free? Read on in the next chapter about performance royalties.

PRO TIPS . . . About Licensing Fees

Sync negotiators are part of a community of people who are invested in helping each other succeed. Transparency, integrity, and empathy are some of my best tools for negotiating, whether on behalf of a production or the writers and artists I represent.

—**James Jacoby**, Music Supervision, Clearance, and Licensing

When an artist asks me to review a licensing agreement for use of their song, I first need to know the backstory—who else may have contributed to the recording and whether the artist needs to obtain signed releases. Understanding and consolidating all of the underlying music rights is the currency for successful music placement.

—**Kenneth A. Helmer**, Esq.

Know that it's not always just the fee that's negotiable. If you feel the fee being offered is lower than you'd typically accept, try to negotiate limiting the rights (especially true with advertising placements). If it's a use where the rights can't be limited (i.e., scripted television), then try to negotiate a most favored nations (MFN) clause so your song is treated on par with other songs being licensed for the same usages.

—**Marc Caruso**, CEO & Co-founder of Angry Mob Music

There is a loose formula for how the music should be arranged for each type of license, and every company has a forte or a focus with licensing.

—**Derek Jones**, Director of Creative Services at Megatrax Production Music

CHAPTER 20

Performance Royalties and PROs

GETTING THE ROYAL TREATMENT

Most logically thinking people would assume that performance royalties go only to performers. And they would be wrong. Much of the terminology used in music licensing is fairly straightforward and intuitive; this one is a bit misleading.

Though some *performance royalties* go to the performers, in the United States most performance royalties are paid to songwriters, composers, and publishers by Performing Rights Organizations (or PROs). The major U.S. PROs are ASCAP, BMI, SESAC, and GMR. These royalties are paid when music is played:

- On television (network, cable, satellite, and audiovisual streaming)
- On radio (terrestrial, Internet, and audio-only streaming)
- As background music in restaurants, bars, hotels, airplanes, amusements parks, fitness centers, stores, shopping malls, and other places of business
- By performers in live-music venues such as concert halls, stadiums, coffee shops, nightclubs, etc.

Visit the PRO websites to see more information about where performance royalties are paid.

Performance royalties are referred to often as *backend* because they are paid months after a show airs. Basically, if someone is making money and music has been used to enhance the experience, then songwriters, composers, and publishers are compensated.

> *If someone is making money and music has been used to enhance the experience, then songwriters, composers, and publishers are compensated.*

The notable exception to the payment of royalties for music placements is in the United States, where no performance royalties are paid when music is placed in films playing in American movie theaters. Licensing fees are still paid. However, royalties *are* paid when films are played in theaters in other countries and territories. There are a few practices in the music business where the United States is not in step with the rest of the world, and this is one of them. The good news is that with so many platforms available to view films, most end up being streamed or aired on TV, where royalties are paid.

PROs collect money from TV networks, radio stations, streaming services, concert venues, restaurants, bars, and places of business that use music.

- This money is collected in the form of a blanket license (not to be confused with the blanket license a music library issues to production companies).
    - For instance, a TV network pays for a blanket license from a PRO.
    - This license allows the network to use all of the music in the PRO's repertoire during the term of the license.
    - Most networks and businesses need to have licenses from more than one PRO.

- The PROs then distribute this money to songwriters, composers, and publishers. Most of these royalties are paid quarterly.
    - To facilitate this, the creators of shows supply cue sheets to the PROs.

RIGHT ON CUE

A *cue sheet* is a list of the songs and instrumentals that have been used in a film or TV show. A cue sheet indicates:

- The title of each piece of music that was used
- How long it was used
- How it was used in the show
- Who wrote it
- Who the publisher is
- With which PRO the writers and publishers are affiliated

It's important that the PROs know the length of a musical use as well as the nature of the placement. Each PRO has its own guidelines, but longer placements earn more money. Also, some types of uses pay more:

- Background vocal placements usually pay more than background instrumentals.
- Visual vocals and visual instrumentals, where the viewer can see the person performing, pay even more.

A very coveted placement is a *theme song* for a film or TV show. There are not many opportunities available, so these placements are very hard to get. However, they can be very profitable, because they pay a higher rate and occur in every episode of a show, including reruns.

DIGITAL FINGERPRINTING AND WATERMARKING

While cue sheets are still the standard for reporting placements of music to PROs, two forms of audio detection technology are available that track when music is broadcast on major, independent, and cable networks. *Audio fingerprinting* is a process that analyzes the audio wave of a sound file and detects it when it is broadcast. *Audio watermarking* places an inaudible digital watermark onto a sound file, which is then detected when it is broadcast. The process of watermarking must take place before the music is released. Though fingerprinting is more convenient and can be implemented after the music has been released, watermarking is more reliable and accurate. Some PROs accept this data, while others do not.

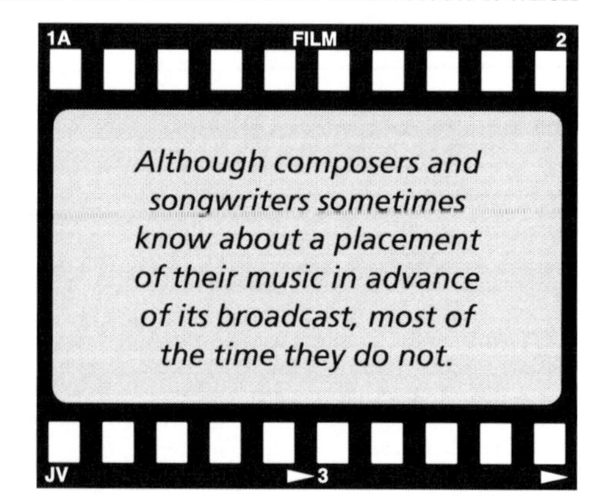

This technology is intended for tracking placements of music for the purpose of payment from PROs; however, it can be a useful tool to help music creators make signing decisions. Utilizing these services allows them to know when their music has been placed without having to wait several months to receive their PRO statement. Although composers and songwriters sometimes know about a placement of their music in advance of its broadcast, most of the time they do not. Knowing when it has been placed helps composers and songwriters make more timely decisions about what kind of music to write and with whom to sign it.

READY FOR PRIME TIME

Another factor that influences how well a music placement pays in performance royalties is how big the audience is for a program. A TV show that airs on a major network in prime time generates more in royalties because of the large number of viewers. One that airs on a smaller cable network at three in the morning pays less. However, in this on-demand world, time of day matters less than it used to. Shows that are streamed thousands of times at any hour of the day can make quite a bit of money.

AND NOW A WORD FROM OUR SPONSOR

The good news about having music placed in a commercial is that it often means a big, fat licensing fee. The not-so-good news about having music placed in a commercial is that the performance royalties are often less than expected. This is not always the case, but it is common.

The same is also true of *promos*—TV network promotions of upcoming shows, usually saying something like, "Tune in next week for another episode of, *Hey! That's My Show!*"

This trend is much more extreme with *movie trailers*. As was noted earlier, there are no performance royalties for music in U.S. movie theaters, including movie trailers. However, shorter versions of trailers usually air on TV, where few or no performance royalties are paid. Fortunately, music in trailers often pays very high licensing fees.

MAKING A STATEMENT

The figure below is from one of our PRO statements. From left to right, it indicates:

- *Series/Film.* The name of the show or movie.
- *Count.* The number of times the episode aired. (Streams are indicated elsewhere on the statement.)
- *Title.* The name of the piece of music.
- *Episode.* The name of the episode.
- *Work number.* BMI's work number for the piece of music.
- *Use.* How the cue was used. In this case, "BI" indicates a background instrumental use.
- *Timing.* How long the cue played.
- *Period.* The financial quarter in which the episode aired. These aired in the first quarter of 2019. (This statement and the accompanying royalty payment were received in September 2019.)
- *Your %.* The percentage of the writer's share to which we are entitled. In this case, it is 50%. (Everything we write is split fifty-fifty between the two of us, so we have another BMI statement that is identical to this one.)
- *Current activity.* The amount paid for this placement.
- *Super usage.* The extra payment for background vocal, visual vocal, or visual instrumental placements that last more than one minute. (These are hard to get.)
- *Royalty amount.* The sum of the "current activity" and the "super usage."

U.S. Performances - Cable Television

Source											
Series/Film		Episode	Work Number	Performance			Your %	WH	Current Activity	Super Usage	Royalty Amt
Count	Title			Use	Timing	Period					
ENTERTAINMENT											
DATING NO FILTER		**DESPERATELY SEEKING SOMEONE**									
18	CRACK UNDER PRESSURE		021540585	BI	00:14	20191	50.00%		$6.69	$0.00	$6.69
18	EDGE OF CRAZY		021540642	BI	00:20	20191	50.00%		$9.56	$0.00	$9.56
18	HOOD CRUISING		021540608	BI	00:12	20191	50.00%		$5.74	$0.00	$5.74
18	JUST HANGIN		024004184	BI	00:10	20191	50.00%		$4.77	$0.00	$4.77
18	WHAT S UP WITH THAT UNDERSCORE		024004300	BI	00:20	20191	50.00%		$9.56	$0.00	$9.56
DATING NO FILTER		**DRAG QUEENS AND D BAGS**									
9	EDGE OF CRAZY		021540642	BI	00:11	20191	50.00%		$3.11	$0.00	$3.11
9	HOOD CRUISING		021540608	BI	00:10	20191	50.00%		$2.82	$0.00	$2.82
DATING NO FILTER		**GOING DOWN UNDER**									
2	EDGE OF CRAZY		021540642	BI	00:57	20191	50.00%		$5.08	$0.00	$5.08
DATING NO FILTER		**KINKS AND KIMONOS**									
7	AKWARDLY COOL		024004153	BI	00:15	20191	50.00%		$2.90	$0.00	$2.90
DATING NO FILTER		**KISS KISS BYE BYE**									
13	AKWARDLY COOL		024004153	BI	00:16	20191	50.00%		$4.60	$0.00	$4.60
13	BADDER THAN YOU		021540557	BI	00:15	20191	50.00%		$4.32	$0.00	$4.32
13	CAUGHT LOOKING		021540654	BI	00:17	20191	50.00%		$4.89	$0.00	$4.89
13	CHEATING AND LYING		024004136	BI	00:39	20191	50.00%		$11.25	$0.00	$11.25
13	COP A TUDE		021540673	BI	00:08	20191	50.00%		$2.31	$0.00	$2.31
13	CRACK UNDER PRESSURE		021540585	BI	00:18	20191	50.00%		$5.20	$0.00	$5.20
13	HOOD CRUISING		021540608	BI	00:25	20191	50.00%		$7.21	$0.00	$7.21

Figure 20.1. *Example of a PRO royalty statement.*

Here are some observations: In this case, several of our cues were used in more than one episode, indicating that whoever chose the music for this show thought these cues were a good fit and wanted more from the same writers. They liked these cues enough to use seven of them in one episode. (Yes, we wrote more cues for the music library.)

The duration of the cues shown here are between eight seconds and fifty-seven seconds—a typical range.

Though the dollar amounts represent half of the writer's share, they are modest. Being successful with these kinds of placements is a volume business.

Though it is not displayed here, the part of the statement that shows international placements does not indicate all of this detailed information.

JUST FOR NOW: DEFINING "EPHEMERAL USE"

The occurrence of incidental music in the background during a live newscast or a sporting event is known as *ephemeral use*. This includes live or recorded music being played under an on-location report, music being performed by a marching band, a crowd singing, or a song coming through the sound system at a stadium. Since the broadcaster does not know in advance which specific music will be heard, no licensing fee is required. *However, performance royalties are still due.* As is always the case, cue sheets must be completed to report the use of music to the PROs in order for the writers and publishers to be paid.

ROYALTIES FOR MUSIC IN THE PUBLIC DOMAIN

Songwriters and composers can receive performance royalties for songs and instrumentals in the public domain that they have arranged or adapted.

When you arrange and record a PD work, register it with your PRO as a traditional song, specifying yourself as the arranger. Be aware that the PROs may pay royalties at a lower rate than if you had written an original piece of music. Include the songwriter's name if you know it.

AMERICAN PIE: GETTING YOUR SLICE

Performance royalties are split equally between the songwriter or composer of a piece of music and the publisher. These are referred to as the *writer's share* and the *publisher's share*. If a music placement generates $100 in royalties, the writer gets $50, and the publisher gets $50. If there is more than one writer, the writer's share will be split between them, based on their agreement with each other.

Co-writers don't have to be affiliated with the same PRO. An ASCAP writer can collaborate with a BMI, SESAC, or GMR writer. However, when registering musical works with a PRO, the percentage of a writer's share from each PRO must match the percentage of the publisher's share.

For example, if Beth is an ASCAP writer and receives 60% of the writer's share and Mike is a BMI writer and receives 40%, then Beth's publisher must be ASCAP and receive 60% of the publisher's share. Mike's publisher must be BMI and receive 40%.

In the same example, if there are two ASCAP writers and one BMI writer, each of the ASCAP writers could each receive 30%, and the ASCAP publisher's share would remain at 60%. If there are more ASCAP publishers, their total publisher's share must equal 60%. The BMI writer and publisher would each still get 40%.

The figure below shows an example of the work registration of a song we wrote with Sierra West; we split the shares evenly, three ways. Our two BMI writer's shares total 66%, and our publisher's share, SongMakerPro Publishing, is also 66%. Sierra's ASCAP writer's share is 34%, and her publisher's share, 21 Monkeys Music, is also 34%. Thus the writer's shares total 100%, and the publisher's shares also total 100%.

SONGWRITER/COMPOSER	PRO	SHARE
Vance Marino	BMI	33%
Tracey Marino	BMI	33%
Sierra West	ASCAP	34%
PUBLISHER	**PRO**	**SHARE**
SongMakerPro Publishing	BMI	66%
21 Monkeys Music	ASCAP	34%

Figure 20.2. *An example of a PRO work registration.*

THE ITCH TO SWITCH

Songwriters and composers can be a member of only one PRO at a time. After a certain length of time, specified by each PRO, an affiliate can switch to another. Most other countries have only one PRO, so their writers have no choice to make. In the United States, there are four major PROs from which to choose—ASCAP, BMI, SESAC, and GMR. (GMR accepts only established hit writers, so we won't discuss it at length here.)

ASCAP and BMI are not-for-profit companies. On the other hand, SESAC and GMR are for-profit companies and have fewer members. SESAC and GMR are invitation only.

ASCAP charges to join as a writer or a publisher. It's free to join BMI as a writer, but it costs to join as a publisher. SESAC is free for both writer and publisher. Any of the above conditions could change, so check their websites.

CHOICES, CHOICES, CHOICES

So, how does a writer choose a Performing Rights Organization? This is not a matter of "looking for the best one that pays the most." For instance, each PRO differs in how it pays for vocal placements as opposed to instrumental placements. If you expect to get more vocal placements than instrumental placements, perhaps one PRO is better for you than another. However, your chosen PRO may change how it pays for vocal placements, meaning you'd be better off with another.

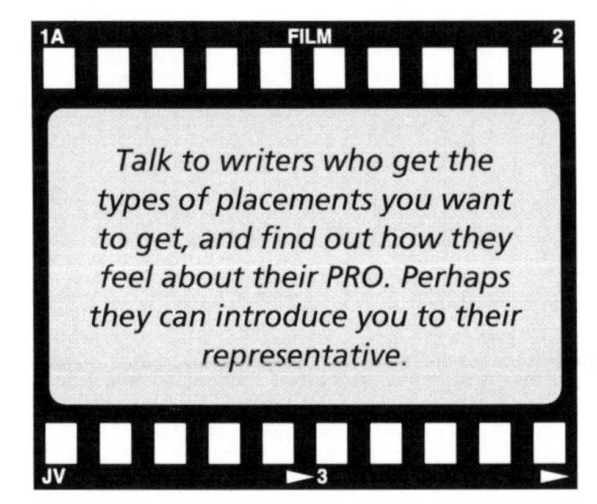

Talk to writers who get the types of placements you want to get, and find out how they feel about their PRO. Perhaps they can introduce you to their representative. This will give you a feel for the company and an idea of what to expect.

Some writers like to join the same PRO that their favorite artists, songwriters, or composers are affiliated with. Though this isn't a very scientific method, going this route is as valid as any other.

IS IT REALLY ALL ABOUT WHO YOU KNOW?

The most important thing to consider when choosing a PRO is the relationships that you may have with their representatives. Ultimately, a PRO is there to collect your performance royalties. If you have any questions or concerns, you need someone at the PRO with whom you can communicate. You can call or email your PRO, but it may be difficult to get through. That's why it's important to meet PRO representatives in person at music industry events. (See the list of music trade organizations and conferences in appendix I.) When they see that you're serious enough about your music career to attend these events, they become more interested in helping you and take you more seriously.

All of the PROs have offices in the major U.S. cities: Los Angeles, New York, and Nashville. Some have offices in Miami, Atlanta, and Chicago—the list goes on. If you are planning a trip to one of these cities, contact your PRO and set up an appointment to meet with a representative.

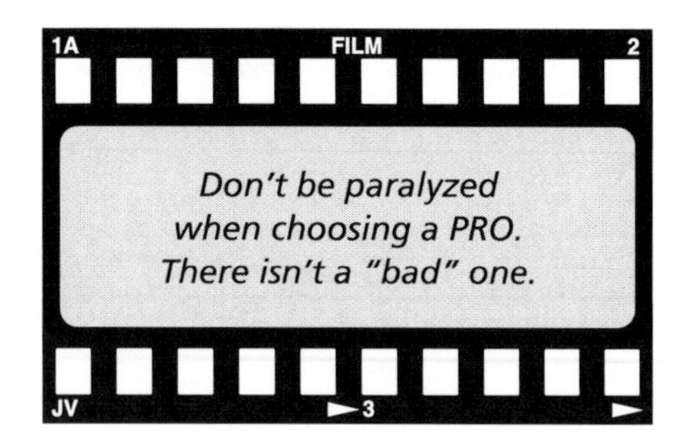

Don't be paralyzed when choosing a PRO. There isn't a "bad" one. As was mentioned earlier, if you're not happy with the one you've chosen, you can switch to another. We know many representatives personally from all four PROs, and they are fine people who love music and the people who create it. Many of them are music creators themselves. They are helpful and knowledgeable. However, they are also very busy, so it's wise to be patient. It can take a month or two before your membership is approved.

JOINING A PRO AS A WRITER AND AS A PUBLISHER

If you are a songwriter without a publishing deal, you are also your own publisher. So when you join a PRO as a writer, it's a good idea to also join as a publisher. Why? You are likely to enter into deals where you will receive some or all of the publisher's share of performance royalties. That's twice as much money as just the writer's share! It is possible to receive publishing royalties through your writer account. However, to increase your chances of getting the money you are due, it's better to be registered as a writer *and* a publisher with your PRO.

Not having correct or complete information with your PRO can be problematic. Something as simple as not providing publisher details or a clerical error on a cue sheet can cause you to be underpaid or not paid at all. Do everything you can to increase your odds of getting paid properly.

ONE STEP AT A TIME: HOW TO REGISTER AS A MUSIC PUBLISHER

Your next mission, if you decide to accept it, is to become a music publisher with your PRO. Remember, you do not have to do this—especially when first starting out in the business. You may not earn performance royalties as a publisher. We thought this would be the case for us. However, we decided to take this step early in our career, and now we literally make hundreds, sometimes thousands, of extra dollars on our PRO statements every year. About two years after we set up our publishing company, we were fortunate to get a couple of placements that gave us our publisher's share. Years after the fact, we still receive publishing money from these placements because the films and TV shows continue to air again and again.

In another case, we developed a great working relationship with a production music library. After we had a proven track record of contributing cues and having them placed in the library's clients' shows, the library gave us some of the publisher's share of performance royalties. This was a sweet and rare deal.

In yet another scenario, some of our publishers split the licensing fee with us, letting us keep 100% of the publishing royalties. This is almost unheard of in the production music world!

Looking back, it was a worthwhile decision for us to establish our publishing company, even though it was not easy coming up with the fees at that time.

I GOT A NAME

The process to set up your music publishing company is not difficult, but in nearly all cases there are some costs. First, you will need a name for your music publishing company. You can choose between using your own name or making up a different name.

When registering with a PRO, using your real, legal name won't be a problem—unless another writer at your PRO has your exact name and is using it for their publishing company. This does happen! Do a search on your selected PRO's website to see if there are any other writers with your name as their publishing company. There are dozens of "Mary Smiths" listed on one PRO's website alone.

KEEPING IT REAL WITH YOUR REAL NAME

If your name is Stevie Songryter, but someone has already claimed the name "Stevie Songryter Music Publishing," you need to present a different take on your name. One solution is to add your middle initial or your middle name. "Stevie S. Songryter Music Publishing" or "Music by Stevie Sammy Songryter" or "Songs by Stevie S. Songryter Publishing Company."

Using your legal name is a practical and inexpensive option, and it's easy to remember. Another plus is that you can use your regular checking account instead of setting up a business checking account. You won't have to do any of the paperwork associated with starting your own business.

However, if you would like to use a stage name, your band's name, or something exotic, creative, or memorable, there are other options. In the music business, especially with music supervisors, it's all about being artistic and standing apart from the crowd. If being perceived as cool or hip is important to you, then, by all means, have an interesting, thought-provoking, original name for your publishing company.

IS IT NOT TRUE? WHEN IT'S GOOD TO BE FAKE AND FICTITIOUS

If you would like to use a fictitious business name as opposed to using your legal name for your music publishing company—such as "Many Moons Music" or "Two Hacks Publishing Company" or "Don't Quit Your Day Job Music Publisher"—you will need to do some paperwork and shell out some fees.

Using a fictitious business name is called a *dba*—or "doing business as." For example, Stevie Songryter, dba (doing business as) Hey! That's My Publishing Company! Here are the steps to setting up a fictitious business name:

1. Select at least three different names for your publishing company. In case one name has already been taken, your PRO is going to ask for some options. For example, if your first choice is Red Guitar Music Publishing, your second choice could be Purple Guitar Music Publishing and your third choice Black Guitar Music Publishing. Obviously, if none of these names is available, you would need to start over again selecting your publishing company's name.
2. Next, establish your fictitious business name with the office of your county clerk (or similar government office). Do an Internet search for the phrase, "How do I set up a dba (doing business as)?" and you'll find information from legal sites to guide you through the process. Or visit your county clerk's website.
3. At this point, you may wish to use the services of a business attorney and/or consult a CPA to set up your publishing company—especially if you decide you want to be an *LLC* (*limited liability company*) or a corporation, rather than a *sole proprietorship*. There are certain advantages and disadvantages to all of these models, and an attorney and/or CPA can assist you. Again, do your research to see what works best for you. Most songwriters and composers use the sole proprietorship business model.
4. After you've decided on your business model, you may have to visit the county clerk's office in person or online for forms and paperwork and file a *fictitious business name statement* in a newspaper. You may be required to apply for a business license or permit with your city. Every place is different regarding rules and regulations of running a business. When contemplating the operation of your business, make sure you are able to do everything from your home.
5. After you have completed the paperwork and paid all the fees, open a business checking account with the name of your publishing company.

Expect to pay anywhere from $100 to a few hundred dollars (or more) to complete this entire process. It can take about a month or more to establish your publishing company and get final approval from your PRO.

STUCK WITH YOU: STICKING WITH ONE PRO AT A TIME

As a writer, you must commit to one PRO. As mentioned before, you can change to a different PRO, but it can be a long and tricky process.

However, as a publisher you may join more than one PRO at a time. Here are some examples of why you would do this:

- You are starting your own music publishing company, and you will be signing writers from each PRO. In this case, you would take some (or all) of the publisher's share of your writers' music.
- You are co-writing with a new writer who joined a PRO as a writer but hasn't yet joined as a publisher. When performance royalties are earned, you could collect the publisher's share on their behalf.

READY, SET, COLLECT YOUR ROYALTIES

Now that you've selected and signed up with your PRO, established your publishing company, paid all the fees, filled out the paperwork, and received the final approval, you're ready for business. You will have earned the respect of music industry professionals, as you will have shown that you know what you're doing. People will want to work with you and help you.

Once you start pitching your music, inking some deals, and getting placements, the next step is collecting royalties. This is where music placement companies earn money for you—and for themselves. They work with the PROs to ensure your music is registered and the information is correct. However, if you are placing your music yourself, you need to take care of these obligations.

FEEL LIKE A NUMBER

Every composer and songwriter, as well as publisher, is assigned a CAE/IPI number when they register and affiliate with a PRO. *IPI* stands for *interested party information* and is the name currently used to refer to this number. *CAE* is the French acronym for "compositeur, auteur, and editeur" meaning, "composer, author, and publisher." Though CAE was replaced with IPI in 2001, it is still used frequently. They each refer to the same number. With most PROs, an affiliate's IPI number differs from their *member account number*. It is important to know your IPI number, as it becomes an extension of a composer's or songwriter's name and is included in most contracts.

Depending on the terms of your deal, you may be responsible for registering your music with your PRO. If you are unsure, consult the company that signed and placed your music. Registering music involves going to the website of your PRO and providing information that includes:

- The name of the musical work
- The name of each writer and their PRO and CAE/IPI number
- The percentage of the writer's share that each writer receives
- The name of each publisher and their PRO CAE/IPI number
- The percentage of the publisher's share that each publisher receives

With BMI, the total writer's share should add up to 100%, as should the publisher's share, resulting in a total of 200%. The percentage of BMI writer's share should equal the percentage of BMI publisher's share.

ASCAP and SESAC are different. Their total writer's share should add up to 50%, as should the publisher's share, resulting in a total of 100%. Again, the percentage of ASCAP writer's share should equal the percentage of ASCAP publisher's share. The same is true for SESAC.

Writers can register their own songs with their PRO, as can their co-writers, if they are with the same PRO. If one of their co-writers is with a different PRO, each writer will need to register the song with their respective PRO. In our earlier example, we are with BMI, so our co-writer, Sierra West, had to register our song with ASCAP as well.

After the music is registered, the PRO assigns a work number and an ISWC number to the musical work, and the registration will be complete within a few days. The work number is used for in-house reference by the PRO, but the *ISWC number* (*International Standard Musical Work Code number*) is used for identification and tracking inside and outside of the PRO. The ISWC is a unique code for a musical work or composition that is recognized throughout the world and identifies information such as:

- The song title
- The songwriters
- The music publisher(s)
- Song splits

This number is available on the website of your PRO for each of your musical works. It is useful to know where to find this information so it can be included in metadata for collection of other royalties.

Some songs have alternate versions and mixes, such as a no vocal mix. There are two ways to handle registering these works:

1. The alternate mix can be included as an alternate title within the registration of the original song. This then automatically retains the same writer and publisher information, as well as work number and ISWC number.
2. The other option is to give the alternate mix a related title, like "My Song—No Vocal," and register it as a separate work with the same writer and publisher information as the original song. It then becomes a new registration with a different work number and ISWC number.

Either approach is valid.

When the publisher registers your songs with your PRO, sometimes they use a publisher name that is not obviously related to the company name you know them by. This is because they must use a different publisher name for each of the PROs. You can usually figure out which publisher name belongs to which company by remembering the ones to which your music is signed. Sometimes this information is included in the agreement. If you're not sure, ask them.

HEY! THERE'S MORE INCOME! (OR HOW DO YOU SAY "MONEY" IN GERMAN?)

ASCAP, BMI, SESAC, and GMR pay performance royalties to songwriters, composers, and publishers for placements of their music not only in shows that air or stream in the United States but also for shows that air in international territories. These can be shows that originate in the United States and go on to air overseas. In other cases, the shows originate in other countries. This is good motivation to consider signing music with a company that distributes music internationally. The world outside the United States is big. There are hundreds of shows being made every day worldwide, and most of them need music. Many U.S. writers make as much—and sometimes more—in international royalties as they do in domestic royalties.

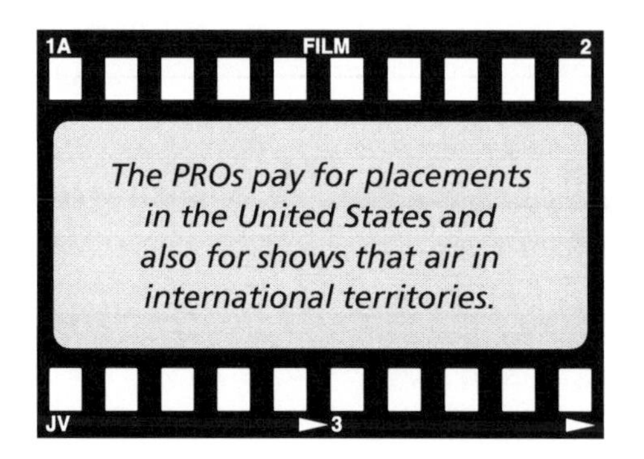

The American PROs have *reciprocal agreements* with PROs in other countries. This means those international PROs make payments to ASCAP, BMI, SESAC, and GMR for music that was written by U.S. writers but is used in shows broadcast in their countries. The U.S. PROs then pay the U.S. writers and publishers. Because the PROs in other countries have their own payment schedules, these international royalty payments often take longer to reach U.S. recipients. Reciprocal agreements also ensure that international writers get paid for their music in shows airing in the United States.

THESE ARE THE PEOPLE (AND MUSIC RIGHTS) IN YOUR NEIGHBORHOOD

When we discussed performance royalties earlier, we mentioned that they are also paid to performers in some instances. *Neighboring rights* are performance royalties paid to performers and master recording owners. They are collected and distributed on a limited basis in the United States, where such royalties are paid for audio streams on noninteractive digital radio. Unlike an *interactive* stream, where the listener chooses the specific songs that are played, a *noninteractive* stream is a predetermined list of songs provided to a customer.

In order to receive neighboring rights royalties, performers and recording owners should register with SoundExchange. Technically another U.S. PRO, SoundExchange differs from the others in that it pays artists, performers, and master recording owners, not songwriters and publishers. It also does not pay for terrestrial radio (AM/FM), TV, movies, or video streams in the United States.

Many publishing companies and production music libraries that aggressively exploit their copyrights also distribute their music to digital radio. Even though these are audio-only streams, songwriters and composers who perform on recordings of their music stand to make some money.

In neighboring rights situations, the owner of the recording receives 50% of the royalty, and the featured artist receives 45%. The remaining 5% is for other performers on the recording.

SO, WHERE'S THE REST OF THE NEIGHBORING RIGHTS MONEY?

The bulk of the neighboring rights money is earned outside the United States. Once again, the United States is not in line with the rest of the world. In many other countries, performers and recording owners *do* receive performance royalties for terrestrial radio, TV shows, and movies. Any U.S. person who has performed on a piece of music or who owns the recording of the music playing on those formats in foreign countries may be entitled to these royalties.

The challenge is that, because the United States doesn't pay international artists and recording owners these royalties, there is no reciprocal agreement in place, which means that in most instances the international societies do not pay U.S. artists and recording owners. Because each country has its own way of making this money available, payment can be very laborious and time-consuming to track down. However, there are companies that will collect your royalties for you for a commission. These commissions are in the 15% range, which is hardly prohibitive. (The not-for-profit U.S. PROs' operating expenses are about 15%.) If you're getting music placements internationally, do an Internet search for "neighboring rights collection companies" to see who can help you find more of your money.

MO MONEY, MO PAPERWORK: MORE INCOME SOURCES

When songs are licensed in movies or TV shows, music fans frequently search for those songs to listen to them again. Some may even purchase physical products (CDs or vinyl records) or pay to download the songs. Many music lovers stream them. The sale of physical products creates a source of revenue for the artists and songwriters; however, collecting money from streaming requires more effort.

The *Mechanical Licensing Collective*, or *MLC*, is the organization that collects and distributes *mechanical royalties* to publishers and self-published songwriters for downloads and interactive streams. Publishers, in turn, pay songwriters. This includes audio-only but *not* audiovisual streams. Like the PROs, your music must be registered on the MLC's website in order for you to be paid. Incidentally, the PROs also pay performance royalties to songwriters and publishers for interactive *and* noninteractive audio streams.

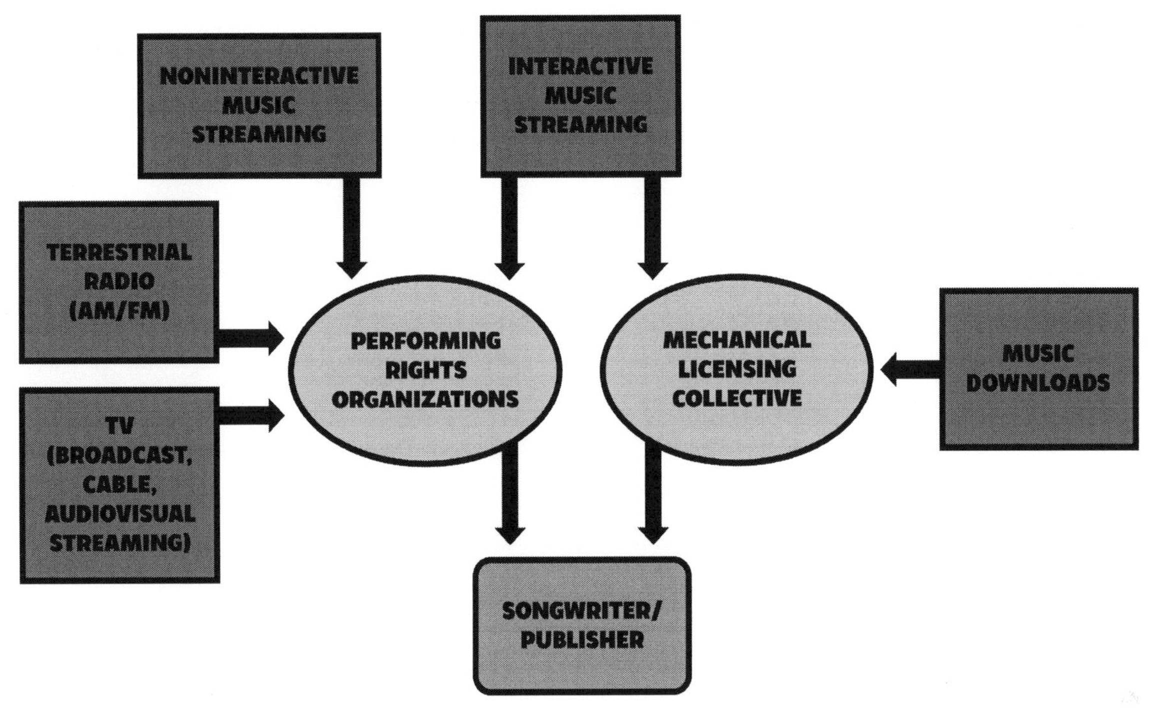

Figure 20.3. *Music royalty distribution to writers and publishers in the United States.*

Artists and master recording owners also receive money when their music is streamed. Royalties for non-interactive streams are paid by SoundExchange in the United States, and royalties for interactive streams are paid by their record label or the organization that distributed the music to the streaming service.

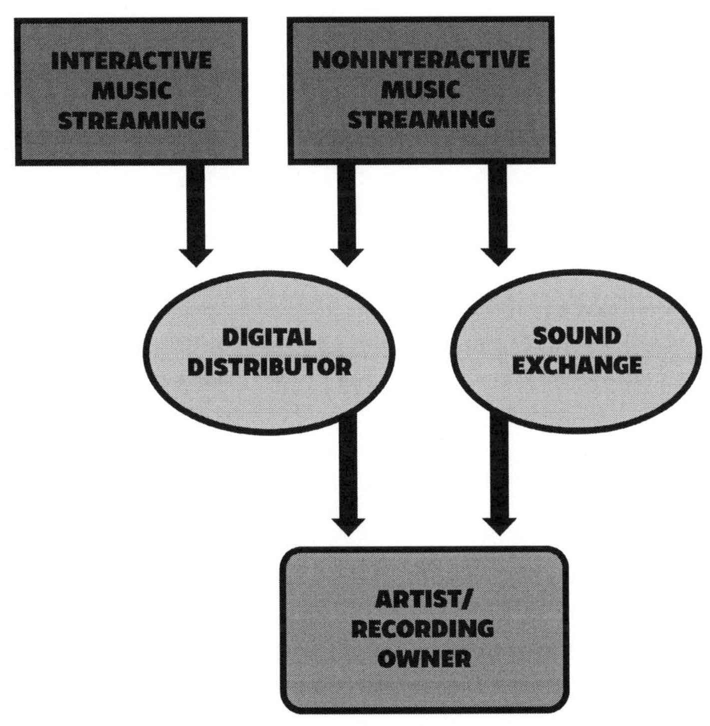

Figure 20.4. *Music royalty distribution to artists and recording owners in the United States.*

RIKKI, DON'T LOSE THESE NUMBERS

The companion to the ISWC number, which identifies a written composition, is the *ISRC number—*or *International Standard Recording Code number—*which identifies a recording. This number is usually issued for free by the entity that distributes music to audio streaming services or may also be purchased online for a fee. The number is requested when registering music with SoundExchange and the Mechanical Licensing Collective.

PRO TIPS . . . About Performance Royalties and PROs

Your PRO rep can be a good source of guidance on a great deal of the music business.

—**James Leach**, Vice President of Creative Services/ West Coast Operations at SESAC

Do your homework and educate yourself. There are four PROs in the United States, and my advice would be to review each of their websites, as they have a wealth of information, tools, and opportunities. Understand their policies and how they pay performance royalties. Learn about their outreach in the music community and who is receptive to creating a relationship with you. Your relationship with a PRO is an important part of your career and is a two-way street.

—**Barbie Quinn**, Senior Director of Administration & Publisher Relations at BMI

All the PROs do the same thing: they collect public performances on your behalf and distribute them to you. They all have agreements with countries around the world, they all are activists protecting your rights, and they all license the same venues and broadcasters. There are differences in size, eligibility, corporate structure, and overall culture.

—**Erin Collins**, Vice President of Film, Television, and Developing Media at SESAC

It is crucial that compositions and sound recordings have accurate, comprehensive metadata. The sound recordings must have ISRCs in order to be correctly identified, and the compositions must have ISWCs. To most effectively track royalties, songwriters should keep track of the recordings and ISRCs that embed their compositions.

—**Abby North**, President of North Music Group

Even though I've been an ASCAP member for my entire songwriting career (and, in full disclosure, I'm on the board there), I still think the best place for a writer to go is where they have the best relationships. Each PRO in the United States has its strengths and weaknesses, but having someone to go to personally when issues or questions arise is a writer's best resource.

—**Michelle Lewis**, Singer, Songwriter, and Composer, Creators' Rights Advocate, Executive Director of Songwriters of North America (SONA), ASCAP Board Member, and Recording Academy L.A. Chapter Board Member

CHAPTER 21

Other Business Models and Income Sources

WILL WRITE FOR FOOD: WORK-MADE-FOR-HIRE

Sync music is a business, and like any other business, different models have emerged. One that appeals to some writers, but not all, is writing music on a work-made-for-hire (or work-for-hire) basis.

This type of arrangement occurs primarily when dealing with production music libraries. The library asks a songwriter or composer to produce one or more pieces of music in a specified style. The library then enters into a *work-for-hire agreement* with the writer and pays a fee to buy both the composition and recording copyrights. The resulting composition is referred to as a *work-made-for-hire.*

There are variables in work-made-for-hire deals. First, the writer receives the up-front work-made-for-hire fee, and then the writer may . . .

- Receive no other additional income. This is sometimes called a "complete buyout," and it is an uncommon deal.
- Receive the writer's share of the performance royalties but no licensing fees. This deal is common.
- Receive licensing fees but no writer's share. This deal is rare.
- Receive the writer's share of the performance royalties and licensing fees. This deal is not typical, but it's nice work, if you can get it.

As is common in business, a work-made-for-hire deal is a risk for both parties. If the music never gets licensed, the writer benefits—although their income will be limited to the work-made-for-hire fee—but the library does not.

If the music generates a lot of licensing fees, the library profits, but the composer may not receive licensing fees, although they will likely receive their performance royalties. Because the library paid for the music, they have an incentive to place it so that they can make their money back. This, in turn, earns performance royalties for the writer.

For some writers, the worst part of this deal is no longer owning the copyrights to their music. With work-made-for-hire deals, there is no reversion of ownership back to the writer. On the other hand, we know of many writers who engage in work-made-for-hire deals on a regular basis, are very successful, and have no regrets.

STRIKE UP THE BAND: HIRING UNION MUSICIANS AND USING DEMO STUDIOS

If you do not perform all your music yourself, you may need to hire outside talent. When you do, you must determine whether or not the singer or instrumentalist is a member of a musician's union (there are several). Always ask before hiring. If the musician or singer is a current member of a union, it's not necessarily a deal breaker. However, hiring union musicians and singers can be problematic and create obstacles. This is because, when your music is placed, union members on your recording may be entitled to additional backend or other royalties (also known as "residuals"). As long as all parties are up-front and have the required permissions and paperwork, union membership should not be a problem.

Also, if you use a demo studio, know that they may hire union musicians. Make certain that you and the studio owner and producer all agree on what you intend to do with the song. These studios are for the purpose of recording a demo of a song to be pitched to an A&R person, artist, or music publisher—and not for the purpose of sync placements. However, many demo studios have come around to recording music for sync, but you may need to pay additional fees and get properly signed releases. Always ask first!

MIND YOUR OWN BUSINESS

How a writer conducts their business is a personal preference. The most important thing is to make educated and informed decisions. Again, find out the types of deals people in your music circle have made, and learn from them. Most experienced sync music writers understand the difficulty in making these choices and are willing to share their experience and offer advice.

Use this information and our earlier discussion about performance royalties to strategize your signings. We write a lot of happy, positive music for commercials. We signed some of this music to a music library on a work-made-for-hire basis that brought us some money up front but no share of the licensing fees. We received some performance royalties, but the larger licensing fees went to the library. Although it was helpful at the time receiving up-front money, had we been more strategic, we would have signed our music intended for commercials to a library that shared licensing fees with us. Knowledge is power!

THE DIRECT APPROACH

Some production music libraries engage in certain dubious practices over which composers and songwriters have no control. All you can do is be aware of a library's business model and exercise your best judgment.

Direct licensing is when a production company or network pays a fee to a library that includes a sync licensing fee *and* the performance royalties. This is a blanket deal that covers some or all of the music in the library's catalog. Like a blanket license deal, the direct licensing fee is often not shared with the writers due to the difficulty in figuring out how to distribute the money. This means no performance royalties for the writers when the shows air in the United States.

A small upside for the writer is that when these shows air overseas, the writer *may* receive performance royalties.

A direct license deal favors the network that will air the show. The network will not have to pay the PROs the fees that other networks pay to use the music in the PRO repertories. Many libraries refuse to engage in this practice, so the network has a smaller number of sources from which to license music. However, they are always able to find some companies to work with.

The main advantage with direct licensing for a library is receiving money up front without having to wait for the shows to air and the PROs to pay. Again, this is a gamble, because the library may possibly receive more in performance royalties over time if they had stayed with the PRO model. The writers would have also received performance royalties with the PRO model.

If you don't want to be a part of this practice and a library you are considering signing with has music in shows on networks that do direct licensing, you probably shouldn't sign with that library.

It's important to note that this model is legal but it is frowned upon by many in the business, as they believe it devalues music.

SHARING IS NOT ALWAYS CARING

Also be aware of the practice of *revenue sharing*. The name might make it sound noble—something that would make your mom proud—but it instead devalues music even more.

Some networks and production companies pay no licensing fee to use music from a production music library's catalog. In addition, they ask for some or all of the publisher's share of performance royalties to be *shared* with them. Some libraries, in turn, take some of the writer's share of performance royalties. (They can't do this unless it's stipulated in the writer's contract with the library that the writer may receive less than 100% of their performance royalties. *Read your contracts!*) Why would a library and its writers choose to involve themselves in this kind of deal? Because some shows generate so much money in performance royalties that even receiving a portion of them is considered profitable by some libraries.

ROYALTY FREE MUSIC LIBRARIES

One of the reasons we decided to write this book was to share information that has taken us years to learn. Here we have another item to add to the list of confusing and contradictory terms in the music licensing business.

Despite the name, *royalty free music libraries* do generate performance royalties and the music is not free. The name is very misleading. The distinction has to do with the licensing fee: When music is licensed from a royalty free music library, the fee covers use of the music *beyond* the current project. A licensing fee is paid, and the client can use the music in a current project and sometimes any future project. This is different from licensing music from other music libraries, where the licensing fee covers the current project *only*—and only for a specified time frame.

This is yet another practice where music is devalued by leaving money on the table. If a show extends beyond the initially agreed-upon term, or if another show is produced, another licensing fee should be paid.

These types of libraries exist to cater to clients whose projects have smaller budgets, so the licensing fees tend to be lower than those in more traditional music libraries.

SUBSCRIPTION MUSIC LIBRARIES

A variation of the royalty free model is the *subscription music library*. As the name implies, clients pay a monthly or yearly fee to use as much music from the catalog in as many projects as they want, no matter how long the project lasts. Songwriters and composers are paid a buyout fee when their music is signed with these companies and receive no licensing fees (because there aren't any) and no performance royalties. In our opinion, this model not only devalues the music, it devalues the writer as well. As one publisher said ruefully, "It's a race to the bottom."

WE'RE ALL IN THIS TOGETHER

Whether or not to sign with libraries engaging in non-exclusive retitling, gratis licensing, direct licensing, revenue sharing, royalty free licensing, or subscription fee licensing is a moral and ethical decision we must each make. Songwriters and composers often sign deals based on what is good for them individually at the moment. So if you plan to be a part of the sync music world for a while, it's worth making decisions based on what's better for the value of your music and the music licensing business overall to ensure that it will be around—hopefully—for a long time.

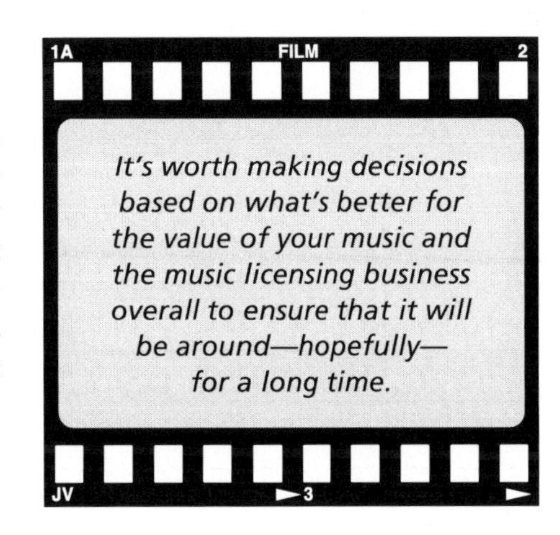

PRO TIPS . . . About Other Business Models

Worry less about what sync model is a good fit for you and more about which relationship is the best fit. If you connect with a sync agent who truly believes in your music, they will move the stars around to help place you among them.

—**James Jacoby**, Music Supervision, Clearance, and Licensing

The more I learn about the music business, the more I realize how elusive an understanding of this business can be. What I believe is important is to know what you don't know; at that point, you create awareness around the need to seek a better understanding. Learn more, understand better, and surround yourself with people who know more than you do.

—**Mirette Seireg**, MSc, and President of Mpath Music LLC

Don't get blinded by the "shiny chrome" of a credit. So many artists/writers, especially those starting out, will accept any license fee amount thinking that adding a credit has more value to their career than their own music. No! Building long-term value in your catalog is the goal—not any single credit.

—**Marc Caruso**, CEO & Co-founder of Angry Mob Music

CHAPTER 22

Understanding the Basics of Sync Music Publishing Agreements

WHEN TO CONTACT A MUSIC ATTORNEY

This is a question of which came first, the chicken or the egg? That is to say, do you hire a music attorney *before* you have a contract from a publisher, or do you hire a music attorney *after* you receive the contract? Does it matter? Obviously, if you're serious about pursuing sync music as a career, a music attorney's services will come in handy at any point, and the sooner you find good counsel, the better. These services can be quite costly; the typical rate is a few hundred dollars per hour. However, some attorneys may review a contract for a flat fee or offer an initial half-hour consultation free of charge. There are legal organizations who will do *pro bono* (free!) work for musicians, songwriters, and composers until they get established.

It is possible to find legal information from just about anywhere, especially on the Internet. But seeking it and using it would be unwise, and it may not even pertain to your particular situation. Only a licensed attorney can give legal advice.

Be cautious when selecting your attorney. It is imperative you find an experienced music attorney or entertainment attorney, because they understand the intricacies of the music business. A qualified music attorney, depending on their connections, can also help open doors, negotiate deals, have access to pitches and briefs, and introduce you to opportunities. They will advise you and negotiate what's best for you and your music. They become part of your team—not just your legal counsel.

One of our friends said money was tight when he was getting started, but he realized he needed help understanding the legalese in his first production music library agreement. He saved up his hard-earned money and booked a few hours with a music attorney. The attorney patiently went over the contract line-by-line as our friend took detailed notes about what everything meant. It was money well spent.

HEY! READ THIS!

One very successful author and music attorney we know said so many of his clients would come to him for help *after* signing all of their music rights away in an ironclad, regrettably binding, long-term contract. He said this is quite common. These clients were frustrated this attorney couldn't just "make a phone call" and "make everything right again." He would tell them, "Okay, then, let me climb into my time machine, go back to the very *second* before you signed your contract, and tell you *not to sign that contract!*"

KEY PROVISIONS IN CONTRACTS

Some contracts are a couple of pages in length; others are over twenty pages. The shorter ones may be clearer and easier to understand, but they could be missing vital clauses. A qualified music attorney can explain what you need to know to protect yourself. Here are some key points to look for and consider before signing on the dotted line:

- *Ownership of the copyrights.* Some agreements allow the composer, songwriter, or artist to retain ownership of the composition and recording copyrights. Others transfer complete ownership to the publisher. Still others split the ownership of the copyrights between the two parties. This is one of the most important details to know about a contract.
- *Exclusivity.* It's essential to know if the musical works are being signed exclusively or non-exclusively. In addition, a writer needs to know if the agreement allows them to sign future musical works with other publishers or if they, as a writer, are signing exclusively.
- *The term or length of the agreement.* Some agreements last a month or two, while others last forever. Most last for three to five years. An agreement may automatically renew at the end of the term and require thirty days' (or more) advance notice in writing to terminate the agreement at the end of the current term. If you're uncomfortable with long-term commitments and want to be sure you have a way out, this is essential information to know.
- *How the money is split.* There are many sources of income when music is synced, but the two most notable are the *licensing fees* and *performance royalties.*
    - In most cases, the licensing fees are split fifty-fifty. Remember that the performance royalties are made up of the writer's share and the publisher's share and are paid directly from the PROs.
    - In most production music library deals, the composer or songwriter keeps all of the writer's share while the publisher receives the publisher's share. In deals with sync agencies and indie and major publishers, a portion of the publisher's share may be split with the writer. Unless there is some compelling reason to renegotiate these standard splits, they should be insisted upon.
- *The payment schedule.* Publishers commonly pay quarterly, biannually, or annually.
    - In other cases, they pay within a specified time period—usually thirty or sixty days, after they receive payment of the licensing fee.
    - In addition, there may be a threshold, below which no payment is made, until an upcoming pay period when the threshold has been met or exceeded.
- *The obligations of each party.* The composer or songwriter is required to deliver a specified amount of music in a stipulated style, in a stated format, within a certain time period, as outlined in the agreement. The publisher is obligated to handle administrative tasks, including registering the musical works with the appropriate societies, and pay the composer or songwriter when the music has been successfully exploited.

READING THE FINE PRINT . . .

Contracts and agreements can be convoluted, especially to people without any legal background. The terminology can be confusing. However, there are legal phrases and deal points that are common in most, if not all, contracts. Once you know this "boilerplate language" (basic text found in most contracts and legal documents), navigating contracts will become much easier for you.

Most contracts begin by designating the parties. The parties are the individuals and/or businesses agreeing to the above-listed terms. There may be a blank line for your name and/or your company, followed by language like, "hereinafter referred to as 'Songwriter' or 'Composer' or 'Licensor.'" The publisher's name and/or company will be stated, followed by language like, "hereinafter referred to as 'Publisher' or 'Company.'" Each party will be referred to by these terms throughout the contract.

Some contracts are broken down into separate sections. Here are some standard categories:

- Grant of Rights
- Term/Territory
- Warranties and Representations
- Indemnification
- Compensation
- Right to Edit Masters
- Non-exclusive Names and Likenesses
- Assignment of Agreement to Another Party
- Schedule A

As an additional note, be aware that publishers may also change the name of one of your works if your title already exists in their catalog by another writer. The new titles may not be desirable. If there is flexibility in the titling of your music, especially instrumentals, check the online catalog of the publisher to see if they already have your proposed title. If they do, consider changing it yourself.

Terms and conditions of the contracts may be negotiable within reason. It's okay to ask politely. This is where a qualified music attorney can be helpful. However, don't be surprised if some companies have a "take it or leave it" stance.

Always get qualified legal help with contracts and licenses.
This information is to be used as a guide only.

SIGNED, SEALED, DELIVERED, THIS MUSIC'S YOURS: COPYRIGHT REGISTRATION

Before copyrighting your music, you need to determine with whom you will be signing. The terms of your contract with a publisher dictate who owns the copyright. If the publisher owns the copyright, it is their responsibility to register it with the U.S. Copyright Office. If you retain ownership, registration is your responsibility.

Your song or instrumental is considered copyrighted when it is created and fixed in a tangible form by having been written down or recorded. Registering it with the Copyright Office is strongly advised, as this will strengthen your case if anyone infringes on your musical work.

Registration can be done through the mail or online at the website of the U.S. Copyright Office (https://www.copyright.gov/). While the review process will take a few months when registering online, doing it through the mail takes considerably longer. Songs can be registered individually, but it may be more cost-effective to register your songs as a group. If you own your composition and the recording, remember to copyright each of these.

THE DREAM WORKS WHEN THE TEAMS WORK TOGETHER

In part 1, you learned who could be on your *creative* team. Now we'll discuss the importance of putting together a *business* team. Your team may include the following members:

- *Music attorney.* Specifically understands and deals with music contracts. The attorney should have relationships with publishers and music supervisors.
- *PRO representative.* Your point of communication when you have a question. They may introduce you to other writers and publishers.
- *Manager.* Knows music producers and has contacts at record labels. They can create marketing plans. Artist managers are often mentors and offer career advice.

- *Booking agent (for bands and artists).* Sets up concert performances and seminars.
- *Sync agent and/or music publisher.* Exploits your music copyrights and handles collecting money and other administrative duties.
- *PR (public relations or publicity) representative.* May assist you in getting the industry's attention, award nominations, and publicity.
- *CPA (certified public accountant) or tax professional.* Has knowledge of the financial side of the music business.

PRO TIPS . . . About Sync Music Publishing Agreements

In my experience, an artist would normally more often need a music attorney who practices in the transactional field (i.e., to assist the artist with contracts, advice, connections, resolve disputes, etc.), as opposed to litigation (as for that, one would probably need an attorney who is experienced in going to court to argue breach of contract and infringement cases, which is a different specialty area and hopefully a rarer occurrence).

—**Ben McLane**, Esq., McLane & Wong

What should an artist look for in a qualified music attorney? Good references, a professional reputation, and compatibility. The music business is a relationship business. An experienced and established music attorney may also bring their client the benefit of relationships they have that might be helpful in the further development of the client's career, either creatively or financially.

—**Garrett M. Johnson**, Esq., Past President of the California Copyright Conference

Some PROs have events to educate creators about the music industry, as well as workshops and social events. They also may help connect writers with other writers, musicians, lawyers, managers, and additional resources. But it is important to keep in mind that PROs are not substitutes for these experts; nor is it their job to pitch music for you or manage your career. Helping writers help themselves is a good way to think about it.

—**Erin Collins**, Vice president of Film, Television, and Developing Media at SESAC

PART 4: RESOURCES

Hey! That Helps!

Useful Information and Additional Tips for Success

CHAPTER 23

Hey! That's a Wrap!

HEY! READ THIS!

A few years after we started writing for sync, our music wasn't going anywhere. So we saved up our money and booked a private feedback consultation with our mentor and hero, the late, great John Braheny, author of *The Craft and Business of Songwriting*. We arrived at his Los Angeles home and nervously waited as he listened to some of our music; then he told us, "This is good!" He asked us what the problem was. We told him each cue or song would take us weeks—sometimes months—to complete because we kept tweaking it, trying to make it "perfect." John peered over his glasses and said, "Don't be so precious with your music! Just write it, submit it, forget about it, then repeat the process." He did not mean we could be sloppy or careless. John meant we should create it, finish it, move on to the next project, and not dwell on it. We took his advice and started finding success. Thank you, John Braheny.

PART OF YOUR WORLD—OR THEIR WORLD: FROM WHOSE POINT OF VIEW?

Memorize this phrase: "In Their World." Tack it on before—or after—just about everything that you hear and read about in the music business. Seriously. It will save you a lot of grief throughout your music career. Why? "In Their World" (or "In My World") means the people giving you advice are doing it from *their* perspective. Their priorities and advice may or may not apply to you at this time—or ever. We went down a lot of rabbit holes early on because we followed someone's well-meaning advice *exactly*, only to find out it was completely wrong for us in *our* world.

Years ago, we were at a music industry lunch and heard an ultra hip and cool, taste-making music supervisor exclaim, "I just can't stand ukulele music. Nobody wants *that* genre anymore!" We were upset! We had just completed an entire collection for a major library. This was our bread and butter—and one of our passions. Our ukulele music was getting used around the world, every day (and still does). We were about to stop writing this type of music when we realized this was just *his* opinion. In *his* world, he was tired of it, but ukulele music still gets placed to this day.

AIN'T NO STOPPIN' US NOW

The music business is tough and demanding. A publisher said once on a panel, "If it were easy, everyone would be a songwriter or composer." You may find and then choose to go down a different musical road than the one you are on now. Talent or musical ability, of course, are a given. Often, luck is involved, too. One of our favorite pieces of advice came from a famous music producer/songwriter who said, "Don't wait for success . . . *Prepare* for it." If you prepare and have persistence, patience, resources, tools, and the desire to write for sync, you *will* be a success.

Here is a recap of what was discussed throughout the book:

- *Do your research.* Know what's getting placed in the sync world. Study and analyze those songs and instrumentals. Pay attention to what's on the music charts, because these songs influence music placements.
- *Be professional.* Develop an excellent work ethic, and never miss a deadline. Do your best with what you have at that time. Strive for quality. Be communicative, direct, honest, and polite. Don't waste anyone's time.
- *Educate yourself.* This is not just about going to school, although taking classes to improve your skills is invaluable. Immerse yourself in the music business. Read books, magazines, articles, and blogs. Get on email lists of music organizations. Attend as many music conferences and events as you can, online and in person. Join songwriter groups. Music industry professionals don't like to explain how the music business works to newcomers (which is one of the reasons we wrote this book). It's okay to not know something, but do research before approaching a music industry person.
- *Accept feedback graciously.* Develop a thick skin. Everyone will face criticism at some point in their music career. Don't take anything personally. Try not to be a "song defender." Music is subjective, and every person has their strong likes and dislikes about it. Negative feedback and reviews can be devastating, but they can also shed light as to what may be holding you back. Figure it out. Move on. Get better.
- *Create and meet your music goals.* It's fine to wish or dream of success, but you need to make a realistic plan with goals and deadlines and then take the necessary steps to make it happen. Your path may change, but keep reaching for what you want—always. If this is something you truly desire but you have certain other commitments or priorities, that's okay; the music business is here to stay. Fortunately, this is a part of the industry that you can do at any stage in your life, and you can do it full-time, part-time, or on your own schedule.
- *Guard your creative time.* Each day, take an hour, a half hour, five minutes—whatever you can carve out—and do *something* with your music. Set a timer, if necessary, and write down ten titles, sing a melody into your phone, open a session in your DAW and start a drum track, or study the music under several commercials. A blank page can be intimidating, but begin by filling a small part of it; then add to it later. Find outlets like tip sheets that will give you a project and a deadline.
- *Be organized.* Keep notes. Scan and keep track of signed contracts. Know where your music is signed and what the terms of the agreements are.
- *Prepare your 10-second introduction and brief, 30-second elevator speech.* Know what you do well, and be ready to describe it quickly. Practice your speech.
- *Keep emails short, polite, professional, to the point.* At the end of every email, always include your name, contact information, a link to your website or where your music can be heard, especially when corresponding with a music industry person.
- *Learn how to network effectively.* Follow up with people you meet. Start conversations at events. Become better at remembering names and faces; it will pay off every time.
- *Build trusted relationships.* Find a community of like-minded friends. They may be some of your best resources, and this is empowering. Search for and nurture these relationships. It may take time, but these friends, collaborators, and music industry colleagues will help you more than you will ever know.
- *Try collaborating.* If you can't do everything yourself, find your musical and business teams. Working with talented, competent, and supportive people is often a secret to success.
- *Remember, only a licensed attorney can give legal advice.*
- *Stay positive.* Optimism and a sense of humor go far in the music business. There can be a lot of rejection and missed opportunities. A hopeful outlook—and a light-hearted attitude—will help you greatly. People like being around enthusiastic people.

DON'T STOP BELIEVIN': CELEBRATE ALL YOUR SUCCESSES

Our final piece of advice: Each week, promise yourself that you'll write down every victory, no matter how small it seems. Then, take yourself out to lunch or coffee, pat yourself on the back, and keep going. This was one of the things that really helped keep our spirits up when we started. There would be weeks and months when not much was happening. Yet, when we wrote down even the tiniest bit of good music news, there was always *something* to celebrate every Friday. And we did. And you will too.

FINAL PRO TIPS . . . Additional Tips for Success

I have never had any song placed or deal made due to the efforts of a manager or publisher. It has always happened because someone heard me play—or someone knew someone. Most deals come through "The Back Door," where someone you know helps you out or passes your song along.

—**Jack Tempchin**, Writer of "Peaceful Easy Feeling," and Member of the Songwriters Hall of Fame

Follow your passions! You'll experience highs and lows, but you'll always be emotionally invested, which is the best way to live.

—**Liz Redwing**, Music Management and Consulting

It's much harder to go it alone. Join a team, collaborate, and use the resources that are in front of you; things will move much faster.

—**Trygge Toven**, Music Supervisor

It's important to keep up with trends and technology in the music business. Do your research.

—**Adam Taylor**, President of APM Music, Chairman of the PMA

The best way to learn anything is to not be afraid of making mistakes. Making mistakes is how you learn, so go for it, and learn.

—**Brian Scheuble**, mixer

Believe in yourself. If you don't, nobody else will. Everyone has an opinion; it doesn't mean they are right. Learn to trust your gut! You never stop learning in life. What you put in, you get out, so don't just settle at being *good*. Be *exceptional* at what you do. Get out of your own way, and get out of your comfort zone too.

—**Pamela Sheyne**, Songwriter, Singer, and Mentor, and Co-founder of SongWriterCamps

The best advice I've ever been given has proven to be far less valuable than any bits of encouragement I've received along the way.

—**Charles Bernstein**, Composer

Imagine there are a thousand songs being considered for a placement, and only one will be chosen. Why should the decision-makers choose yours? They won't—unless you provide compelling reasons for your music to be chosen over the competition. Being perfectly crafted is not enough. Explore unique sounds, melodies, rhythms, and chords that will jump out of the pile and demand attention. If your song includes lyrics, seek fresh, original ways to express your ideas without saying anything that might eliminate it from working for a scene.

—**Jason Blume,** Emmy®-winning Hit Songwriter and Author

Be great at what you do, and be easy to work with.

—**Tom Villano,** Emmy®-winning Music Editor and Music Supervisor, and Instructor at the Musicians Institute

Foster as many relationships as you can, as this is a people and relationship business. Network and educate yourself. Attend events, showcases, and webinars, and become a member of different organizations that support the music community. Be persistent but respectful, assertive without being aggressive, and always put your best foot forward.

—**Barbie Quinn,** Senior Director of Administration & Publisher Relations at BMI

As clients increasingly seek "real music" (music by artists) over generic "production music," composers have an opportunity to shed the practice of producing "utility music" in favor of creating music with an "authentic edge"—an approach that will always lead to original-sounding tracks.

—**Juan Carlos Quintero,** Composer and Producer, Moondo Music LLC

Be prepared to pick yourself up and dust yourself off a hundred times a week. This is a business of rejection!

—**Steve Dorff,** 2018 Inductee to the Songwriters Hall of Fame

I think I learned this from multiple people I admired: When an issue is complex or you are not 100% clear about something multifaceted, you have to pick up the phone and speak with the person you are dealing with and talk it through for a dynamic solution. Text and email will fail you; those communication forms are only for simple, binary issues, but too many people think they can solve complicated issues.

—**John Houlihan,** Music Supervisor

Composers need to ensure that all aspects of their composition are 100% original—intro, melody, lyrics, bass line, signature hooks, etc.—especially if they are using any existing tracks for inspiration or reference during the composition process.

—**Ron Mendelsohn,** president and CEO of Megatrax

Be authentic. Authenticity is so important, and it applies both to your creation of music and to your business relationships. On the creation side, the best music that'll come from you is the music that you're passionate about making—the music that speaks to your soul. On the business side, I always say that you're not going to be a fit for everyone, but you'll be a fit where you belong, and there will be opportunity within that authenticity.

—**Morgan McKnight,** Executive Director of the Production Music Association

Realize this part of the industry is a slow burn. It takes *years* before your music gets used. Let's call it the "Patience Factor."

—**Ken Jacobsen**, Composer and Producer

The best advice I've received was from Jim Long, who always told me, "When in doubt, do without." This advice applies to everything—from creating music to licensing to working with clients to making everyday decisions.

—**Tanvi Patel**, Owner and CEO of Crucial Music Corporation

Read everything. Stay abreast of technology. Books are great but can become outdated quickly. Visit music forums. Read blogs. Watch YouTube videos. There will always be something new to learn. Be part of the solution, not part of the problem. Be kind to people.

—**Steve Barden**, Composer and Author

I have had many ups and downs, and it has been a very difficult, yet rewarding, road. But if I were to distill everything I was told and everything I learned along the way into one concise principle, I would have to borrow from Nike's slogan: "Just do it."

—**Michael Eames**, President of PEN Music Group, Inc.

Be willing to invest in yourself, whether that is taking the necessary time to develop your craft, finding your own initial resources to be able to create your work product, or making a commitment of your own time to find resources before looking to others to join in. If you're not willing to invest in yourself, it is not reasonable or ultimately fruitful to expect others to do so.

—**Garrett M. Johnson**, Esq., Past President of the California Copyright Conference

The best piece of advice was from my father when I was so frustrated that I was neither rich nor famous (nor solvent) that I was going to "call it a day." He urged me to be patient and said that if I just kept working hard and looking for opportunities it would all work out. He was right: I did—and it did.

—**Michael A. Levine**, Curator, Mpath

Don't perform for free just to get "good exposure." (Would a brain surgeon perform a surgery just to get good exposure?)

—**Dr. Jonathan Rathsam**, Acoustician

Always think about what value you bring, not just what someone else can do for your career. Being of service to others and lifting each other up is so important. So, get out there, be a good listener, be kind and authentic, and your network will grow. When I first started writing songs, one simple message I heard at a conference from hit songwriter Allen Shamblin was, "If you want to be successful, be kind." Words to live by.

—**Nitanee Paris**, Award-Winning Songwriter, and Partner and Director of A&R, ArtistMax

One of the best things you can do to improve both your craft and career is to be a part of projects that actually get out into the world. Find ways to be a part of "real" work with real goals. Do whatever you can to collaborate with people who are more talented and successful than you.

—**Ronan Chris Murphy**, producer and engineer, Veneto West

The career success is a function of the power of your music, the power of your relationships (as most opportunities would come to you via referrals), and your worldview—tenacious, grateful, resourceful, creative, inspired.

—**Penka Kouneva**, Composer for film, TV, and video games

Songwriters need to understand that they are in the music *business*. They must read as much as they can about the business. And do not be afraid to ask questions.

—**James Leach**, Vice President of Creative Services/West Coast Operations at SESAC

These days, my favorite quote is what Angela Davis said (the opposite of the Serenity Prayer): "Let me change what I can't accept."

—**Lisa Aschmann**, songwriter and author, Nashville Geographic

An important key is to *send your strongest material*. We know that many composers cover many genres, but everyone has a strongest style or genre. That's what we want to hear.

—**Ron Goldberg**, Vice President of Manhattan Production Music

This is a business, and your (potential) clients are all busy, have deadlines, bills to pay, etc. So if you make their lives easier, they will probably call you again. Most of the people in this space are friendly, easygoing, and down-to-earth. Follow their example! Also, never stop learning. Do what you love and what genuinely interests you. This also pertains to writing music you enjoy. Don't write in a genre you hate just because you think it will make you money, because it probably won't!

—**Matt Hirt**, Composer, Songwriter, and Producer, and Co-owner of Catapult Music

Don't be afraid to extend yourself; it's how you will learn and experience growth. Once you get your foot in the door, it's up to you to write your own ticket in this industry. It's true. Be grateful, be thankful, and you will be blessed.

—**Teri Nelson Carpenter**, President and CEO of Reel Muzik Werks, Past President AIMP, Executive Vice President of the Independent Music Publishers International Forum

If you want to be a professional songwriter, remember that as a professional you are paid for the services you give others, not for what feels good to you. Start writing from inspiration absolutely, but remember when you're editing the final version that its professional purpose is the impact it has on others, so craft it accordingly.

—**Jai Josefs**, Songwriting Coach, Mentor, Author

My favorite piece of advice is this: Check your ego at the door. For composers and songwriters getting into sync, it is ultimately not about you. You are part of a team that elevates someone else's vision, be it a music supervisor, producer, or director. Be flexible, accommodating, and willing to try new ideas.

—**Erin Collins**, Vice President of Film, Television, and Developing Media at SESAC

After being on this planet for eighty years, and sixty of them in the music business, I can't say there is one piece of advice but rather a philosophy that has worked for me: (1) Visualize your goals, (2) work on them every day, and (3) trust your instincts.

—**Art Munson**, *MusicLibraryReport*

Show up, and step up. Commit to a bold vision, and hold onto it. Tap into intuition. Ride with luck. Mitigate frustration. Practice patience. Be prepared to sort out a fair amount of chaos. When a creative inspiration knocks on the door, invite it in as a welcome visitor. Be curious about what happens, and enter into a vortex of creative intimacy. Do what you need to liberate whatever it is that you're channeling, and boldly take your work to the next level. There's always romance involved in placing your music in a bottle, releasing it, and seeing when—and where—it lands. Above all, listen to your spirit, lead with your heart, and stay true to the friends and collaborators you meet along the way. It is a soulful journey.

—**Mirette Seireg**, MSc, and President of Mpath Music LLC

It's a *long* process. You can't be in this industry to score big money fast; it just doesn't work that way. But if you can't imagine doing anything else for a living other than making music, then this is the career path for you. If you stick with it long enough, it will happen. It might take six months, it might take six years, it might take sixteen years.

—**Derek Jones**, Director of Creative Services at Megatrax Production Music

Ask yourself, "What feeling am I conveying? Am I feeling it strongly enough to make the listener feel it? Have I said it the best I can?" If you haven't, try again in a brand-new song about the same feeling. A photographer takes sixty frames to pick one image. The same is true for a songwriter. Keep expressing the same feeling from different perspectives.

—**Suzan Koç**, Publisher and Songwriting Mentor

Working relationships require networking, and sometimes that can be a long game. I may hear from someone that I haven't spoken to for five or ten years, and they think of me and have a project they'd like me to help with, or maybe I hear from someone new whom I have been recommended to. As long as I do my best and am easy to work with and share their goals of making it great, my career will keep moving.

—**Les Brockmann**, recording engineer, mixer, and score mixer

The industry is much smaller and more interconnected than you imagined it to be. Most everyone in the industry is only a degree or two separated from each other, and the reality is that your reputation, both good and bad, gets around. Set a high standard for yourself, and live up to it. The industry will know and reward you!

—**Marc Caruso**, CEO & Co-founder of Angry Mob Music

One of my favorite expressions is, "You don't know what you don't know." While writing lots and lots of songs is critical to improving as a songwriter, if you continue to make the same mistakes with no one to help point you in the right direction, the process will be a much slower one.

—**Cliff Goldmacher**, award-winning songwriter and producer, and songwriting consultant

I wish I had found mentors when I was beginning my career. Most of what I learned, I learned through trial and error. That's not a bad method, but it's not the most streamlined.

—**Abby North**, President of North Music Group

I live by the exact same mantra in business that I live by in life: Do good in the world, be kind to others, and be a beacon of light in the darkness. You'd be amazed how far just treating people with kindness and respect will take you, especially in a tough business like the music industry. People are *drawn* to kindness and positivity. If you practice them, you'll automatically attract the right kind of people to your business—and to your life. If you become known as a decent, considerate person who's easy to work with, people (and business) will come flocking to you. If your goal in everything is to *help* people rather than to "get something from them," you'll already be ahead of 90% of the people in the music industry.

—**Fett**, Producer, Engineer, Author, Teacher, and Coach

My best advice is to write hand-written thank-you notes! Hand-written because no one does it that way anymore. And sent through the U.S. Postal Service. It *will* get noticed. It makes a powerful, positive impression. Most people don't say anything at all. Some people will say thank you in the moment. That's nice, but it doesn't take a lot of effort. And some people will send an email thank-you. That's better, but it's not as good as a hand-written, hand-addressed, sent-by-snail mail thank-you note! Do it! Trust me on this. You will make friends for life.

—**Nancy Moran**, Singer-Songwriter and Artist Development Coach

Composer agent Richard Kraft's response to rejection and disappointment is simple and quite memorable, paraphrased here for all audiences: "Oh, Poop. Darn. Next!"

—**James Jacoby**, Music Supervision, Clearance, and Licensing

I usually paraphrase something I heard James Taylor say about going into the music business when I was a teenager: "Keep your expectations high and your overhead low." I think it still applies!

—**Michelle Lewis**, Singer-Songwriter and Composer, Creators' Rights Advocate, Executive Director of Songwriters of North America (SONA), ASCAP Board Member, and Recording Academy L.A. Chapter Board Member

Surviving in the music industry takes courage, a passion to keep learning, and the ability to remain open and adaptable to the opportunities that come your way. Prepare for the long road ahead, but enjoy the journey while you get to live out your dream of making music.

—**Richard Harris**, Artist, Songwriter, and Producer

My dad (composer/arranger Bruce Miller) has given me a lot of advice over the years, but one thing he said that really stuck with me is this: "The ones who make it in this business are the ones who can stomach it." It reminds me that, when times are tough (and there will be tough times), I just need to keep pushing. Everyone goes through it, but not everyone keeps going. That one piece of advice really resonated with me.

—**Jason T. Miller**, Composer, Producer, and Songwriter

This is a marathon, not a sprint. Detours and delays from unforeseen obstacles will occur. Persistence and flexibility are required.

—**Gerard K. Marino**, Composer

My best advice: Show up!

—**Ben McLane**, Esq., McLane & Wong

Be honest and compassionate, and trust the outcome. There is a letting-go and connection that happens when we start from that space. A path we lay that is built upon those things is pretty special to witness and partake in.

—**Katie Herzig**, Artist, Songwriter, and Producer

Diversify your business opportunities and creative pursuits. Seek balance, be grateful, and enjoy the journey.

—**Brian Thomas Curtin**, Composer and Songwriter, Eaglestone Music

ABOUT THE PRO TIP QUOTE CONTRIBUTORS

Many of our music industry friends who contributed their endorsements and Pro Tip Quotes have helped us significantly on our musical journey. To them we owe a debt of gratitude. They are talented, successful, accomplished, and at the top of their game. All genuinely want to help educate composers and songwriters and are visible in the music community. Many volunteer their time and give back by serving on boards of important organizations. We have heard them speak on panels only to witness them staying for hours afterward to answer questions. Some are trailblazers. Several have written books and write blogs. Others are teachers and mentors. We've learned so much from them over the years, and it is our hope that you will gain insight and inspiration from their words as well.

For more Pro Tips and information, please visit the *Hey! That's My Song!* website at https://www.HeyThatsMySong.com/.

Glossary of Terms

A/B testing The process of comparing an aspect of one audio recording with another.

a cappella A vocal performance with no instrumental accompaniment.

accidentals Notes that are not part of the scale or mode of a specific key signature. In music notation, they are indicated by a flat (♭), sharp (♯), or natural (♮) sign appearing on the staff.

acoustic treatment Panels and other devices, commonly made of materials such as foam, wood, fiberglass, and fabric, that are placed on the walls and ceiling of a room where recording or mixing takes place. The treatment is intended to absorb and reduce the reflection of the sound in the room.

active speakers Speaker enclosures that contain built-in amplifiers and do not require external amplification.

administration agreement An arrangement between a publisher and a songwriter wherein the songwriter retains full ownership of their composition(s) and the publisher handles the day-to-day administration duties for a fee.

advance A prepayment of royalties made to a songwriter or composer by a publisher, music library, or record company upon the signing of a contract. This money is recoupable from the income the works later earn for the songwriter, composer, or artist.

AIFF (Audio Interchange File Format) file An audio-file format standard that is used for storing sound data for personal computers and other electronic audio devices. These are large, high-resolution, lossless, and uncompressed files with an extension of .aif or .aiff.

alliteration A lyric-writing device in which words within a phrase contain the same consonant sound, usually at the beginning of a word or stressed syllable, creating sonic patterns that are pleasing to the listener, as in *ball, bat, above.*

alternate (alt) mix A mix of a piece of music with some of the tracks muted or removed from the full mix to give a music editor more options.

ambience The echoes and reflections of sound indicating the nature and characteristics of the room or environment in which audio originates. In mixing, this is controlled with reverb and delay.

amp modeling Recording-software plug-ins that take a direct signal from an electric guitar or bass and simulate the sound of being plugged into a physical amplifier.

analog-to-digital converter (A/D converter) A device that converts the analog signal from a microphone and preamp to a digital signal a computer can understand.

arc In arranging, the progression and development produced by the variation of layers, textures, and intensities throughout a piece of music.

arpeggiator A function of a synthesizer or virtual instrument that steps through a defined sequence of notes in a rhythmic, mechanical manner. The result is that the notes of a chord are played one at a time.

arranging The art and craft of adapting and developing an existing musical composition.

ASCAP (American Society of Composers, Authors and Publishers) A Performing Rights Organization that collects and pays performance royalties to songwriters and publishers.

attack time The time it takes for a compressor to work after the signal reaches the threshold.

audio fingerprinting A process that analyzes the audio wave of a sound file and detects it when it is broadcast.

audio interface A device that routes audio signals from microphones and instruments to a computer and from the computer to the speakers.

audio track A channel on a physical or virtual mixer where audio is recorded from a microphone or instrument source and played back.

audio watermarking A process that places an inaudible digital sound pattern ("watermark") onto a sound file for the purpose of identifying ownership of copyright and for tracking.

automation On a track in an audio mixer, user-defined instructions to the DAW that change parameter settings of the tracks and plug-ins during playback and recording.

aux (auxiliary) track A channel on a physical or virtual mixer that contains no audio of its own, but audio from other sources is routed through it for processing. Also known as a *bus track*.

background vocals Vocal harmonies that run parallel to the melody, or vocals that are independent of the melody that bring a unique texture to a song. They sometimes contain the same lyrics as the melody, but they can also have different lyrics or no lyrics at all, such as "oohs" and "ahs."

bandwidth In equalization, a range of frequencies.

bell curve In equalization, the result of a boost or cut at a specified center frequency.

bi-amped The state of having two amplifiers in a speaker enclosure, one for each of its two speakers.

bit depth The number of bits of information in each sample in an audio file. Common bit depths are 16 and 24 bits.

blanket license (PRO) Permission granted by a PRO to companies that have music broadcast or played in their businesses for use of the music from the PRO's repertoire. These include TV, radio, and other network broadcasters, as well as restaurants, bars, transportation, and live music venues.

blanket license (publisher) Permission that is granted by the copyright owner of a music catalog to a client to sync that music to video.

BMI (Broadcast Music, Inc.) A Performing Rights Organization that collects and pays performance royalties to songwriters and publishers.

boosting In equalization, increasing the level of a frequency band of audio.

bouncing Exporting an audio file from a digital audio workstation. Also known as *printing*.

boutique music library A small music library with a very specific collection of curated music.

bpm (beats per minute) Used to measure the tempo or speed of a piece of music.

brickwall limiter An extreme limiter that does not allow any audio signal over the threshold to proceed to the output.

bridge A song section that occurs later in a song and happens only once. The lyrics in the bridge contain new information, and the music is in contrast to the rest of the song.

broadcast quality A characteristic of well-recorded, -mixed, and -mastered music in which there are no unintentional noises. The mix is clear, well balanced, appropriate for the genre, and ready for audio broadcast in any medium.

bus compressor A compressor designed to be used on a group of tracks, like those of a drum kit.

cardioid A microphone polar pattern in which the mic picks up sound coming from the front but rejects sound from the back and sides.

channel strip A section of a mixing console that the audio passes through in order to be processed, including the processors.

chord A combination of three or more notes played simultaneously.

chord formula A numeric representation of the notes from a scale that can be combined to create a chord. For instance, the formula for a major chord is 1–3–5.

chorus A song section that is repeated throughout the song and usually has the same melody and lyrics each time it appears. It often contains the hook or the title.

circumaural A headphone design in which ear cups cover the ears.

click track A track of audio that plays a short, percussive sound in steady time, usually indicated in beats per minute. It is intended to keep musical performances synchronized.

clipping The waveform distortion that occurs when an amplifier is overdriven and attempts to output an audio signal of a level beyond its maximum capability, leading to a lowering of audio quality.

closed-back A headphone design in which ear cups seal around the ears so no sound leaks in or out.

comp In audio editing, the process of selecting the best recorded takes and compiling them to make sure the best performance of each part ends up on a final recording. Short for "compile" or "compilation."

compression The process of reducing the difference between the softest and loudest parts of an audio signal.

condenser microphone A microphone in which incoming sound waves cause a variation in the distance between a vibrating diaphragm and a solid backplate, changing their capacitance and creating an audio signal.

consonant Harmony that sounds pleasing and satisfying.

construction kits Virtual instruments that in addition to containing instrument samples also contain composed, pre-recorded instrumental pieces of a song, such as a verse, chorus, and bridge. These song pieces are composed by the maker of the plug-in.

co-publishing agreement An agreement between a publisher and a songwriter or composer that allows both parties to co-own musical copyrights and to each receive a portion of the publisher's share of performance and other royalties.

counterpoint A secondary, independent melody that complements the main melody. Also known as *countermelody*.

cover song A recording of a reinterpretation of a preexisting song.

crescendo In musical performance, to gradually grow louder.

crossfade At an audio edit point, the process of applying a fade-out of the signal level at the end of the first piece of audio and a simultaneous fade-in at the start of the next piece of audio to reduce the likelihood of pops or clicks and to provide a smooth segue.

cue A piece of instrumental music used to underscore a video scene.

cue sheet A document that lists the songs and instrumentals that were used in a film or TV show, including song titles, duration, usage, songwriters or composers, publishers, and PRO affiliations.

cutting In equalization, reducing the level of a frequency band of audio. Also known as *attenuating*.

DAW See *digital audio workstation*.

dba "Doing business as"—the fictitious name of a company. Also DBA or d/b/a.

decibel (dB) The unit of measurement of the amplitude of a sound wave, which determines volume or loudness.

de-esser A very specific compressor that allows dynamic control of the sibilant frequency range of the human voice.

default The setting with which a plug-in opens and that is often considered a neutral starting point for making adjustments.

delay A device or plug-in that reproduces original audio as repeats and plays them back fractions of a second later with discernable reflections that are distinct and separate.

DI (direct input or direct injection) The process of plugging an instrument, usually an electric guitar or bass, into a preamp or interface.

diaphragm A capsule within a microphone that converts sound waves into an electrical signal.

digital audio workstation (DAW) A computer and the software used to record music and audio.

digital signal processing (DSP) hardware Hardware that assists in providing extra power for plug-ins and recording software.

digital-to-analog converter (D/A converter) A device that converts the digital signal from a computer to an analog signal that can be amplified and sent to speakers or headphones.

direct licensing The practice of combining a licensing fee and performance royalties into a single up-front payment. No additional performance royalties are earned when the shows containing the music are broadcast.

dissonant Harmony that sounds odd and somewhat unpleasant.

dramedy A genre of show, film, or library music that combines elements of drama and comedy.

driver A speaker transducer element that converts an audio signal into sound waves.

drum groove The rhythmic feel of a drum performance and the vibe it contributes to a piece of music.

drum loop A recording of a drum performance that is repeated throughout a piece of music, usually one to four bars in length.

dry The lack of reflections or reverb in a room or on a recording. Also, no audible reverb or delay effect.

dynamic microphone A microphone in which incoming sound waves cause a movable wire or coil to vibrate in a magnetic field, creating an audio signal.

dynamic range In mixing, the difference between the strongest and weakest audio levels in a recording.

dynamics In mixing, devices and plug-ins that control the difference between the highest and lowest levels of an audio signal. Tools used in this process include compressors and limiters.

ear candy Unexpected, subtle textures that occur throughout a piece of music that can be synthetic or acoustic in nature and have been processed using special effects.

edit In sync usage, a variation of a full-length piece of music, usually created by changing its length to a specified duration, such as to 30 or 60 seconds.

edit point A clear delineation between the sections of a piece of music that may include a very short silence. They are helpful places for music editors to make a cut.

electronic press kit (EPK) An online presentation of a music artist that includes a picture, biography, and samples of their work.

elevator speech A 30-second pitch to a music industry professional about who you are, what you do, and the reasons why they might want to work with you.

ephemeral use The occurrence of incidental music in the background during a live newscast or a sporting event. This includes live or recorded music being played under an on-location report, music being performed by a marching band, a crowd singing, or a song coming through the sound system at a stadium.

EQ (equalization) The process of adjusting the balance between frequencies of an audio signal.

evergreen A term used to describe music that is not tied clearly to any time or place and therefore has an ongoing need and will likely not become dated.

exclusive agreement (production music library) An agreement in which the musical works assigned to a production music library by a songwriter or composer cannot be assigned to any other library. The songwriter or composer, however, is free to write new material for another production music library.

expander A device or plug-in that makes loud audio louder and soft audio softer, thus increasing its dynamic range and doing the opposite of a compressor.

exploiting Marketing a music copyright with the goal of getting many sync placements.

fader A control on a physical or virtual mixer that slides in two directions and controls the level of the audio signal that passes through the track on which it resides. Also known as a *slider*.

feedback A reaction and advice that comes from a knowledgeable and experienced music industry professional. The most effective feedback indicates what's working with a song and what can be done to improve its quality.

feel The emotional response of a listener to a piece of music, often associated with the kind of scene under which the music may fit.

fictitious business name A name that is not a person's true, legal name that can be used when setting up a business, such as a music publishing company.

fictitious business name statement A statement filed with the county clerk's office, or other appropriate government agency, that declares a person's intention to start a business using a name other than their own.

figure 8 A microphone polar pattern in which the mic picks up sound from the front and back but rejects sound coming from the sides. Also known as *bidirectional.*

file format The structure of a computer file that determines how the data within the file is encoded and tells a program how to display its contents.

filtering EQ An EQ that reduces the level of frequencies in a specified range.

first person A narrative in lyric writing in which the perspective is that of the singer, using the words "I" or "we."

frequency The speed of the sound vibration of a sound wave, which determines its pitch and is measured in cycles per second or hertz.

frequency range A span or spectrum of sound between two specified audio frequencies.

gain A control that adjusts audio signal level.

gain reduction meter A display that shows the amount of compression applied by indicating how much the incoming signal is being reduced.

gain staging The process of monitoring the audio signal level along its path to make certain that it is not too low or too high.

gate An expander device or plug-in that completely removes the soft parts of audio.

genre A category or style of music that is identified by shared characteristics, such as hip hop, rock, or country.

GMR (Global Music Rights) An invitation-only Performing Rights Organization that collects and pays performance royalties to songwriters and publishers.

Graphical User Interface (GUI) The display on a plug-in that shows the available parameters that can be adjusted.

gratis license Permission granted for music to be licensed or synced for various uses with no payment.

grid In recording software, a graphic display of audio and MIDI notes indicating their timing.

guide track A basic, rough recording of a song used as a starting point to record final instruments and vocals. It is often removed from the finished recording. Also known as a *scratch track.*

half step In traditional Western music, the smallest interval between the pitch of two notes. Also known as a *semitone.*

harmony The sound created by combining two or more simultaneous musical notes.

hertz (Hz) The measurement of the frequency of a sound wave equal to one cycle per second.

high pass filter An EQ that removes low frequencies. Also known as a *low cut filter.*

high-resolution file format (hi-res files) Computer audio files that are large and high quality.

hook A catchy part of a song that repeats.

humanize A feature in some DAWs that allows the timing of notes to be loosened to sound as if the instrument were being played by a person instead of a computer.

hybrid music Music in which elements from two or more different genres are incorporated into one composition and recording.

independent or indie publishing company A stand-alone publishing company that does not have the sizable song catalog or may not have far-reaching distribution of larger corporate publishers but may offer more flexibility in the terms of their deals.

inner rhyme A rhyme that falls in the middle of a line instead of at the end.

input The point at which audio enters a track on a mixer or other audio device.

insert The location on a track in a DAW where plug-ins are instantiated.

instrument level The moderate audio-signal level coming from instruments, like electric guitars and basses.

instrument track A channel on a virtual mixer used to host a virtual instrument plug-in. MIDI information is recorded to an instrument track, and audio is played out of it.

instrumental cue A piece of instrumental music used to underscore a video scene. Also known as a *bed, track,* or *underscore.*

instrumental mix An alternate mix of a piece of music with the melody or other vocal elements removed. Also known as a *bed mix*, an *underscore mix*, a *TV mix*, or a *no melody mix.*

interactive Audio streaming that allows the listener to choose the specific songs that are played.

inversion The rearrangement of notes in a chord such that they are played in an order different than the root position.

IPI (interested party information) number A number that identifies a songwriter, composer, or publisher for the purposes of collecting royalties; usually issued by a PRO. Previously known as a *CAE* (using the French words for "composer, author, and publisher)" *number*.

ISRC (International Standard Recording Code) number A number identifying a recording for the purposes of collecting royalties and that is usually issued by the entity distributing the music to audio streaming services.

ISWC (International Standard Musical Work Code) A number that identifies a musical work or composition and includes information such as the title, songwriters or composers, publishers, and how the shares are split. Usually issued by a PRO.

key In music, a group of related notes derived from a given scale, including the tonic note, that gives it its name. A song that uses notes from the C major scale is in the "key of C major."

key signature The grouping of sharps and flats at the beginning of the staff that indicate which notes are to be raised (sharps) or lowered (flats) to correspond with a specific scale in order to follow its pattern of half steps and whole steps.

key switch A method used in some virtual instruments to change to a sample with a different articulation or other characteristic. A MIDI note outside of the playable range of the instrument is struck directly before a different sample is wanted.

keywords A list of terms that describe a piece of music.

kilohertz (kHz) A frequency of 1,000 hertz.

latency An audible delay between the moment a sound is performed while recording and when it can be heard through the headphones or speakers. This is caused when the computer is not fast enough to keep up with the audio.

layering Combining two or more instruments that play the same notes to create unique and interesting textures.

LCR panning Limiting the panning of audio to only the left, center, or right.

legato The performance technique of playing musical notes in a smooth, connected manner.

license In sync music, permission granted by the party representing a music copyright to another party to use that music in a specific manner, often to synchronize it to video.

licensing fee In sync music, a fee paid by one party to the parties representing a music copyright for use of that music in a specific manner—often to synchronize the music to video. Also known an *all-in licensing fee* or a *sync fee*.

limited liability company (LLC) A business structure whereby the company owners are not personally liable for the company's debts or liabilities.

limiter An aggressive compressor with a ratio setting of 10:1 or more.

line level The strengthened audio signal that comes out of a preamp and is most common and compatible in audio systems.

linear phase EQ An equalizer that aligns the delays of all frequencies and harmonics passing through it to reduce phase smearing. Often used in mastering.

loop To repeat the same one to eight bars of a musical performance.

loop record A recording function that allows the user to record a section of a song over and over.

lossless A characteristic of an audio file that has not lost any frequency range as a result of being compressed.

low pass filter An EQ that removes high frequencies. Also known as a *high cut filter*.

major chord A three-note chord using the first, third, and fifth notes from a major scale. In the sync world, this chord is described as having a happy, bright, uplifting, and positive feel and quality.

major publishing company A large music publisher that has offices in dozens of countries and represents tens of thousands of songwriters and over one million songs. They own many of the copyrights they represent and usually have a large legacy catalog.

major scale A series of eight notes, with the last being an octave above the first. Each consecutive pair of notes is a whole step apart, except the third and fourth, and the seventh and eighth, which are a half step apart. In the sync world, the major scale is described as having a happy, bright, uplifting, and positive feel and quality.

makeup gain A control that allows the output level of a compressor to be brought back closer to the incoming level.

marketing In sync licensing, the act of promoting and exploiting music for the purpose of licensing.

master bus A channel on a physical or virtual mixer that is the final destination for audio before it is sent out to the audio interface and speakers. Also known as a *master fader*.

master license An agreement whereby a record label or recording owner, on behalf of the artist on a recording of a piece of music, grants permission for the master recording to be synchronized to video, usually with very specific terms and for a fee.

master recording The final mixed and mastered recording of a song or instrumental. Also known as a *sound recording*.

mastering The process of using equalization, compression, and limiting to balance the elements of a stereo mix to ensure the sound is optimized for playback on all speaker systems.

Mechanical Licensing Collective (MLC) The organization that pays mechanical royalties from download and interactive audio streaming services to self-published songwriters and publishers in the United States.

mechanical royalty A royalty paid to a songwriter or publisher whenever a copy of one of their musical works is reproduced in some form. This includes CDs, MP3 downloads, and interactive audio-only streams. In the United States, royalties for MP3 downloads and interactive audio-only streams are paid by the Mechanical Licensing Collective (MLC). This does not include audiovisual streams.

media The means by which something is communicated.

melody A linear succession of single musical notes.

metadata Information about a piece of music, including title, songwriters or composers, publisher, names of the artists, length, and contact information, all of which may be digitally embedded in the audio file, presented on a spreadsheet, or included in the Schedule A (list of tracks or songs) addendum to a publishing agreement.

metaphor A figure of speech in which a word or phrase is used to describe something that is not literally true by stating that one thing *is* another. For example, "Love *is* a fuzzy blanket" or "You *are* my sunshine."

meter In mixing, a visual display on an audio interface or within a computer that indicates the strength of the audio signal passing through it.

mic level The weak audio signal level that comes out of a microphone.

microphone isolation shield A product that forms an acoustically absorbent semicircle around the back of a microphone to reduce the sound of the room on the recording. Also known as a *reflection shield*.

microphone signal booster A device that strengthens the signal coming out of a microphone.

midfield monitors Monitor speakers that are intended to be used a moderate distance from the listener.

MIDI (Musical Instrument Digital Interface) The language that digital devices use to communicate with each other, such as computers, synthesizers, and other digital music instruments.

MIDI controller A keyboard or interface used to trigger sounds from a synthesizer or virtual instrument in a computer.

MIDI mock-up A preliminary version of a recorded piece of music in a DAW containing parts recorded with virtual instruments that will later be replaced with acoustic instruments.

MIDI track A channel on a virtual mixer where MIDI information is recorded and used to trigger samples from a virtual instrument or hardware synthesizer.

midsized publishing company A music publisher that performs the duties of a major publisher but with a smaller song catalog, smaller staff, and fewer offices in foreign territories. Sometimes known as *mini-major publishers* or *major indie publishers*.

minor chord A three-note chord using the first, flatted third, and fifth notes from a major scale. In the sync world, this chord is described as having a sad, dark, dramatic, and negative feel and quality.

minor scale A series of eight notes, with the last being an octave above the first. Each consecutive pair of notes is a whole step apart, except the second and third, and the fifth and sixth, which are a half step apart. In the sync world, this scale is described as having a sad, dark, dramatic, and negative feel and quality.

minus mix A mix created by removing selected tracks from the full mix.

mix The recording that results from combining multiple recorded tracks together while adjusting and balancing individual track levels.

mix control A control that balances the blend between wet and dry effects.

mixing The combining and blending of multiple recorded tracks together while adjusting and balancing individual track levels to create a unified, cohesive, balanced, and focused final recorded product that sounds professional when played back on any sound system.

mixing console An electronic device that combines and blends multiple audio signals. Also known as a *mixing desk.*

mnemonic device A tool or technique used to aid in memory retention.

mode A type of scale with a specific arrangement of intervals.

modulation wheel (mod wheel) A control on a MIDI keyboard that can be used to transition smoothly from one sample to another or to add expression and dynamics to musical phrases.

monitor speakers Professional-quality speakers intended for use in a recording or mixing studio that produce a flat, uncolored, unhyped, transparent, detailed, accurate representation of how a recording sounds. Also known as *reference monitors* or *studio monitors.*

mono An audio signal containing one channel.

most favored nations (MFN) A clause in an agreement that requires one party to receive the same payment as another in a similar situation.

motif A short musical idea, theme, or phrase that is repeated in a piece of music.

movie trailer An extended advertisement for an upcoming film.

MP3 (MPEG-1 Audio Layer 3) An audio file-format standard used for storing sound data for personal computers and other electronic audio devices. These are small, lossy-compressed files with lower audio quality using the extension .mp3.

music creator Anyone involved in writing, performing, arranging, producing, recording, mixing, and mastering music.

music editor The person who compiles, edits, and syncs music with the video of a TV show, advertisement, video game, or movie.

music supervisor The person who selects, clears, licenses, and otherwise handles the processing of music that is placed in movies, TV shows, advertisements, or video games.

music user In sync licensing, the person who selects the music that is placed in movies, TV shows, advertisements, video games, and other visual media. The music user may be a music supervisor, music editor, video editor, producer, director, or showrunner.

mute To silence the audio of a track during playback or recording using a button or other control on an audio mixer.

natural notes Music notes that are neither sharp nor flat. On a piano keyboard, these are the white notes.

natural reverb Reverb that is created by modeling real spaces, such as concert halls, chambers, churches, recording studios, rooms, and other physical spaces.

nearfield monitors Monitor speakers that are intended to be used in close proximity to the listener.

near rhyme Rhyme in which the vowel sound is the same, or very close, but the last consonant is different. Also known as *close*, *imperfect*, *false*, or *lazy rhyme.*

needle drop license Permission granted by the representative of a song to a client to sync all or part of a song to video for a one-time use.

neighboring rights Performance royalties paid to performers and master recording owners. These royalties are collected and distributed on a limited basis in the United States, where neighboring rights royalties are paid by SoundExchange for audio streams on non-interactive digital radio but are paid for more uses outside of the United States.

non-exclusive agreement (production music library) In music publishing, an agreement between a songwriter or composer and a publisher in which the musical works being assigned to the publisher may also be assigned concurrently and non-exclusively to another publisher.

non-interactive Audio streaming that does not allow the listener to choose the songs that are played.

omnidirectional A microphone polar pattern in which the mic picks up sound from the front, back, and sides.

on the nose The undesirable quality of lyrics of a song too literally reflecting the scene they are intended to underscore, likely preventing the song from being placed in that scene.

one-stop licensing and music clearance The ability to obtain permission from all parties involved in the creation of a piece of music to license that music by contacting a single party.

online file-delivery service A service that allows a user to upload large files and receive a Web link to send to parties interested in downloading the files.

open-back A headphone design that allows airflow through the ear cups to release sound pressure.

open fifth In music, an interval comprised of the root and fifth notes of a chord. "Open" refers to there being no third to determine whether the harmony created is major or minor. "Fifth" is used to indicate that this is the interval between the first and fifth notes of a major scale. Having only two notes, the open fifth is not technically a chord, which gives it an ambiguous, indefinite, and neutral sound.

outline In sync usage, a road map of where a song or cue starts, where it goes, and how it ends.

output A setting that controls the amount of signal leaving a compressor or other audio processor.

pad A long synthesizer sound that fades in slowly and sustains.

pad switch A control on some microphones that reduces their output signal. Also known as an *attenuation switch.*

pan To place audio to the right or the left in the stereo field.

parallel processing A mixing technique that combines an affected copy of a signal with the original signal.

passive speakers Unpowered speaker enclosures that require a signal from an external amplifier.

pentatonic scale A five-note scale within an octave.

perfect rhyme Rhyme in which the vowel sound and the last consonant of the words are exactly the same.

performance royalties Payment collected by Performing Rights Organizations for distribution to songwriters, composers, and publishers when their music is played on TV, the radio, video streams, and audio streams and in transportation venues, live performances, and the background at restaurants or other places of business. These royalties are also paid to performers and recording owners in certain situations. Also known as *backend.*

Performing Rights Organization (PRO) A company that is responsible for collecting and distributing performance royalties to songwriters, publishers, artists, and recording owners. In the United States, the major PROs are ASCAP, BMI, SESAC, and GMR.

perpetuity In contract agreements, having no expiration date; forever.

phantom power The power supplied by some interfaces that is required for some microphones to work. This is sometimes indicated as 48V, or forty-eight volts.

phase cancellation An acoustic phenomenon whereby sound waves recorded from two microphones are out of phase, causing some of the frequencies to be weakened.

pitch correction A device or plug-in used to adjust the pitch of out-of-tune sound sources—most frequently vocals.

pitch (tip sheet) service A person or company that provides music requests to creators and sends qualified submissions to industry decision-makers, usually for a fee.

pitching to a project The process of submitting music directly to the decision-makers of a video project instead of through a third-party representative.

plate reverb An unnatural reverb that emulates the effect created by a large metal plate suspended by springs in an enclosure, giving the audio a metallic sound.

plosives The sounds that result from a sudden release of breath from a vocalist that overwhelms the mic and distorts the signal, most commonly, from the letter P.

plug-in Software commonly used in digital audio workstations to create and process audio.

polar pattern The directions in which a microphone is sensitive to sound.

pop filter A circular screen that often attaches to a mic stand and is positioned between the singer and the microphone to reduce the effect of plosives.

post-chorus A song section that follows usually after a chorus. Its lyrics may contain: the title and/or the hook, nonsense words (vocalises), or some lyrics from the chorus repeated in a catchy way.

post fader A mode of a track in an audio mixer whereby the position of the volume fader on the track changes the amount of signal going to the send.

preamp (preamplifier) A device that strengthens the audio signal from a microphone, or DI instrument, to line level.

pre-approved vendor In sync music, production music libraries and sync agencies that have been vetted by production companies and networks and frequently have ongoing licensing agreements in place.

pre-chorus A section of a song that leads to the chorus. The pre-chorus is situated between the verse and chorus and is also known as a *lift* or a *climb*.

pre-cleared In sync music, the state of having all permissions and signed agreements in place to allow a piece of music to be licensed prior to any such opportunities arising.

pre fader A mode of a track in an audio mixer whereby the position of the volume fader on the track does not change the signal level delivered to the send.

preset A predetermined setting in a plug-in for a specific purpose.

pro bono The practice of rendering professional services without charge. Latin, meaning "for the good."

producer In music, the person who oversees the creation of a recording by an artist. The producer renders some or all of these services: the writing or selecting of the songs, determining the musicians who perform on the recording, arranging the music, booking the studio and equipment that is used, and overseeing the mixing and mastering of the music.

production music Pre-cleared recorded music that has been specifically written to be licensed into media projects, is of a defined genre, and is broadcast quality.

production music library A company that controls many styles and genres of music organized and categorized in a searchable database and that represents and markets the music for the purpose of placement and licensing in various media.

promos On-air commercials that promote upcoming shows on TV and radio networks.

prosody In the songwriting world, the marriage of the music with the lyrics and how appropriate they are with each other. Prosody can also apply to the production and mixing elements that support the vibe and mood of the music.

proximity effect The increase in lower frequency response when a sound source is close to a microphone.

public domain (PD) Musical compositions for which the copyright has expired and ownership now belongs to the public. The copyright expiration varies from country to country.

publisher In the music industry, a person or company that owns or represents music composition copyrights and markets and exploits them for profit.

publisher's share The portion of performance royalties to which the publisher of a piece of music is entitled.

publishing administration The collection and distribution of royalties earned by musical works, including the registration of those musical works with the appropriate royalty companies. These tasks are performed by a publishing company or a third-party company that offers these services to an independent artist or catalog.

pulse A steady beat produced by an instrument or group of instruments playing notes in a rhythmic manner. A synthesizer is commonly used for this purpose.

punch in In recording, the process in which a performer records a short piece of audio in the middle of a good take to replace an undesirable part of the performance.

quality factor (the Q) A parameter of equalization that adjusts the shape of an EQ curve and its bandwidth.

quantize In digital audio, the process of correcting the timing of a musical performance.

QWERTY keyboard A computer keyboard used to type and enter letters, numbers, and symbols into a computer.

ratio The amount of compression, expressed as a ratio, applied to an incoming signal relative to how much it exceeds the threshold.

reciprocal agreement An agreement that a Performing Rights Organization or other royalty collection company in one country has with its counterpart in another country, which allows music creators in one territory to be paid for the use of their music in another territory.

record enable A control on an individual track on a recording device that enables audio or MIDI to be recorded to the track during the recording process.

record label A company that owns or represents master recording copyrights and markets and exploits them for profit.

recording engineer The person who shapes music recordings, creatively interfacing with the artists and producers. Additionally, the recording engineer is responsible for handling the technical details, setting up the DAW, and overseeing the physical setup of the studio for the sessions.

reference track or song Music used as a guide and inspiration to create a new, original piece of music that contains a similar vibe and feel. The term may also refer to a recording that is used as a model when mixing or mastering a song or instrumental.

reflections Sound bouncing off of walls, floors, and ceilings.

relative (major or minor) key In music, the key that shares the same scale notes as another key but starts on a different root note. For instance, C major and A minor use the same notes, so they are relative keys.

release time The time it takes for a compressor to stop compressing after the signal falls below the threshold.

retitling A practice that allows non-exclusive publishers or music libraries to receive performance royalties for music placements they secure by changing the title of a piece of music and registering the new title with a PRO.

revenue sharing The frowned-upon practice in which networks and production companies receive a portion of performance royalties from music providers in exchange for placing music in their shows.

reverb (or reverberation) The echo effect created by sound reflections bouncing off of walls, floors, and ceilings. Also used to refer to an electronic device or software intended to re-create this effect.

reverse In audio editing, playing a sound backward to create a building of intensity.

reversion clause A contract clause that allows the ownership, control, or representation of a piece of music to revert back to the creator after a specified period of time.

rhyme scheme The pattern of rhyming the last word in lines of lyrics.

rhythm A repeating pattern of regular pulses that contains strong and weak beats.

ribbon microphone A microphone in which incoming sound waves cause a light metal ribbon suspended between the poles of a magnet to vibrate, creating an audio signal.

riser A synthesizer sound that ascends in pitch.

root position A voicing of a chord in which the lowest note is the root or tonic note.

round-robin samples In some virtual instruments, the feature of having two or more samples assigned to the same MIDI note. When the same MIDI note is repeated, a different performance of the same sound is heard each time.

royalty free music library A music library that charges a licensing fee covering use of the music beyond the current project. However, performance royalties are sometimes earned.

rubato A rhythmically loose musical performance style that does not adhere to a strict tempo.

sample (MIDI) A pre-recorded sound or note, usually triggered to playback through a MIDI keyboard or within a DAW on a computer.

sample (recording) A pre-recorded piece of music, often from another party, that is incorporated into another piece of music. This can only be done legally by obtaining a license from the owners of the original composition and master recording.

sample rate The number of samples of audio carried per second in an audio file, expressed in kilohertz. Common sample rates are 44.1 and 48 kHz.

scale An orderly series of notes within an octave that follows a predetermined pattern of intervals. A scale is named for its root or tonic note.

scene-setter music Music that lets the viewer know where a scene is taking place.

Schedule A A list of the titles of musical works subject to the terms of a contract and which may include additional information about the song, the songwriters, and other metadata.

score Custom music composed to video that enhances the emotion in scenes.

scource A combination of score and source music that the characters can hear and that also underscores the emotion of a scene.

second person A narrative in lyric writing that is directed to the listener using the word "you."

send On an audio mixer, the path that delivers a virtual copy of audio on a track to an aux bus for separate processing and is later combined with the original audio.

SESAC An invitation-only Performing Rights Organization that collects and pays performance royalties to songwriters and publishers. Originally the name was an abbreviation for the Society of European Stage Authors and Composers, but this is no longer the case.

shelving EQ In equalization, a filter that adjusts all of the frequencies below or above a specified frequency.

showrunner The person who has creative control and is the main decision-maker in the production of a video, TV, or other project; frequently a director, producer, writer-producer, creative director, or executive producer.

simile A figure of speech in which two unlike things are compared by using the words "like" or "as." For example, "Her eyes were as dark *as* midnight" or "His voice was *like* gravel."

slant rhyme Rhymes where the words sound similar, like "yours" and years," but the vowel sounds are not exactly the same. Also known as *half rhyme*.

slope In equalization, the range and degree to which frequencies around the one selected are affected by the filter.

sole proprietorship A business enterprise in which there is no legal distinction between the owner and the business entity. As a result, the owner is personally responsible for the company's debts and liabilities.

solo In recording, a button (or other control) on an audio mixer used to isolate an audio track so that it can be heard apart from the other tracks in a mix.

songwriter split sheet (writers' split agreement, writer splits) A written and signed document that indicates how the performance royalties and other income from a musical work are shared between two or more writers.

sound effects Artificial or enhanced sounds that are heard in a show, other than dialog or music, that make the scenes seem more realistic.

SoundExchange A nonprofit collective rights-management organization in the United States that collects and pays performance royalties for non-interactive use of sound recordings on digital audio platforms. These royalties, also known as "neighboring rights," are paid to featured and non-featured artists and master recording rights owners.

source music Music in a film, TV, or live show that can be heard by the characters, as well as the audience. It comes from a "source"—visible or implied, such as a jukebox, a piano player, a band on stage, or a group of musicians or singers.

speaker level The high level audio signal that comes out of an amplifier and is sent to speakers.

spring reverb An unnatural reverb that emulates the effect created by a small coiled-up piece of metal suspended in an enclosure, giving the audio a somewhat twangy sound.

staccato Playing musical notes in a short, detached manner.

stems The individual tracks, or groups of tracks, from the recording of a piece of music that a music editor uses to create an alternate mix including only the desired instruments.

stereo An audio signal containing two channels, usually left and right.

sting (stinger) A shortened edit of a piece of music, usually the last two to four measures leading up to the last note, and generally six to twelve seconds in length.

structure In music composition, the sequence of sections that create the form of a piece of music; most commonly, the series of verses and choruses in a song.

studio monitor controller An interface that routes an audio signal to one or more pairs of speakers, as well as to headphones.

sub-publisher A publisher who represents the works of another publisher in a different territory.

subscription music library A music library that charges a monthly or yearly fee allowing clients to use an unlimited amount of music from the catalog in an unlimited number of projects. No performance royalties are earned. This practice is looked upon unfavorably in the sync world.

subwoofer A very large speaker driver that reproduces the lowest frequencies.

supercardioid A microphone polar pattern in which the mic has a narrower area of sensitivity in the front and on the sides than a cardioid mic and a small amount of sensitivity in the back.

supra-aural A headphone design in which ear cups rest on the ears without completely enclosing them.

sync Short for *synchronization*, which means "matching the music to the picture."

sync agency A company that represents and exploits music for the purpose of licensing it for sync placements. They work with artists and bands and usually allow them to retain control of their music and the copyrights. Also known as a *sync licensing agency*.

synchronization license An agreement with a music publisher, on behalf of the songwriter or composer of a piece of music, that grants permission for the written composition to be synchronized to video, usually with very specific terms and for a fee.

synchy A characteristic of a song that sounds like it was obviously written for sync, while not sounding like a song by an authentic artist.

synthestration The process of creating a MIDI mock-up of a song or cue using virtual instruments entirely. Real instruments may be added, blended, or substituted later into the mix.

template A previously created file in a digital audio workstation that serves as a starting point for sessions.

theme song A piece of music occurring in every episode of a show, always at the beginning, that identifies and brands the show.

third person A narrative in lyric writing that is directed to someone not immediately present, using the words "he," "she," or "they."

threshold The input level at which a compressor starts working.

through-composed A music composition technique in which each section is new, resulting in no repeated sections.

tonic note The first note of a scale that gives it its name. Because the tonic sounds finished and resolved, it is often the last note in the melody of a piece of music. Also known as a *root note* or *keynote*.

topline The melody and lyrics of a song (without the underlying track or chord changes).

track In a digital audio workstation, the place where an audio signal passes through to be processed.

tracking Another term for recording.

traction The momentum that comes when a song or artist is gaining interest due to a pattern of exposure and success.

trailer music The music that accompanies an extended advertisement for a film. It can consist of an intro, a buildup, and a climax from a single cue, or edited together from bits and pieces from dozens of cues.

trailerize To create an epic, over-the-top, moody, or dramatic treatment of a song or instrumental for the purpose of placement in a film trailer.

transient The very first, sudden sound that can be heard at the beginning of a piece of audio.

triad A three-note chord.

tweeter A small speaker driver that reproduces high frequencies in a speaker enclosure.

uncompressed A state of digital audio files that have not been made smaller, resulting in their retaining their size and high quality.

unnatural reverb Reverb that is not modeled after a physical space but instead through synthetic means, such as plate and spring reverbs. Also known as *synthetic reverb.*

unsolicited A music submission to a publisher that was not requested and will likely be returned to the sender unopened.

USB microphone A microphone that plugs directly into a USB port on a computer and is powered by the USB connection.

velocity How hard a key is struck on a MIDI keyboard or interface, which affects the volume and other characteristics of the sample playback.

verse A song section that has the same melody but different lyrics each time it occurs. The lyrics in the verses explain and point to the title of the song, usually without actually containing the title.

virtual instrument A software plug-in that creates electronic or acoustic instrument sounds.

vocal producer During the recording process, the person who coaches and gives guidance to a singer about vocal performance techniques and other details.

vocalise A vocal passage consisting of a melody without words, often using individual syllables, nonsense words, or vowel sounds.

voice leading The process of writing melodies and single-note harmonies that move smoothly through their chord progressions.

voicing The order and arrangement of notes in a chord.

vox Abbreviation for "vocal."

WAV (Waveform Audio File Format) file An audio-file format standard used for storing sound data for personal computers and other electronic audio devices. These are large, high-resolution, lossless, and uncompressed files with an extension of .wav.

waveform A graphic representation of audio.

wet A full reverb or delay effect.

whole step Two half steps. Also known as a *whole tone.*

woofer A large speaker driver that reproduces midrange and low-range frequencies in a speaker enclosure.

work-for-hire agreement (music creators) An agreement between a songwriter or composer and a collaborator, such as a singer, instrumentalist, producer, mixer, recording or mastering engineer, who is paid to help create a musical work.

work-for-hire agreement (publishers/production music libraries) An agreement between a publisher and a songwriter or composer in which the publisher purchases the musical copyrights and receives all of the publisher's share of performance royalties—and, in some cases, the writer's share.

work-made-for-hire A musical work that is specially ordered to be purchased for use and, therefore, owned by the party by whom it was commissioned.

writer's share The portion of performance royalties to which the songwriter or composer of a piece of music is entitled.

APPENDIX A
Sample Lyric Sheet

Jingle Bells

By James Pierpont / Sammy Songwriter / Lydia Lyricist

VERSE 1
Dashing through the snow, in a one-horse open sleigh
O'er the fields we go, laughing all the way
Bells on bobtail ring, making spirits bright
What fun it is to ride and sing a sleighing song tonight, oh

CHORUS
Jingle bells, jingle bells, jingle all the way
Oh what fun it is to ride in a one-horse open sleigh, hey
Jingle bells, jingle bells, jingle all the way
Oh what fun it is to ride in a one-horse open sleigh

VERSE 2
A day or two ago, I thought I'd take a ride
And soon Miss Fannie Bright was seated by my side
The horse was lean and lank, misfortune seemed his lot
He got into a drifted bank and then we got upsot, oh

CHORUS and INSTRUMENTAL INTERLUDE

BRIDGE
Now the ground is white, go it while you're young
Bring your friends tonight, and sing this sleighing song, oh

CHORUS

©1857 Snowglobe Music Publishing, James Pierpont, Sammy Songwriter, Lydia Lyricist
For licensing, contact the administrator: James Pierpont at Pierpont@JingleBellsSongwriter.com
[*NOTE: Personal contact information below may be omitted.*]
Website: www.JingleBellsSongwriter.com / Email: Pierpont@JingleBellsSongwriter.com
Phone: (617) 555.BELL / Mailing address: 19 High Street, Medford, MA 02155 USA

[*The following information is helpful for Film/TV pitches but only if it is true and correct*]
One-stop clearance and licensing available. The publishing, composition, and master recording are owned and controlled by James Pierpont (BMI 34%, IPI #000.00.00.00), Sammy Songwriter (SESAC 33%, IPI #100.00.00.01), and Lydia Lyricist (ASCAP 33%, IPI #200.00.00.02).

APPENDIX B
Sample Agreements

TYPES OF NECESSARY SYNC MUSIC AGREEMENTS

Sample Songwriter Split Sheet

Note: In the sync world, it's imperative for music users to know who wrote the composition (the Song) and what the percentages (splits) are for clearance purposes. Split percentages may be assigned to anyone and for any percentage amount, as long as these terms are signed, dated, and agreed upon by all parties. Below is one example of how a songwriter split agreement may be done. Always get qualified legal help with contracts. This is to be used as a guide only.

This agreement is made and entered into on [*Month/Day/Year*] ____________________ by and between or among the following Songwriters regarding their original Song composition titled "____________________________." Songwriters agree to the following song split percentages:

Name: ____________________________________ / [*optional*] Title: ______________________________

Applicable Percentage [*Spell out amount*] _________________________ percent [*Numeral*] (________%)

Name: ____________________________________ / [*optional*] Title: ______________________________

Applicable Percentage [*Spell out amount*] _________________________ percent [*Numeral*] (________%)

Name: ____________________________________ / [*optional*] Title: ______________________________

Applicable Percentage [*Spell out amount*] _________________________ percent [*Numeral*] (________%)

IN WITNESS WHEREOF, the parties hereto have executed this Agreement on the day, month, and year first above set out.

READ AND AGREED by:

Signature: X ______________________ / Date: __________ Percentage: _____%

Print Name: ______________________ / Title [*optional*]: ______________

Email: __________________________ / Phone: __________________

Mailing Address: ____

PRO (BMI/SESAC/ASCAP/Other): ______________ / IPI/CAE #: ____________

[*If applicable*] Publishing Company Name: ____________ / Pub. Co's IPI/CAE #: _______

READ AND AGREED by:

Signature: X ______________________ / Date: __________ Percentage: _____%

Print Name: ______________________ / Title [*optional*]: ______________

Email: __________________________ / Phone: __________________

Mailing Address: ____

PRO (BMI/SESAC/ASCAP/Other): ______________ / IPI/CAE #: ____________

[*If applicable*] Publishing Company Name: ____________ / Pub. Co's IPI/CAE #: _______

READ AND AGREED by:

Signature: X ______________________ / Date: __________ Percentage: _____%

Print Name: ______________________ / Title [*optional*]: ______________

Email: __________________________ / Phone: __________________

Mailing Address: ____

PRO (BMI/SESAC/ASCAP/Other): ______________ / IPI/CAE #: ____________

[*If applicable*] Publishing Company Name: ____________ / Pub. Co's IPI/CAE #: _______

Sample Work-for-Hire Agreement

(for a Producer, Musician, Vocalist, etc.)

Note: A written, signed, dated, and agreed-upon work-made-for-hire (or work-for-hire) contract is necessary in the sync world, especially if the person being hired (a) did not contribute to writing the composition (Song) in any way, and/or (b) will not be able to claim ownership of the Master Recording in any way, and/or (c) may have possible future entanglements as a result of having worked on the project. Always get qualified legal help with contracts. This is to be used as a guide only.

This agreement is made and entered into on [*Month/Day/Year*] ________________________ by and between [*Name of Songwriter (or Person doing the hiring)*] ___________________________, hereinafter referred to as "Songwriter," and [*Name of Person being hired*] _______________, hereinafter referred to as "Producer" [*Note: or applicable title such as "Musician," "Vocalist," "Mixer," "Recording Engineer," "Mastering Engineer," "Arranger," "Orchestrator," etc.*]

Whereby we, the parties hereto, agree as follows:

1. Songwriter hereby engages Producer's services as an independent contractor [*Note: Check laws regarding independent contractors*], and Producer hereby accepts such engagement to [*Note: describe the duties person being hired will be performing, such as*] perform on and record Songwriter's song [*Title of Song*], "_______________," hereinafter referred to as "Song," for the purpose of creating a recording of Songwriter's original song. Producer agrees to diligently, competently, and to the best of Producer's ability, experience, and talent, perform to Songwriter's satisfaction all of the services required of Producer hereunder.
2. Conditioned upon Producer's full and faithful performance of all the terms and provisions hereof, Songwriter shall pay Producer the sum of [*Enter fee amount here, spelled out and numerically*] _______________ ($_______) for Song as full and complete consideration for Producer's services hereunder.
3. Producer agrees that his/her/their performance and recording shall be considered as a work-made-for-hire (or work-for-hire) as contemplated and defined in Section 101 of the United States Copyright Act of 1976. Producer hereby grants to Songwriter all rights of every kind and nature in and to the results and proceeds of Producer's services and performances rendered hereunder, including, without limitation, the complete, unconditional, and exclusive worldwide, beyond, and everywhere, ownership in perpetuity of any and all recordings and audiovisual reproductions and technology known or yet to be discovered embodying Producer's performances hereunder. Songwriter shall accordingly have the sole and exclusive right to copyright any such recordings or audiovisual reproductions embodying Producer's performances under Songwriter's name as the sole owner and author thereof.
4. Producer hereby grants to Songwriter the right, worldwide, beyond, and everywhere, in perpetuity, to use and publish and to permit others to use and publish Producer's name, likeness, voice, and other biographical material, in connection with Producer's services and performances hereunder.
5. Songwriter shall use his/her/their best efforts to credit Producer as performing on the recordings herein in the event such recordings are released for sale to the public and, if applicable and/or possible, shall include Producer's name on Songwriter's website, metadata, recordings, and promotional materials. No casual or inadvertent failure by Songwriter and no failure by or of any third party to accord the requisite credit herein shall be deemed a breach of this agreement.
6. Producer fully understands that Songwriter would not have employed Producer without an agreement on Producer's part to give, grant, release, and assign to it and/or him/her/them all rights of every kind in and to the work performed by Producer for Songwriter, together with all results thereof and incidental thereto.

7. Producer hereby warrants, represents, and agrees that Producer is not under any disability, restriction, or prohibition, whether contractual or otherwise with respect to Producer's right to execute this contract, to grant the rights granted hereunder to perform each and every term and provision required to be performed by Producer hereunder. No materials, ideas, or other properties furnished by Producer and utilized by Songwriter will violate or infringe upon any common law or statutory right of any person, firm, or corporation, including without limitation contractual rights, copyrights, trademarks, and rights of privacy and/or publicity. Producer shall hold Songwriter (and any assignee, licensee, or third party) harmless and hereby agrees to indemnify Songwriter (and any assignee, licensee, or third party) for all costs in connection with any breach of the above warranties and representations.

8. Producer acknowledges and agrees that nothing in this agreement shall obligate Songwriter to employ or otherwise engage Producer's services in connection with any other future recording or agreement.

9. Producer acknowledges and agrees that if he/she/they provide(s) musical and/or recording equipment or other property of any nature in connection with services required hereunder, Songwriter shall not be liable for any loss or damage to such equipment or property.

10. This agreement sets forth the entire understanding of the parties hereto relating to the subject matter hereof and supersedes all prior and contemporaneous negotiations, understandings, and discussions. No modification, amendment, waiver, termination, or discharge of this agreement or any of its terms or provisions shall be binding upon either party if not confirmed by a written agreement signed and dated by Songwriter and Producer.

11. Producer is not entitled to any future revenue generated by the composition of the Song and is not a co-writer of Songwriter's Song in any way.

12. [*Optional text:* "This agreement does not prevent Producer from receiving potential income, royalties, and/or residuals that may be due as a result of Producer's performance on the recording of the Song. It is the responsibility of Producer to research, join, and/or register for these potential revenue sources. To the best of his/her/their ability, Songwriter shall provide pertinent information about the recording of the Song to Producer to facilitate this process."]

13. Any and all disputes between the parties arising under and/or relating to this agreement shall be determined in accordance with the laws and the courts of the State of [*Insert the name of State here*] ____________________, USA.

IN WITNESS WHEREOF, the parties hereto have executed this Agreement on the day, month, and year first above set out.

READ AND AGREED by:

[*Person being hired*] Signature: X________________________________ / Date: ____________

Print Name: ______________________________ / Title [*optional*]: ______________________

Email: __________________________________ / Phone: ___________________________

Mailing Address: ____

READ AND AGREED by:

[*Person being hired*] Signature: X________________________________ / Date: ____________

Print Name: ______________________________ / Title [*optional*]: ______________________

Email: __________________________________ / Phone: ___________________________

Mailing Address: ____

Sample Master Recording Split Agreement

> *Note: Generally, whoever records the full and complete song is the Master Recording owner. However, Master Recording split percentages may be assigned to anyone and for any percentage amount, as long as these terms are agreed upon by all parties. For instance, if the songwriters pay a Producer/Recording Engineer in a work-for-hire situation, and all parties have agreed and signed a valid "Work-for-Hire" agreement, the songwriters may own the Master Recording. Below is one example of how the Master Recording splits (percentages) may be done. Always get qualified legal help with contracts. This is to be used as a guide only.*

This agreement is made and entered into on [*Month/Day/Year*] __________________ by and between or among the following persons [*Note: List each person's name below. Optional throughout the agreement: include a title such as "Songwriter," "Singer-Songwriter," "Producer," "Artist," "Musician," "Songwriter/Musician," "Producer/Songwriter," "Recording Engineer," etc.*]

[*Note: The person's title may be included or omitted*]

Name: ________________________________ / [*optional*] Title: ____________________________

Name: ________________________________ / [*optional*] Title: ____________________________

Name: ________________________________ / [*optional*] Title: ____________________________

Whereby we, the parties hereto, agree as follows:

1. We, the parties named above, each hereby acknowledge and agree that we are the owners of the recording (hereinafter "Master Recording") of the Song titled "__________________," and that we shall each be deemed to be the Master Recording Rights Owners of the Master Recording in accordance with the applicable percentage set forth below ("Applicable Percentage").
2. We agree that we will jointly register and own the copyright in the Master Recording. All rights in the Master Recording shall be held jointly by the parties hereunder, and we shall participate in all receipts from the exploitation of the Master Recording in proportion to our respective ownership interest in said copyright in the Master Recording which is as follows:

   Name: ____________________________ / [*optional*] Title: ____________________________

   Applicable Percentage [*Spell out amount*] ________________ percent [*Numeral*] (______%)

   Name: ____________________________ / [*optional*] Title: ____________________________

   Applicable Percentage [*Spell out amount*] ________________ percent [*Numeral*] (______%)

   Name: ____________________________ / [*optional*] Title: ____________________________

   Applicable Percentage [*Spell out amount*] ________________ percent [*Numeral*] (______%)
3. Except to the extent that the material is in the public domain in the United States, each of us hereunder represents and warrants that the material contributed by each of us shall be original with us and shall not violate or infringe the copyright, common law copyright, right of privacy, or any other personal or property right whatsoever of any person or entity, or constitute a libel or slander, and that we fully own and control such material and all rights therein and have the full right to enter into this Agreement and other contracts and consents to be entered into hereunder.
4. We agree that we each shall have the right to administer through our respective companies our respective share of and exploitation rights in and to the Master Recording, except no exploitation rights individually administered shall be exclusive and all such agreements shall provide for all proceeds to be paid directly to the parties in their respective shares and a true copy of each agreement issued by one party shall be promptly furnished to the other parties.

5. All expenses which may reasonably be incurred pursuant to this Agreement shall be shared per each party's respective ownership hereunder.
6. All parties shall share in proportion to their ownership percentage all costs and expenses, damages, losses and attorney's fees incurred in protecting the Master Recording, with respect both to responding to infringement claims brought as to said Master Recording and as to bringing suit against an infringer of the Master Recording.
7. Nothing herein contained shall constitute a partnership or joint venture between the parties hereunder.
8. The parties to this Agreement shall each have the right to assign their respective interest in the Master Recording to any third party provided that such assignment is subject to the applicable provisions of this agreement.
9. This Agreement shall be for the full term of copyright throughout the world, including renewals and extensions to extent owned or controlled by the parties.
10. This Agreement constitutes the entire understanding between the parties hereto and may not be modified except by a written instrument duly executed by the parties hereto or their assignees or authorized representatives.
11. This Agreement shall be construed, interpreted and enforced in accordance with the laws of the State of ________________, USA, applicable to agreements executed, delivered and to be performed within such state. This agreement may be executed in any number of counterparts, each of which shall be deemed an original, but all of which shall constitute one document. Delivery of an executed counterpart of a signature page to this agreement by telecopier or digital transmission shall be effective as delivery of a manually executed counterpart of this Agreement.

IN WITNESS WHEREOF, the parties hereto have executed this Agreement on the day, month, and year first above set out.

READ AND AGREED by:

Signature: X ______________________________ / Date: ____________ Percentage: ______%

Print Name: ______________________________ / Title [*optional*]: ____________________

Email: ______________________________ / Phone: ____________________________

Mailing Address: ____

READ AND AGREED by:

Signature: X ______________________________ / Date: ____________ Percentage: ______%

Print Name: ______________________________ / Title [*optional*]: ____________________

Email: ______________________________ / Phone: ____________________________

Mailing Address: ____

READ AND AGREED by:

Signature: X ______________________________ / Date: ____________ Percentage: ______%

Print Name: ______________________________ / Title [*optional*]: ____________________

Email: ______________________________ / Phone: ____________________________

Mailing Address: ____

APPENDIX C

Keywords: Basic Objective Information about the Music

DESCRIPTIONS OF THE MUSIC

Instrumentation

accordion, various
acoustic guitar
bagpipe, various
balalaika
band (rock, pop, swing, big, etc.)
banjo
bass (electric, standup, etc.)
bassoon
bells, various
brass
calliope/steam organ
celesta
cello
Chapman stick
cimbalom
claps
clarinet
didgeridoo
double bass
drum, various
dulcimer, various
ektara
electric guitar
ensemble
ethnic, various
fiddle
flute
glass harmonica
glockenspiel
guitar, various
handbells
harmonica
harp, various
hurdy-gurdy
kalimba
kazoo
keyboard, various
koto
lap steel
lute
mandolin
marimba
musette
oboe
ocarina
orchestra
organ, various
pad
panpipes/pan flute
pedal steel
percussion, various
piano, prepared
piano, grand/upright, etc.
resonator guitar (Dobro)
saxophone
sitar
slap bass
snaps
spoons
steel guitar, slide guitar
steelband/steel orchestra
steelpan/steel pan drum
string quartet
strings
synths, various/vintage
theremin
Tibetan singing bowl
trombone
trumpet
tuba
ukulele
vibraphone
viola
violin
whistle (human, synth, etc.)
wind chimes
woodwinds
xylophone
yueqin (moon lute)
zither

Key of Music

major
minor
mixed keys
mode
specific key (C major, A minor)

Tempo

beats per minute (bpm)
loose tempo/rubato
varying/fluctuating

The following is the tempo range from slow to fast:

extremely slow/grave (est. under 45 bpm)
very slow/largo/lento (est. 45–60 bpm)
slow/down-tempo/larghetto/adagio (est. 60–75)
medium slow/andante (est. 70–85 bpm)
medium/mid-tempo/andantino (est. 85–100)
medium fast/moderato/allegretto (est. 100–120 bpm)
fast/up-tempo/allegro (est. 120–150 bpm)
very fast/vivace (est. 150–170 bpm)
extremely fast/presto (est. over 170 bpm)

Unique Characteristics of the Music

à la . . . (in the style of/similar to/like . . .)
alt mixes (unusual ones)
arc at 00:00 (time)
atonal
breakdown/stripped-down section at 00:00 (time)
break/stop (at 00:00 time or throughout)
build/crescendo/increased intensity at 00:00 (time)
buildup at 00:00 (time)
bumper/bump (10–15 seconds long)
button/hard ending
canon (repeated theme with layered buildup)
choppy/detached/staccato notes
cinematic
climactic
climax at 00:00 (time)
climb/stop/sub-stinger/climb/final stinger
col legno (percussive bow on wood sound)
complex/sophisticated
contemporary
cutdowns/edits available (:10, :15, :20, :30, :60, etc.)
cutting edge (sounds, production, etc.)
decreased intensity/decrescendo at 00:00 (time)
dramatic climax ending
dynamic/varying dynamics
ear candy (briefly describe)
ebb and flow (rhythmic/recurring pattern)
edit point(s) at 00:00 (time)
electronic
ending, coda/false/tag
fade-out ending
glissando/notes gliding (piano, harp, strings)
hits/stabs
hooky/catchy (melody/production, etc.)
intro/signature riff or hook
jump scare chord (for horror, video games)
key change at 00:00 (time)
legato/smooth
melodic
musical interlude/instrumental at 00:00 (time)
orchestra hit (stabs)
ostinato/continuous repeated pattern
outro/coda/false ending
pizzicato/plucking strings
rubato/out of time
signature riff or hook (intro/interlude(s)/outro)
simple/stripped-down
singer-songwriter style
slowing down/rallentando/ritardando
smooth/flowing/legato notes
solo section/musical interlude
sporadic breaks/hits/vocalises
stabs/horn stabs (on downbeats)
staccato/detached
stops/cuts/cesura/caesura/breaks
suddenly louder/sforzando/strong accent
surprises (ear candy, hits, etc.)
swell/swelling at 00:00 (time)
swooshes/whooshes (transitions)
syncopated/rhythmic
tempo change at 00:00 (time)
thematic

traditional
trailerized/epic
transitional
vamp/improvised section
vocalise section/nonsense singing
windup/big ending

Vocals (if applicable)

a cappella choir/solo/group
acapella (alt. spelling)
balladeer
barbershop quartet/chorus
beatbox/vocal percussion
boy group/band
cantorial singing
carolers
chanting/chant singing
children's choir
choir/choral group
church/congregational singing
crooner, male/female
crowd vocals
doo-wop
duo/duet
emceeing/MCing
ensemble
ethnic, country/region various
falsetto (high voice)
female vocal
gang vocals
girl group/band
glee club
group
male vocal
opera chorus/soloist
quartet
rapping
recitative
scat singing
soloist/solo voice (or a cappella)
spoken singing
spoken voice
surf harmonies
talking blues
toasting
torch singer
trio

APPENDIX D

Keywords: Sync Music Genres and Subgenres

MAIN MUSIC GENRES

Americana
Blues
Children's/Kids'
Cinematic
Classical
Commercial/Advertising
Country
Dance
Drum and Bass/Percussive
Easy Listening and Lounge
Electronic Dance
Folk
Funk
Fusion/Hybrids/Mixed
Gospel
Hip Hop/Rap
Island
Jazz
Latin
Light/Mood Music
New Age and Neoclassical
Orchestral
Pop
Reggae
Religious/Inspirational
Rhythm and Blues/Soul
Rock
Specialized Styles
World

MAIN MUSIC GENRES AND THEIR SUBGENRES OR STYLES

Americana Music Subgenres

acoustic folk/folk pop/folk rock
Appalachian music
ballad
bayou
bluegrass
Cajun
country
Creole
folk, traditional/indie/contemporary
gospel
heartland folk/pop/rock
hillbilly music
indie folk
indigenous
Indigenous music of North America
Native American
New Orleans
old Western
old-time music
regional genres, various
rhythm and blues
roots
swamp
yodeling
zydeco

Blues Music Subgenres

acoustic
beach/Carolina shag
boogie
Chicago
Delta
dirt road, back road blues
electric
regional genres, various
rhythm and blues
shuffle
solo instrumental/vocal
Texas
traditional
twelve-bar blues

Children's/Kids' Music Styles and Subgenres

acoustic folk/pop/rock
ballad
bubblegum pop
electronic
fairytale
folk songs
kids' pop
lullaby
novelty
orchestral
nursery rhyme
rock
sing-along
solo instrumental/vocal
story song
tweener pop

Cinematic Music Styles

action
adventure
electronic
epic
fantasy
fusion/musical hybrids/mixed genres
horror
modern
mystery
retro
suspense
symphonic metal
tension
thriller
traditional
trailerized
various genres

Classical Music Styles

21st century classical
aria
art song
avant-garde
Baroque
chamber
chant
choral
contemporary
early music
ensemble, various
fugue
Impressionist
medieval
Minimalism
Modern
opera
operetta/light opera
orchestral
Postmodern
Renaissance
Romanticism
solo instrumental/vocal
string ensemble
trailer music
waltz
wedding music/marches

Commercial/Advertising Songs and Music Styles

acoustic folk/pop/rock
alternative, various
ambient
art pop
avant-garde
cinematic
cross-genre/genre-busting/crossover
dreampop
electronic
fusion/musical hybrids/mixed genres
genreless
indie
indie folk/pop/rock
inspirational/motivational
light orchestral
orchestral
positive/positivity pop
power pop
quirky (pop, folk, rock, etc.)
solo instrumental/vocal
sunshine pop
synthpop
worldbeat, global fusion

Country Music Subgenres

alt country
Americana
ballad
bluegrass
bro-country
Cajun
campfire ballad
classic
Christian country music
country-Western
countrypolitan
dances, various
folk
fusion/musical hybrids/mixed genres
gospel
hick hop/country rap
honky-tonk
indie folk/rock/pop
inspirational country
jug band
modern
Nashville sound
neotraditional country
old-time
outlaw
pop
progressive
rock
rockabilly
roots rock
singing cowboy
solo instrumental/vocal
Southern hip hop
traditional
Western swing

Dance Music Styles

ballroom, various
ballet, various
breakdancing
bunny hop
cha-cha-chá dance
classical dances, various
club
conga line
contemporary, various
country Western, various
ethnic, various
fashion show
flamenco
folk, various
jazz

jitterbug
Latin, various
limbo
line dancing
mambo
modern dance
polka
recital
regions/countries, various
salsa
square dancing
street dancing
swing, various
tap
two-step
waltz

Drum and Bass/Percussive Music Styles

acoustic drum pattern
bass music
bassline
beatboxing
cajón
djembe
drum n bass, DnB
drum circle
electronic drum kit pattern
human drums, percussion
percussion and bass
promo
regional, various
rock drum kit pattern
snaps and claps
solo drum/percussion
solo jazz percussion
stomps and claps (style)
taiko drum pattern
vocal drums, percussion
vocal or body percussion

Easy Listening and Lounge Music Subgenres

ambient
bachelor pad
background
beautiful music
bossa nova
cha-cha-chá
chill-out
electronic
elevator music
exotica
fusion/musical hybrids/ mixed genres
light music
mood music
piped
Polynesian music
poolside/resort music
solo instrumental/vocal
space-age pop
symphonic strings

Electronic Dance Music Subgenres

ambient
atmospheric
breakbeat
dance club
disco
down-tempo
drone
drum n bass, DnB
dubstep
electroacoustic
electronica action
electronica drama
electropop
freestyle
fusion/musical hybrids/ mixed genres
future bass
Goa trance
hardcore
house
IDM (Intelligent Dance Music)
industrial
lounge
rocktronica
synth-pop
techno
trance

Folk Music Subgenres

acoustic folk pop/folk rock
contemporary
dance or song
folk metal/pirate metal
fusion/musical hybrids/ mixed genres
indie
North American folk/ old-time music
regional, various
rock
roots revival
sea shanty
solo instrumental
traditional
yodeling
world

Funk Music Subgenres

boogie
breakbeat
contemporary R&B
electro
disco
funk metal
funkstep
funky house
fusion/musical hybrids/ mixed genres
hip hop funk
jazz funk
liquid/liquid DnB
post-disco dance funk
psychedelic funk
retro
synth-pop

Fusion/Musical Hybrids/Mixed Genres and Subgenres (Common)

country rock
dramedy
ethnic electronica
folktronica
Gulf and Western
hick hop
hip hop rock/country/pop
Jawaiian
Neoclassical new age music
orchestral hip hop
smooth jazz
trop rock
tropical house
worldbeat, global fusion

Gospel Music Subgenres

bluegrass
Christian country
hymns
praise
progressive Southern
solo instrumental/vocal
Southern
spirituals

Hip Hop/Rap Music Subgenres

alternative
crunk
dancehall
dirty South
dramatic
dramedy
drum and bass
dub
dubstep
East Coast
electronic
emo hip hop
freestyle rap
fusion/musical hybrids/ mixed genres
gangsta rap
hip pop
indie
jungle
Latin
mumble rap
old-school, old-skool
reggaetón
trap
trip hop
West Coast

Island Music Subgenres

Afro-Caribbean
calypso
Caribbean
cumbia
dancehall
electronic
fusion/musical hybrids/ mixed genres
Hawaiian
Indo-Caribbean
Jamaican
Jawaiian
rake-and-scrape
reggae
reggaetón
rocksteady
ska
slack-key guitar
soca
solo instrumental (marimba/ steelpan/ukulele)
tropical

Jazz Music Subgenres

acid
bebop
big band
big band swing
boogie-woogie
bossa nova
cocktail
contemporary
cool
crooner
crossover jazz
Dixieland
easy listening
exotica
funk
fusion jazz
fusion/musical hybrids/ mixed genres
gypsy swing
hard bop
hot club
improvisational
jazztronica
Las Vegas lounge
Latin
lounge
modal
modern
New Orleans
nu
piano trio/quartet
progressive
ragtime
Rat Pack sound
scat singing
smooth
solo instrument or vocal
soul jazz
standards
swing
traditional
West Coast

Latin Music Subgenres (Common)

banda
bossa nova
cha-cha-chá
conjunto
cumbia
dances, various

electronic
flamenco
fusion/musical hybrids/
mixed genres
jazz
mariachi
meringue
Norteño
pop
reggaetón
regional, various
rock
rumba
salsa
samba
solo instrumental/vocal
tango
Tejano
Tex-Mex
tropical

Light Music/Mood Music Styles and Subgenres

ambient
background music
beautiful music
classical crossover
concert
dramedy
easy listening
electronic
elevator music
exotica
fusion/musical hybrids/
mixed genres
game show
incidental music
Minimal
New age
operetta
parlour music
pizzicato strings
pops orchestra
solo piano/harp/guitar/other
string quartet/ensemble
string orchestra
talk show
theme music
Western classical

New Age and Neoclassical Music Subgenres

ambient
atmospheric music
background
Celtic fusion
chill
contemporary classical
drone
easy listening
electronic
fusion/musical hybrids/
mixed genres
healing/relaxation/
meditation music
Minimal
modern classical
resort
solo piano/harp/guitar/other
soundscape
spa/massage music
space music
world

Orchestral Music Styles and Subgenres

action
adventure
animation
chase
circus music, traditional
comedy/comical
crime
drama
dramedy
drone
epic
exotica
fanfare
fantasy
film noir
fusion/musical hybrids/
mixed genres
horror, various
hybrids, various
jazz
marching band music
melodrama
military
modern
mystery
political
pop
psychological thriller
romance
rom-com
science fiction/sci-fi
score
spaghetti Western
spy thriller
superhero
suspense
thriller, various
trailer music
Western

Pop Music Styles and Subgenres

acoustic folk pop/pop rock
adult contemporary
art pop
ballad
Baroque pop
British
bubblegum
California sound
classical crossover
contemporary
country
dance
disco
electronic
folk pop/pop rock
Great American Songbook
hip hop
indie pop
jazz
Latin
MOR, middle-of-the-road
orchestral pop/ork-pop/
chamber pop
positive pop/commercial

power
progressive
punk
rhythm and blues/R&B
rock
sentimental ballad
soft rock
soul
standard
sunshine pop
synth-pop/techno-pop
Tin Pan Alley
traditional

Reggae Music Subgenres

dancehall
dub
fusion, various
Jamaican, various
lovers rock
mento
ragamuffin/ragga
reggaestep
rocksteady
roots reggae
ska
solo instrumental/vocal
toasting

Religious/Inspirational Music Styles and Genres

(See also "Gospel")
bluegrass gospel
CCM/Contemporary Christian Music
CEDM
chant, various genres
children's Bible songs
Christian holidays
Christian hip hop, metal, pop, rap, rock
Christian music, various denominations
Christmas
church music
Christian country
classical
contemporary Catholic liturgical
contemporary worship music
Easter
ecumenical
faith-based
funeral/memorial dirge
gospel
gospel beat music
Gregorian chant
Hanukkah
High Holy Days
hip hop, various religions
Holy Week
hymns
Jesus music
liturgical music
metal, various religions
meditation music
plainsong
pop, various religions
praise/worship
psalmody/psalms/Book of Psalms
rap, various religions
religious ceremony, various
rock, various religions
Rosh Hashanah
sacred
Southern gospel
spirituals
Yom Kippur

Rhythm and Blues/Soul Music Subgenres

alternative blues
ballad
contemporary R&B
doo-wop
fusion, various
gospel
jazz
jump blues
Memphis soul
Motown sound
new jack swing
neo soul
pop
quiet storm/late night
rap
retro-soul
Southern soul
Stax/Volt sound
trip hop
vintage

Rock Music Styles and Subgenres

1950s styles
1960s styles
1970s styles
1980s styles
1990s styles
2000s styles
alternative/alt
Americana
AOR, album-oriented rock
arena
blues
British
British Invasion
chamber pop
classic
corporate
country
death metal
desert
emo
extreme metal
folk
funk metal
garage
glam
gothic rock/goth
grunge

hair metal
hard
heartland
heavy metal
indie
indie folk
industrial
jangle pop
jazz fusion
Latin
new wave
nu metal
oldies
power ballad
prog, progressive
psychedelic
punk
rap
rockabilly
roots
screamo
sentimental ballad
soft
Southern
solo instrumental/vocal
speed metal
surf
swamp
symphonic metal
yacht

Specialized Music Styles

anime music styles
award show music
barbershop, quartet/group
Broadway/New York City sound
cabaret style
call-and-response songs
camp/kitsch style
carnival/circus/carousel
Christmas, secular/pop/classic
clown/comic/zany/slapstick
corporate/selling music
dirge, sacred/secular
drone, electronic/acoustic
eclecticism
elevator/background music
era/epoch/decade, specific (1920s, 1930s, etc.)
esoteric music
fashion show/runway
festivals, various
fife and drum
game show music
Halloween/horror/pop/rock
Hollywood/red carpet
holidays, secular/religious/other
hymn (PD)
industrial/corporate musical
jingle/hooky ad music
loop music
lullaby (PD)
marching band/parade
military cadence/march
motivational music
musical theater styles
national anthem (PD)
nursery rhyme (PD)
old Hollywood glamour
overture
parody/comedy/burlesque
patriotic (PD)
party (various genres)
public domain (PD)
reality TV
religious, various
silent film
solo instrumental/vocal
sports/sports team songs
talk show music
theatrical/musical
torch song style
trailerized music
trailers
wedding music, ceremony/marches
work songs

World Music Subgenres

(See also "Latin," "Island," "Reggae")

African, various
Afro-Caribbean
Asian, various
Australian/Oceanian
ballad
Bollywood
Brazilian carnival
C-pop, various
calypso
Caribbean
Celtic
Central American, various
Central Asian, various
chant, sports/kids/crowd/regional
continental, various
country, various
dance, various regions
East Asian, various
ethnic folk
European, various
folk dance
folk instrumental
folk song
folktronica
fusion/musical hybrids/mixed genres
global fusion/worldbeat
highlife
instruments, various
island, various
J-pop, various
K-pop, various
Mediterranean, various
Mexican, various
Middle Eastern, various
Native American
North American, various
regional, various
solo instrumental/vocal
South American, various
South Asian, various
Southeast Asian, various
traditional
West Asian, various

APPENDIX E

Keywords: Mood, Feel, and Vibe of the Music

SPECTRUM AND RANGES OF THE MUSIC'S OVERALL FEEL

Extremely Positive

alluring
amped
astonishing
awesome
awestruck
beautiful
blissful
bold
bravura
breathtaking
brilliant
bubbly
bustling
celebratory
celestial
chic
classy
cosmic
courageous
daring
dazzling
deep
determined
driven
ecstatic
effervescent
elated
electrified
elegant
enchanting
energized
engaging
enthusiastic
excited
exhilarating
extraordinary
exuberant
fabulous
fanciful
fantastical
fearless
fired up
glam
glittery
glorious
gorgeous
grand
groovy
gutsy
heroic
hilarious
inspirational
jazzed
jubilant
lively
luminous
lush
magnificent
majestic
marvelous
motivational
noble
oomph
outgoing
overjoyed
passionate
peppy
plucky
polished
pomp
posh
powerful
prestigious
prideful
pumped
purposeful
racing
remarkable
resilient
robust
rock out
rousing
shiny
showy
sleek
soaring
sparkling
spirited
splendid
sprightly
stirring
stunning
sunshiny
superfine
swagger
terrific
thrilling
trendy
triumphant
unstoppable
valiant
valor
vibrant
victorious
vivacious
winning
wondrous
zesty

Positive

affable
airy
brave
breezy
bright
carefree
careful
caring
charming
cheerful
comforting
confident
cool
cute
delicate
delightful
dignified
distinguished
dreamlike
endearing
enjoyable
fancy
fashionable
feel-good
festive
flirty
friendly
frisky
fun
funny
genteel
gentle
glad
glamorous
gliding
glowing
graceful
grooving
happy
heartening
heartfelt
heartwarming
heavenly
honest
hopeful
humorous
impressive
inviting
jolly
jovial
joyful
joyous
light
lighthearted
likable
lilting
lovely
magical
optimistic
outgoing
peaceful
perky
playful
positive
quaint
relaxing
satiny
shimmering
silly
slick
soothing
springy
steady
summery
sweet
tasteful
tasty
tender
tinkly
twinkly
upbeat
uplifting
wishful

Slightly Positive

adventurous
animated
astonished
at ease
believable
calm
careful
casual
cautious
clean
comfortable
compelling
content
corny
cozy
curious
dumbfounding
dynamic
earnest
easy
effortless
elaborate
embellished
energetic
enormous
epic
exotic
fizzy
flabbergasting
flamboyant
flashy
free spirit
freewheeling
giddy
good-natured
hokey
insistent
juiced
laughable
lively
lofty
mod
neat
nice
ornamental
passionate
pastoral
pensive
pleasant
proud
spicy
stimulating
striking
stunning
stupefying
sultry
swanky
vigorous
whimsical

Neutral

ambient
ambiguous
ancient
anthemic
anticipating
atmospheric
attitude
authentic
awestruck
big
bouncy
brand-new
brassy
casual
childlike
classic
colorful
common
contemplative
contemporary
current
cutting edge
dancy
detailed
different
down-home
down-to-earth
dreamy
driving
droning
earthy
epic
ethereal
evergreen
evolving
faithful

familiar
fast
filmy
fine
flowing
fluctuating
folkie
folksy
formal
free
fresh
full
funky
futuristic
genuine
giant
gigantic
global
grandiose
hardy
hazy
hearty
high
high-energy
highbrow
hip
historical
homespun
hot
huge
humble
hypnotic
idyllic
immense
important
in limbo
in the pocket
indifferent
informal
innocent
intense
intricate
intriguing
irregular
jamming
jangly
jazzy
laid-back
light
loose
massive
mature
mechanical
meditative
mellow
melodic
metallic
misty
moderate
modern
moving
mysterious
mystical
natural
neutral
new
newfangled
nonchalant
noncommittal
normal
nostalgic
old-fashioned
old-school
old-timey
old-world
open
ordinary
organic
percussive
plain
pressing
primitive
pulsating
punchy
pure
quiet
quirky
real
realistic
refined
reflecting
repetitive
retro
reverent
rhythmic
rich
ritzy
rocking
rocking out
romantic
rootsy
royal
rugged
rushing
rustic
sacred
schmaltzy
sedate
sensational
sensitive
sensual
sentimental
serene
serious
sexy
shady
showstopper
simple
sincere
sliding
slow
smoky
smoldering
smooth
soft
solid
sophisticated
soulful
sparse
sporadic
sporty
state-of-the-art
stately
stealth
stirring
strong
stylish
subtle
surprising
swaying
swelling
swirling
thin
tight
timeless
touching
traditional
trance
tranquil
transparent
twirling
unbelievable
unconcerned
unexpected
unique
unprocessed
unusual
vacillating
vague
vibey
warm
whirling
wholesome
worldly

Slightly Negative

bawdy
bewildering
bittersweet
bizarre
bland
boisterous
booming
brazen
busy
campy
capricious
cartoony
cheesy
climactic
coarse
complex
complicated
crazy
critical
crude
ditzy
dizzying
doubtful
dull

dumbfounding
edgy
emotional
erratic
esoteric
flat
flighty
forceful
frenzied
frivolous
frothy
fuzzy
goofy
haughty
heavy
hesitant
imposing
jammed
jarring
jerky
jolting
juiced up
jumpy
lofty
ludicrous
melodramatic
peculiar
piercing
poignant
preposterous
prideful
provocative
rambling
raw
repetitious
risk-taking
rowdy
sassy
saucy
shocking
showboating
sketchy
spacey
startling
stiff
suggestive
superficial
surreal
syrupy
tentative
twangy
uncertain
uncivilized
uncomfortable
uneasy
unfriendly
unpredictable
unreal
unrefined
unsettling
unsophisticated
unsteady
unsure
urgent
wacky
wistful
zany

Negative

aching
afraid
aloof
apprehensive
awkward
bad
bitter
blindsiding
blue
bumpy
charged
cheeky
childish
chilling
choppy
classless
cold
confused
dark
defeated
deflated
detached
disenchanted
disillusioned
disoriented
distasteful
distorted
distracted
distressed
eerie
foolish
freakish
frosty
ghostly
gloomy
gross
grumpy
haunting
hurting
immature
inane
indecisive
insipid
introverted
irreverent
irritating
jealous
lazy
lethargic
lonely
longing
losing
lost
loud
mad
mean
melancholy
messy
mischievous
moody
mournful
naïve
nasty
naughty
negative
nervous
obscure
painful
pessimistic
prideful
regret
remorseful
restless
ridiculous
risqué
rough
rude
sad
sappy
scared
secretive
sinking
sloppy
smoldering
sneaky
snooping
somber
sorrowful
sorry
spooky
stiff
strange
suspenseful
tacky
tasteless
tearjerker
tense
tension
tipsy
tired
tough
trashy
uncaring
uncouth
upsetting
untamed
vampy
weary
weepy
weird
wild
wintry
worked up
worried
wrong
yearning

Extremely Negative

abrasive
absurd
aggressive
agitated
alarming
angry
anguished
annoying
anxious
arrogant
awkward
beastly
bombastic
brooding
burned-out
buzzkill
chaotic
clanging
clashing
cocky
confrontational
cranky
creepy
dangerous
delirious
demonic
depressing
deranged
desperate
devastated
devilish
diabolical
dirty
disastrous
distraught
distressing
disturbing
downtrodden
evil
exasperated
fearful
foreboding
frantic
freaking out
freaky
frenzy
frustrated
fury
grating
grieving
gritty
grotesque
gun-shy
hard-hitting
harrowing
harsh
hateful
haunting
heartbreaker
heartbreaking
heartbroken
heated
hectic
hell-raising
hopeless
horrifying
icy
idiotic
inconsolable
insane
intimidating
irritating
jolting
jumpy
lowlife
madness
martial
menacing
monstrous
nerve-racking
obnoxious
obsessive
ominous
oppressed
ostentatious
outlandish
overbearing
panicky
pompous
pounding
prickly
puffed up
pushy
racy
rambunctious
raunchy
rebellious
reckless
rejected
relentless
risky
rotten
scary
severe
sinister
sleazy
slimy
snarky
snarling
solemn
souped-up
standoffish
stormy
stressed out
stubborn
stuffy
suffering
suffocating
terrified
terrorizing
tragic
trampy
trapped
trashy
twisted
uncontrollable
uneasy
unhinged
unraveling
unruly
vengeful
vicious
wacko
warlike
wicked

APPENDIX F

Keywords: Lyric Themes and Additional Sync Music Styles

Lyric Themes for Sync Songs

adventure/journey/exploring
alone/isolated/solo
angry/hostile/livid/outraged
belonging/fitting in
betrayal/infidelity/two-timing
boasting/bragging/prideful
bold/having confidence
breakup/heartache
celebration/party/good times/fun
change/new beginning/fresh start
character definition (ex. crazy, evil, heroic)
cheating/broken trust/unfaithful
confidence/self-assurance
conquering/overcoming something
courageousness/being brave/stepping up
daring/taking a chance/risking it all
defeat/being discouraged/disappointed
desperate/anxious/dire situation
discovering/exploring self
drinking/imbibing/getting inebriated
drunk/intoxicated
encouragement/support/comfort
escaping/getting away from it all
excluded/ostracized/not fitting in
first . . . kiss/date/time meeting someone
flirting/teasing/suggestive
forgiveness/pardon
freedom/liberation/independence
friends/friendship/togetherness
goodbye/leaving/closure
gratitude/thank you/appreciation
happiness/joy/feeling good
hateful/despising someone/something
hello/inviting/welcome
heroism/saving someone
holiday themes, various
home/family life/living
hopeful/upbeat/optimistic
hopeless/despair/dark/dismal
impulsive/wanton/loose morals
infidelity/immoral/shameless
insecurity/lack of confidence/self-doubt
jealousy/envious/possessive
last . . . kiss/time seeing someone
lifestyle: easy/laid-back/relaxed/simple
lifestyle: fast/freewheeling/rough
lifestyle: free spirit/unconventional
lifestyle: jet set/wealthy/rich/powerful
lifestyle: wanderer/vagabond/unsettled
lifestyle: wild/unbridled/out of control
loneliness/not belonging
losing someone/grieving/major loss
losing something/defeated
love/affectionate (non-romantic)
love/passionate (romantic)
loyalty/faithfulness/devotion
lust/intense desire
missing someone/something
money/riches/wealth/bling
moving on/acceptance
nostalgia/remembering/longing
obsession/infatuation
philosophical/life experience
rebellion/against authority
remorse/contriteness
revenge/payback/retaliation
security/safe/familiar
social/cultural issues
sorry/apology/regret
soul-searching/introspection
surviving/enduring something
suspicious/distrusting
taking a risk
taking control
tired/worn out/fatigued
trapped/being stuck
traveling/driving/road trip
tribute/toast/homage
triumph/victorious/winning

trying something for the first time
uncertainty/doubting/in limbo
unrequited/one-sided love
upset/frustrated/worried
using a mind-altering substance
wanting/needing someone/something
wisdom/advice/offering insight
wishing/dreaming/hoping

Additional Sync Music Styles

action music
adventure music
chase music
chilling music
climactic music
comical music
competition music
countdown music
defeat/losing music
drama/dramatic music
dramedy/sneaky music
fashion/runway music
fight music
high-energy music
horror music
low-energy music
moving around music
news music
reveal music
rom-com music
romance music
showdown music
surprise music
suspense music
tasking music
tension music
thriller music
winning music
victory music

APPENDIX G

Keywords: Music Placement Possibilities

(Note: Some of the keyword entries below will overlap each other and/or some of the entries above. If this is the case, avoid using the same descriptive word more than once in any of the metadata fields.)

Locations and Specific Places

amusement/theme park
art gallery/art show
bar/grill
biker bar/motorcycle club
billiard hall/poolroom
boat/ship/watercraft
bowling alley/lounge
business/office building
campground/campsite
car/truck/vehicle
carnival/fairground/circus
casino/gambling room
castle/palace
cemetery/graveyard
church/chapel/cathedral
city/town/village, specific
classroom/schoolhouse
club/nightclub/limo
cocktail party/upscale bar/lounge
coffeehouse/café
college/high school campus
concert venue, various
country/nation, specific
convention/trade show/expo
cruise ship
diner/coffee shop
dormitory/dorm room
downtown/metropolis/city center
elevator
factory/manufacturing plant
farm/ranch/barnyard
fashion show/runway
food court/cafeteria/fast food place
funeral parlor/mortuary
gasoline/service station/truck stop
geographical region, specific
grocery store/corner market
headquarters/command center
home/habitat
hospital/doctor's office/medical facility
hotel/resort/motel/lodge/B&B
house/mansion/apartment/condominium
island resort/getaway
laboratory/science lab
landmark: national/international
landscape: arctic/tundra/glacier
landscape: beach/seashore/coastal
landscape: desert/wasteland/wilderness
landscape: forest/woods/timberland
landscape: island/tropics
landscape: meadow/pasture/prairie
landscape: mountain/hillside
landscape: plain/savanna/moor
landscape: rainforest/jungle
landscape: rural/backcountry/wilderness
landscape: suburban/city/rural
landscape: swamp/wetland/marsh
movie theater/drive-in/cinema/art house
newsroom, print/radio/TV
neighborhood/residential area
office lobby/place of work/job
old West/saloon/ghost town
party/celebration/life event
pier/boardwalk
race track/racing
region/area, specific
religious/holy/sacred place of worship
restaurant, casual/fine dining/fast food
roller/ice skating rink
saloon/pub/tavern/public house
shops/stores, various
shopping mall/department store
small-town/hamlet/village
spa/gym/exercise class

stadium/ballpark/sports arena
stage/auditorium
state/territory, specific
station, radio/TV/fire/police
suburb/countryside
theater/amphitheater
zoo/aquarium/animal preserve

Subject and Situation Placement Possibilities (How the Music May Be Synced)

action/action drama
adventure
advertisement/promo/infomercial
agriculture/farming
alternative lifestyle/subculture
ancient civilization/ruins/gladiator games
animals/pets
animation/cartoon
anniversary party/dinner
antiques/collectibles
architecture/design
art, various
artisan/craftsperson
arts and crafts
award shows/red carpet
baby/infant/toddler
baking/bake-off
baseball/softball
basketball
beach activities
beauty/fashion styles/trends
biographical/historical
birthday/anniversary
boating/sailing
boxing/fight
branding/marketing
building/construction
business/corporate event
campaign
camping/glamping/campfire
car/automobile
casino/gambling/slot machine/card game
celebration/gathering
celebrities/famous people
challenge
chase
children/kids
children's party
Christmas
Cinco de Mayo
civilization/society/culture
clown/hijinks
cold weather/freezing/snow
comedy/slapstick
competition/contest/tournament
concert, various
conflict/fight
cooking/culinary arts
cuisine, various
corporate/corporate culture
costume party/cosplay/dress-up
cowhand/cowboy/cowgirl
crime/courtroom
dance recital
dancing/dance-off
dating/relationship
detective/private eye
dinner party/dining
disaster, natural/unnatural
dream/dreaming
driving/highway/road trip
duel/showdown
educational/learning
election/voting
engagement/bachelor/bachelorette party
equity/fairness/justice issues
ethnic/cultural/indigenous event
extreme sports/games
fairytale/storybook time
family/family-friendly
family drama
fantasy
fashion/runway/catwalk
festivities, various
figure skating/ice skating
film noir
fishing/hunting/outdoors
fitness/exercise
flashback/flash-forward
flora and fauna/plants and animals
food/beverage, general/artisanal
football
fortune-teller
funeral/graveside service/burial
funny/silly/slapstick
futuristic
game show, correct/incorrect answer
games, various
gardening
ghosts/spirits/séance
gourmet/foodie
graduation ceremony
gymnastics
health/wellness
heavenly/sky/clouds/aerial
hero/heroic act/protagonist
historical/period
hobbies, various
hockey
holidays, secular/religious/other
homecoming, military/family/school
home improvement
horror/suspense/thriller
hot/desert
human interest story
Independence Day/Fourth of July
indigenous/native/ethnic events
industry/factory/manufacturing
inequity/unfairness/injustice issues
infamous/notorious person
international events/sports/games
investigative reporting
jet set/elite/upper crust/rich/famous
journey/exploration
jukebox
jungle/tropics/rainforest
law/legal issues
leisure, various events/activities
life celebrations/bridal shower/baby shower
lifestyle, various types
loss/breakup/heartbreak

magic/wizardry/illusion/sleight of hand
makeover/transformation
martial arts, various
media, radio/print/TV/film/Internet
medical drama
medical news/information
memorial/tribute/commemoration
military service branches
mixed martial arts
montage/panorama
music box/musical clock
music event/concert
mystery/thriller/whodunit
nature/environmental
nautical/maritime/aquatic/marine life
New Year's Eve
news/information/current events
newsreel, vintage/historic
on hold/phone music/answering machine
outdoors/hunting/fishing
outer space/space/universe/cosmos
outlander/stranger/non-native/foreigner
parade/marching band/drumline
paranormal/supernatural
party, various types
playing/play time
playoffs
podcasts
police/cops/law enforcement
politics/government
poverty/poor/disadvantaged
prank/satire/spoof/parody
product development
progress/moving forward
racing, motorsports/horses, etc.
radio, in a car/truck/home
radio, stand-alone/vintage
radio show, old time
rally/demonstration/protest
ranching/farming/livestock
reality TV
record player/turntable/gramophone
recreational activities/events/shows
religious holidays/observances
renovation/remodel/redecorate
restaurant, ethnic/casual/fine, etc.
retail background music
reunion, school/family/various
rich/wealth/fortune/opulent
ringtone
romance
romantic comedy/rom-com
royal/royalty/kingdom
rugby
running/marathon/jogging
sales pitch/selling on-camera
science/scientific news/events
science fiction/sci-fi
sea/ocean/harborside
seasonal events
seasons, spring/summer/autumn/winter
showbiz/show business
silent film/melodrama
situation comedy/sitcom
skiing/snowboarding/winter sports
sneaky/snooping around
soap opera, vintage/current
soccer
social issues/justice/classes
social media platforms
socialite/magnate/high society
sporting event/show
sports figures/athletes
spy/espionage/undercover/secret agent
St. Patrick's Day
storytelling/bedtime story
striptease/burlesque
sunrise/sunset
surfing events/scenes
swimming, leisure/competition
talent show/recital
talk show
tasking, chores/cleaning/office work
teaching/teachers/grades
teams/team sports, various
technology/high tech
teen/tweener
tennis
Thanksgiving
theater/live entertainment
thinking/clock is ticking/time's up
toasting/honoring/saluting
toys, various
track and field
tragedy/tragic event/news
trailer
transportation, various
travel, various locations
underwater/deep sea
vacation
Valentine's Day
variety show/entertainment
vaudeville
video games, vintage/contemporary
villain/bad guy/antihero/antagonist
walking/hiking
war/battle
weather events/climate
weight training/working out
wedding, ceremony/reception
wildlife/nature
world/global/international issues
young adult
youth

APPENDIX H

Recommended Reading

For more recommended reading, please visit the Hey! That's My Song! website at https://www.HeyThatsMySong.com/.

Aschmann, Lisa. *1000 Songwriting Ideas*. New York: Hal Leonard, 2008.

Barden, Steve. *Writing Production Music for TV: The Road to Success*. Foreword by Kevin Kiner. Anaheim Hills, CA: Centerstream Publishing, 2017.

Blume, Jason. *6 Steps to Songwriting Success: The Comprehensive Guide to Writing and Marketing Hit Songs*. Revised and expanded, 3rd ed. New York: Billboard Books, 2008.

Borg, Bobby. *Business Basics for Musicians: The Complete Handbook from Start to Success*. 2nd ed. MusicPro Guides. Lanham, MD: Rowman & Littlefield, 2020.

Borg, Bobby, and Michael Eames. *Introduction to Music Publishing for Musicians: Business and Creative Perspectives for the New Music Industry*. Lanham, MD: Rowman & Littlefield, 2021.

Brabec, Jeffrey, and Todd Brabec. *Music, Money and Success: The Insider's Guide to Making Money in the Music Business*. 8th ed. New York: Omnibus Press, Schirmer Trade Books, 2018.

Frederick, Robin. *Shortcuts to Songwriting for Film & TV: 114 Tips for Writing, Recording, & Pitching in Today's Hottest Market*. Los Angeles: Taxi Music Books, 2010.

Henry, Barbara. *First 15 Lessons: Piano; A Beginner's Guide, Featuring Step-by-Step Lessons with Audio, Video, and Popular Songs!* Milwaukee: Hal Leonard, 2018.

Krippaehne, Dean. *Demystifying the Cue: Thoughts and Strategies for Creating Competitive Film and TV Music in Today's New Media World*. Seattle: RMC Publishing, 2014.

McLane, Ben. *Music Business in 10 Easy Lessons: The Deal*. N.p. Artisthead Press, 2018.

Passman, Donald S. *All You Need to Know About the Music Business*. 10th ed. New York: Simon & Schuster, 2019.

Pattison, Pat. *Writing Better Lyrics: The Essential Guide to Powerful Songwriting*. 2nd ed. Foreword by Gillian Welch. Cincinnati: Writer's Digest Books, 2010.

Sokolow, Fred. *Fretboard Roadmaps—Beginning Guitar: The Essential Guitar Patterns that All the Pros Know and Use*. With editorial assistance by Ronny S. Schiff. Milwaukee: Hal Leonard, 2012.

Thomas, Amanda Krieg. *Thinking in Sync: A Primer on the Mind of a Music Supervisor*. Foreword by P. J. Bloom. N.P.: Self-published, 2019.

Winogradsky, Steve. *Music Publishing: The Complete Guide*. 2nd ed. Edited by David Lowery. Van Nuys, CA: Alfred Publishing Company, 2019.

APPENDIX I

Music Trade Organizations, Conferences, and Additional Resources

ASSOCIATIONS: EDUCATION AND ADVOCACY

AIMP (Association of Independent Music Publishers // L.A., NYC, and Nashville)
https://www.aimp.org/

CCC (California Copyright Conference)
https://theccc.org/

GMS (Guild of Music Supervisors)
https://www.guildofmusicsupervisors.com/

NSAI (Nashville Songwriters Association International)
http://www.nashvillesongwriters.com/

PMA (Production Music Association)
https://pmamusic.com/

SCL (Society of Composers and Lyricists // L.A. and NYC)
https://thescl.com/

SONA (Songwriters of North America)
https://www.wearesona.com/

MUSIC CONFERENCES AND EVENTS

ASCAP Experience
https://ascapexperience.com/

Durango Songwriters Expo
https://durango-songwriters-expo.com/

Game Developers Conference (GDC)
https://gdconf.com/

GameSoundCon
https://www.gamesoundcon.com/

Guild of Music Supervisors "State of Music in Media" Conference
https://www.gmsmediaconference.com/

Hawai'i Songwriting Festival
http://www.hawaiisongwritingfestival.com/

Hollywood Music in Media Awards (HMMA)
https://www.hmmawards.com/

MIDEM (Marché International du Disque et de l'Edition Musicale in France)
https://www.midem.com/

MUSEXPO
https://www.musexpo.net/

NAMM Show (National Association of Music Merchants // Winter in Anaheim and summer in Nashville)
https://www.namm.org/

NARIP (National Association of Record Industry Professionals)
https://www.narip.com/
NSAI's Tin Pan South Songwriters Festival
https://www.tinpansouth.com/
PMC (Production Music Conference by the PMA)
https://pmamusic.com/
SXSW (South by Southwest)
https://www.sxsw.com/
Sync Summit
http://syncsummit.com/
TAXI Road Rally
https://www.taxi.com/taxi-road-rally/

PERFORMING RIGHTS ORGANIZATIONS

ASCAP (American Society of Composers, Authors and Publishers)
https://www.ascap.com/
BMI (Broadcast Music, Inc.)
https://www.bmi.com/
GMR (Global Music Rights)
https://globalmusicrights.com/
SESAC (Society of European Stage Authors and Composers)
https://www.sesac.com/
SoundExchange
https://www.soundexchange.com/

COPYRIGHT REGISTRATION

U.S. Copyright Office
https://www.copyright.gov/

MECHANICAL RIGHTS ORGANIZATIONS

Harry Fox Agency (HFA)
https://www.harryfox.com/
MLC (Mechanical Licensing Collective)
https://www.themlc.com/
MRI (Music Reports)
https://www.musicreports.com/

PUBLISHING ADMINISTRATORS AND RIGHTS MANAGEMENT COMPANIES

Exploration Group (Media management and technology)
https://exploration.io/
Songtrust
https://www.songtrust.com/
TuneCore
https://www.tunecore.com/music-publishing-administration/

NEIGHBORING RIGHTS COLLECTION AGENCIES

All Right Music
http://www.allrightmusic.com/
Global Master Rights
https://www.globalmasterrights.com/

NRG
https://www.nrg-agency.com/
Premier Muzik
https://www.premiermuzik.com/

AUDIO DETECTION SERVICES

BMAT
https://www.bmat.com/
SourceAudio
https://www.sourceaudio.com/
TuneSat
https://tunesat.com/

PITCH SERVICES AND TIP SHEETS

NARIP (National Association of Record Industry Professionals)
https://www.narip.com/
Songtradr
https://www.songtradr.com/
TAXI
https://www.taxi.com/

MUSIC SEARCH SERVICES

Shazam
https://www.shazam.com/
Tunefind
https://www.tunefind.com/

FILE TRANSFER SERVICES

Disco
https://disco.ac/
Dropbox
https://www.dropbox.com/
WeTransfer
https://wetransfer.com/

FORUMS AND MISCELLANEOUS RESOURCES

Hey! That's My Song!
https://www.HeyThatsMySong.com/
MasterWriter
https://masterwriter.com/
Music Business Registry
https://www.musicregistry.com/
Music Connection Magazine
https://www.musicconnection.com/
Music Library Report
https://musiclibraryreport.com/
Songtrust
https://www.songtrust.com/
TAXI Forums
https://forums.taxi.com/

Special Thanks

To our family and lifelong cheerleaders (some of whom are with us only in spirit): Carlene Marino, Manuel and Ethel Souza, Melvin Souza, Laurie and Bill Spinks, Melanie and Jim Piva, Bryan and Laureen Marino, Clement Marino, Leilani Marino, Tomi and Richard Weddleton, Anne Weddleton, Bennett C. Ashley, Joan Vandermolen, Diane K. Ward, Mark Weddleton and Teri Bannister, Victoria and Chris Colman

To our longtime friend Brian Thomas Curtin, for the wisdom, pep talks, and laughs over the years, especially during the tough times

To our friends who inspired us to write this book, especially Steve Barden, Matt Hirt, Ken Jacobsen, Dean Krippaehne, Juliet Lyons, and Nitanee Paris

To our supportive colleagues, collaborators, and companions on this musical journey, especially John Allan, Volker Barber, Charity Chapman, Steve Collom, Vince Constantino, Carrie Cunningham, Al Di Cicco, John DeFaria, Randy Fischer, Barry French, Mark Hattersley, Chuck Henry, Larry Hopkins, Trevor Wayne Howard, Inbal-Rotem Sagiv, Jeanna Isham, Cliff Keller, Cher Klosner Lane, Panos Kolias, Lew Lazarus, Jeff Lizerbram, Andy Machin, John Mazzei, Margaret McClure, Paula McMath, Stan Morris, Francisco (Cisko) Rodriguez, Adryan Russ, Robin Sandoval, Chuck Schlacter, Jocelyn Scofield, Michael Silversher, Patty Silversher, Tyler Traband, Jacqueline Van Bierk, Dave Walton, Sierra West, Chris Wirsig, and Elizabeth Zharoff

To the late John Braheny, who told us exactly what we needed to hear, when we needed to hear it. A special thank you to JoAnn Braheny for keeping John's legacy alive

To Michael Laskow, for creating the TAXI music community

To our teachers, mentors, and expert sages, especially Charles Bernstein, Jason Blume, Dr. William (Bill) Bradbury, Dr. David and Ann Chase, Jai Josefs, Roy Miyahira, Ralph Murphy, Marty Panzer, Esther Rhinelander, John Riggle, Eric Shimamoto, and Matthias Weber

To those who have graciously shared their pro tips, guidance, friendship, and creative and music business knowledge with us over the years, especially Lisa Aschmann, Jim Attebery, Les Brockmann, Charles Brotman, Teri Nelson Carpenter, Marc Caruso, Rob Case, Anne Cecere, Erin Collins, Michael Crepezzi, Aaron Davis, Jerry Davis, Steve Dorff, J. C. Dwyer, Michael Eames, Christopher Farrell, Chas Ferry, Fett, Gary Fitzgerald, Dan Foliart, Ron Goldberg, Cliff Goldmacher, Benoît Grey, Richard Harris, Sinéad Hartmann, Kenneth A. Helmer, Esq., Katie Herzig, John Houlihan, Kevin Houlihan, James Jacoby, Garrett M. Johnson, Esq., Derek Jones, Dan Kimpel, Suzan Koç, Leisa Korn, Penka Kouneva, Debra Young Krizman, James Leach, Cassie Lord, Michael A. Levine, J. Carlos "Charley" Londoño, Esq.,

Bob Mair, Gerard K. Marino, Morgan McKnight, Ben McLane, Esq., Ron Mendelsohn, Jason T. Miller, Nancy Moran, Wenty Morris, Art Munson, Ronan Chris Murphy, Peter Neff, Abby North, Elisabeth Oei, Eric Palmquist, Tanvi Patel, Shelly Peiken, David Quan, Barbie Quinn, Juan Carlos Quintero, Dr. Jonathan Rathsam, Liz Redwing, Allan Rich, Julia Riva, Andrew Robbins, Paula Savastano, Brian Scheuble, Mirette Seireg, Pamela Sheyne, Alison Smith, Adam Taylor, Tess Taylor, Jack Tempchin, Trygge Toven, Edwina Travis-Chin, Dean Truitt, Tom Villano, Marcy Rauer Wagman, Adam Weitz, Beth Wernick, Hunter Williams, Steve Winogradsky, Esq., and D.A. Young

To Kay Hanley (SONA), Bart Herbison (NSAI), Ashley Irwin (SCL),
David Israelite (NMPA), and Michelle Lewis (SONA) for their
tireless support of songwriters and composers

To our editor, Ronny Schiff, who is tough, witty, and astute.
This book would not exist without her.

Acknowledgments

In appreciation for their professional advice and input in the writing of this book:
Brian Thomas Curtin, Michael Eames, Garrett M. Johnson, Esq., Suzan Koç,
Ben McLane, Esq., Ron Mendelsohn, David Quan, Juan Carlos Quintero,
Brian Scheuble, and Scott Wilkinson

Index

About the Authors

Tracey and **Vance Marino** are a husband-and-wife music-writing and -producing team who met at a concert at the Belly Up Tavern in Solana Beach, California. They started talking with each other after they realized they had been stood up by their friends. But it soon became clear that they could work with—and learn from—each other's various musical backgrounds. They are full-time composers and songwriters with two Pro Tools studios in San Diego, south of Los Angeles.

Tracey is a singer, keyboardist, and classically trained pianist who studied with the late Grammy®-winning concert pianist Earl Wild and with John Garvey, composer and conductor of the La Jolla Music Society.

Originally from Boston, Tracey received a BA in liberal arts and sciences with emphasis in journalism from San Diego State University. While at SDSU, she studied music composition with David Ward-Steinman, student of famed Parisian music teacher Nadia Boulanger. Tracey also studied jazz piano privately with SDSU professor Rick Helzer, and she plays many different types of keyboard instruments. She also earned a graduate paralegal certificate at the University of San Diego. She was a vocal coach and staff piano accompanist at MiraCosta College and Palomar College where she studied harpsichord, tracker organ (steam calliope), pipe organ, MIDI, music production, and choral performing arts. Tracey is well versed in hymnody of nearly all denominations and still directs choirs. She has performed in Finland, Russia, Latvia, Estonia, and Sweden. Tracey was a member of the invitation-only Monday Night Group in Los Angeles, led by songwriting teacher, author, and mentor Jai Josefs.

With more than three thousand titles in their BMI catalog, the Marinos have had thousands of music placements in film, TV, video games, broadcast commercials, websites, film trailers, and theater productions. Their music is heard daily around the world.

Vance Marino, a seasoned rock, blues, and country guitarist, is originally from O'ahu, Hawai'i, and studied music performance and theory at Kamehameha Schools and Leeward Community College. Vance performed with bands for many years throughout Hawai'i, Arizona, and California. He played classical guitar at the famed Rancho Bernardo Inn resort for eleven years. Vance spent seven years directing and arranging music for a ten-voice contemporary youth choir and a 25-voice traditional choir. For years Vance has been teaching songwriting and music lessons and continues to do so. Several of his students have become successful in the music industry.

In addition to guitar, Vance sings and plays bass, drums, percussion, keyboards, ukulele, resonator guitar (Dobro), banjo, mandolin, guitalele, banjolele, bouzouki, and other stringed instruments.

Tracey and Vance studied lyric writing with hit songwriter Marty Panzer at UCLA Extension. They also studied film and TV synthestration composition with Emmy®-winning composer Matthias Weber and studied music in film with composer, author, and member of the board of governors of the Academy of Motion Picture Arts and Sciences' music branch, Charles Bernstein.

For more information, please visit Tracey and Vance Marino's company, SongMaker Productions, online at http://www.SongMakerPro.com/ or the Hey! That's My Song! website at https://www.HeyThatsMySong.com/.

Tracey and Vance are regular contributing columnists for music newsletters and have been panelists at music conferences in San Diego, Nashville, Los Angeles, and around the world. For many years they have been judges for the San Diego County Fair's annual Music and Singer-Songwriter contests.

As a way to give back to the songwriting community, they became coordinators of the San Diego Chapter of the Nashville Songwriters Association International (NSAI). They are members of Songwriters of North America (SONA), the Society of Composers and Lyricists (SCL), the SCL SongArts Committee, the Association of Independent Music Publishers (AIMP), the Production Music Association (PMA), the California Copyright Conference (CCC), Friends of the Guild of Music Supervisors (GMS), and several other music organizations.

To access the online media visit:
www.halleonard.com/mylibrary

Enter code: 4703-8562-0804-3959